Mountains of Music

Music in American Life

A list of books in the series appears at the end of this book.

Mountains of Music

WEST VIRGINIA

TRADITIONAL MUSIC

FROM *GOLDENSEAL*

Edited by John Lilly

University of Illinois Press

Urbana, Chicago, and Springfield

Publication of this book was supported by a grant from
the West Virginia Commission on the Arts, which is funded
in part by the West Virginia Division of Culture and History
and the National Endowment for the Arts.

∞ This book is printed on acid-free paper.

Library of Congress Cataloging-in-Publication Data
Mountains of music : West Virginia traditional music from Goldenseal /
edited by John Lilly.
p. cm. — (Music in American life)
Includes discography (p.   ) and index.
ISBN 978-0-252-06815-7 (paper : acid-free paper)
1. Folk musicians—West Virginia—Interviews.
2. West Virginia—Social life and customs.
I. Lilly, John, 1954-
II. Goldenseal.
III. Series.
ML394.M75   1999
781.62'130754—dc21   99-6043
CIP

P 8 7 6 5 4

CONTENTS

Introduction • JOHN LILLY   1

PART 1   FIDDLERS

Melvin Wine • SUSAN LEFFLER   7

Woody Simmons: Recollections of a Randolph County Fiddler • MICHAEL KLINE   12

Clark Kessinger: Pure Fiddling • CHARLES WOLFE   25
   I Remember Clark Kessinger • BOBBY TAYLOR   28

Wilson Douglas: Mountain Man and Mountain Musician • NANCY MCCLELLAN   34
   How I Came to Be a Fiddler • WILSON DOUGLAS AND NANCY MCCLELLAN   37

Sarah Singleton: A Fiddler All Her Life • TERESA HAMM   43

John Johnson: "A Pretty Good Thing All the Way Around" • MICHAEL KLINE   49
   A Musical Look at John Johnson's Fiddling • JOHN A. CUTHBERT   54

Robert Byrd: Mountain Fiddler • DAVE WILBUR   62

Ernie Carpenter: Tales of the Elk River Country • GERALD MILNES AND MICHAEL KLINE   66
   Thinking about Music • ERNIE CARPENTER   72

PART 2   BANJO PLAYERS

Clarence Tross: Hardy County Banjoist • KIP LORNELL JR. AND J. RODERICK MOORE   81

Sylvia O'Brien: "We Lived Good Back Then" • KEN SULLIVAN   87

Elmer Bird: The Banjo Man from Turkey Creek • PAUL GARTNER   96

Aunt Jennie Wilson: "I Grew Up with Music" • ROBERT SPENCE   103
   "A Real Fine Looking Man": Aunt Jennie Remembers Frank Hutchison • ROBERT SPENCE   106

Andrew F. Boarman:
The Banjo Man from Berkeley County • PEGGY JARVIS & DICK KIMMEL   109

Charlie Blevins at the Red Robin Inn: The Coon Dog Truth • MICHAEL KLINE   116

PART 3   DULCIMER PLAYERS

Russell Fluharty: The Dulcimer Man • KEN SULLIVAN   127

Worley Gardner: Mountain Music, Dance, and Dulcimers • MARK CRABTREE   136

Patty Looman: Carrying on the Music • DANNY WILLIAMS   141

PART 4   GUITARISTS

Doc Williams: A Half Century at the "Wheeling Jamboree" • IVAN TRIBE   147

Blackie Cool: "Whoop It Up a Little Bit" • SAM RIZZETTA   156

Carl Rutherford: Music from the Coalfields • JIM MCGEE   165

Nat Reese: Something to Give • MICHAEL KLINE   171

PART 5   FAMILY BANDS

The Lilly Brothers:
"We Sing about Life and What It Means to Us"   •   CARL FLEISCHHAUER AND TOM SCREVEN   181

Lynn Davis & Molly O'Day:
"Living the Right Life Now"   •   ABBY GAIL GOODNITE AND IVAN TRIBE   188

   Remembering Molly O'Day   •   DAVE PEYTON   192

The Currence Brothers: "The Spark to Play Music"   •   JACK WAUGH AND MICHAEL KLINE   196

The Welch Brothers Band: "Always Come Home after the Dance"   •   BILL WELLINGTON   208

   *"A Good Clean Square Dance Is a Very Fine Thing":
   Saturday Night at New Creek Fire Hall*   •   BILL WELLINGTON   214

Suggested Listening   219

Contributors   221

Index   225

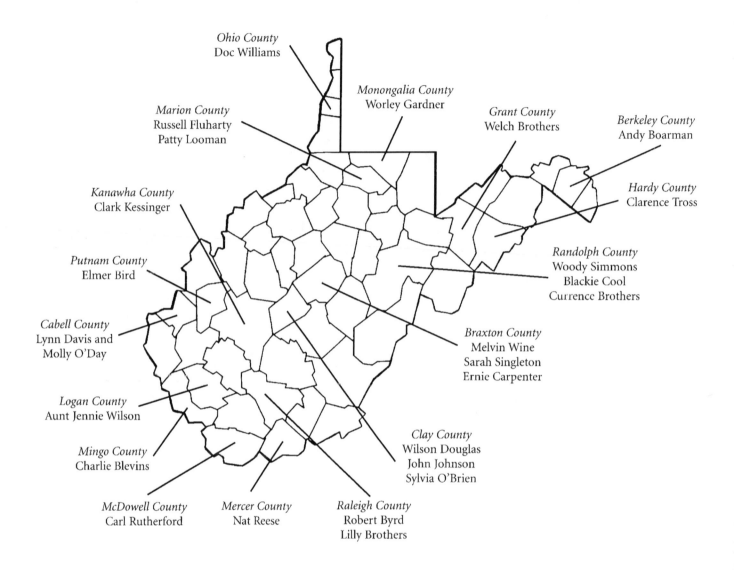

Ohio County
Doc Williams

Monongalia County
Worley Gardner

Grant County
Welch Brothers

Berkeley County
Andy Boarman

Marion County
Russell Fluharty
Patty Looman

Hardy County
Clarence Tross

Kanawha County
Clark Kessinger

Randolph County
Woody Simmons
Blackie Cool
Currence Brothers

Putnam County
Elmer Bird

Braxton County
Melvin Wine
Sarah Singleton
Ernie Carpenter

Cabell County
Lynn Davis and
Molly O'Day

Logan County
Aunt Jennie Wilson

Clay County
Wilson Douglas
John Johnson
Sylvia O'Brien

Mingo County
Charlie Blevins

McDowell County
Carl Rutherford

Mercer County
Nat Reese

Raleigh County
Robert Byrd
Lilly Brothers

Introduction

John Lilly

EST Virginians love their way of life, and traditions here are very strong. From the northern panhandle to the southern coalfields, West Virginians relish a sense of joyful independence, freely indulging in local pleasures, from ramps to venison and from ginseng to yellowroot.

Nowhere is this blessed individualism more apparent than in West Virginia's traditional music. And nowhere has this legacy been more thoroughly examined or more lovingly celebrated over the past 25 years than in the pages of *Goldenseal*, West Virginia's quarterly magazine of traditional life.

Begun in early 1975, *Goldenseal* is published by the State of West Virginia's Division of Culture and History and is read by more than 20,000 people per issue. Founding editor Tom Screven (1975–1979), longtime editor Ken Sullivan (1979–1997), and I (1997–present) have worked to create a journal for the general public that reflects the real lives of 20th-century West Virginians as told through oral history by freelance writers and recent and historic photographs.

Goldenseal, named for the indigenous yellowroot plant,

was an outgrowth of a broad interest in roots culture during the early to mid-1970s. It was initially sustained by state funds and mailed free of charge to anyone who cared to read it. Over the years, state funding has dwindled, but enthusiasm for West Virginia folk culture remains strong. *Goldenseal* continues to highlight the work of the finest freelance writers and folklorists in the country (as evidenced by this volume), and fascinating stories about folklife in West Virginia continue to come in the door faster than they can be published. Today, readers across the state and throughout the country support the publication in the form of annual subscriptions. (For information about *Goldenseal*, write to The Cultural Center, 1900 Kanawha Boulevard East, Charleston, WV 25305-0300.)

Goldenseal covers considerable ground, presenting music as part of the full range of life experience in West Virginia. The magazine also publishes articles about farming, mining, religion, politics, sports, herbs, crafts, immigrants, and other topics. According to former editor Ken Sullivan, "I saw the music as a vehicle to tell the broader cultural story,

Goldenseal founding editor Tom Screven (left) with musician Everett Lilly in 1975. Photograph by Carl Fleischhauer.

and that broader story was infinitely more important to me than was the music itself. Music was one thread of the tapestry; and the tapestry was the story of West Virginia's traditional culture."

That musical thread remains in a class by itself. Perhaps no other expression of local culture has drawn so many visitors, enthralled so many researchers, elicited so much comment, or established such cross-cultural rapport as the music of the Mountain State. From Wheeling radio station WWVA's "Jamboree U.S.A." to the Augusta Heritage Arts Workshops in Elkins, from the weekly international radio broadcasts of "Mountain Stage" to the annual Appalachian String Band Festival at Clifftop and the state-sponsored Vandalia Gathering, tens of thousands of people each year are drawn through music to the mountains and culture of West Virginia.

In the 100 issues since its beginning, *Goldenseal* has published scores of articles about music in West Virginia. To recognize the magazine's first quarter century, we have chosen 25 of these articles for this book. Selecting a representative grouping from that extensive catalog was difficult, but I believe we have managed to put together a fair and balanced collection, one that spans the work of all three editors. Together, these 25 articles form a "core sample" that shows the depth and variety of the unique musical expression of West Virginia life.

These articles are reprinted as they appeared in *Goldenseal,* along with a representative sampling of 150 photographs. Because some of the pieces date back as far as the mid-1970s, story and subject updates are included at the end of each article.

Mountains of Music might have been arranged geographically, chronologically, or by musical style; instead, we chose to divide the book into five sections highlighting fiddlers (8), banjo players (6), dulcimer players (3), guitarists (4), and family bands (4). The musicians represent 17 different counties from one end of the state to the other; and their music displays a surprisingly wide variety of styles. There is no single or dominant statewide tradition in West Virginia. Instead, these stories present a spectrum of musical approaches that could have evolved only in this remote mountain region.

Don't be misled by the book's arrangement into believing that instrumental music in West Virginia takes precedence over vocal styles. In fact, song in the mountains is so pervasive that if we had included a section on singers, nearly half of the collection would belong in that section. The duet harmony of the Lilly Brothers, the full-throated gospel singing of Molly O'Day, the smooth radio-style songs of Doc Williams, the rough-and-ready ballads of Charlie Blevins, the original coal-mining songs of Carl Rutherford and others give voice to the real-life concerns of these musicians. To quote Everett Lilly, "We sing about life and what it means to

Longtime editor Ken Sullivan (left) examines a fiddle with *Goldenseal* story subject Ernie Carpenter. Photograph by Michael Keller.

us." Others interpret their favorite songs instrumentally, creating a unique repertoire. Fiddler Melvin Wine, for example, performs hymns on the fiddle, such as "I'd Rather Be an Old-Time Christian" or "Uncloudy Day," and John Johnson recorded a spectacular solo fiddle medley of Jimmie Rodgers's "Blue Yodels."

Folk culture in West Virginia, as elsewhere, reflects strong family and regional influences. As a result, the crooked and haunting fiddling styles found in the rural central counties stand in contrast to the smooth, accomplished fiddling associated with the relatively urban Kanawha Valley. A distinctive hammered dulcimer tradition thrives in the ethnically diverse northern counties, while the blues influence is felt most strongly in the southern coal areas.

Folklorist Alan Jabbour, a fiddler and long-standing scholar of West Virginia musical styles, points out the contrast between the valley farming tradition and that of the state's hills and hollows, which have always been adjacent but competing subcultures. Jabbour suggests that unaccompanied vocal and instrumental performance styles, with their ancient cultural roots and musical irregularities, echo the individualism of the rural and mountainous areas with which they are associated. Indeed, the state motto, *Montani Semper Liberi* (Mountaineers Are Always Free), underscores this emphasis on independence.

Musicians from the more urban areas understandably show the influence of radio, recordings, and professional performance styles in their music. Still others, especially the dulcimer players in the north-central counties, reflect the ongoing rediscovery and revival of folk music in their choice of instrument and repertoire.

Historically and geographically, West Virginia is at a crossroads. It lies strategically between the Union North and

Editor John Lilly (right) shares a tune with retired railroad engineer Gilbert King. Photograph by Michael Keller.

the Confederate South, between the colonial dignity of Old Virginia to the east and the "wild frontier" beyond the Ohio River to the west. These influences, and many others, are still felt throughout the state and occasionally run together in unexpected ways. It's possible, for example, to hear a blues tune played on the dulcimer, a polka picked on the banjo, or an unaccompanied ballad sung by a coalfield bluesman.

Some of the musicians included in this collection have achieved widespread recognition for their artistry. These include Melvin Wine (National Heritage Award recipient), Clark Kessinger (national fiddle champion), Lynn Davis and Molly O'Day (influential country and gospel music recording artists), Elmer Bird (banjo ambassador), the Lilly Brothers (bluegrass pioneers), Doc Williams (WWVA radio star), and Robert C. Byrd (fiddling U.S. Senator).

The majority of the musicians in this book, however, are local heros. They play and sing for each other, entertain at community events, and occasionally venture out to a festival to share their unique talents with a slightly wider audience. They often play instruments that they made themselves or that were handed down to them by a relative or loved one. They play tunes and sing songs learned many years ago from members of their families or communities, which revives in them the closeness and affection they hold for their teachers.

Faced with an increasingly technological world and the relentless pressures of popular culture, these musicians and the communities they represent rely on folk traditions, especially music, for a large measure of their cultural identity. It's not uncommon to hear fiddles and banjos supplying the background music for local ads on the radio. A recent primary election in Summers County included a candidates' debate complete with "refreshments and string music." The town of

Elkins boasts a Wednesday night "Pickin' in the Park" series of informal jam sessions that draw hundreds of people with folding chairs, guitar cases, and video cameras; the sessions are taped and broadcast on local television each Sunday evening. Rural churches throughout the state resound with soul-stirring congregational singing each Sunday morning.

By reading and learning about the musicians in this book, we also discover something about the private lives and family histories of a population that lives "below the radar" of contemporary media or popular culture. We learn from fiddler Ernie Carpenter about the early settlers along the Elk River who ate elk meat and traveled in hand-hewn flatboats called gunwales. We learn of the challenges faced by the Currence Brothers as they coped with hemophilia. We learn how banjoist Andy Boarman repaired instruments in between haircuts at his barber shop.

Music and real life are one and the same in this area of Appalachia, one of the few regions of the United States where a true folk culture persists in the waning years of the 20th century. While contemporary society seems to strive for an ever-narrowing range of cultural values and acceptable behavior, mountain traditions are stubbornly digging in for the long haul.

There is a certain level of tenacity—even defiance—required of those who live "below the radar." Here in West Virginia that means proudly participating in a folk culture that won't let go and a musical tradition that remains strong and vibrant. Older musicians seem to get better with time. Younger musicians learn the tunes and carry on. Children pull in close and wait their turn.

As Ken Sullivan points out, this culture is "remarkably durable. [It] is alive and well despite everything that is pushed at us. It changes as it's supposed to, but the music and the culture of West Virginia persist."

PART 1

Fiddlers

Melvin Wine

Susan Leffler

O n a chilly spring evening last April, musicians and fans of traditional Appalachian tunes packed the old wooden pews of the former Methodist Episcopal Church in Sutton, now the Landmark Arts Center. It was a mixed crowd. There were young women with dangly earrings and faded denim skirts, gray-haired ladies in polyester pants suits, balding men with "Support Our Troops" printed on their T-shirts and tobacco bulging in their cheeks.

A few rows from the stage, in the middle section, sat a beaming silver-haired gentleman in an old felt hat and a red plaid shirt. His hands, gnarled from years of work, quietly thumped his knees, keeping time to the music.

This was the guest of honor, Braxton County fiddler Melvin Wine. The occasion was his birthday, which friends and family have celebrated for the last few years with an informal concert. Melvin turned 82 this year.

"Come on, Grandpa, play something," shouted one of Wine's 77 grandchildren and great-grandchildren. "Yeah Dad, do 'Whiskey Before Breakfast,'" yelled another member of the Wine clan.

So Melvin Wine quietly walked to the front and started to play his fiddle. The crowd jumped up stomping and cheering. Brandy, an 11-year-old granddaughter in ruffled pink satin and patent-leather tap shoes, clogged across the stage. Baby Danielle, the youngest Wine at the celebration, gurgled and headed for Grandpa at a fast crawl before being grabbed by her mother.

Melvin Wine has played for very different audiences. Government officials, diplomats, and college students have applauded him at the Smithsonian Institution, the Wolftrap Farm Park near Washington, D.C., Swarthmore College in Pennsylvania, and other places far from his central West Virginia home.

The crowd attending Wine's birthday celebration included many of West Virginia's top traditional musicians. They came to pay tribute to the man as much as the fiddler.

One of those present was Mack Samples, president of the West Virginia State Folk Festival at Glenville, and a fine old-time fiddler himself. Samples called Wine "a true traditional musician," one who worked hard and lived close to the soil and to his family.

"While he is an excellent fiddler, he views other segments of his life as more important," explained Samples. "This is

Melvin Wine won the first Vandalia Award in 1981. This award, West Virginia's highest folklife honor, recognizes a lifetime of accomplishment in the perpetuation of the state's traditional culture. This official Vandalia portrait was made by Michael Keller in 1986.

what separates the real traditional musician from those who play traditional music for a living, or who try to."

Wine lives with his wife of more than 60 years, Etta (pronounced Etty) and their granddaughter, Toni, near Copen. They raise cattle, chickens, and hay on their 120-acre farm nestled in a hollow at the end of a gravel road. But Melvin says his sons and a hired hand do most of the outdoor work these days.

"I just run out of steam," he says. "I got black lung and arthritis, and when I try to work out on the farm much I just give out."

The Wine household may be short of steam and even breath but not of love or cooperation, as I found out on a recent visit.

It's late afternoon and Toni, who's 33, comes home from her work at a job-training and rehabilitation center in Sutton. She's had a learning disability and speech impediment since childhood and has spent most of her life with Etta and Melvin.

"They taught me everything I know," she says. "I wouldn't be able to talk or walk if it wasn't for them." She's now taken over the responsibility of caring for Etta when Melvin's away.

Toni sets the table and Melvin takes some cube steaks out of the freezer. Etta supervises from the next room. "Honey, you get that pan nice and hot before you try to fry those steaks," she cautions Melvin.

Etta had a stroke eight years ago and is partially paralyzed. She spends most of her days in a recliner chair facing the front window. "My job now is watching the hollow," she jokes.

And from the looks of it, teaching her octogenarian husband to cook. She listens carefully to the grease sizzling and then warns him not to put too much flour on the meat or "it won't brown up nice."

Melvin grins and says he hasn't quite gotten the hang of fixing country-fried steak, but that he gets up every morning and makes biscuits that are as good or better than anyone's. I've tried them. He's right.

After dinner Toni does the dishes and Melvin starts to tell me about his life and music. He says that he was born in 1909 near Burnsville. His father Bob played the fiddle and his mother, Elizabeth Sandy, sang ballads and hymns. Some of Melvin's earliest memories are of lying in bed at night and hearing his father make music.

"Some of those tunes he'd play in the night would just touch me," he remembers. "I don't know why. One of them, 'Lady's Waistribbon,' used to make me cry. There was just something about it that bothered and overjoyed me."

Melvin never really went to school. When he was nine he started playing the fiddle while his father was out cutting timber or working as a farmhand for neighbors.

He taught himself to play "Bonaparte's Retreat" and finally worked up the nerve to play for his father. After that Bob Wine taught his son the tunes he'd learned from his own father, Nels, and Grandfather "Smithy." These included "Cold Frosty Morning," the title tune on Melvin's first album, and "Hannah at the Springhouse," the title tune of his

Melvin and Etta Wine were married in 1930. Etta played the banjo and guitar and called square dances in earlier years. Photograph by Susan Leffler.

Melvin Wine has balanced his life of hard work, traditional music, and a commitment to church and family. He turned 82 about the time this photograph was made by Susan Leffler in 1991.

cassette. Like most old-time musicians, Melvin never learned to read music.

"My dad, if I didn't play right, why, he'd get behind me and grab a-hold of my arm and show me how to do it," he says. "We played so near alike that he could note the fiddle and hold it and I could use the bow, or vice versa."

Sometimes Melvin's love for music carried him a little beyond what he was willing to admit to his dad. "My father had a sorrel horse. It had a red tail and it had some white in it," he recalls. "I went out and I snooped some hair out of that horse's tail and put it in the fiddle bow. Dad was really wondering about that, how I got that nice bow string. It was really pretty."

When he was 13 Melvin won a fiddler's contest at Gassaway, beating an old man named Bailey, the longtime champion. Bailey told Melvin that he was having a hard time making a living, so the teenaged fiddler gave him the prize money.

"I've felt good about that ever since," chuckles Melvin, dark eyes twinkling under huge bushy eyebrows.

About that time he and his brother Clarence started playing music at the Burnsville movie theater. Clarence played the banjo and mandolin, and together they'd entertain the audience while the projectionist changed reels.

Although there were 10 children in the Wine family, Melvin was closest to Clarence. They shared many good times, including playing music at fairs, log rollings, and bean stringings.

Melvin often played for parties. Soon he started courting Etta Singleton, who called square dances and played the banjo and guitar. In 1930 they walked three miles to a preacher's house and got married. The newlyweds set up housekeeping in a two-room shanty where years before loggers had come to warm their hands while timbering the area.

Melvin went to work in the mines. His boss tried to spread the scarce work around by hiring more people than he needed. Unfortunately, this reduced the amount of coal each miner could load and thus reduced each man's pay. Melvin often earned no more than a dollar a day.

He got discouraged and hit the road with Clarence and with Etta's brother, William "Ace" Singleton. They played music on the streets of Fairmont, passing the hat. On weekends, Melvin took his meager earnings home to his new bride.

The three musicians' most memorable adventure was their first airplane ride. They were walking to a square dance when they spotted a crowd gathered around two small open-cockpit planes. The trio started playing, and eventually the pilots invited them to go for a spin. Melvin and Ace climbed into one plane, and Clarence crawled into the other. Melvin has never forgotten what came next.

"When that thing started up, why me and Ace both tried to dive into the little space under the control panel," he

Brothers Clarence (left) and Melvin Wine were music-making buddies. They played together in Braxton and neighboring counties. Photographer and date unknown.

recalls. "But we couldn't fit. I tell you, we was scared! Well, we got over that once we got level and everything was going alright. Then my neck scarf blew off somewhere over Gassaway. When the pilot lit down, he dipped too low and the propeller caught some old swamp weeds and turned her right up on her end. We was up in the air and the nose was right in the ground."

They climbed out and pulled the plane down on the level. Meanwhile the other plane landed near them. The pilot told them to get back in and they'd taxi to the landing field. Melvin declined, saying he'd walk. "And Clarence looked right at his pilot and said, 'I ain't no buzzard, and I ain't flying no more,'" laughs Melvin.

A little while later, something happened that changed Melvin's life for the next two decades.

He was playing for a party when an older man started dancing with a 12-year-old girl. As Melvin tells it, the old man was bragging at the top of his lungs about the fact that he could dance with someone so young and pretty. A woman on the other side of the room told him he shouldn't be talking like that, at which point he swore at her.

"And he fell dead right there," says Melvin. "I tell you, people run over me and knocked me down trying to get out of there. It was a scary time. That man, he left this old world in a hurry."

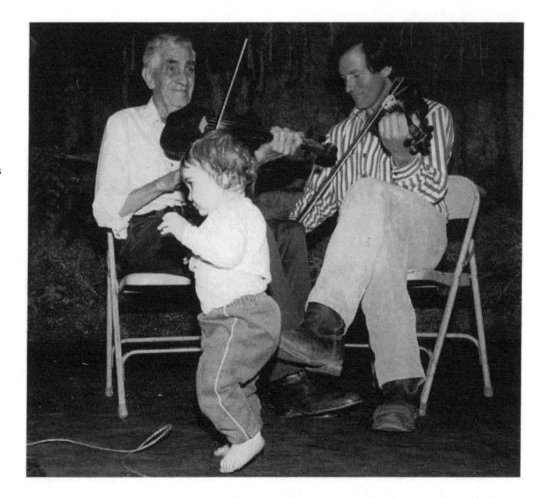

Passing good music and sound values down to younger generations is important in Melvin Wine's mature years. Here he plays with apprentice John Gallagher for the obvious enjoyment of his great-granddaughter Danielle. Photograph by Susan Leffler.

Melvin took the incident as a sign and stopped playing the fiddle for more than 20 years.

"Then I became a shovel operator in the mines," he chuckles. "A *hand* shovel operator."

He worked in and around the mines for 37 years in Webster, Gilmer, Braxton, and Lewis counties. He was seriously injured only once. He still has a huge knot on one knee that he shows to spice up the story of the day an iron bar sliced into his leg. The injury kept him off his feet for nearly three years. By then, he and Etta had four children.

"We lived on $8 a week during that time. Workmen's Compensation. Can you imagine that, with all those mouths to feed?"

Melvin finally was able to start working again by having friends help him get down into the mine and riding out on a coal car at the end of the day. "I stuck to it," he says. "I loaded more coal than anybody there on the hill. I had a strong back and a weak mind."

For nearly 10 years he had to work away from home for weeks or months at a time. When he was working nearby, he'd leave on foot before dawn and get home after dark.

Etta remembers those hard times well. "I've picked 500 bushels of corn with the kids and then stayed up canning all night," she says.

The couple eventually had 10 children. Nine were born at home, some with the help of Melvin's mother who was a midwife. Etta says she taught them all to share and to work. "I couldn't be raising no lazy kids in those days," she says.

She also made sure they went to school and kept up with their studies. Nearly all the Wine children graduated from high school and several went on to careers in nursing or electrical work.

"Their mother was a hard boss," laughs Melvin. "She ramrodded 'em. But they all say now they wouldn't have been raised any other way."

At one point Etta almost died of typhoid fever. She had been misdiagnosed and was taken off the operating table minutes before having surgery that the doctor later said would have killed her. The experience was so powerful that both Etta and Melvin turned to the church and were saved. Both were baptized in the creek near their house.

"It really made a change in our lives," Melvin says. "The lights burnt brighter. People's faces shone more."

Etta goes to church several times a week and Melvin has been superintendent of the Copen United Methodist Church for 50 years.

During the time that their children were growing up, Melvin went from mining to timbering. Then he tried running a sawmill and a trucking company. He "almost lost his shirt" several times but eventually purchased the farm where they still live. He paid the place off in four years.

Religion, raising a family, and his lingering memory of the rowdy old man collapsing on the dance floor had cooled Melvin's interest in music. It was the early 1960s before he started playing the fiddle again on a regular basis. He gives credit to his granddaughter, Kelley, whom he was babysitting at the time.

"She got unruly, and I was trying to get her to quiet down. So I went and got my fiddle and played for her. It did the trick. I thought that this must be a gift, and I shouldn't give it up."

Melvin started playing at the nearby West Virginia State Folk Festival at Glenville, and to his surprise, started winning fiddle contests. Soon he found himself surrounded by eager young fiddlers anxious to learn the old tunes he'd picked up from his father.

"One song I played, 'Jump Jim Crow,' the young people just hungered after that one," Melvin says. "I played it so many times at Glenville, I wore the feathers off the crow."

He says the young players' enthusiasm really inspired him. Gradually he started remembering tunes he hadn't heard or played for years. The stories that went with the songs also began to come back. Sometimes these are of great interest themselves, often offering theories about the origins of a tune.

For example, Melvin says that "Soldier's Joy" got its name from a Civil War incident involving his great-grandfather Smithy. According to the story, the Yankees caught Smithy helping Confederate troops. The Northerners forced him to walk to Virginia to sign an oath that he would never collaborate with the enemy again. During the long trek, the Yankees learned that their prisoner was a fiddler and asked him to play for a dance. One tune they especially enjoyed didn't have a name so they dubbed it "Soldier's Joy."

Melvin's music and recollections made him a popular attraction wherever he went. He soon became a regular at the prestigious Glenville festival, winning the fiddle contest for players over 50 years old an unprecedented seven times. You'll also find him at the Vandalia Gathering in Charleston and the Augusta Heritage Arts Workshops and Festival in Elkins.

Last year Melvin taught fiddle as part of the West Virginia Folk Arts Apprenticeship Program, instructing 34-year-old John Gallagher, an Elkins carpenter. John says he was attracted by Wine's music, which he describes as having a "beautiful ancient quality." He was also drawn to Wine himself because of his warmth and openness. Gallagher, who grew up mostly in metropolitan Washington, D.C., was fascinated by the Wine family's attitudes toward each other and toward life. He wanted to understand where the music came from, so he'd often spend all day playing music with Melvin and then stay the night.

"I guess spending so much of their lives near the earth really challenged them to try harder at everything and to get their priorities straight, to figure out what was really important in life," says Gallagher. It seems that Melvin Wine, who says he feels an obligation to pass his music on to the younger generation, is passing on the values of a simple lifestyle as well.

EDITOR'S NOTE: This article first appeared in the summer 1991 issue of *Goldenseal* (vol. 17, no. 2). Melvin Wine, the 1981 Vandalia Award winner, was honored with a National Heritage Fellowship from the National Endowment for the Arts in 1991. He continues to appear with his fiddle at the annual Vandalia Gathering and is an active participant at musical events across the state. His wife, Etta, passed away in March 1992.

Woody Simmons

RECOLLECTIONS OF A RANDOLPH COUNTY FIDDLER

Michael Kline

THE following article was transcribed from a taped interview with Woody Simmons on January 23 of this year [1979] at his home on Mill Creek, 16 miles south of Elkins in Randolph County. Laverne Simmons was present at the interview and recalled many details of her husband's long musical career, in which she was briefly a singing partner during the early years of their marriage.

At 67, Woody Simmons is perhaps the most highly decorated local fiddler to come up in central West Virginia. His legendary smooth bowing style and effortless soaring phrases and his combative approach to contest playing have won him the admiration of a large following of contest and festival audiences throughout the state. Plagued with a recent heart condition, Mr. Simmons has had to curtail his physical activities considerably. Yet he has kept his musical spirit together in the past year, and with quiet determination and twinkling smiles has walked off stage after stage with ribbons and trophies of every description. At the Vandalia Gathering this past Memorial Day, Simmons won three prizes and an honorable mention in stiff fiddle and banjo competition.

But more importantly, Woody Simmons has displayed a warmth and hospitality toward musicians of all kinds that have served to foster the oldest and best traditions of music in his community and state. Mr. and Mrs. Simmons have opened their home as a kind of haven to both ordinary and extraordinary musicians and, as the two of them readily offer, they have yet to meet any visitor from whom they didn't learn something about music or life, or both.

Woodford Simmons was born on Becky's Creek, just south of Huttonsville, in 1911, and grew up with two older sisters, one of whom married Gus McGee, a fine fiddle player in Elkins. Florence Tacy and William Ison Simmons, the parents, were married on Becky's Creek in 1896, and lived out their married lives there. Woody Simmons revered his parents and has fond memories of the isolated home place.

෴

Michael Kline: Tell me about the musical traditions in your family on both sides that you can remember anything about.

Woody Simmons: My grandfather and grandmother on either side never played any music. My father played an old

Woodford "Woody" Simmons in 1979. Photograph by Doug Yarrow.

accordion a little bit and he could pick out a few tunes on the banjo.

MK: Where did he learn, I wonder, if he didn't learn the accordion from his parents?

WS: I wouldn't have any idea. He played an old tune he called "Fee-be-l," or something like that. I remember that. And he played some hymns on the accordion and "Irish Washer Woman," I believe he played that, and some polkas.

MK: Well, when did he come to Becky's Creek?

WS: Well, I'd say in, maybe in the 1880s. They just decided they didn't like it over in Virginia, so they moved back to

West Virginia in a wagon and two horses. My dad owned a place up at the head of Becky's Creek. And from what my dad said, they had it pretty rough at that time. I heard him say they had no matches or anything, go and borry some fire coal from a neighbor and bring and start a fire in the morning if the fire would happen to go out. And they'd shoot in the chimney with a muzzle-loading rifle to start a fire. Heard him speak of that and heard him talk about wolves. Why, the wolves would be around so thick when they got ready to go to the house they'd have to get a big pole and set the pole a-fire and carry it on their shoulder to keep the wolves off of them until they got to the house. And they made sugar.

MK: The sugar camp was back further up in the head of the mountains, was it?

WS: Uh huh, and big timber! They just cut the old sugar camp out here about 20 years ago. Awful big trees, big timber back at that time.

MK: You must have some recollection of Randolph County before all the timber was cut off then, do you?

WS: Oh, yeah. I worked in the woods for the Wilson Lumber Company a couple of years. Cut timber and drove grab and drove team and done about everything. This big store down here on the corner was the company store. I walked from there to the head of Becky's Creek, about seven miles one way then. And we worked from daylight 'til dark. Working in the woods, yeah.

MK: What sort of character was your father, anyway? You told me once you never heard him swear an oath.

Laverne Simmons: He didn't.

MK: Was he stern or did he have a sense of humor? Was he hard working?

WS: He was a hard working man, yes sir. He worked hard and he liked to drive teams of horses. He was an awful good hand with the horses. He was a blacksmith, he done a lot of blacksmith work, built wagons.

MK: Where do you suppose he learned that trade? Is that something his father knew?

WS: No, I don't think his father was a blacksmith, knew anything about blacksmithing. I don't know where he picked it up, but ever since I can remember he had a blacksmith shop and shoed a lot of horses. I put shoes on one horse in my time. But I could turn the shoes and toe 'em and weld and everything like that. I learned a lot of blacksmithing work.

MK: He had a shop right there on the place, did he?

WS: Yes, sir, right on the farm, pretty close to that old granary. Had a blower and everything. Made his own tongs and everything that he worked with.

MK: He even made the first instrument you had?

WS: Yeah, he made the first banjo I ever had, yeah.

MK: Can you describe how he did that?

WS: Well, he split out a piece of white oak. And I don't remember how thick it was, probably one-half inch thick.

And then maybe he used a saw on it to saw all the way around it and make it bend easier. And then he put it in a kettle and boiled it. And bent it around, and pinned it together some way, and then all the metal parts he made in the blacksmith shop. He used an old groundhog hide on it for a head, tanned the hide and made the head, and made the neck out of locust. And he only put five frets on it and made them out of fencing wire. And, of course, it had wooden tuning pegs, I think they was made out of locust. And the first strings he used on it was screen wire.

MK: Screen wire?

WS: Old screen out of a screen door, raveled out, but you couldn't tune them up very high. And the first tune I learned to play was "Silent Night."

MK: Where did you hear that?

WS: Well, I heard it around Christmas [school] programs, you know. And then finally we walked to the I.P. Russell store here in Mill Creek to get a few things, and seen he had banjo strings, and the brand was *Sunrise*. They was 20 cents a set. That Russell still lives in Mill Creek, he'd remember about it. And I bought a set of them strings and put on that old banjo and I really thought I had something! Oh, my, I thought that was the finest banjo in the world. Then the next one I got when I came home from school one evening. Why, my dad had traded a feller 10 chickens for a banjo, a factory-made banjo. It had 38 brackets on it.

MK: You didn't have anybody to teach you to play. What kind of finger style, picking style did you work out for the banjo?

WS: Well, I first started out by using three fingers and my thumb. I used the third finger on the first string only and the second finger on the second string only, and the first finger on the third string, and the thumb on the fifth string and fourth string. Never crossed over at any time.

MK: So you got a sort of roll going with your fingers?

WS: Yes sir. Then I played the clawhammer style. Some of them called it frailing.

MK: Where did you first hear that?

WS: Seems like the first feller I seen do that was Cletus Johnson. And maybe Floyd Swecker, that was my brother-in-law. Seemed like I seen him do the clawhammer style . . . I didn't play that very long 'cause everybody seems to not like that style of playing.

MK: What do you mean they didn't like it? That was the old-time style, wasn't it?

WS: Old-time style, yeah, but they kind of got away from it. They just seemed to didn't pay any attention to it. They said they didn't like the banjo played that style. They made fun of you playing that way, yeah. They called it "n-----style."

MK: But by that time you were hearing a different style on the radio?

WS: I was hearing a different style on the phonograph. It was an old Edison Victrola. Played on them rolls. [Fred Van Epps] sounded to me like he was playing with two fingers and his thumb. That's when I started playing like that, around in the '20s. Played "Golden Slippers" and "Blue Ridge Mountain Home." Sounded like he was using two fingers and his thumb, and that's where I got picking that style.

MK: You started to tell me a little about hearing "Silent Night" at Christmas programs in your school. Was the school there on Becky's Creek? What was it like?

WS: Yes, it was there on Becky's Creek, about a mile and a half from my home. Some days I'd ride the horse to school, in bad weather.

MK: Who was your favorite teacher back at Becky's Creek?

WS: Ethel Rosencrantz, Ethel Rosencrantz See. She married Roland See.

MK: Did Ethel board in the community some?

WS: Uh huh. She'd go home and stay all night with each one of the students during the school session. She went home and stayed all night with us when I was about 13 years old. And me and her walked about five miles that night to a dance on the mountain. She taught me to dance. I danced three sets with her. Yeah, she was a fine schoolteacher.

MK: Was she a young-like person, or an older woman?

WS: She was 21 years old when I went to school with her.

MK: Uh huh. I can see maybe why you paid attention. Well, now, tell me about this dance. What kind of music did they have?

WS: Arnold and Lilburn VanPelt played the music. I believe Arnold used an old mandolin. It was one of them that was made like a gourd, and we called it a "taterbug" back at that time. But I don't believe he had a guitar, though. I think the first guitar he ever had he made it himself. Arnold lives in Pennsylvania now and Lilburn, he still lives here in Mill Creek. He's up in his 80s, Lilburn is, and he won't play anymore. Not interested in it at all.

MK: Can you tell me what it was like when you were a small child growing up on the farm? Did you work pretty hard as a youngster?

WS: Oh, yeah, had to work all the time. You only got one pair of shoes a year and you went barefoot most of the time: When you went to Sunday School, why you'd carry them in the summer. You'd tie the string together and put them over your shoulder and carry them 'til you'd get almost to the church. After you got a ways from the church, why you'd take the shoes off and go home barefooted. You went barefooted until it started frosting, getting cold.

Yeah, pretty rough. At the age of 13, when school was out, I went to work for old Battershel. He was a contractor and graded the road from Huttonsville to Mingo. And I worked on the roads 'til school started. The wages then was about 25 cents an hour. You worked 10 hours a day. I grubbed stumps and done a little bit of everything. We had mules and wagons they hauled dirt in.

On Saturday, why, and of an evening after school, there's something to do all the time on the farm. In the winter months we'd clear off a piece of ground. When my dad bought that farm, it was all woods. You started building right in the woods and cut the timber off of it. There was a sawmill moved in and sawed all the lumber, and then the lumber was dried—of course not dry kilned, it was just air dried. My father started building a house right in the woods. We'd clear out a plot of ground in the winter, and in the spring of the year, then we'd plow it up with one horse and a shovel plow. He made his own hoes to hoe with, and those stumps were still there and you'd dig them sprouts off the stumps. It's called "new groundin'." You didn't have to use no dust nor anything on the beans to keep the bugs off. There'd be no bugs or anything on them and you raised real good beans and corn, anything you'd plant growed real good. Then, the next winter, why, you'd clear up another place. Plowed it up and kept on 'til you got enough land cleared that you could raise hay.

MK: And some pasture, maybe?

WS: Yeah, and pasture fields. We had sheep, cows, and a team of horses. And on the buildings you'd use shingles split out of red oak. I helped on the shingles for the old buildings. They're up there yet today. I've still got the tool we used, they called it a "froe," I believe. They used that to split those shingles with, and they've been on there 65 years at least.

MK: Did you put them on in the new of the moon, or did you pay attention to the phases of the moon?

WS: At a certain time you used to put them on. They claimed that if the moon was ruling up, that if you put them on, they'd all turn up. Yeah, we put them on when the moon was ruling down.

∾

The new moon is said to be "ruling up" with its tips pointing in a generally upward direction. According to traditional folk belief, this is the proper time to plant, since the moon will pull the plants upward, and a bad time for roofing, since the shingles will buckle upward. The waning moon is "ruling down"—a bad time for planting but a good time for roofing.

∾

MK: What about in the mountains? Was there a lot of game to hunt back then?

WS: There was plenty of game back at that time. You'd kill squirrels right there at the house. They'd come into the corn field on the old rail fence, and you could kill a mess of squirrels any time. There wasn't too many deer, though, but in later years they's a lot of deer.

The old Simmons homeplace at Becky's Creek, Randolph County, where Woody grew up. Photograph by Doug Yarrow.

MK: Did you hunt a lot of bear at that time?

WS: Well, no, I didn't, but the old fellers did. They'd talk about how they'd catch 'em. An old bear is awful fond of honey. Well, they'd put honey in a nail keg and drive the nails in sloping, and the old bear, he'd tee his head in there and he couldn't get it back out. He couldn't see where he was going. Then they'd track him down and kill him, you know. They'd eat the bear. Used bear and deer and everything for food.

MK: What about fiddling? Can you remember your first fiddle?

WS: Yes, sir, the first fiddle I ever owned I bought off an old man by the name of Smith Shreve. I built fires in the schoolhouse and done the sweeping, and paid him for the fiddle in the spring of the year when I got my check. I was 13 years old. I believe I give $15, wasn't very much. I've still got it. It's a fine old fiddle.

MK: What made you want to fiddle so bad that you built fires every morning and swept out?

WS: Well, sir, I really enjoyed music back at that time. I thought, there's nothing like it! And I just wished and wished that I could have a violin. Old man Smith Shreve told me he'd sell me that one.

MK: Did he give you some lessons along with it? Who taught you to play?

WS: Well, I just picked it up myself.

MK: Now, Woody, how could you just learn to play the fiddle? I mean, could anybody do that? I know I couldn't.

WS: Well, sir, I tuned it up the first thing I got it. Then, of course, I heard Gus McGee play, and John Geer, he lived there close, and he played the fiddle. I learned an old tune off of him called "Ninety Days in Georgia." But I believe the first tune I learned was "Soldier's Joy." And then the "Mitchell Clog," that was one of Wren McGee's tunes. He was, along about them days, a champion fiddler. He lived on McGee Run and played the fiddle. I was at Dave's house several times, and then Ballard McGee, that was Gus's dad, he made a fiddle out of poplar. The old fiddle sounded pretty good. I heard him play a lot. Then Clint McGee, he played the old fiddle that his dad made. I stayed there a while. Clint and I cut timber, and we'd play a little music of the night. He'd play the fiddle and I'd play it. We didn't have no guitar or anything.

MK: What were some of the pieces you played with him?

WS: "Sally Goodin" and "Sally Ann," that's an old tune I heard Dave McGee play. I've heard it several different styles on the fiddle, but [the McGees] had a style different from everybody else on "Sally Ann." They tuned the fiddle up in a high bass and played it. I used to play "Turkey in the Straw" tuned up that way because everybody else did. Old Fiddlin' John Carson, that's the way he tuned his fiddle. "Sugar in the Gourd," he tuned it up high bass to play it.

MK: When did you first hear him?

WS: Probably 1918 or '20, somewhere around there. Smith Shreve, now he had a phonograph. When he first started out he had one he carried. It was pretty heavy, though. It was a Victor, and he had it fixed some way another he could put a hole through that old Victrola. Had it fastened to it and put it over his shoulder, the records over his other shoulder in a sack. He'd carry that around to people's houses and play those phonograph records. He really enjoyed it. I met Smith one time up there on the Huttonsville straight, had mud roads back at that time, and he said, "Come over tonight," he said, "got the best 'Turkey in the Straw,' you ever heard. Fiddlin' John Carson!" We'd all meet there, a whole lot of people'd go to Smith's to hear those phonograph records. He kept right up with them. When a new one came out, why he'd have it.

MK: Who were the great fiddle players over here in Mill Creek? Was Charlie Bell one of them?

WS: Charlie, he lived up on Elkwater at the time he was doing the fiddle. He taught them all to play, his wife, Howard, Lee, and Bobby played. He had a band of his own family. And they played pretty good music. I'd go over to Charlie's and play with him of the night, walked about three miles one way. Yes, Charlie's a mighty fine man. I don't know how he learned his music, but he composed an old tune called "Susie's Band," and I put it on the record. I rearranged the tune, he wanted it recorded awful bad. I've got permission to record it. Charlie's 93 years old. He lives down near Valley Bend. He played up until he cut his fingers off in a saw. He can still play accordion some, but now Charlie was a pretty good fiddle player.

MK: So after Smith's Victrola, people got radios, did they?

WS: Yeah, they got a radio that operated off of batteries, and only one could listen at a time on it. You had to use earphones. Then finally they got one that had a big horn on it, and everybody could listen in the house. But it wasn't too good. There was a lot of interference back at that time, you know. But we'd listen to a station that had the old country music on, you know, hillbilly music. I heard John Carson and Arthur Smith. They had a station at Hopkinsville, Kentucky, used to hear a lot of good music over that but I just couldn't remember who did the playing. But the "Grand Ole Opry" was the main place.

MK: What about the Carter Family and Jimmie Rodgers?

WS: I worked a long time to learn "The Wildwood Flower" on the guitar. I finally worked it out. [Then a piece] that

Jimmie Rodgers could pick out on his guitar. I learned that from records, see. The Carter Family put out a lot of records and I learned all of their songs. I could play all them on a guitar, could pick them with a straight pick or my finger picks, either one . . . Yes, and I played with Clayton McMichen in Virginia. They'd have fiddlers' contests, and Clayton, he'd always win. Couldn't beat him on a fiddle. He'd always hand it down to Emery Street—we called him "Stroupy"—he was from Harrisonburg. He was in the monument business there. That's what caused his death, that old dust. He done the work with chisels, you know. Terrible thing. Stroupy was an awful good fiddle player.

MK: So you just soaked up every bit of music you could find locally. You were interested in everybody who played anything, whether it was guitar or banjo or . . . ?

WS: Yes, anything. Accordion or anything. Feller by the name of Bernard Kuhn come in here from Cameron, West Virginia. I'd play the fiddle and he'd play the accordion. He was mighty fine, he'd play any fiddle tune, could read any music. I played a lot of music. Every spare minute I got I'd put it in on the music. 'Course I never went out and played for a living, I just played for the fun of it mostly.

MK: While you were growing up you sought out all the people that played locally, but you were also listening to the gramophones and then to the radios, so you were getting two kinds of influences. I guess everybody who played was paying attention to the radio music, weren't they?

WS: Oh yes, they'd set up 'til . . .

MK: And try to play like Fiddlin' John Carson or . . . ?

WS: And music back in them days was harder to learn than it is now, because you couldn't see nobody play and you just had to figure out what he was doing the best you could. It's much easier nowadays because you can see them play, 'bout how they're bowing the fiddle, or picking the banjo or guitar, everything like that, you know.

MK: Well, when did you first notice a class of professional musicians who did nothing else but travel and play on the radio?

WS: Back in, oh, 1936, somewhere along there. You could make more money back in '28, in the '30s, up in '35 and '36, at playing around just the local places, houses and square dances. I've played for dances by myself a lot of times. And then maybe we'd have a guitar player and would take up a collection. Some of the fellers, them Sees up here, was very liberal with their money. They liked to dance and they'd throw in a $10 bill. That was a lot of money back at that time. Ten dollars was 10 days hard work. Ralph See, he was Circuit Clerk for years here at Elkins. And he'd say, "Now boys, we got to pay the fiddler." He wore one of them hard-shelled straw hats and he'd take her round. They'd always throw in a $10 bill apiece, them Sees would. I made more money back then than you could make in the '40s or '50s. Back in the '50s

Motorcycling was a passion second only to fiddling in Woody Simmons's younger days. Photographer unknown.

now, why music went over pretty good, but still there was no money in it. I tried it down through Bluefield and around, and a man could starve to death playing.

MK: Well, by 1930 you were a pretty swell young feller, weren't you? You played music a lot, what else did you do for fun?

WS: I'd fish and hunt. Oh, yes, and rode them motorcycles. Yes, sir, I even tried out riding the walls—just about a day. I seen I wasn't going to last long at that.

MK: Riding the walls? What was that?

WS: Oh, that was over the Pocahontas County Fair. It was a thing like a silo, about 50 feet high, the walls were straight up and down. The motorcycles belonged to the company.

MK: How did you get started up the side of the wall, did you have sticky tires?

WS: [You started up a ramp] slanted like that, and then as you got on the walls, why, no trouble to ride on the walls.

MK: And you could actually do that?

WS: Yes, I could ride a motorcycle, stand up on it or anything.

LS: Tell him what you did, tell him how you rode the motorcycle.

WS: I rode it every way you could get on it . . . stood up on it and played the fiddle.

MK: No!

WS: Stood up on the seat, yes, and rode it right down through Mill Creek. Lot of them fellers can tell you.

LS: He rode it from Huttonsville to Valley Bend standing up on the seat.

WS: Backwards.

MK: Was that a big old Harley, or what was it?

WS: Big Harley-Davidson, yes. I rode it on rock road or anything standing up on it. Most perfectly balanced feller in this country! I could have rode a wire, where you walked a wire, no trouble for me to balance anything. Keith Ambler brought his motorcycle over here from Buckhannon, to get me to dress it up for him a little bit. I did, and we took it up the road. He was in the car, had two other fellers with him. I drove it up to the foot of Cheat Mountain and adjusted the carburetor up real good, set the points, and maybe put a new set of spark plugs in it. Coming back down, why, at about 60 miles an hour, I stood up on the seat and passed him. And old Keith, he couldn't hardly get over that. He come back up and said, "Wood, please don't do that again. You don't know how that scared me!" But it wasn't no trouble to me, I could ride it. Any way I wanted to get on, it didn't make any difference.

MK: Tell me more about the Pocahontas County Fair.

WS: We was playing music all at the same time. Gander Digman, Bill Rosencrantz, Tuck Withrow, and Bob Carr. Stayed in a tent there part of the time. Part of the time we slept in the barn with the horses. Yes, and Gander Digman, he'd get there usually before I did. The Fair lasted a week, and maybe I wouldn't get there 'til on Tuesday. And he'd be there, they'd have him dressed up. He played the steam organ. He'd play for the hoochie-koochie girls, you know.

MK: What do you mean, "hoochie-koochie girls," Woody?

WS: Well (laughs).

MK: What do you mean by that?

WS: They were the girls that done the dancing on the stage, you know. Yes, and they'd come on . . .

MK: Was that an imported act, or were they local Pocahontas County girls?

WS: No, no. That was a big carnival. And they'd come out on the stage and do these dances, you know, and he'd play the steam organ for them. And he was a champion dancer. There was nobody in the world could beat him at dancing.

MK: He stayed pretty steamy himself, I guess?

WS: He was a regular clown up there. He'd join up with us and play with us when we got there. He'd always win the dancing contest. Sometimes, well, Hemp Carpenter might have beat him a time or two. But Gander was pretty hard to beat. And Pete Mosder, he was playing in the band. He had a Gibson tenor banjo. I've never seen him from that day to this. He lived at Independence, West Virginia. We had our pictures taken together.

S.P. Wallace was a wholesale druggist. He was president of the fair, I believe, and he let me sleep in his office one night. And then fiddled in them fiddlers' contests, and fiddled agin a mighty hard old feller, Edwin Hammons. Sometimes I beat Edwin, sometimes he'd beat me. Then one year they had a banjo contest. I went to see Jay Richards in the hardware store, and I bought a brand-new banjo to play in the banjo contest. They were also going to have a fiddlers' contest the next day. Well, they ruled me out and wouldn't let me play in [either] contest. I took the banjo back, told them to give me my money back, but they wouldn't, I had to keep it. The old banjo's still around. Paul Collett down here at Elkins owns the banjo now. He give me $40 for it. And I offered him $50 back for it. I would give him that back, to have the old banjo back again.

MK: Was it about that time that you met Laverne?

LS: When you rode the motorcycle and played the fiddle, well, we were already married then. We had been going around together on Becky's Creek for about a year before we even thought we was courting. We'd known each other all of our life. He'd dated every girl around but me. Finally he settled down with me.

MK: Did you play music together?

WS: She played the mandolin. She'd have been a fine singer, a fine musician if she'd kept on playing—why, if she'd kept on I'd probably be singing, too. Quit playing.

MK: Why did you stop?

LS: Just did . . . I played with him for a long time, but I was young and Woody was young then when we was married, and I'd get mad easy and he would, too. And I guess I just quit. I played a few dances with you, didn't I?

WS: Yeah.

MK: You know, a lot of fiddlers I've talked to over the years tell me they quit for a while. Did you ever quit playing?

WS: Yes sir, I quit, but I don't remember how many years. I thought maybe about 10, but I don't think I did. Didn't quit that long, did I, Laverne?

LS: No, because you began playing dances when William was tiny little. You started playing with Zillah Hutchinson. You never quit no more, you played steady.

WS: But they'd be a lot of times I'd quit for a long time. Now one time I quit and went to work on a strip job at night. Went to work on a shovel, could make more money working on the shovel. Back at that time there wasn't much money in playing. You'd play at those club houses, why they'd maybe pay you $5 or $6. You'd burn gas coming and going, and you didn't make anything out of it. Far as going out to make a living playing music, I never did fool with that.

❧

Fiddle contests at the Mountain State Forest Festival in Elkins drew large crowds and lots of local fiddlers. The prize money was good and the competition stiff. The festive spirit brought people together from all over the countryside de-

spite unpredictable, spitty October weather. The downtown section was blocked off for street dances and other exciting events. Simmons attended the very first Forest Festival in 1930, when he was just 19, and won the fiddle contest. He recalls interesting details of early festivals.

❧

WS: I don't remember what the prize money was. Wasn't much, though. I believe I played "Mississippi Sawyer." And we played several years. Dewey Hamrick was just talking last summer like he got a big laugh out of it. He played in the contests, too. He lives over in Princeton. At that time he lived on Point Mountain.

[In 1932] me and Brownie Ross tied for first place. Brownie, he was from Wendell, West Virginia. Worked in the coal mines. He was a real good fiddle player. That year they judged by the applause of the crowd, and you couldn't tell any difference. They's both the same. So it was decided we'd play another tune, said we had to play the same tune in the play-offs. Brownie said, "How about 'Mississippi Sawyer,'" and I said alright. So we played it, and still Dick Collett, the feller that was doing the judging, couldn't tell any difference in the applause. And he said we'd just flip a coin, so they flipped the coin and I won.

MK: What were those early Forest Festivals like?

WS: They had street dances. I played for the street dances for years and years. They have it up in a building now, and nobody goes hardly. But there was an awful crowd there when they had it on the streets. We played on a platform up to the YMCA and they danced on the street. There sure was a lot of people attending, I know that. Usually it was pretty weather, only it was kind of cold. One year I remember the second day of the Forest Festival there was three inches of snow.

MK: When did your radio career begin?

WS: In 1935, I believe it was, I played with the Leary Family over in Harrisonburg, Virginia. I played for them regular when Wilma Lee was [a girl]. Wilma Lee Cooper, she's still playing over the "Grand Ole Opry." Jake Leary was her dad, you know. She played the guitar and I done the fiddle. They was great singers. Nobody could beat them.

LS: Wilma Lee started out playing the guitar, playing radio shows.

WS: Yeah, they was the greatest singers there was ever in this country. They could sing most any style, they sung Carter Family songs. They would sing a lot of hymns.

Then I fiddled for Joe Phillips and the Dixie Pals in Fairmont. Was on the air at 5:30 to 6:00 in the morning, then from 9:00 'til 9:15, and 4:00 to 4:30 ["Sagebrush Roundup"]. I didn't play there very long, didn't even join the union. They wouldn't let me carry my fiddle case even then, 'cause they was checking there all the time. There were several

Woody Simmons's group at WDNE, Elkins, in 1950. From left to right: Woody Simmons, William Simmons, Rusty Helmick, and Arnold Selman. Photographer unknown.

groups on the air in Fairmont at the time. Snap and Ginger was there, and another group. Arnold Selman, the banjo picker, he went with me. He didn't have no job. And we stayed there in Fairmont. We got to playing bluegrass with Snap and Ginger some, and was going to kind of organize as a band. Frankie Moore, he was over the whole group of us. He got after us and said no more "criss-crossin' around," playing with first one group and then the other. I decided I was quitting, and we come up here to Elkins and went on Radio WDNE.

MK: Was that in '49, the year you opened the restaurant in Mill Creek?

WS: Yes, I was at Huttonsville, and then in 1950 we moved to Mill Creek. [Managed] a Pure Oil station down on the corner, was there a couple of years.

LS: He had the gas station and I had a restaurant down there.

WS: Then we moved up above the Post Office here behind the restaurant for 25 years.

MK: Was that where the deer got in?

WS: That was before we had the restaurant.

LS: Now tell him about it, just like it was.

WS: Well, I had sold a car to a feller, and I was coming down here and meet him to fix the title up. Got up here to the high school building, why a deer jumped across the road in front of me. There was a real steep bank on the other side, and he run up agin that bank and a barbed wire fence up

there. The bank was so steep that he couldn't jump over the fence, and he run back down into the road in front of my car. I kept after him down through town.

LS: Blowing the horn at him.

WS: Blowing the horn. And the show building was on the left of the road at that time. 'Bout time for people to go to the show. I wanted to run the old deer down by the show building so everybody could see him. Now the police, his name was Red, he heard the horn a-blowing and he thought it was somebody speeding. He got behind a telephone pole there and he said he meant to blow the tires off that car when it came along. Said about that time he seed something pass that looked like a big Jersey cow. The deer was running 35 miles per hour, was what he was doing. I kept the car right up to his heels. He didn't seem to want to get out of them bright street lights, you know, and my car lights. He just stayed right in the middle of the road right down through there. 'Course there was no cars coming either way, only me. I slowed up before I got to the show building. I wanted everybody to see the old deer, that's the reason I was blowing the horn. When he got to the bank corner up here, why he jumped up on the sidewalk. He took the sidewalk and Ham Gum, he can tell you about it. Ham's getting up in years. Ham, he was standing on the corner. He and somebody was talking, and the old deer jumped through this big window, oh, it must have been, I don't know, it's an awful big glass window.

LS: Post Office.

WS: Post Office window, yeah. Ham said he thought it was somebody threwed a damn big rock through the window. Ham talks kind of rough. About that time the police, he was hid down there, he said, "What's going on here?" And I said, "There's a big deer jumped in the Post Office." People, you know, commenced to gathering around this commotion. In half an hour, why there must have been 150, 200 people there, cars a-stoppin', you know, and parking in the road. Red was just a-running round through the people spreading them with his arms, telling them to get back off the street, that deer would jump out of there and cut them all to pieces with his hooves. Finally he said, "Go get Wrightmeyer to unlock the Post Office and get the deer out." So they had to go after Wrightmeyer, and they unlocked the door and opened up and the floor was slick with oil. The old deer, his hooves, you know, he couldn't walk. He'd fall down. He was cut a little bit, he was bleeding, and Red said that deer'd die, said his throat was cut and he'd die. I said, "Ah, he won't die." The old deer wouldn't come out at all. George, that was Red's brother, he come up around there and started to look in to see what was going on, said "What's going on around here?" Red said, "Get back from there, George, that deer'll jump out of there and cut you all to pieces with them hooves. Get back off the streets! Get back off the streets!"

And by gracious, Ray Amos, he come up around there. He had been to Helen Bell's store and he had a sack of groceries on his back. He hadn't even attempted to go over and look in. Red grabbed Ray by the arm and reached for his blackjack. "Now I told you two or three times to get back off the streets here," Red said, "I could take you to jail here in a minute." Ray says, "Well, I haven't been doing nothing!"

"Woody, I'll have to get a warrant for you," Red says. "All right, Red," I says, "I've had a hundred dollars worth of fun out of this." But he says, "I'll have to get a warrant for you now. I'll have to call the state police and the game wardens." I says, "All right." He says, "That deer's gonna die." Still the deer wasn't out of the Post Office yet. Couldn't get it out, you know. Well, they deputized Ralph Brady, went and got him to go in to the Post Office, see if he could get the old deer out. As soon as Ralph went in the Post Office, that deer jumped out the other big glass window, broke it. You can see the windows as you drive by, how big they are. And the deer ran off up the road. There must have been, I'd say at least 150 people there. Never seed such a crowd in my life.

Red went to old man Luther's office and wanted to get a warrant for me, the deer jumping in the window, me running the deer down through there. I come down the next morning and seen what went on. The game wardens come up and the polices, but they never done nothing about it.

⌒

In 1949 Simmons went on the road again in search of radio work, this time with the encouragement of old friends Jack and Helen Williams, natives of Oklahoma, who had previously played music over the radio in Bluefield. The Williamses said there was radio work to be had if they would all travel and play together. In the company of his old banjo-picking friend Arnold Selman and his 12-year-old son, William, Simmons set out to tour Bluefield, Princeton, Beckley, and other music meccas in southern West Virginia. Woody describes the circuit-riding adventure as a terrible struggle, even to find a place to stay. But the three of them finally found a room near Princeton with a kind woman who charged only $2.50 apiece a week. "She took a liking to us, and she'd stay up at night 'til we come in and feed us, and didn't charge us anything for food." Using Princeton as a base, Woody, William, and Arnold booked shows across the southern counties to Williamson. But they ran into stiff competition. Ezra Cline and the Lonesome Pine Fiddlers were on the road at the time, as were Rex and Eleanor Parker. Lester Flatt was working Bristol, Tennessee. The Simmons group was footing all its own bills, ". . . and we just couldn't make any money at all." So Woody left William to travel for a while longer by himself and went home to Laverne in Mill Creek. After a few weeks, they drove over to Princeton to rescue their exhausted, star-struck son, and they brought him home.

At the age of 13 William was a kind of child prodigy in the world of country music. Laverne had gotten him started chording the mandolin when he was a very small child, and it wasn't long before he had a guitar in his hands. Woody says he ". . . played the fiddle, too. I taught him to play the fiddle when he was four years old." William could fiddle like Benny Martin, pick like Lester Flatt, and sing like Bill Monroe, according to his father.

⌒

WS: Music was just real easy for him, yes, sir, he never had no trouble learning anything. He'd hear a song once and he'd know the tune and know the words. He never had to work hard at playing music, he could play any style, rock 'n' roll or any style, it didn't make any difference. And he could read music, I think that advanced him some. He wouldn't play with nobody that played the least bit out of time, now that was just out with him. If I'd break time the least bit in a tune, why he'd stop me right then. After he got crippled up he couldn't use his arm no more, but he'd listen to us play and tell us where we was losing time. He'd straighten me out not later than a year before he died. He said nobody could dance the way we was playing the tune.

MK: How old was he when he was injured?

WS: Twenty-seven. He played right up 'til that time, played with all kinds of groups. I've got 45 rpm records he cut with the Pelferry Brothers in Kentucky. He done the fiddling for them. And the next week after he got crippled they was over at the hospital and wondered if he'd be able to cut another album, another record with them.

MK: You told me Bill Monroe was William's idol?

WS: Yeah, [Bill Monroe] was at our place all day one day, down at the restaurant. 1951. He played two shows and didn't have an amplifier with him, and used my equipment. He was there all day. And William had boxing gloves. Bill put the gloves on him and, I believe, Gordon Terry. Got out there and boxed. Had a big time that time. Rudy Lyle was with him. He had a Gibson banjo, and on the second show he asked William if he thought I'd care if he'd go down and get my Bacon banjo, he'd like to play it. And William took him down. When they come out on the second show, why he had that gold-plated Bacon & Day banjo of mine. He really liked it. Gordon Terry was with him at the time doing the fiddling.

MK: Did you fiddle some with Bill, did he like your style?

WS: Yeah, I played with him, I played all his songs back at the time. Any of them songs he sang, I could play them.

MK: What happened after that? What kind of style did William develop?

WS: Well, he started out in bluegrass music. Then when he went into the service he stayed in Newfoundland. Why, he got a rock 'n' roll band. And then in Goose Bay, Labrador, he played western and country music. Then he was in Texas and he played different styles of music there. He also had a group of musicians in Florida. But when he went to Newfoundland he had a rock 'n' roll band. It was an awful good band. I have the tapes out there.

MK: Did you tell me you went to visit William there?

WS: Yes, I went in 1959. I drove a 1941 Ford up there. I built that car. Took the car body in the garage and taken the body off the frame and cleaned the frame up real good and cut it out. Had to change the master cylinder and put power brakes on, power brake unit off a Chrysler. Put a Lincoln transmission and overdrive in it. Cut the torque tube and drive shaft. Welded the torque tube back. Re-splined the drive shaft. Cut 12 and $^3/_8$ inches off the drive shaft and the torque tube. And bored an Olds 88 engine to four inches. Put a three-quarter cam in it and solid lifters with adjustable tappets and two Cadillac four-barrel carburetors on it. Had windshield washers on it, back-up light, adjustable springs— make them any tension I wanted. Power steering. Had Lincoln hubs and drums on it. Adjustable shocks. It would do most anything you wanted it to, that car would.

The engineer here on the Penn Line said I'd never make it up there and back in it, the brakes would burn out in it. I told him they wouldn't burn out any quicker in it than they would in a Chrysler. So I left at 1:30 on a Sunday morning. Two o'clock Sunday afternoon, I was going through New Haven, Connecticut. Monday morning I called back from Augusta, Maine, at 7:00. And Tuesday morning at 8:00 I was at North Sydney, Nova Scotia. Got on a ship there at 8:00 that night, and got off at Port aux Basques, Newfoundland, at 8:30 the next morning. Hit blacktop road, it only lasted 17 miles. Oh, I had 135 miles of rock base road to drive on. William met us out of Stephensville, Newfoundland, about 4:00 that evening. And we went into Stephensville to his home.

William said we could go to the dance with him that night at the road house, the Rose Club. Said he had a rock 'n' roll band. I told him then, I said, "Now, that's going to be a joke." When they pulled back the curtain I really had a surprise. He had a good rock 'n' roll band. He kept his violin there beside of him, and he played lead guitar. Then he said I'd just as well play with them. I played a few waltzes on the fiddle and got by with that, got $15 a night while I was there.

MK: Sounds like you really enjoyed the trip.

WS: Yes, I really did. I caught a lot of nice salmon fish. And Martin, he was a guide, he tied my flies for me—it was unlawful to fish with spinners in the Harry's River—and I'd catch fish, because he knew how to tie flies. We caught a lot of nice salmon. Then there was no law on brook trout. Caught some 18 inches long. You catch as many of them as you want, catch them any way you want.

And then I got acquainted with a lot of musicians. When I was up to St. John's [Newfoundland] I cut a tape for the Canadian Broadcasting System. They wanted to know where I had been in Newfoundland, and the only place I could think of was Port aux Basques.

We left the first of September, the day moose season come in. They wanted me to stay there and moose hunt with them, to go with them before the season come in, but I was afraid to go. Because if they caught me killing a moose out of season up there, they'd have kept me a lifetime.

MK: Woody, you've had a lot of setbacks in your music through the years, haven't you?

WS: Sure have. In 1968 I got paralyzed, got my spine broke in two places in a truck wreck hauling coal for the Carnation Milk Company. Hauled coal for them for 15 years. And I just got down the road here a mile and a half and a feller come around on my side of the road. I tried to stop. Wasn't much of a wreck. Everybody said they didn't know how in the world I ever got hurt. But the doctor said I was born with a narrow spine and didn't take much to snap it. Well, I couldn't use my hand and couldn't even walk for a time. And then when I did get so I could use my left hand a little bit, I couldn't use my right one. I couldn't lift the music, or anything like that, and it kind of throwed me off 'til I didn't even know the tunes, you know. I forgot all the tunes.

People would put the fiddle in my lap, Kenny and Merle,

and I couldn't do anything with it, couldn't even lift it. And one night I was watching television, and they was there trying to get me to play. I seen Paul Warren on the television and he played an old tune, "Take Me Back to Tulsa." And I said, "I used to play that tune." I got the fiddle and sawed around a little on it and got so I could sort of play it just a little bit. Well, from that time on I kept working on that tune and got so I could play it again—I played it for, oh, two or three months.

And then I went over to Marlinton Pioneer Days and got in the fiddlers' contest. Some of them played two tunes, some of them played three, but I could only play just the one tune. I had to walk with a cane at that time, and I got out in the crowd and sit down in a chair. They said the contest would be judged on smoothness and tone quality. And they named over the third place winner. Of course, I knew, well, I thought, no chance of me winning anything. And named over the second place winner. And they named over the first place winner—it was me! Won first place on that old tune. But actually that was the only tune I could play. Well, I kept a-gaining a little all the time then. I got so I could play, but it was mighty hard because my fingers just wouldn't hardly work at all. Some of the tunes I never did gain back to this day. And "Fire on the Mountain." I had one awful time with that. I had to hunt up an old disc that had it on to get it figured out. That's the way I got back on to it again after I got disabled.

MK: Just felt your way back.

WS: Uh huh. Still bothers me yet in my hands. Just don't work good. Jim Andy says to me, says, "I want to get up close to you and watch your fingers because," he said, "I know you're doing a lot of work with them fingers, but I can't see them." And he got up close and watched them. I don't raise them very high off the fingerboard, because I lose time if I do, see. And the closer I can keep them to the strings, why, I can make the notes much quicker. And he says, "I see what you're doing now, you're not clearing the strings very much." And he said, "That's an advantage." But I had to learn to do that because I couldn't move my fingers as fast.

MK: And you just got back from all that trouble and then your heart gave out?

WS: Yeah, I had a heart attack in 1978, February 12. Had open-heart surgery the third day of August, 1978. Yes, they said it was the worst heart surgery they'd ever performed in that hospital. Said they came awful near losing me.

MK: But you came right back and have been winning steadily at contests ever since.

WS: I went over to Morgantown last fall, I went in the hospital down here, and the doctors decided they'd put a monitor on me and let me go. And they said, "Well, let him go. Better be over there than laying in the bed, and if he dies, well, he'll die happy." So I went over there [the Mountaineer

Days Festival in Morgantown] and played about 30 minutes in the afternoon, and I had to make a report every hour how I was doing and feeling. I did. And the next day, then, I went over there, the next night, and won first place in the fiddlers' contest on Saturday night, November 4.

MK: Looking back over all your musical life, who do you think are the great fiddlers who influenced you?

WS: Edwin Hammons. He was the best old-time fiddler that I ever heard, I believe. He played here in Mill Creek in a contest. He won a competition or two here in Mill Creek.

MK: Beat you on your home ground, huh?

WS: Yes sir. Well, he did beat me.

MK: Did you ever go down home with him? What were his people like?

WS: None of his boys didn't play the fiddle, as I know of. But Burl, that's his nephew, he's a pretty good fiddle player. Burl Hammons, yes. But old Edwin, now, he had some tunes he was hard to beat on, "Billy in the Low Ground," and then he made that old "George Washington March" up himself. One day I said, "Edwin, play me the 'George Washington March.'" He said, "I'll play her for you, but I won't play her fer"—he called Dewey Hamrick 'Jewey'—he said, "I won't play her fer Jewey, but I'll play her for you." And he did, he played me the "George Washington March," and I learned it from him. I won a fiddlers' contest in Glenville with it. I could never win nothing at Glenville, only with the old "George Washington March." You tune the fiddle altogether different to play that. Edwin Hammons would drop the G string down to D, and the E string down to D.

A lot of them says that Burl Hammons can play as good as Edwin. But I'll tell you the same I'd tell Burl, that he couldn't play noways near like Edwin. Burl'd agree to that, too. Burl's a real good fiddle player but nothing like Edwin. Edwin could play a lot of tunes, and he used his fingers properly, and he done a good job bowing the fiddle.

MK: Who were the other great ones from that time?

WS: Wren McGee. Wren would play a piece and Edwin would say, "Let me have the fiddle." He'd play the same piece and try to beat him, and if he got a little something different, why Wren would say, "Let me play her again." Wren, he was pretty hard to beat. Couldn't ever keep up with him, because anybody that'd play a tune like him, why, as soon as they'd play it like him, he'd play it some other way. Wasn't no use to try to learn to play like him, 'cause if you'd learn to play a tune just exactly like he did, why the next time you heard him he'd play it different. Wren, he'd win most of the contests back in them old days.

MK: What about the great radio fiddlers? You mentioned Arthur Smith and Clayton McMichen.

WS: But you couldn't leave Chubby Wise out! Chubby Wise was a mighty fine all-round fiddler, I think.

MK: He prospered during the 1940s, was it?

WS: Yes, he fiddled for Hank Snow for 16 years. Big Howdy Forrester was fiddling for Bill Monroe, and Chubby, he was down in Florida. He heard on Saturday night that Forrester had to go to the Army on Monday, so he drove to Nashville on Saturday, and he asked at the door where Monroe was. He said they told him back behind the curtain. And he asked if he could go in and see him. They said yeah. And he went in there and asked Monroe, "I hear you need a fiddle player." Bill said, "Yes, I do." Said, "Can you play?" Said, "Yes." Said, "How about playing me a hoedown." He said, "All right." Said he played "Katy Hill." Monroe said to him, he said, "How about playing one of my songs that I sing, and let me sing and you play it." And he said he done "Footprints in the Snow." Bill said, "Where's your clothes at?" So he fiddled for him for several years. Then he done fiddling for Lester Flatt and them, too, I think.

To me, when it come down to bluegrass music, I don't think there was anybody can beat Bill Monroe. And any of the boys he trained, I think, is the best. I never thought that none of them could play as good after they left Bill Monroe. 'Course, that's just my opinion of the thing. Seem to me like he could train them to play real good.

MK: Did the bluegrass music challenge you, Woody? You were always kind of an inventor, weren't you, always changing tunes a little bit, trying to develop your own style?

WS: Yes, sir. Yes, I play a tune different from what a lot of fellers do. Just like "Gold Rush," I can play it the way it was played on the record, but I have a style of my own to play. I can play it either way.

MK: I know that you made up at least one fiddle tune,

because a few months ago I was in Bemis, a little place where I had never been before. And there standing by her gate was a woman named Mrs. Shifflet. We got to talking, and she told me that she had helped name one of your fiddle tunes and had won some kind of prize.

WS: Yes, yes. Arnold [Selman] and I worked on an old tune and got so we could play it together. We played over Radio WDNE every day. We didn't have no name for the tune, so I decided to give a prize to who'd send in the best name. And this Shifflet woman from Bemis sent in the name "The Fiddler's Hornpipe," and I chose that for the name of the tune, and I give her a gold necklace. And I played this tune, well, 28 years, I reckon. Yeah. But somebody come out with a tune something near it. I don't know what they call it. I don't know whether they learned it off of me, or where it comes from, but it's almost like mine. So I kind of dropped my tune, don't play it much anymore.

MK: Woody, how do you feel about what's happening with music these days?

WS: Well, I'm going to tell you one thing, I'm awful glad that the young generation has picked up the music. Somebody's got them interested in it, and I think they're doing wonderful. The boys and girls that's playing now, they're way advanced in the music. Back when I was their age, there was very few people could play music like them. They're learning quicker, 'cause they've got somebody to instruct them and teach them, I think.

MK: Woody, you're in the midst of putting out your first record, and you've had some help from the Currence Brothers. Can you tell me something about them?

Jimmie Currence of the Currence Brothers accompanies Woody Simmons. Photograph by Doug Yarrow.

Woody Simmons pauses at the front door of his Mill Creek home. Photograph by Doug Yarrow.

WS: I've known Jimmie and Loren Currence since before they played.

MK: Since they were young boys? Did you know their daddy?

WS: Oh, yeah, their daddy, Jacob Currence. He never missed hearing our program. He'd be out in the cornfield, Jimmie said. We'd come on at 12:00 in the day, and he'd say, "Boys, it's time for Woody to be on the radio. Let's throw these hoes down and get to the house." And Jimmie said he'd pull his chair up close to the radio, it was a battery radio, I figure. At that time, they lived over back in the "High Germany" country, over here back of Blue Rock. It's a real rough country to get in and out. And his dad said, "Now, boys, be right still, you're going to hear something here in a little bit." Soon as we came on the air we'd always play a hoe-down tune. Jimmie said his dad said, "Now it's going to take something to beat that feller." I've played off and on with them for years. Jimmie used to play the mandolin along with me.

MK: Did their dad play any?

WS: No, but he was a good singer. His mother was a fine singer. I have an album here of them singing hymns. Jimmie

and Lody [Loren] was singing on it, too. First time they played on the radio or television they went to Pittsburgh and I let Lody have my old Gibson guitar. He didn't have any music back at that time. And they had it pretty bad. They was crippled up and was lucky to live as long as they have. They're fine musicians, a good bunch of boys. They always played as hard as they could with me to help me win a contest. And they've never made me feel a bit bad from beating me in a contest.

MK: What is the toughest contest you ever played in?

WS: Well, my toughest contest was down here in Elkins. Lions Club had it, they built me up pretty big, and I'd won it a couple times, and they give a big write-up in the paper. I just had to play real good to win that contest, and then tied with a feller. We had to play a waltz and a hoedown, and I'd played these old waltzes so many times that I'd get kind of tired of them. So I played the "Roxanna Waltz," and I got Gerry Milnes to play the guitar. I trained Gerry to play the guitar after me, and on the play-off on the tie, why, Gerry, he played with me and I won that contest. It was right smart competition there, a feller name of Jim Hilders.

MK: Woody, if you had it to do all over again, would you play it like you did, or do you think you'd have gone on the road and shot for the Nashville scene, or what do you think?

WS: I'd just do it the same, I believe.

MK: That's what I like to hear.

WS: Believe I got more enjoyment out of it. That's right. I'd go out here and play just as quick all night for nothing as if somebody'd say, why I'll give $200 if you go and play. Back when I was playing around it was kind of like PTP. Promise to pay. Somebody'd say, "I'll give you $5 if you come over here and play a dance." Well, they'd all get a drink or two, and they'd forget to pay the fiddler, you know. And you'd go home without any money.

I always played with anybody, it didn't matter, now, they didn't have to be the finest players. Or if they could just play a little bit I still played and tried to enjoy playing with them. There'd always be a good note made somewhere on the fiddle. I'd listen. There would always be somewhere in the tune something that interested me. A lot of people would just hear a tune and say, "Why, you can't play," and wouldn't listen no more. There's no fiddler that I've heard but what I couldn't find something that he made sound good somewhere along the way.

EDITOR'S NOTE: This article first appeared in the July–September 1979 issue of *Goldenseal* (vol. 5, no. 3). Woody Simmons continues to win fiddling awards around West Virginia and western Maryland. He was the 1983 Vandalia Award winner and is frequently featured as a master artist for the West Virginia Folk Arts Apprenticeship Program. Laverne Simmons passed away in 1994.

Clark Kessinger

PURE FIDDLING

Charles Wolfe

Iⁿ the summers of the late 1960s, the great Southern fiddle contests found themselves awash in new fans. Thousands of young enthusiasts, caught up in the throes of the folk music revival, hitchhiked and drove their way into the humid Southern summers bound for festivals in places like Union Grove [North Carolina], Pulaski [Virginia], Richwood [West Virginia], Pomeroy [Ohio], even up in Weiser, Idaho.

It was an age of rediscovery, and the young fans searched out and coaxed into playing musicians from Eck Robertson to Arthur Smith to Clayton McMichen. But one of the few veterans who could really hold his own at the contests, who needed no patronizing or special consideration, was a lively, lanky fiddler who always wore a small-brimmed hat. He loved to play, and was a master showman; he would shake his hips, crouch like a batter, dance a little, and occasionally let out a spontaneous whoop. He ripped into a tune like a hungry man faced with a plate of fried chicken. He played "Ragtime Annie" with a feverish tempo and launched into "Sally Ann Johnson" in a way that dared anybody to keep up.

People who had heard his old records from the 1920s swore that, unlike the other resurrected fiddlers of those summers, he was actually playing better than he had then. He didn't have to be coaxed out of retirement; he roared out of it. By 1971, many of his fans had no qualms about using superlatives. "He is the greatest old-time fiddler around today," announced Rounder Records founders Ken Irwin, Bill Nowlin, and Marion Leighton after hearing him. Many agreed, and few in those days didn't know his name: Clark Kessinger.

His was pure fiddling, with no real concessions to popular taste. In the 70-plus sides he recorded for the old Brunswick company between 1928 and 1930, and the five LPs he made during his comeback in the 1960s, he had no novelty numbers, no funny vocals, no cute trick playing, no harmony singing. Except for a few square dance calls on his first records, it was all pure Kessinger; if you didn't like fiddling, it wasn't your music.

He came by it honestly. He grew up in rugged Lincoln County, south of Charleston, across the Kanawha River. "I was born in Kanawha County, Charleston, right out of Charleston, South Hills, and I was raised there," he recalled in 1971. "I stayed up around Boone County as much as I did

Knees bent and fingers flying, Clark Kessinger was a consummate musician and a master showman. He is pictured here during a 1960s fiddlers convention in Union Grove, North Carolina. Photograph by Jerry Galyean.

Possibly the earliest known photo of Clark Kessinger, this 1912 portrait shows him with a fiddle on the steps of the family's home. Other family member are unidentified. Photographer unknown; courtesy of Rosie Kessinger.

around Kanawha. We lived around Lincoln County when I was a boy. When I was about 10 years old we moved there. We moved back to Charleston then. South Hills that is. I was born 27th of July 1896. I was the youngest boy." Clark's father spent most of his time working as a molder in a local foundry, making wheels.

In later years, Kessinger was a little cagey about just where he learned his fiddling. He admitted that "my great-grandfather fiddled. Also my great-uncle on my mother's side, in Lincoln County. That was way back." He admired local fiddlers like George Dillons and the brothers Dave and Bob Glens. "One played slow music and the other played hillbilly [country music]." But probably his most important mentor was the legendary Ed Haley, the blind fiddler who never recorded commercially but whom many today consider perhaps the finest of all West Virginia–Kentucky fiddlers. "He was from over around Logan, close to the Kentucky line. He was a great fiddler, he was a smooth fiddler." Young Clark certainly inherited some of Haley's tunes, and most likely some of his unusual bowing technique. For much of his life Haley stayed around the Ashland area, and in later years openly admired Kessinger's playing, though he occasionally complained to friends that Kessinger always seemed to shy away from playing in front of him.

Clark had started playing music when he was only five and was playing for country dances by the time he was 10.

Though his first instrument was the banjo, he later switched to violin. "I just started playing, not to learn it. Just come natural to me." His first attempts at making money with music came when he was seven, in local saloons. "My dad used to take me there. My dad didn't drink; he used to take me there just to make money. I'd get 10 or 15 dollars a night, more than he made in a week, back in them times. The people who came in . . . throwing money at me. I used to dance, why I'd get out there and dance a little bit. That was quite a thing . . . I'd play and dance, carry on just a little bit." Ironically, young Clark didn't even own his own fiddle through all this; he would borrow his brother-in-law's, or "someone would just hand me one."

When America entered World War I, Kessinger was 21, and he found himself serving a stint in the Navy. By the time he got back to West Virginia he was starting to get a serious reputation for his fiddling. French Mitchell, a well-known fiddler from the area, recalled that by the early 1920s, he was known throughout the Kanawha Valley as a fierce competitor in local fiddling contests. At one such event, at Point Pleasant, Mitchell recalled that many of the contestants who had signed up suddenly dropped out when they learned that Kessinger was playing.

By this time he had started performing a lot with the son of his brother Charles, Luches "Luke" Kessinger (1906–1944). Nine years younger than Clark, Luke lived in Charleston and

South Charleston. Unlike a lot of the older West Virginia fiddlers, Clark Kessinger did not like to play solo; he enjoyed a guitar accompaniment and especially liked Luke's playing. "He played it clear, clear as he could be. That's what I liked about him. He was right there with the notes . . . every note that I hit, why he'd hit 'em. He didn't slack down on you, he didn't speed up or nothing. Well, we were used to one another. We used to have a time playing around in different places. Play for nothing. Never get no money out of it."

The pair also got their own radio show on the new station in Charleston, WOBU, when it opened in October 1927. The station was not all that powerful at first, but Kanawha County, full of factory towns and coal camps, could boast of around 10,000 radios, more than any other county in the state. The people in the area who had somehow missed Kessinger at fiddling contests and dances now had their chance to hear and admire him.

Next came the single most important event in the career of Clark and Luke: in February 1928 a major league recording company set up shop in Ashland, Kentucky, about 40 miles from Charleston. The company was Brunswick-Balke-Collender, which released records on the Brunswick and Vocalion labels. In charge of the activity was James O'Keefe, accompanied by Richard Voynow, a former piano player on some of jazzman Bix Beiderbecke's sessions.

For several months prior to the Ashland session, O'Keefe had networked through the region lining up talent. It would include an important cross section of key musicians from as far away as North Carolina and Tennessee. A temporary studio was set up at Carter's Phonograph and Music Shop at 217 Sixteenth Street in Ashland. Clark and Luke had been recommended to O'Keefe by a local violin teacher, Richmond Huston. "He wanted us to make some records. He said he could get us on. And sure enough, he did, he got us on."

The Kessingers were asked to report at 9:30 A.M. on February 11, at the very start of the session. O'Keefe's roster was short on fiddlers, and he was interested to hear the Clark Kessinger everyone in the area was talking about. He also had a specific problem he hoped the Kessingers could solve. Arch-rival Columbia had just issued a hot new seller which was threatening to become the biggest hit of 1928: an instrumental by a Mississippi fiddle band called the Leake County Revelers and entitled "Wednesday Night Waltz."

O'Keefe had sent a copy of the Columbia hit to Clark Kessinger and asked him to work up a version of both sides. It was no problem for Kessinger, who loved waltzes anyway, and he and Luke added it to the session. It became Brunswick 220, the first Kessinger recording. (It was O'Keefe, incidentally, who decided to name the pair the "Kessinger Brothers" because "it just sounded better.") It took off about as fast as the Columbia original, and soon Brunswick had a best-seller on its hands. In fact, it became the Kessinger Brothers' most

Clark Kessinger's recording career began on February 11, 1928, when he (left) and Luke Kessinger (right) recorded 12 sides for Brunswick records. Many of these early recordings included the dance calling of Ernest Legg (center), but their most successful record was a version of the popular "Wednesday Night Waltz." Photographers unknown.

popular record. "We'd have made a fortune if they'd paid us royalties," Kessinger said. There was no fortune, but its success did guarantee the Kessingers a recording career, and a chance to preserve some of the South's best fiddling.

Many of the early fiddle records released by the companies were designed for a practical purpose: square dancing. To that end, they were festooned with dance calls, sometimes with the caller right up in the mike, often frustrating listeners who were trying to appreciate the fiddling. On about half the Kessinger sides from this first session, a caller named Ernest Legg was brought in. Fortunately, Legg was a local man who had experience doing square dances with the Kessingers, and his calls did not distract all that much from the music. Indeed, they even added to the effect. Legg almost sang his calls, using a laid-back mountain tenor and long, cascading, internally rhymed phrases that actually echoed Kessinger's bowing patterns. Of the first 12 Brunswick sides, all but two featured calls on at least one of the sides. Soon the Brunswick bosses figured out that Kessinger's fiddling was attractive on its own terms and did not need to be marketed as a means to an end. After this first session, there were no more recordings using a caller.

The Kessingers' second record was also a best-seller: it was a fine reading of "Turkey in the Straw" backed with the first commercial record of a tune that would become a standard, "Hell Among the Yearlings." Kessinger's arrangement featured a much-copied technique where he brushes the string with his forefinger, creating a subdued pizzicato effect. Other releases from the first session included more common tunes, such as "Arkansas Traveler" and "Forky Deer," "Chicken in the Barnyard" and "Devil's Dream," and "Girl I Left Behind Me." Even these familiar standards were played with a drive and intensity that earlier versions lacked. Two of the more unusual tunes were "Garfield March" and "Kanawha March"; the former dated from the assassination of President James Garfield in 1881, and was originally a piece of sheet music called "Garfield's Funeral March." Kessinger had learned it from local fiddler Abe Glenn in 1903, when he was seven.

Though these and future records would carry his name and his music across the country, Kessinger didn't know that at the time. He was working hard at a day job as a caretaker for a wealthy Charleston resident, Harrison B. Smith. Smith knew Kessinger as a good painter and all-purpose handyman, but did not know he was a fiddler. One of the best legends about Kessinger describes how he found out about it. Researcher Nancy Dols tells one variant: "One day the cook

I Remember Clark Kessinger

Bobby Taylor

My introduction to the music of Clark Kessinger was at the age of 13 when my younger brother Michael ordered *The Legend of Clark Kessinger,* an LP with 18 tunes. My father, fiddler Lincoln Taylor, always said that there was more music on this record than any other.

I first met Clark Kessinger in person in 1969. This was when I got my driver's license at the age of 16. I drove to his home right off Kanawha Terrace in St. Albans. He lived in the lower level of a duplex apartment. We always referred to his home being located at Twin Maples. Actually, this was a little night club that stood in front of his house where Clark sometimes played. It got its name from the twin maple trees standing in the front yard.

Clark's little apartment was shared by his second wife, Rosie, and Dolly, their small dog.

With a little coaxing, I was able to get him to play "Arkansas Traveler." As long as I live, I will never forget his incredible bowing and noting. As our visits progressed over the next six years, I learned more of Clark's tunes and techniques. He was always very nice to me and willingly shared all of his secrets, for which I felt very privileged. Clark always told me to put the emphasis on the down bow. With this bow action accenting the down beat, he could achieve the ultimate of drive and dynamics.

A large part of my style and repertoire came from Clark's records and the instruction I received during our visits. I will

mention a few tunes that are very special to me. I always thought that Clark's version of "Arkansas Traveler" was unsurpassable. "Durang's Hornpipe," "Red Bird," and "Poca River Blues" were Clark's show tunes. Clark played "Hell Among the Yearlings" the best I have ever heard the tune. Clark composed "Turkey Knob" and "Wilson's Hornpipe," both of which I try to keep alive.

I learned a great deal about bowing from learning "Ragtime Annie," "Mississippi Sawyer," and "Rickett's Hornpipe." His "double back bowing" (as I call it) was one of the hardest things to learn. Only on one of my very good days am I able to perform this technique close to Kessinger's style.

In 1974 the late Tom King and I

was playing one of Clark's records in the kitchen when Mr. Smith came in and asked, 'Who's that wonderful fiddler?' He was amazed to find out it was Clark, and immediately hired him to teach his son to play."

Throughout the rest of 1928, the Kessinger Brothers' records continued to sell better than any other fiddle records in the Brunswick catalog. Some were issued on Sears labels under the name "Birmingham Entertainers," and later some of the sides would even be issued on French Canadian labels under the name "Les Deux Paroissiens." Convinced they had a major act on their hands, Brunswick invited Clark and Luke to come to New York in early 1929 to make a new round of discs. This session, spread out over several days, produced some 23 sides, none with any square dance calls. It, too, produced its share of classics. One was "Tugboat," in its first commercial recording. This record would make its way to, among other places, Texas, where the influential Texas fiddler Benny Thomasson would learn it and insert it into the Texas fiddle contest repertoire, where it remains to this day. Another was "Salt River" (later redone), an old Irish tune which would eventually make its way to bluegrass star Bill Monroe, who would record it as "Salt Creek."

There was "Dill Pickle Rag," "Old Jake Gillie," "Chinky Pin" (some Brunswick clerk's mangling of the word "chinquapin," a type of mountain chestnut), "Done Gone," "Sally Goodin," "Sourwood Mountain," "Mississippi Sawyer," "Richmond Polka," and "Soldier's Joy."

Other sessions followed in June 1929 (24 sides) and September 1930 (17 sides) before the Depression, and the sale of the Brunswick company, put a premature end to them. Even though these later recordings sold only a fraction of the earlier ones, due mainly to the Depression, many of them are considered true Kessinger masterpieces.

In addition to traditional fiddle tunes, Kessinger drew upon a number of sources to fill out his sessions, with fascinating results. One was the body of quirky, unusual West Virginia-Kentucky fiddle tunes he had grown up hearing in the Kanawha Valley. These included items like "Poca River Blues," "Birdie," "Three Forks of Sandy," "Portsmouth," and "Brownstown Girl," as well as the aforementioned "Old Jake Gillie." A second source was old pop songs, which Kessinger rearranged into fiddle tunes: Kerry Mills's "Whistling Rufus," "Steamboat Bill," "Little Betty Brown," Billy Reeves's 1869 hit "Shoo Fly," and "Little Brown Jug." A related source was Kessinger's unusual fondness for marches and polkas; not only did he do the popular "Garfield March," but he did

went to visit with Clark. This was to be a most special visit. I knew Clark had not been able to play since his stroke in 1971. The stroke affected his left noting hand. His bowing arm had not been affected, and I had studied his noting patterns for several years.

I decided to stand behind his chair holding the fiddle in front of him, my hand doing the noting and his doing the bowing. It was here I learned the "triple bowing" technique. There were several tunes we played in this manner. I was able to see what he did on "Hell Among the Yearlings," which has a very challenging bowing pattern. This was perhaps the highlight of my life to be able to note while Clark bowed. Together we played a pretty good tune. Tom was very impressed and continued to tell this story until his death in July 1993.

I had the pleasure of playing with Clark Kessinger's bow on June

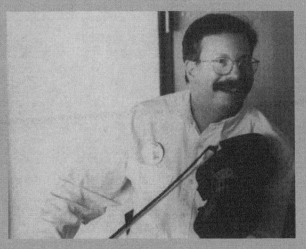

Today, Bobby Taylor is an accomplished fiddler in his own right. He plays and teaches Clark Kessinger–style fiddle at every opportunity. Photograph by Phil Swango, 1995; courtesy of the Augusta Heritage Center, Davis and Elkins College, Elkins, West Virginia.

13, 1997, at St. Albans City Park. This bow belongs to Jewel McClannahan, who bought it from Clark personally. It was an evening of reverence. The bow seemed to pull soul and tone from above. Even with the rain pouring down, it sang with the richest of tone. Clark's triple bowing, which I call the "bow jump," was never so easy. The bow seemed to possess the

spirit of the greatest master of all time. Since Clark showed me this incredible bowing after his stroke, it is a very important part of my presentation. I feel much gratitude to Clark for showing me his special secret which only he and I have shared to this day.

Benny Thomasson, the great Texas fiddler, went to visit Clark after his stroke in the early 1970s.

"Under the Double Eagle," "Polka Four," and others. A final source was original pieces, or constructs, where Kessinger pieced together parts of different tunes: "Everybody to the Puncheon," "Kanawha County Rag," and "West Virginia Special."

Kessinger occasionally complained that the three-minute length of the 78 rpm records actually caused him to repeat a tune more times than he thought necessary. But often when he did this he managed to infuse the different choruses with subtle variations. A typical Kessinger arrangement often featured a series of short, rhythmic bow strokes where he actually lifted the bow from the strings, followed by a long, breathtaking, cascading run (as in "Tugboat"). Unlike those of modern Texas fiddlers, his variations stayed close to the original tune outline; as Nancy Dols notes, "the smooth, clean exterior of his playing sometimes almost hides the intricate things he does with the melody, rhythm, and bowing." He was fond of devices such as the "brushing pizzicato" effect heard on "Hell Among the Yearlings" and "Going up Brush Fork," and of using entire lines of double stops to enhance a melody. Like many of the older mountain fiddlers, he was fond of adding an extra beat to a phrase, creating an irregular meter, making it hard for a competing fiddler at a contest to duplicate his style.

In later years, admirers of Clark Kessinger, noting his bow control, tone, and precision, assumed that he had had some formal training. Even today it is not clear how much he had. Kessinger himself insisted he was a "natural" musician, a self-taught country fiddler. By his own admission, however, Kessinger knew and studied the records of such popular classical violinists as Fritz Kreisler, Joseph Szigeti, and Jascha Heifetz. All three toured widely in the 1920s, and all three had a wide variety of popular recordings on the market.

Kessinger not only knew the records of these masters, but he heard them in person and actually performed before Szigeti. When Kreisler and Szigeti gave concerts in Charleston, the son of Kessinger's employer was able to get him into the concerts. On one such occasion Kessinger met Szigeti. Billy C. Hurt tells the story:

"After the concert was over, he [Smith, Kessinger's em-

This was such an historic event with two legendary fiddlers meeting for the first and last time. This was truly a fitting acknowledgment from one great master to the other. I can only think of the years Benny had thought and waited for this moment.

Clark influenced many great fiddlers with his recordings and performances. I will name a few local fiddlers he influenced. French Mitchell was quite renowned, and regarded Clark as the best old-time fiddler. Fiddlin' Mike Humphreys always had great respect for Clark's playing. Emmett M. "Lefty" Shafer, Reece B. "Sam" Jarvis, John Johnson, Glen Smith, Woody Simmons, Wilson Douglas, plus scores of others borrowed from Clark's vast collection of tunes and techniques.

I remember Clark talking about a rival fiddler (who will remain nameless) coming to visit him. I later went to see Clark to get his side of the story. Clark only said that yes, he was here, playing on an old loud fiddle. He said his dog was so disturbed, that it had intestinal distress (to be polite) ever since. The rivalry between fiddlers was always a source of entertainment for me as a young fiddler.

I talked to one of the judges at the Galax Old-Time Fiddlers Convention who judged Clark when he made his comeback to the stage in 1964. He said all was quiet about 2:00 A.M. The young music fans had already sacked out in front of the stage fast asleep. Clark Kessinger, Gene Meade, and Wayne Hauser hit the stage with a thunderstorm of spirit.

The first few notes Kessinger hit aroused everyone far and near. People rushed to the stage; the sleeping hippies started dancing. The festival was back to life. Well, with no doubt in anyone's mind, Kessinger "took the blue." This was the start of an incredible comeback.

I guess it is no wonder that musicians and listeners alike were truly taken by his incredible style.

John Morris, a well-known Clay County fiddler, went to visit Clark.

Clark stated some very memorable words regarding old-time music. John shared these words with me. Clark and John were discussing music, and Clark said, "If you are going to play this old-time music, you've got to put the power in it." To me, this describes Clark's philosophy of music.

Clark Kessinger died on June 4, 1975, at the age of 78. I will never forget how saddened I was to hear this news. I could no longer visit and get insight from this musical genius. With Kessinger's passing, more talent departed this world than I could imagine. I do my best to keep his memory alive.

I am very saddened that Kessinger's name has become somewhat unknown in the old-time music community. I hope Clark Kessinger can regain his rightful spot in the limelight.

EDITOR'S NOTE: This article first appeared in the fall 1997 issue of *Goldenseal* (vol. 23, no. 3).

Lester Flatt (right, with guitar) and Earl Scruggs (left, with banjo) accompanied fiddler Clark Kessinger when he appeared as a guest artist on the "Grand Ole Opry" in 1966. Kessinger was the only performer in the four-hour show to receive an encore—in fact, he received three. Photograph by Jerry Galyean.

ployer] wanted Clark to meet Szigeti. So he went up and got word to Clark that Szigeti was going to be there and he wanted him to meet him, so we went up to the house and met Szigeti, one of the greater violinists, and Szigeti wanted him to play a tune and Clark played the 'Mockingbird.' And Clark said old Szigeti like to pulled his hair out, and he said, 'How in the world do you do that?' Clark said, 'I just do it by ear, I don't know one note from the other.' He said Szigeti got his genuine Strad out, and he said Szigeti started playing that violinist stuff. He said Szigeti didn't know it, but he [Clark] was watching every move he made. He was getting all this stuff off of him. He was watching them hands and them double-triple stops he's putting on the violin. And that's where Clark got a lot of this violin touch that he had."

Kessinger himself later admitted his debt to Szigeti and Kreisler: "[I] caught the touch they had . . . Some of their kind of bowing, I could kind of add it in with hillbilly. Made it a lot better."

On September 20, 1930, about a year after the stock market crashed, the last of the Brunswick recordings were completed, and Clark Kessinger effectively dropped out of the national music scene for the next three and a half decades. He married in 1929, and began a family that would eventually number six children, none of whom showed any special interest in playing an instrument. "I was a painter by trade," he explained. "I painted for years and years. I painted for one man for about 18 years. One contractor. Mostly inside painting, decorating. I don't like the outside work. I never was no highclimber." His hand was so steady with the brush that he

Always looking for an audience, Clark Kessinger prepares to embark on one of his many fiddling excursions with guitarist Gene Meade. Photographer unknown; 1965 photograph from the James F. and Ola Comstock West Virginia History Collection, Booth Library, Davis and Elkins College, Elkins, West Virginia.

did not even have to use tape to protect the windows. During World War II he briefly left this trade to work as a guard at a local plant.

Not that he ever gave up fiddling. He and Luke played for a time in the 1930s over Charleston radio WOBU's "Old Farm Hour" and engaged in several of the highly promoted "fiddling showdowns" against Natchee the Indian. He appeared on stage shows with the Delmore Brothers, the Mc-Gee Brothers, Arthur Smith, Clayton McMichen, and others. They often played at City Hall for the mayor of Charleston. "One of the mayors was a good friend of mine," he remembered. "He was the Mayor Copenhavery [John T. Copenhaver, mayor of Charleston from 1951 to 1959]. I used to play for him. I'd always played for him when he'd have any doings going on. He liked the old-timey music. He was crazy about hillbillies." Clark and Luke also continued to play at dances and clubs, and in the late 1930s they actually appeared at the National Folk Festival in Washington, D.C. The end to the chapter came in May 1944 when Luke died.

Still, Kessinger kept his skills sharp by playing with different accompanists, whomever he could pick up, at various dance halls and clubs. Rock 'n' roll, with its electric guitars and Elvis imitators, came on the scene in the 1950s, but in West Virginia and other parts of Appalachia, many of the rural dance halls still preferred fiddle bands. In 1963 Kessinger was working at a club called Westfall's, down on U.S. Route 60 just east of Hurricane. It was a center for local square dances, big enough to have three sets on the floor at one time. Kessinger had been playing there for some time, and word had gotten out. One of the people who perked up at the news was Guthrie Meade, then working for the Library of Congress and a devotee of Kessinger's old records. At the National Folk Festival that year at Covington, Kentucky, Meade passed on the information to a young man named Ken Davidson.

Davidson was a young Charleston resident who was deeply interested in traditional music of the area, and was responsible for discovering some of the area's best performers. He had discovered the remarkable fiddler French Carpenter, as well as instrumentalist and singer Jenes Cottrell. He not only encouraged his finds to get out and perform more, but he took them to fiddling contests and festivals, including ones as far away as the Newport Folk Festival in Rhode Island. He also recorded them and formed a company called Folk Promotions to release his field recordings.

Acting on Meade's tip, in the spring of 1964 he drove to Westfall's Inn and introduced himself to Clark Kessinger. He was amazed at how well Kessinger was still playing and urged him to go up and compete in a fiddle contest at Pulaski, Virginia. He agreed and took first place. A second win at Richwood, West Virginia, soon followed. By August he was ready for the granddaddy of all Virginia contests,

"When I Grow Too Old to Dream." Clark Kessinger returns from Weiser, Idaho, clutching his trophy. Photograph by Jerry Galyean.

Galax, and lit out down Highway 19. There he formed an impromptu string band with two younger musicians, guitarist Gene Meade (from Draper, North Carolina) and banjo player Wayne Hauser (from Winston-Salem, North Carolina). Though Kessinger had never recorded with a full string band, it fit his fiddling like a glove, and after a few rehearsals the group took first place in the string band category, beating out 60 other groups.

Later that year Davidson recorded the band in Charleston, and released the results as *The Legend of Clark Kessinger* on his Folk Promotions label. Guthrie Meade wrote a booklet of notes and included a complete discography of the old Kessinger Brothers 78s. By the end of the year fiddle fans knew that Clark Kessinger was back; fiddle novices knew there was a new gunslinger in town and that the level of play at Southern contests had just gone up.

Kessinger was 66 when Ken Davidson met him for the first time, and his comeback was to last about seven years. He quickly became the most colorful and intense fiddler on the contest circuit, winning dozens of prizes, including the World's Champion prize at the 47th Union Grove affair in April 1971. He continued to record, including three more LPs for Davidson's label (which had by now changed its name to

Kanawha). Some of the albums were later reissued on Folkways Records, and then on County. They were popular, and some of them probably reached a larger audience than did the original 78s. Gene Meade became Kessinger's regular guitar player, both at contests and on records, playing in a fluid flatpicking style. Even today, many fiddle fans can still remember where they were when they first heard Kessinger play at one contest or another.

By 1971 Ken Davidson's company was effectively out of business, and he encouraged a newly formed company to take over his chronicling of Kessinger's music. The new company was owned by Ken Irwin, Bill Nowlin, and Marion Leighton—a trio of young Bostonians who were all veterans of the festival circuit and who had named their company Rounder. They drove to Union Grove and met Kessinger. After the finals, they drove over to the Vance Motor Inn in nearby Statesville and began recording the new LP. They got 12 good cuts, 11 fiddle tunes and a guitar solo by Gene, and left with the tapes, planning to return in a few weeks for a follow-up session. A week before the scheduled session, though, Kessinger had a stroke and collapsed on stage at a convention in Virginia. He recovered, but his left hand was severely affected and he had trouble playing. Hoping against hope that therapy would improve Kessinger's condition, the Rounders waited for several months. Only when it seemed Kessinger would not play well enough to continue, they released the album as *Clark Kessinger: Old-Time Music with Fiddle and Guitar* (Rounder 0004). It contained several lively hoedowns, plus some of the lovely, obscure waltzes Kessinger loved to play. One of them might have served as a theme song: "When I Grow Too Old to Dream." Kessinger died June 4, 1975.

EDITOR'S NOTE: This article first appeared in the fall 1997 issue of *Goldenseal* (vol. 23, no. 3) and is based on a chapter that appeared in *The Devil's Box: Masters of Southern Fiddling* by Charles Wolfe, © 1997, used by permission of Vanderbilt University Press and the Country Music Foundation. The Kessinger legacy continues in West Virginia through the talents and performances of the Kessinger Family, consisting of Clark's nephew Bob Kessinger and Bob's sons Robin and Dan.

Wilson Douglas

MOUNTAIN MAN AND MOUNTAIN MUSICIAN

Nancy McClellan

O F all the riches in Clay County none are of more
value than her music and the men and women who
keep it alive; among these, none is more worthy of
interest than Wilson Douglas, mountain man and fine fiddler. The highest compliment Wilson can pay is to say of
someone, "He's a real mountain man," and Wilson can be
accorded that title by almost any criterion you might wish to
set: by heredity and birth, by his own life, and by that most
powerful claim of all, his love for the mountains.

Well before the Civil War the Douglas family had settled in
what is now Clay County. By 1917 Wilson's grandfather had
bought a farm on a fork of Rush Creek at Booger Hole, a
farm still so isolated that, standing there on a windy November hill, you can well believe the tales of ghostly teams and
riders and of unseen women who cry and walk the roads. On
this farm which lies beneath Painter Knob and overlooks a
cemetery holding the graves of many of his family and earlier ones dating back to 1810, Wilson was born in 1922 to Shirley and Goldie Morris Douglas.

At the age of 13, Wilson moved from this farm on Booger
Hole to a home on Otter Creek where he stayed until he
entered the Army in World War II. Upon his return from the
Army in 1945, he lived for a number of years in Ivydale; there
he married and brought up two sons, one who practices law
in Morgantown and one serving in the Marine Corps. He
now lives with his second wife, Delma, on Hansford Fork
near Maysel, less than 20 miles from the place he was born.

Thus Wilson's roots run deep. In part perhaps because he
has spent all his life essentially in one place, Wilson is im-
bued with an unusually keen sense of the past, his own and
his community's. What distinguishes him, however, from
many others with similar experiences is his balanced view
toward that experience. He sees clearly that the good old
days were equally hard old days. And while he feels pride,
almost reverence, in his heritage, Wilson does not romanti-
cize.

In the following passages, tape recorded in March 1975
and November 1976, Wilson speaks of a portion of that heritage, first of his early life on Rush Creek and later of certain
contrasts between the past and the present. Like many another mountain man, Wilson is a natural-born tale-teller,
but his musician's ear and an artist's eye for vivid detail
make his reminiscences especially memorable.

Delma and Wilson Douglas at the Brandywine Mountain Music
Festival at Concordville, Pennsylvania, July 1975. Photograph by
Carl Fleischhauer.

Wilson Douglas: This country, it's so lonesome now. I like
to come back, occasionally. But when you get to thinking
about things, you hate to walk back down the road. You
know. You hate to walk back down the road.

See this knob here in front of us? That's called Painter
Knob. The old-timers called a panther a "painter." The panther, they bred and denned on this knob and there's rocks
back in there you can crawl back in. And over there is Buzzard Rocks. The buzzards congregated there in the nesting

time; it was the high place. In the spring of the year the buzzards come there and in the fall they gather there and leave. Those rocks are the oldest, most designated point in Clay County. They was an old trail on that ridge during the Civil War. The old-timers traveled on it going from Clay County to Calhoun County. And down yonder's the old picnic ground—years and years ago when my father was a boy the old hard-shell Baptists had their meetings there. And that's the family cemetery up above.

See, when we moved here there was a three-room house my grandfather had. My father built two rooms. It was a five-room plant house with a cut stone chimley and a porch all around.

Yeah. 'Course, we had no refrigeration, no electricity. 'Course you can't see it now, but that cellar—these rocks came from big rocks back up to the foot of Painter Knob. They was churned with a churn drill. They wasn't no jackhammers or air compressors. And they were shot out with black powder. And this here rockmason by the name of Wayne—he's dead now—he handpicked these rocks, picked them out and laid them up there. It took one whole summer to cut them rocks. And we had a little trough, we'd put cold water in there to set our milk in to keep it from spoiling, and my mother kept that milk in these big crocks. I've put many a potato in there; I put many a canned stuff in there. Me and my mother has canned and we would carry that cellar full of vegetables, muskmelons, cucumbers. And we got up before daylight, and you can picture that, I believe. It's just like it was, only the house is burned down. And I've seen that cellar so dang full that the floor was full!

And we had a bucket and a windlass. That's an old dug well, was dug in 1920, two years before I was born. And that—well, there was the finest water there was.

I was going to tell you—you know, nowadays—this is no slur to anybody—when people wash clothes, they put about everything in the washer *but* the clothes, you know. And my mother, we used to have an iron kettle, before the washing machine comes out, and she had to wash on her hands but we went clean. We didn't have very many clothes. And you'd build a fire under this brass kettle and if they wasn't boiled, they wasn't satisfying, they wasn't sanitary. We would take this old white P&G soap, white naphtha, and we'd shave off big chunks of that soap, let it boil in that water. Lord-a-mercy, them clothes! White, you know, just like lye. Yeah. They had to be just right, now. You had to carry water, start shaving that soap, about half a bar. Them clothes had to boil so long; while they was boiling you took a stick, took them out of there, put them in the rinse tub, see. Yeah, she was particular. Scrubbed the floors. And if I'd of set my foot on the carpet, I'd of died! Them old wooden floors, they were scrubbed with sand and P&G soap. And brother, she was clean, now. She was clean.

Wilson Douglas in November 1975 at the cellar house foundation below Painter Knob, Clay County, his birthplace. Photograph by Rick Osborn.

A view from the hillside of Wilson Douglas's birthplace near Booger Hole. Photograph by Rick Osborn.

Them tales sound like fairy tales, but they're true. Times were hard. And Lord-a-mercy, a dime was bigger than a million dollars! Dad made his living farming, and he'd work in the mines. Well, when we'd get too hard up—Widen's a mining camp over here. And my father and me would—he had an old '26 model Chevrolet car—we would gather them vegetables up and take them to Widen and sell them to all those black people. In them mining camps you'd draw scrip, but we had to take a 10-cents-off-a-dollar discount—scrip, see—to get the real money. And if we had to have lamp oil, we'd take half a dozen eggs around to the store and we'd get a gallon of oil. If you had money coming to you, you'd get a due bill.

You couldn't read after dark, unless you read by firelight, so's not to waste lamp oil. Had to self-educate yourself. It was hard getting an education. I walked from here to Rush Fork School, me and my two sisters, a mile. And you'd carry a six-pint lard container for a lunch bucket—would have eggs and cornbread or an apple or apple butter, and a big Dutch onion. And I got $3 a month for sweeping and cleaning the school.

And, as I recall, in the summertime we'd work late-like and the frogs would be hollering. And barefooted—we just got one pair of shoes a year. Well, before we went to bed Mother'd see that we washed our feet. And we went through the front room and out on the porch to this well and poured water in a washpan and washed the dust off our feet. And we'd set on this front porch till late. Of an evening, why,

we'd set out here and look to the head of Booger Hole. And you could hear people farming back at that time, you know. Nowadays there's too much noise in the air—you can't holler and make anybody hear you. But once I could holler and you could hear me clear to that valley there. But now there's too much noise in the air—you can't holler no distance. And if our clock stopped, well, we'd holler down here to these Ashleys lived down here, holler down and ask what time it was, to reset our clock, see. And my father used to set here on this front porch, and when he'd tune that old five-string banjo up, he'd play that banjo—it was so doggone lonesome that it was pitiful; and you could hear it all over this country. But he had his mind on getting ready for winter. It was a burden. He looked ahead, and my mother canned.

But there's no question that people were closer then than now. My parents done the best they could by me and I'm grateful. They never raised their voice. But you better not let my mother holler at you twice! There was no hollering to get you out of bed. And Dad's word was Law and Gospel. His "Children, it's time to go"—that was it. And I used to think he was too hard on us. Until I got a man, I saw he wasn't. He was firm, he was good to us, but he never told us twice.

But my kids—I got one that's a lawyer and one that's a Marine—they can't understand. But I *liked* it here, them days, you know. But there wasn't anything to look forward to, really. And I had to work awful hard, never will forget it. But my children, they can't see it; they say, "Dad, how'd you ever live like that?" I said, "What else was there to do? Everybody with the same dang dream, with the same high hopes,"—and they don't understand, you know.

The people that wanted to learn got out. I didn't know anything really. And when I went to the Army, I took every dang school I could get in. I studied. I learned how to get along in this world, to live in this world, to get along with people. I pick out, select what I can get along with, and what I can't, I let alone. And I study every man. You know you've seen people you didn't like, but you'd study them. I try to get that man's turn, and I try to find out what he *likes* and then I try to study up enough to cope with him and just touch him here and yonder till he'll get to liking me, and then I'll find out something about him. You see? And if you don't do that, you're lost. Yeah . . .

∽

Besides being an abundant source of such stories as the above, Wilson presents a perhaps more profound link with the past in the depth of his woods lore and his folk knowledge—knowledge, once widespread, the more valuable now because it is so nearly lost. Both he and Delma are deeply aware of the most minute signals of the seasonal cycles of the mountains. And Wilson's love and knowledge of nature are intricately woven in his whole philosophy of life.

∽

Harvey McClellan: I want Wilson to retell a little bit what he was talking to me about. I told him I was interested in these woods. And then we were—Wilson and I were talking about how different a tree looks growing in the forest from the way it looks when it's all by itself and can branch out, you know. When it's confined by its brothers and sisters, how it grows so straight.

WD: Yeah, that's right.

HM: And Wilson mentioned the way you can smell a forest.

WD: Right. You can smell the plants. You can smell them.

How I Came to Be a Fiddler

Wilson Douglas and Nancy McClellan

My grandfather and Saul Carpenter were half-brothers and Saul's wife was an Indian. And my grandfather, Martin Stephenson Van Buren Douglas, was one of the greatest ballad singers of all times and he couldn't play anything. But he sang songs during the Civil War and before. Tunes like the old "Willow Garden" and "Barbry Allen."

My grandmother, now, she was a good fiddler and all her brothers were top fiddlers on my mother's side, the Morris side. My mother, she used to be a pretty good ballad singer, she couldn't play music. She'd sing "The Little Blossom" and those old songs. But my dad was one of the best, the plainest, old-time banjo players you ever heard. He played it slow, but he'd put everything in it. And then he lost his thumb and he quit. But, now, he had an ear for music.

In the evening we'd sit out there and look to the head of Booger Hole and my father used to sit there on that front porch—but when he tuned that old five-string banjo up, he'd play that banjo—it was so doggone lonesome that it was pitiful and you could hear it all over the country. He'd play a few of them old tunes, pick the old "Barbry Allen," "Gunboat Going Through Georgia," "Pretty Polly," and the "Little Birdie." When he played four or five and he got tired, he'd quit! But that banjo would almost speak.

And like I said, Grandmother Morris was an old-time square dance fiddler. And 1935–1936 was a severe cold winter. I was 13 years old. I had played guitar up until that time for various fiddlers. During that winter I lived about a mile from my grandmother's. Every night I would take my guitar over there and play; I had learned how

Wilson Douglas at the Brandywine Festival, 1975. Photograph by Carl Fleischhauer.

There is so many different odors that it is just wonderful. Well, I'm going to put it this way; there is no perfume that was ever made that will smell like it. *Nothing* smells like the forest in the spring of the year. And you see everything is different. There is no tree exactly alike. The bark will be different or the grain will be different, the leaves will be different, or the branches will be more or fewer. Am I right, Delma? And the green willow is the first to show.

And you see these sparrows and cardinals and various types of birds. But in the woods you see an entirely different race or different variety of birds. You see the little sapsuckers, the little twig-pullers. And you'll see all different kinds of birds. The bluejays. And you'll notice the hawks. The hawks and, well, thousands of things that you'll notice. And each has its own time. Right. And, well, this is getting back to the almanac, the signs.

Well, now, a lot of scientists will say there's nothing to the signs being in the feet or the bowels or the heart or the eyes.

But according to where the sun is in the seasons on each side of the earth, it works. You know. The signs. Well, now, you can cut out board timber out of blocks, out of white oak—they roof their houses, some of the old-timers in this country, with split oak boards; you split them out with a froe. You rive them. They call them riven boards; we call them clapboards, too. Yeah, and if you put them on when the moon is light, they'll curl up; but you put them on in the dark moon, it'll lay flat till it seasons. And you plant corn in the dark moon it won't get as high as my head, it won't do no good; plant it in the light moon, the fodder'll be 10 foot high and no ears, you see. And now you go with your pickled beans and pickled corn—you explain that to them, Delma.

Delma Douglas: Yeah. If you pickle things when the signs are in the bowels, you cannot eat them. You go with all these old people, now. Sylvia Cottrell [O'Brien], you know, she's an old-timer and she makes *the best* pickles, and—

WD: That's right, she can't be beat.

to tune it with her fiddle. At that time she had the only old fiddle in the country. To my knowledge. The old instrument was patched with solder, carpet tacks, and various other things. She and her son lived alone. Each cold winter night I'd get in wood and coal for the old potbellied Burnside stove. I would stay all night and go to school from there in the morning. She would play hoedown fiddle tunes half of the night. She played mostly dance tunes on two or three strings. She seldom played the bass.

That winter passed and we continued to play. The following winter her health failed her and she began to lose interest in the violin. However, that fiddle began to sound good to me. Then I suddenly decided I would quit playing the guitar and try to make some kind of a fiddler out of myself. Times were hard, money was scarce. The only work I could get at that time was on a farm. I got five cents an hour or 50 cents a day. So I started saving my money to buy me a fiddle.

And I lost a lot of sweat getting it. I saved, I believe it was $10.40

with postage, in order to buy a violin. So I saved $10.50 and ordered a $9.95 fiddle from Sears Roebuck. And then I had to work me out a bow; you could buy a top bow then for $2.65. Then I got the bow, and I didn't have any case. So I carried the violin in a 24-pound Sunny Field flour bag! Until I got me a case. And this violin case that I bought later was $2.35 plus postage, and I kept it up to about a year ago, then I gave it away. Fiddle strings were 25 cents and at that time there was one penny tax plus. I'd buy them over at Clay, at King's Jewelry Shop; his son's still got the shop. You got Black Diamond strings for 26 cents and now they're $3.

And I couldn't tune the violin at that time. Now there was an old gentleman by the name of Charlie Drake lived about two miles from where I lived—now this was before I got with my grandmother to learn—he could tune the violin, but he couldn't play it, really; just a little tune or two. I'd take the old fiddle up there and get it tuned. Maybe the wind would be blowing. Put her down in that flour bag and

start home. By the time I got home, the variation in the temperature would throw the E or A string, mostly, a little out. But I didn't know the difference! I'd saw on her until she didn't sound good, take her back.

And I did that until my grandmother taught me, until I got the sound. And, like I said, she was a good fiddler and I was a guitar player at that time. I started on the guitar when I was nine years old; I played the Carter fashion—but that fiddle got through to me. I liked it! And after she quit playing she taught me the notes to start the "Soldier's Joy." Well, I wore the "Soldier's Joy" out!

And then she said, "Well, Wilson, as time goes on," said, "I can't tell you every little thing. If you want to play bad enough, you'll learn." So I kept improving. And she was 91 years old when she died; her health got to failing and she just completely quit playing.

Well, I finally learned to play "Soldier's Joy." After this, everyone I knew that could play a fiddle, I managed to visit them and listened

DD: And you talk to her, she'll tell you the same thing.

WD: And in the dark moon the brine won't raise on your cabbage to sour your kraut. It won't raise.

DD: Put it in your crock in a light moon and it'll raise. And it'll boil the brine out.

WD: They's so many things like that. And in this country, now, during the summer, Harvey, if you see the leaves turning up—you can see the bottoms of the leaves—inside of 12 hours it's going to come a real severe storm. You can bet on it. In 12 hours. Every time. And now, this is my saying here: these hoot owls in this holler—you might hear them tonight, you might not—when he hollers in the north side of the hill, look out! It's going to be a winter if he hoots over there a few days. But if he goes to the south, the weather's going to break up. It'll do it every time.

And if you're logging in the summer, when you cut this poplar timber when the sap's running, you'll peel that bark right off, you see. Why, there's no ice that was ever froze as slick as that there log is. You can start it down the hill, it'll jump 20 feet in the air! It'll go right on to the landing. Some of these loggers aim the logs when the sap's running. And then they use them to make tanbark from the bark and paper and what have you.

And, well, you see, they are all come to color. And you take a white walnut tree, nothing grows under that tree. They's nothing grows. Each night as the dew falls, an acid—that acid will eat up anything. Park your car under it a few nights and the paint's gone. Ain't that right, Delma? That's a white walnut, a butternut. We don't have too many. And the nuts are fine, boy, they're delicious! And then you have the persimmon, you know. They're good in a certain time of the year. The wood's no good, it's a rough grain. And then you have your sassyfras, your ash, your white ash, your black walnut, your white walnut (which Jenes Cottrell makes all of his banjo necks out of), and the elm. And we have what's called a hackberry, it's a slick-bark tree, grows real tall. And

to get a new tune in my mind. I tried to make it a habit to play four or five hours each day in a room to myself. And during that time there were only two battery radios in the country to my knowledge, and my father owned one of them. So every Saturday night we would listen to the WSM "Grand Ole Opry" until it went off the air at 1:00. All the neighbors would gather in to listen to the mountain music.

Then during that time, about 1939 or 1940, Ed Haley came in the country and that put me *on,* see! I was 17 the first time I saw Ed Haley. There was an old gentleman lived in Calhoun County joining Clay County by the name of Lorie Hicks. He was a good old-time rough fiddler. I would ride a bicycle over to his home to hear him play the fiddle. Then somehow Lorie Hicks contacted Ed Haley in Ashland, Kentucky. In about a month Haley came to Calhoun County. So the news got around through the country that Ed Haley was at Lorie Hicks's. Everybody around went to hear him play.

I told my mother, I said, "I heard old man Mr. Ed Haley play the fiddle and," I said, "I'm going to learn." She said, "Wilson, it's hard—I doubt it. Maybe Mother could teach you." "Well," I said, "I'm going to learn or there ain't no bull in Texas!" So I started making every arrangement. Now, I wouldn't spend a penny for nothing till I got that $10.40 to order that violin. I thought it was something, but it wasn't really.

One day it came from Sears Roebuck. I'd walk to the mailbox and I'd hear the mailboy coming and I was there to meet him. It used to be carried by buggy and team. I counted the days until that violin came, I think it was nine or 10 days. It was in the carton and the mailboy said, "Here, Wilson, is your package." Oh, man! I commenced tearing that thing open. All shiny and nice, you know! But it wasn't, really.

There's so many things come into my mind—it was 12 miles from where I was raised over to Lorie Hicks's where Ed Haley'd come to. He'd play until about 12 o'clock at night, and he got tired, he'd quit. I was really not conscious

of coming back home—I'd ride a bike, had an old trap of a bicycle; and if a gang didn't gather up to go in an old '29 Model A Ford truck, we'd start walking, maybe somebody'd come along in an old car and pick us up. Or we'd start in time to walk it. Lord! IT WAS 12 MILES!—And I'd come back home and I wasn't really conscious of when I left and when I got there. I was just *dazed* with that fiddle.

And it was just like a dang carnival, you know. We just sat and never opened our mouth and, like I said, he'd scare them fellers, them fellers never tried to play. Doc White asked him one night, said, "Ed, how do you play them tunes without changing keys?" "Well," he said, "Doc, I change them with my fingers!" He wasn't being sarcastic with Doc, he liked Doc.

Well, when he'd take a notion to go back to Kentucky, we'd all beg him to stay another week. Doc White would say, "Now Ed, listen. They's a gang of people coming from Roane County, you can make some money. Now, you stay another week." Ed was bad to swear.

you have your sarvis [service] and dogwood. And my Lord! How many more? Shellbark, slick-bark. And then we have a gum. A gum tree, with the mistletoe in it, you know. And a gum tree has no grain in the wood and you couldn't burst it with dynamite. There's no such a way of splitting one of them open, you can't do it. And, now, it makes good firewood after it seasons, but there's no way to burst one of them. It has no grain. Just like a rock that's cut, it has no grain. And we have the spruce, the jack pine, the hemlock, the needle pine, the black pine. And well, the sour gum, which is a bassy wood, it splits good; the sour gum, which has little countersunk marks all through it. Water beech. Water birch. Delma, there, she can tell a tree, what it is, as far as she can see it. And I can too.

DD: It's a beauty here in late spring to look up this holler. And different trees come out in leaf at different times and they are different colors. There'll be ever so many different shades of green, you know.

WD: Yeah. And Delma has some beautiful flowers here of a summer. And the wild rabbits, they lay out there and waller and dust theirselves, you know, six or seven of them in a game!

And in the fall of the year this country is fantastic. You'll see one tree's fiery red, the next one will be yellow, the next one will be brown, the next one will be a variety of colors. And the animals, you know, the squirrels, they have a certain time to feed on a certain thing. They know when it's right, you see.

And when you dig into that—they's something that very few people ever stops to notice, what makes this planet tick. Really how beautiful it is! In other words, what I'm trying to say, what life really means if you stop to look at it. And I believe, I believe that this world was made for—it was made to harmonize, to live in harmony, to get along, and not be in some kind of a confusement or disagreement all the time.

Well, they'd talk him into it. Maybe he'd make four or five dollars a night.

The last night, the last time I seen him—I was a big boy and I'd got over there, had went with some fellers. I was sitting in this old split bottom chair, sleepy, you know, but every time he'd play a tune, I'd survive. And he said, "Son, what's your name?" I didn't know that he knew that I'd been sitting in front of him. I told him. He said, "You've been over here every night, haven't you?" I said, "Yeah," and I said, "Mr. Haley, you've played tunes for everybody," and I said, "and I don't have no money. I'm saving up money to buy me a fiddle." He laughed! I said, "How about you playing me a tune?" "All right, what is it?" I said, "Play the 'Black-eyed Susie.'" Well, that's really no tune. It's just a little old thing. "Well," he said, "dammit, I'll play it. I don't like to play it. But I'll play it." Said, "Them's single-line tunes. But I'll play it for you." And he did; because I was interested, you see.

And some of these old music fans, some of them—maybe you've noticed it—it touches them. Some of them will cry and everything else. Maybe somebody of these old farmers would come along; they'd had a tune and maybe their father played or some of their ancestors, and they'd heard it. They'd say, "Well, Ed, play me this tune," and they'd hand him a dollar. Well, he'd play it for 15 minutes! They'd sit there with big tears, you know. And somebody else, "Well, Ed, play this tune." And they'd hand him another dollar. Well, he'd play till the money ran out and he'd quit!

And Carpenter, he was in and out of this country a lot; he worked up around Oak Hill. Sometimes he'd come to Clay County for a weekend. I would go and stay the weekend with him; and he started to teach me to play the fiddle.

French Carpenter was an interesting man. Had been a bugler in the World War. He was not a large man at all. And I guess he could have put on a flour bag and it'd look good on him. Had been a handsome man. Fair complected, hair combed straight back. And big blue eyes. Fair every way. And he

was a man you couldn't hear him walk on nothing. And this don't make no sense: he was a feller could walk in the mud, but yet he wouldn't get his shoes dirty! And walk across the floor, it was like cats! And dance. Lord have mercy! That man could dance!

And right after the war and when I got discharged, why, after I found out Ed Haley was dead, well, Carpenter came back in the country and in 1958 he retired—lived in a little old house over here right where Rush Fork and Otter meet, house is still there. And he'd take that fiddle out about dark, you know, and all them frogs hollering—you know in the spring of the year—I thought that was the lonesomest dang thing I ever heard.

So I practically stayed with him. Oh, I was with him off and on for eight or nine years. And we'd get together from one to three times a week to play the fiddle. And he had a first cousin was a hot banjo player. And we'd play all night! Play the god-blessed night. And he'd make me tune my fiddle with *him*. And he'd say, "Now, Wilson, don't you

Above all else, Wilson Douglas is a musician. He first played guitar, "Carter style," and was "a fair ballad singer" as a young man. And he now even repairs instruments when his friends can talk him into it. "They put me in the middle. They say, 'Can you fix it?' 'Yeah, well, I probably can, it'll take me a month. Don't be in a hurry, I can't get it out for a while.' When you get nervous you have to quit working on them, they're delicate." But it was the fiddle that, as he says, "took me and set me right" and the fiddle which has held him for nearly 40 years.

In Clay County for a man like Wilson there was always the music—the hoedown after a neighbor's barn raising, the gospel sings at Little Laurel Church and the all-day meetings with dinner on the ground; above all, the front porch picking of a summer's evening or the warm fiddling of a winter's night. Despite the pervasiveness of music, however, Wilson notes the age-old conflict between the artist's temperament and community attitudes. These attitudes stem primarily from the drinking and carousing sometimes associated with music making and from the reputation for general all-around shiftlessness imputed to musicians. Wilson laughingly comments about a fellow fiddler, "Lord, he's not a bit afraid of work! He'll lay down and sleep by it." And of another, "He takes care of his hands: he won't lift nothing no heavier than a piece of light bread!" But the dominant Calvinist work ethic also enters in; and Wilson has felt the conflict keenly within his own life.

∾

WD: Musicians are people that are in search of something. They're wound up tight. They'll stop and search for things, really get down to the bottom of the Good Lord's creation. Yeah. And musicians are high-tensioned, they're *touchy* about whatever they do.

try to copy me. For you can't. That's ruined a many good fiddler. We have a different time. If you happen to be something like me, fine. *Play yourself.*

So we got to be so doggone good it just sounded like one fiddle, you know. I'd miss a note, he'd stop, he'd say, "Now, play that over again, you missed it, Wilson." He'd make me get it, wouldn't let me see no peace till I did—he was that way.

And Carpenter and me'd play, and Carpenter had his time, you couldn't push him, he had a certain time. And if he got with a musician didn't suit him, he'd say, "Well, I don't feel good. I'm going to quit for tonight." You know? He wouldn't offend nobody, he was very kind.

Oh, I worked every day. And I'd go up there, I was all out of steam! I'd work six days a week and I was always up one or two o'clock in the morning with that fiddle. Well, I'd come home and I'd go to bed and that fiddle tune would keep pushing me; I couldn't sleep. I could just almost put my finger on it. And I've got up at four o'clock in the morn-

ing and played that tune. And after I got it, I'd go to bed.

Carpenter drove me all the time and he kept telling me he had a bad heart condition and he said, "I want to push you all I can." And the man died in 1964 and had a couple of tunes I never got to learn. He was a wonderful old-time musician.

And now I go to these conventions, and when you walk in a place—competition makes any individual good at anything you do; if you've got competition you want to get good right then! And if you ain't good, it'll put your best in you. And then—you know what I'm talking about—when you feel that chill, boy! Look out! When I feel that chill, I'm ready! I can play the fiddle then. I'm just like two preachers wanting to preach! And sleep, hunger, fatigue leaves you. It don't bother you till you quit and then you're *dead.* By gosh, you're dead. I've gone to these places and I couldn't see no way of ever getting home without stopping along the road—and Lord! I was give out, I was sleepy—and them tunes that them old gentlemen would play

would ring in my ears for a week. And when I'd come home, I don't know, it seems like I just, like I just dropped in a hole. There wasn't nothing there. It's hard for me to explain.

And the way I feel about music, I think these musicians—I do it myself—each one is expressing his past, his present, what he should have been, and what he hopes to be. And he's expressing all of his sorrows, all of his happiness—if you study him close you can almost read his life. And I think when they're all playing good, clean, honest music—banjo-picking, guitar-playing, fiddling, what have you—I think you're just as close to heaven on this earth as you'll ever be. If you've got the music in you. You know what I mean? I believe that. I don't mean I put that above a hereafter or above an eternal life. But in *this* world, that's my Paradise. In this world.

EDITOR'S NOTE: This article first appeared in the January–March 1977 issue of *Goldenseal* (vol. 3, no. 1).

Wilson Douglas playing at the Brandywine Festival, 1975. Photograph by Carl Fleischhauer.

And Dad would get on me when he thought I was playing too much. In this country if you participate in too much music, you're not too high thought of. As long as you're prudent, as long as you're having hard times, that's fine. But, brother! Don't relax too much!

And, now, you get to the place, you come to the place sometimes, you just think—well, heck, I believe—well, I just can't play music and work both, you know. You get to thinking, well, I'll just quit the music. But you won't do it. That's right, it's kinda a bug, it's actually a bug.

∾

Wilson has come by his music naturally. Because the Clay County area is singularly rich in musicians and traditional music (much of it heard but rarely outside the region), Wilson has taken his some 400 fiddle tunes from many sources. He has been most directly influenced, however, by the

several-generations-long tradition of music on both sides of his own family and by his encounters with three other particularly splendid fiddlers.

Wilson's maternal grandmother, a fiddler herself, was his first teacher, and both his parents were highly regarded traditional musicians. His father was a banjo player; his mother, who still lives in Ivydale, was a ballad singer. But his real inspiration to learn came from the fiddling of Ed Haley, an almost legendary blind musician from Ashland, Kentucky. In recent years Wilson has especially admired the fiddling of J.P. Fraley, of Rush, Kentucky. The most telling influence on Wilson, however, was the master fiddler from Clay County, French Carpenter. In a relationship quite uncommon today he virtually apprenticed himself to Carpenter for a period of several years.

It is the dedication and discipline implicit in such a relationship that sets Wilson apart from many other mountain musicians. Music for him is decidedly not just an avocation, it makes demands. It's not uncommon, for instance, for him to bundle Delma into his little red VW and drive 100 miles or more to listen and learn from a respected fiddler like Burl Hammons, "the lonesomest fiddler I ever heard." Finally, what Wilson Douglas knows in his bones is the bittersweet truth that joy received is balanced fully by sacrifice paid.

∾

WD: Now, I don't claim to be a top fiddler, but I fiddle it from the heart, the way I want to and, you know, the way it does me good. There's a lot of things I could have been. But I'm not. I'm not and I'm not going to worry about them. I could have been many things, probably. But them hoedowns always kept me from being those things. And I'm not going to worry about them.

I know what makes me happy. And they ain't nothing more interesting to me than to try to get a complicated note on a violin. And never rest till I do get it. A man learns a little. He never learns it all. And nowadays the young people don't have no interest to stop and play music. They ain't got no patience; they think they have to play it overnight. But, now, I'm telling you the truth. I've played the fiddle *hungry* and enjoyed it, I couldn't tell you when I'd eaten. In other words, I've sacrificed a lot to play music. But it done me a lot of good.

EDITOR'S NOTE: This article first appeared in the January–March 1977 issue of *Goldenseal* (vol. 3, no. 1). Wilson Douglas, who received the 1992 Vandalia Award, was an active participant at music festivals and gatherings around the state. He passed away in March 1999 at the age of 76. Delma Douglas passed away in October 1995.

Sarah Singleton

A FIDDLER ALL HER LIFE

Teresa Hamm

SARAH Singleton of Bragg's Run has been a fiddler all her life. Born and raised in Braxton County, "the 13th child from the top and the fourth from the bottom," she says that she used to sit in a corner and listen to her father, John Jackson Blake, and his friend George Morris make music. "When I was little I was always right there, listening to the fiddles. It didn't matter about other instruments. Just so the fiddle was there, I was there."

Sarah's dad and his people had walked from Greenbrier County to Braxton. John Blake was a farmer, fiddler, and rock cutter. Sarah's mother, Biddie Jane Bragg, played the jaw harp and sang for the younger children when the work was done in the evenings. Sarah remembers her mother singing lonesome "Wildcat Holler," perhaps when her father was away on a rock-cutting trip:

> Wildcat Holler is the meanest place on earth,
> Where the mountain dew's a-plenty and you get your
>   money's worth.
> The rattlesnakes rattle and the grizzly bears roam,
> And Wildcat Holler is the place I call home.
> I'm going crazy, don't you wanna come along?
> I'm going crazy, there's something wrong.

"She used to be a pretty singer," Sarah says of her mother. "She sang old ballads that I never did hear anymore after she sang them. I wish I'd had sense enough to write them down, but I couldn't write then. She would just sit and sing—just to entertain us, you know."

Since the Blake family was so large Sarah remarks that there was never a time when all of them were together at one time. But there were always plenty of brothers and sisters around to make up a square dance band or a detail.

And the work was hard on a farm in the mountains. "We dug our living out of the ground," Sarah recalls. "Dad would rent a corn patch. We'd have to sprout it off, and then we'd have to dig it up with hoes to plant the corn in, broad hoes. We'd have to stretch a string out along the hill to plant with a corn planter. That's the way we raised the corn. He'd clear off maybe an acre or two to plant the corn, and then we would have to dig it up [without plowing]. People don't know what we had to go through with when we growed up. Nobody knows but us."

Sarah Singleton is proud to stand with the mountains of Braxton County behind her in this 1992 photograph by Michael Keller.

Times were hard, but laughter was plentiful. Sarah tells a story about the time a scorpion ran up sister Loni's leg, and another story about a muskrat running up brother Hobart's pants leg. When Hobart threw the muskrat off it narrowly missed his sweetheart Beulah's head, but Beulah later became Hobart's wife anyway!

This last incident occurred while hunting snapping turtles. Sarah remembers that they used to go in "big gangs" to catch turtles, some wading in the water and some remaining on shore. Those in the water would reach back under the creek bank to grab the turtles, sometimes getting bit in the process, then throw them out to whomever was waiting on the bank. Sarah gave me a blow-by-blow description of how to butcher a snapping turtle in case I should ever need to know.

The Blake sisters brought their music to the students of Bragg's Run School at the request of teacher Eulah Mick (far left). The musicians are Loni (seated on the left), Sarah (with the fiddle), Macel Blake (with the dulcimer), and Mabel Dean (seated on the far right). Photogapher unknown, late 1920s.

Turtle was an occasional treat, but mostly the Blakes ate what they raised. Sarah's mother grew and stored many garden vegetables. Apple butter was kept in stone jars sealed with wax. I was surprised to find that canning, which I usually think of as "old-time," was not in much use back in Biddie Jane Blake's time. Instead, delicacies such as pickled beans were stored in big wooden barrels that sugar and salt came in down at the store. John Blake bought these barrels "for little or nothing," Sarah says.

Make-do comes through loud and clear when talking to Sarah. She grew up in a four-room house "stuffed with people," she says. "Yeah, it was crowded. We had two beds in this room, two beds in that room, and sometimes there was four to the bed. We got used to being like that, and we thought we was supposed to do that. So it didn't bother us a bit.

"You learned to give and take," Sarah says. She tells about when brother-in-law Jake Dean came and worked with her dad and stayed with the family. Every night Sarah's brother Basil would put a small pumpkin under Jake's pillow. Every night Jake would lay the pumpkin down on the floor without making a fuss before he went to bed. But one night he got mad. "He got up on the bed, stood up, and hit that pumpkin

down on the floor and just busted it all to pieces," Sarah says.

Lora, one of Sarah's brothers, would often trick the older brothers by putting beans between their bed covers at night. When the tired workers would try to crawl into bed the racket began. "Mom got to raking their heads for that because she said [they were] wasting the beans. You didn't waste nothing at our house. We didn't throw nothing away."

Time was the one thing that got wasted, but only occasionally. When the children went to the store they would get into "some of the awfullest messes you ever saw," Sarah says. A bunch of kids would be sent to nearby Burnsville for groceries, she recalls. Along the way they would run, fight, make up, "piddle off," and talk about what they wanted to be when they grew up. Sarah at first thought she wanted to be a nurse but when she got to playing music she decided she'd rather be a musician.

Her childhood memories include making music, even before she had a proper musical instrument. "We used to get our old cornstalk fiddles and sneak out behind the barn, you know, and they'd dance. Didn't you ever make a cornstalk fiddle out of a cornstalk? It's the way we did." The kids learned to dance by mimicking their elders. They would sing an old song like "Skip to My Lou," replacing each verse with a figure call:

Grand change, skip to my Lou,
Grand change, skip to my Lou,
Grand change, skip to my Lou,
Skip to my Lou, my darling.

John Blake's fiddling was Sarah's main early musical influence. She remembers sitting in a corner while five or six fiddlers held forth around the fireplace.

"They would start fiddling over here and they'd fiddle clear around," she says. "And they'd play the same tune and see who could play it the best. I swear, I'd laugh! Then they'd argue: 'Now that's not the way it's supposed to be played.'" Sarah says that she always liked her father's fiddling the best.

By the age of 11 or 12 Sarah was learning to play. She was given her first fiddle by her brother-in-law Jake Dean. Jake had told her that if she learned how to play the fiddle, he'd get her one, so she'd been practicing with her father's fiddle. John Blake would sit down with her and play a tune and she would listen. "Jenny Lind Polka" wasn't an easy tune to learn, she recalls. "My dad sat with me one time for two hours and tried to teach me to play that and I still can't play it!"

Difficult tunes notwithstanding, Sarah Blake was fiddling for square dances by the age of 14. She and some of her siblings would walk out of an evening to entertain somewhere. "Me and Loni and Bas and Berth, we'd walk maybe three or four miles to this house and we'd play for square dances, and then we'd walk back home that night." When asked how long the dances lasted, she laughs. "Whenever we'd quit, then they'd have to quit, because they wouldn't have any music."

Sarah tells me about one time when her sister Bertha was going to spell her on the fiddle for a while. "We was over at Vern Harris's one night, playing for a square dance. I was the only fiddler there, so Berth said, 'Sary, if you want to rest I'll play one.' I said, 'Okay.' She played 'The Old Black Cat.' Tunie Harris was turning the figures. Directly Berth was going to play again and Tunie got up and says, 'The next damn time "The Old Black Cat" is played I ain't a-calling figures.' So Berth didn't play, she let me play. That was the only tune she could play."

Sarah also remembers going to fiddle contests when she was young. When she was 16 or so, she and her father and her brother Hubert attended a fiddle contest in Summersville. She played against her dad and 25 or 30 other old-time fiddlers in that contest. "We got up on the stage. All of us lined up and stood up, and we just played the tune we wanted to play."

There was no sound system, no accompaniment, and no other female fiddlers at the contest. Sarah was used to that, because fiddling was mostly a man's pleasure in the old days. "Back then I was about the only girl that ever played the fiddle," she says. "Everybody was just flabbergasted. Everybody'd walk for miles just to hear me play the fiddle and I just sounded awful, you know, squeak-squeak, squeak-squeak. It was awful to listen to, I'll tell you."

Sarah tells about later meeting the fiddler for Flatt and Scruggs at an open-air theater between Gassaway and Sutton. She was married by then to Jim Singleton, and her husband liked to brag on her music. "My wife here can play the fiddle," Jim said to the professional. Sarah remembers that the Flatt and Scruggs fiddler replied something to the effect that, "He always liked to see a woman play the fiddle, he could just laugh up a storm at 'em, said they hold a fiddle in a funny way."

Sarah Singleton fiddles for the Town and Country Pickers. Zita McQuain plays guitar at left and Marian Long at right. Photograph by Michael Keller.

Whitey Radcliff, Howard Knight, Sarah Singleton, Ernie McCall, and Jim Adkins (left to right) made up a busy local band in the 1960s. Here they play a Weston "remote" for Buckhannon radio station WBUC. Photographer unknown.

When radio came in, Sarah's ears were open to the new sounds. On Saturday nights people would descend on those lucky enough to own radios and listen to the "Grand Ole Opry" out of Nashville. Arthur Smith and Hank Williams are mentioned as we talk about music over the airwaves.

It seems that performances on radio (and later television) refreshed and stimulated individual musicians, while undoubtedly altering local styles in general. But Sarah was fortunate to grow up in an area with strong, persistent musical traditions of its own. She remembers so many fiddlers "just born and raised around here." Among them were the Allen men, George Morris, Bob and Melvin Wine, Ernie Carpenter, and others.

So Sarah never had to travel very far in search of music and dance. "Back then, about every Saturday night there was a square dance on Bragg's Run some place, up at Hub Stout's, or at our house or some place else. All we'd have to do was go out and holler at our neighbors, get up a little bank there and holler, 'We're gonna have a square dance tonight!' And everybody'd be there. Or they knowed the signal—Lora would whistle by blowing on his hands and they knowed there was going to be a square dance."

Most dances were held in people's homes, the furniture having been moved out of the largest room. These were usually crowded affairs, with neighbors catching up on the local news.

While attending high school for one year in Akron, Ohio, Sarah met and married Jim Singleton in 1934. She says that she thought she wouldn't be playing square dances after she got married, but people would still hunt her up to come and play. The whole family, which eventually included daughter Sue and son Reetis, would bundle up and go. Sarah relates that she would nurse her daughter and then lay her down in another room and go out and play for the dance. With her son Reetis it was the same, she says, "only he was like a fairy-diddle, he wouldn't stay put."

Gradually dances ceased to be held in people's homes. Sarah says that the house dances went out about the same time that beer gardens and dance halls were being built. She mentions that sometimes dance platforms would be built on the outside of a building, as in the case of Falls Mills. Upon occasion these dance hall dances could be quite rowdy, Sarah reports. "The whole bunch'd get drunk. Did you ever play for a bunch of drunks? The people who didn't drink pulled the other ones through the dance."

Women, on the whole, didn't drink back then, so roughly half of the dancers remained sober. When I asked Sarah about her opinion of women imbibing she replies, "Didn't seem like it would hurt a woman any worse than a man."

By the 1960s Sarah was playing in a band that performed a variety of musical styles. There was Sarah on the fiddle, Ernie McCall on snare drums, Whitey Radcliff on steel guitar or five-string banjo, and "Little Howard" Knight on guitar and vocals. Their other guitar player, Jim Adkins, also acted as announcer. They would play for Ernie's dance hall, the Shangri-la, in Weston, on Saturdays. On Thursdays they would travel to Buckhannon and make a tape for WBUC to broadcast on Saturday night.

Sarah describes the range of their music. "Used to be I could play some of them twists, you know. 'The Peppermint

A Braxton County community dance is the place to have a good time. These dancers were photographed in Flatwoods in April 1992 by Michael Keller.

Twist,' I used to play that on the fiddle. We played dance tunes and they'd play and sing. Some of it was bluegrass, some of it was old-time. We just had a mixed-up band."

At about the same time Sarah was also busy playing more traditional square dances at Adrian and Weston with her brother Basil on banjo and second cousin Gerry Dean on guitar. There was just no telling what would happen at a dance. "I used to play over at Gassaway in the community building," Sarah says. "They took somebody out of jail one night over there to play the guitar with me. The jail's down underneath, and they went down there and took him out of jail. He played the guitar with me, and then they put him back in jail again!"

Sarah also remembers a particularly rough evening down at Falls Mills. "They was fighting over there one night, Old So-and-So got Mr. What's-His-Name down in the floor and jumped on him with both feet. He was bleeding all over. I went and got a pan of water and washed him and washed the blood up out of the floor and went to play for the square dance again. We left before the state cops got there. Everybody left. Back then they didn't have no telephones, they couldn't call, you see. So we was all gone by the time they got there."

In addition to nursing the wounded, there are other special skills needed to be a dance fiddler. Sarah's father played hornpipes and polkas with a lot of rhythm in the bow, and she thinks that is essential.

"A lot of fiddlers said to me, they said they could never play for a square dance, they didn't have the right rhythm. Well, I was brought up with it, see, I knowed what to do." Sarah says that one of the lessons John Blake repeated over

The Pickers proudly carried Sarah Singleton's banner on a foray into Ohio. Photographer unknown, 1980s; courtesy of Sarah Singleton.

and over was: "If you don't have a certain time to a tune, you might as well not play it."

Endurance is also a key factor in being a dance fiddler. "One night me and Willard Montgomery was playing 45 minutes for one dance. And you're only supposed to play 10 minutes for each set! Well, they was out there in a great big, long ring and they just kept a-dancing and a-dancing. I winked at Willard and I thought, 'We'll just play and wear them out.' But they wore us out!"

Although Sarah has mainly played fiddle over the years, she has recently brought out her mountain dulcimer for performances at the Augusta Heritage Center's Spring Dulcimer Week, which is held each April in Elkins. She plays a dulcimer handmade by her brother, the late Basil Blake.

Basil brought the pattern for the dulcimer back from France after World War I and eventually became a West Virginia dulcimer maker. Shoe tacks were used to hold his first instruments together and fret markers were cut out of comb, as were the bridges. Basil made hundreds of instruments and shipped them as far away as California. Sarah recounts that when she was about eight or nine years old she and her sisters would "get them down and hammer on them until we'd get a tune."

Over the years, Sarah has played music at home, at school, at church, and at dances, festivals and fundraisings. The band she plays with now, the Town and Country Pickers, recently helped the Flatwoods Elementary School raise money for new playground equipment.

At 77, Sarah Singleton stays busy—she helps cook for community dinners, meets with her women's club, worships at the Heaters Methodist Church, works in her garden, and fiddles up a storm. Recently she was designated a master folk artist by the Augusta Heritage Center and I apprenticed with her in the summer of 1990. I came away with a much greater appreciation of the effort involved in learning another's music and a great appreciation for Sarah in particular.

One day I asked her just when she decided to take up the fiddle. "I used to be out in the yard of a night and my dad would be playing," she told me. "He would get out and play for his own pleasure, you know. If he didn't want to play, he wouldn't play for you at all. Sometimes he would and sometimes he wouldn't, it just depended on how he felt.

"But one night he was playing this fiddle tune, 'Nellie Gray.' I was out in the yard. And that was the most beautiful tune I believe I've ever heard. Something went through me and I said, 'Oh, I wish I could do that.'"

EDITOR'S NOTE: This article first appeared in the summer 1992 issue of *Goldenseal* (vol. 18, no. 2). Sarah Singleton died on March 10, 1995, at the age of 80 at her residence in Braxton County.

John Johnson

"A PRETTY GOOD THING ALL THE WAY AROUND"

Michael Kline

THE first time I heard John Johnson playing the fiddle in his little trailer on top of a ridge near Sutton I thought of an uncut forest and the flow of primeval energies. The measures from his long-drawn bow seemed to roll over me and to soar and dip like the wind and rain. Some of the crooked musical turns with bent time tumbled out of his fiddle like water cascading over rocks of different colors and shapes. After a while John's music began to live in my mind like a melodic blueprint of the mountains themselves and I felt deeply touched by the power of his driven cadences and the craggy beauty of his images.

John Johnson was born 65 years ago, December 29, 1916, in an apartment above the jail in Clay, where his father, Seymour Johnson, was the Clay County jailer. John claims to have hit about every jail in the country since then. He was the sixth in a family of 10 children.

John has lived a restless and intensely artistic life, having rambled and fiddled his way through 46 states and much of Canada and Mexico. He is a prolific poet—from a large family of poets—and paints vivid primitive scenes of mountain life in oil colors. He is also a timberman, sawyer, cowboy, and carpenter of seasoned experience and considerable knowledge. Mostly he is a shy person possessed of an astonishing ability to communicate through his music, verse, and art. He lives currently with his daughter and her family in Craigsville, but says he may soon hit the road again for Kansas, California, and "who knows where else."

Excerpts follow here from a taped interview made March 7, 1981, at the home of Susie Johnson Hicks in Craigsville, with John recalling some of his earliest memories of music making in Clay County.

John Johnson in 1981. Photograph by Doug Yarrow.

∾

John Johnson: My dad bought an old fiddle from Joe Carte, the ferryman there at Clay. Ferryman Joe, I called him. He was one of the first men that lived in Clay and he had a ferryboat there. He lived on the Clay side of Elk River. Over on the Dundon side, across the river from the mouth of Buffalo, his bell was over there. People would come there and ring the bell and he'd shunt them across the river. It was 10 cents to ferry the river. [...] So Ferryman Joe, as I called him, lived there for years and years. And he's the one my dad bought the old violin from.

My dad's name was George Seymour Johnson. And most of the people called him Semer. He could play the fiddle some, but he wasn't a fiddler. Very few times I ever heard him play in my life. When he brought that old fiddle home off of Joe Carte, that was the first time I ever heard him play. After that I doubt if I ever heard him more than three or four times. He never did play the fiddle hardly any, but he could play pretty good. He knew a lot of them old tunes like "Soldier's Joy" and the "Boatsman," and all those kind, you know.

My mother's father, now he was a famous fiddler. His

John Johnson was living with his daughter, Susie Johnson Hicks, when this photograph by Doug Yarrow was taken.

name was Alexander Hamrick. They called him Alex. He was born and raised over there in Swandale where that bandmill used to be. And then he sold about 2,000 acres there to the Elk River Coal and Lumber Company at Widen. And he kept about 150 acres back on top of the mountain and built a house up there. People would come from all over the country and get him to play the fiddle—he was hard to beat on that fiddle—and they'd always bring their jug of whiskey and like that. Later on he was converted and made a preacher. And he quit playing the fiddle. Soon the fellows that come there with their jugs, you know, would stay at home. He says, "I'm done, I'll never play no more." So that was the end of his fiddlin'. It's something similar to about all the old fiddlers: most of them usually quit when they get a little bit old. I'm figuring on quitting myself.

Michael Kline: Where did Alex learn? Did his daddy play?

JJ: I don't know where he learned to play from. All I know he played the fiddle and was hard to beat at it. My dad, now, when he was a boy, learned what tunes he knew from old Sol Carpenter. Old Sol Carpenter, you know, he was another famous fiddler. Sol said he'd never see the day when he could fiddle like Alex Hamrick. When Grandpa Hamrick pulled a bow across a fiddle your hair started tickling. That's the way it was when Dad drawed a bow across the fiddle strings first time I ever heard him. It just seemed like my hair started feeling funny, see, like your hair is raising up now. And it just thrilled me all over, you see. My mother noticed it. I was the only one of the kids that was much interested in it. So my dad said, "Do you want to try a tune, son?" And that was something very unusual for Dad to allow us to

touch anything that he had. Tools, or anything like that, he didn't allow us to bother them. But I took the fiddle and played "The Unclouded Day" right off the rib. So from then on I played the fiddle.

Along when I was 12 or 13 they'd come there at night and steal me away. Dad wouldn't allow me to go, but they'd come in at night and steal us away, me and Charles, my brother. He was a guitar player. And they'd take us to play for dances all over the country. They come here and got us one time, a bunch of them did, and went down—it was winter—we got down there to what's called Eagle's Bend on the Elk River. It's about a mile above Clay. And the river had so much ice floating, we couldn't get across the river, which had a boat on the other side. My brother James pulled his clothes off and swum the river in that ice and got that boat over there and come over and got the rest of us and our instruments. And we went over to the place they call the Old Fields dance hall and played for a dance over there that night. If you made a quarter then you was doing good. I didn't ever have any money. None of us ever had any money. That's the way it was at home. If I went anywhere to play they had to steal me away at night.

MK: Didn't you tell me one time that your dad brought a lot of fiddlers home, though?

JJ: Oh, I couldn't mention, I don't know how many old fiddlers used to come there. Lee Triplett, he was always there. One time my dad brought Lorie Hicks from Calhoun County. He was left- and right-handed, both, he'd just flop her over and play the other way, left and right. He was a good fiddler. And then old Jim Lyons, he'd come there all the time.

Old Chaney Armstrong from Richwood, he come there and stayed two months. I learned about 500 tunes from him. Afterward we had a '21 model Pierce Arrow, seven-passenger, and we took Chaney home. My dad gave him two pigs for coming to teach me the tunes, you know. I think Edden Hammons was at our house one time. There was a fiddler's contest at Clay. Chaney Armstrong and Ed Hammons, I think, came from Richwood. Every Sunday there was a big gang there, maybe. In the summertime especially there was 100 to 150 to feed. My mother and all the girls done all the cooking for them. We had an ice pond. We'd cut ice, store it in the icehouse in the summertime. Strawberry time, we had ice cream and strawberry shortcake. And they came from everywhere especially to hear music. Everybody brought an instrument of some kind. And we really had a time on weekends.

MK: Sounds like your dad had a lot of interest in seeing you learn to play the fiddle.

JJ: At that time my parents was really proud that I was able to play. Then we got us a band after that. I was about 15 then, I guess. Me and my brother Charles and Noble Knotts, he played the harmonica, and Lee Legg was the banjo. We played at WCHS in Charleston several times. We used to get a large box of Baby Ruth candy bars for playing down there. That was the pay we got.

Then about 1931 we moved to Richmond, Virginia, just outside Richmond on a farm there in Louisa County. I played at WRVA in Richmond several times. Could have played steadily all the time with Grandpa Jones and Sunshine True and the Oklahoma Sweethearts. I was about 17 when we moved to Virginia. We was out there about four year and moved back to West Virginia.

MK: What caused your dad to move over there?

JJ: Well, one of Dad's brothers, Uncle Rice, traded for that farm out there and wanted my dad to move on it. My dad sold his property he had in Clay and moved out there. It had a mansion on it and two big tobacco barns, a big cattle barn and all that stuff. There was a $4,000 lien against it. My dad didn't know, see, Uncle Rice didn't tell him anything about it. My dad was pretty old then. He was in the sawmill business and he wasn't making no money. People just robbed him. And me and my mother and two sisters stayed out there. I cleared 27 acres of land by myself with an axe. Chopped her down. Four acres of pine I grubbed with a mattock.

A man come in there one day and wanted a payment on the place. He had the papers right there. We didn't know anything about it. My dad wasn't making enough to pay and they wanted the money right off the reel, quick as they could get it, or they were going to seize the place. So we moved back to West Virginia. He lost all that. I couldn't number the times he lost thousands of dollars. Hundreds of thousands. It come into his hand and went right out. My mother always

John Johnson started fiddling at an early age. Here, his brother Charles plays guitar, while brother James and sister Maxine look on. Photographer unknown.

John Johnson's life on the road never left as much time with his family as he would have liked. This undated photograph, with the car standing ready in the background, perhaps represents a parting scene. Photographer unknown.

said to him, "It's a good thing you didn't get all that money in your hand." Then he would say, "I want to know why it wouldn't have been good for me?" "Well," she says, "if you'd a had all that money at one time you'd a got the big head and we'd a never lived together: You'd a been one place and I'd a been somewhere else." So that's the reason all his fortunes went down the drain. But he was a fortune hunter. He liked to hunt them fortunes.

MK: Run down your sisters and brothers for me. I've heard you mention several.

JJ: Well, the girls was Ernestine, she was the oldest. She died when she was young. Ernestine, Josephine, Clementine, Irene, Maxine, and Lorriane was the girls. And the boys was Charles, George, James, and John. Ten altogether. I was the sixth one down.

When we come back from Virginia we lived above Clay on top of the hill. Then my dad bought 76 acres and lumber enough to build a five-room house. I went to work at Swandale, walked six miles each way for three years, and bought lumber enough to finish the house. Carried a lot of it on my back across them hills. Carried all the lumber from Swandale for the doors and windows and the baseboards and all that. My dad got him a couple of little Jersey calves. We broke them to work, made a yoke to haul logs with to build a barn, smokehouse, all that. And the stones that went under the house, them calves pulled them. We lived there a long time, and Dad finally sold that and bought his old home

place down here on Kingers Ridge, where he died. My mother stayed there till she died, at the same place.

I lived with them sometimes and helped out. I built a big barn there, and after I built the barn I had to go away to work. I had a woodworking shop there and turning lathe that would weigh, I expect, 700 pounds. It was in a building just out from the house a little piece. I come in one night and mother said, "John, what do you reckon happened to your shop?" I said, "I wouldn't have any idea. What happened to it?" She said, "You don't have any shop now." "Well, how come I don't have any shop now?" She says, "There's nothing out there." I got a light and went out and there was nothing there. The ground was clean. No building. No nothing. We had a big granary over top and my shop underneath. Every kind of tool a man could need, blacksmith shop and everything. She said just a whirlwind come down and picked it up and took it away. There was never a piece of that house or a tool or a lathe ever found, but one auger bit. My mother just happened to be down in the holler there below the house a quarter of a mile 'senging [digging ginseng] one day, and found an auger bit where the twister had turned it loose. That's all that was ever hear tell about that stuff. We never did know what happened.

MK: Getting back to your childhood a little bit more, you said that you could learn a fiddle tune just by hearing it one time?

JJ: Yeah, it used to be I had no trouble learning a fiddle tune. I'd just hear a tune one time, I had it right then. And I used to go down below Clay there, a place called Pigtown. It's still there yet. It was a coal mining place. There was a fellow lived there by the name of Dorvel Hill. I was bashful back then and wouldn't go in anybody's house hardly. I'd sit on the railroad and listen to Dorvel play the fiddle at night. And I learned most all of Dorvel's tunes. I just set down there and listened to all his tunes and then go home and play them. First one I ever learned from him was "Ragtime Annie." I don't remember all of them. "Under the Double Eagle." Some of them good old tunes, "Dill Pickle Rag." I couldn't name all of them.

Old man Lee Triplett, I learned a lot of tunes off of him, "Wild Horse and the Red Trace," some of them like that Lee played. One time me and my dad went over to Catlettsburg, Kentucky, to see Blind Ed Haley. We found out about him from old man Jim Ryans. Used to work for my dad. He played the fiddle a little and fixed fiddles. Then I heard Natchee the Indian play a lot of times. I think he was a Sioux Indian. And another fiddler you probably know, Clark Kessinger. I played with him along in the '40s and the first part of the '50s. He was a fast, smooth fiddler. I went to see him just a week before he died. He was playing in a contest and had a stroke, and the fiddle fell right out of his hand. He lived in St. Albans, just a little ways from my sister there. I went and played the fiddle for him, played "The Forked Deer." Clark said, "That's not 'The Forked Deer.'" "Well," I said, "I don't know whether it's 'The Forked Deer,' or not, but I learned it from a record that Arthur Smith made when I was a kid, and I know that tune's way older than I am." And Clark said, "That ain't 'The Forked Deer.'" But you see, I play six parts of "The Forked Deer" and he just played two. So I suppose that's the reason why he said that wasn't "The Forked Deer." I learned that whole tune just like Arthur Smith played it. I've heard lots of other fiddlers put just two parts to it.

MK: Tell me more about your childhood memories of Clay.

JJ: Well, back then Clay was just exactly like it is now. It never did change. People always had to go somewhere else to work, if they had any work. Never did have anything there for people to work at. Someone wanted to put a big paper mill in there, plenty of timber, but they wouldn't let them do that. So it's right now today just like it was when I was born. Never changed a bit, except they built a new high school and a new courthouse. That's all the change that's ever been made in the place.

Eustas Murphy ran a store up there. He could undersell just about anybody around. A fellow come in there one time to buy a bunch of stuff, and he got it pretty near all bought and he saw a crosscut saw hanging there on the wall. And he said, "How much is that saw, Mr. Murphy?" "Well," he said, "that's $3.95." "Ain't gonna pay it, not a-gonna pay no such price. I can get it at Sears Roebuck for $3.49." "Well, if you was to buy at Sears and Roebuck go right ahead. I'll sell it to you the same price as Sears and Roebuck." "If you sell it to me at the Sears Roebuck price, I'll take it!" "Okay." Eustas went ahead and got all his groceries. He just left the saw hanging there. Fellow says, "Well, I'm ready for my saw." Eustas says, "You haven't bought an envelope yet." "Well, what do you want with an envelope?" "Well," he said, "how you gonna mail that order? You got to have an envelope to mail that order." He says, "That's a penny, and two cents for the stamp, that's three cents." "Well, I'll pay three cents." "Well," he says, "the money order, that's 15 cents." "I'll pay that." "Now," he said, "you haven't paid the shipping charges on that saw yet." "Well, add it on." Eustas finally got it figured up and after the fellow got it all paid for Eustas still left the saw hanging there. "I'm ready to take my saw now . . ." "No," says Eustas, "you have to wait two weeks for the saw. If you'd a ordered that from Sears Roebuck you'd a had to wait two weeks for it." "Give me the saw, I'll pay your price!" And he took his saw.

In the early days the school children, the ones that went to Clay from the Dundon side, either had to ring that ferry bell down there and get across the river—and Ferryman Joe could only haul about two or three across at a time in the boat—or, if the river was up, they couldn't ride the ferry at all. They had to walk all the way around the railroad and be late for school. And lots of times a freight train was switching there on the tracks and they couldn't get across the bridge. Sometimes they wouldn't get to school 'til noon. So my mother wrote a poem about how they needed a bridge at Dundon. My dad took it and had it published in the Clay paper. I know a few words of the first one she wrote, but I don't remember the rest. She wrote five poems altogether. The first one started out:

> Near the yawning outlet of Big Buffalo,
> Where the crowds of people come and go,
> The people of Clay County need a bridge,
> To splice the road to Punkin Ridge.

Then she told in the poem about how the river was up, and about the train switching there and how them railroad ties was covered with ice, and how the children might slip and fall and break their arms and legs. She told all that in this poem, and how they had to walk the extra mile around the railroad and up through town to high school, and get there late, and how they were degraded and everything else. All in poetry. My dad would take them and have them published.

Every time a poem was published they'd build a little more on the bridge. The first time they built the piers. They built for a grade-crossing bridge that went right across the railroad. And before they got a chance to lay another piece of steel she wrote another poem and told what danger there was in that grade-crossing. About how they needed an overhead bridge. And my dad took that to the paper, and, boy, that there O'Connor was his name, he was the big bridge man, and how he roared when he heard that one. She had the whole court there at Clay in an uproar over that bridge. Well, they started the addition to put the bridge up across there on the hill, and finally they got that part of the pier made, and there it set again. We never heard no more about it for a while. And Mother asked my dad, "What's the reason we haven't heard anything about that bridge down there?" "Well," said my dad, "they say this and they say that and they say the other, and I don't know what they're going to do about it."

So she wrote a poem titled, "They Say." And it started out:

> They say that Gabriel's horn will blow,
> The time we know not when,
> They say they'll build a bridge to Clay,
> The time we know not when . . .

And it was "they say" from there on with every man's name on it that was in West Virginia. Never missed a one. When they read that, buddy, they burnt their feet. And they started to work on the bridge again. And then she wrote another one, I forget the title of it. And then the last one she wrote was in thanks for the bridge. The bridge is right there today, and they wanted to put her name on the head of it. But she wouldn't let them do it.

Her name was Missouri Edith Hamrick Johnson. She's the one I was telling you about the writing spider writing her name. The spider wrote M-O-Z-U-R-A, so she went by the name Mozura ever after that.

MK: Wait a minute, John, what do you mean the spider wrote her name?

JJ: Well, she called her children out on the porch one morning, and there in the morning glory vines she showed us the writing spider. It had her name wrote big in the web in wide, white letters: M-O-Z-U-R-A. And she never went by any other name any way after that. I saw one of them writing spiders here last summer but you couldn't tell what it had wrote. It had just started to write. Very seldom you see them. They're a large yellow spider, real pretty spiders. And, of course, a lot of people think they're phoney, they think they can't write, and all like that. But they do. They really write.

MK: Did your mother attach some significance to the spi-

der writing her name? Did she think it was a sign of good luck?

JJ: No, she didn't believe in luck. There wasn't any such thing as luck to her. All that she believed in was God-sent. She believed that's the way her name was wrote on the book of life in heaven. That was her belief.

MK: And you saw the spider?

JJ: Yeah, we all saw it, the whole family saw it.

MK: Do you get your writing ability from your mother?

JJ: I don't know, I can't write nothing, really.

MK: Just books and books and books of poetry!

JJ: Well, sometimes I get in the mood to write something, a song, maybe. I've wrote a few. Would you like to hear about my horse I had?

MK: Oh, yeah.

JJ:
I used to have a good old horse,
I called him Faithful Dan.
I was just a kid, of course.
But I felt more like a man.
I'd ride him all the live-long day,
Old Dan could not be beat.

A Musical Look at John Johnson's Fiddling

John A. Cuthbert

In the summer of 1947, Louis Watson Chappell, a folklorist from West Virginia University, met John Johnson in Strange Creek, West Virginia. Having heard of Johnson's musical prowess from other fiddlers in the Braxton County area, Chappell had come equipped with a disk recording machine with which he had been engaged in documenting and preserving West Virginia's musical tradition for over a decade.

Chappell is perhaps best known for establishing the factual basis and circumstances surrounding the John Henry legend in his book *John Henry: A Folk-Lore Study* (Jena, Ger.: Frommansche Verlag, 1933; rpt., Port Washington, N.Y.: Kennikat Press, 1968). Professor Chappell's archive of 647 aluminum disks recorded throughout

West Virginia from 1937–1947, embracing nearly 100 performers, is preserved in the West Virginia Collection at West Virginia University.

On this occasion, his efforts were well rewarded. Johnson proved to be not only an abundant source, but also one of the most skilled musicians Chappell had ever encountered.

Oddly enough, according to Chappell's notes, Johnson did not possess a fiddle when the two met one August morning; thus, their first job was to borrow one. This task was evidently accomplished in short order for before the day was out 20 12-inch aluminum disks, embracing some 80 tunes, had been recorded. In addition to being remarkable from a technical standpoint, the recordings emphasize the

wide variety of sources, styles, and types of fiddle music which flourished in West Virginia in the 1940s.

The Johnson recordings are as varied as they are numerous. Classic old-time fiddle tunes such as "Forked Deer" and "Fisher's Hornpipe" are interspersed with more modern pieces like "Dickson County Blues," "Down Yonder," and "Honeysuckle Rag." Also included are many play party and dance songs, including "Cumberland Gap," "Granny Will Your Dog Bite," and "Hop Light Ladies," as well as traditional ballad hymn tunes: "Barbara Allen," "Amazing Grace," and "The White Pilgrim" —altogether an eclectic mixture of old and new, sacred and secular.

Stylistically, the recordings exhibit a hybridized manner of playing which was derived from many

I did not have to feed him hay,
Because he could not eat.
Now old Dan was homely,
And he was precious to my soul.
But you know the horse was only
A long, slim hickory pole.

MK: That's nice. When did you make that?

JJ: Back in the '30s, somewhere along about '32.

MK: Did your brothers and sisters write poems, too?

JJ: Yeah, about all of them, every one of them can write something. I don't know if I ever saw a poem Clementine wrote or not. But all the rest of them wrote.

MK: Did you sit around and talk verse in your house, or what? Make up songs all the time? How did this get started?

JJ: No, I really never wrote a song 'til I was about 20 years old. I wrote some songs been copyrighted by somebody else, you know, like "The High Cost of Living," I wrote that song.

MK: Tell me a little about the school you went to.

JJ: Oh, I went to school down in Dundon, West Virginia, when I first started. 'Course, I didn't know anything about school, and I didn't know what you went there for. When a

person done wrong there the teacher'd flip them on the ear with a rule. First day I ever went to school I was crawling around on the floor, and got a whipping for that right off. I never had much schooling, didn't know much. Never did learn anything in my whole life. Still don't know nothing. Can't imagine anything, and can't see straight: I'm all the time looking around a curve and sliding down a hill or something. Never do anything right. 'Bout all I can draw is flies, and then only in the summertime. That's just about all I know about myself.

When I went to school in Dundon they pronounced me totally blind. And the teacher wrote a note home, "This boy absolutely has to have glasses for he is practically blind and cannot see the letters." My mother wrote on the other side of the note, she says, "If you'll teach him his letters he can read them." Well, I couldn't learn anything in school, that was for sure. So my mother told me she would buy me a pair of gloves that had a fringe on the cuff of them, like an Indian made them, if I would learn my letters. In 15 minutes I knowed every letter there was in the book. All she had to do was tell them to me one time and I knew them all. And in school I couldn't learn anything.

John Johnson. Photograph by Doug Yarrow.

different sources. As Johnson has stated, his style was nurtured in the midst of a mountain fiddling tradition for which central West Virginia is famous, characterized by modal melodies, persistent drones, and highly accentuated rhythms produced by relatively short, irregular, bowing patterns. His debt to this tradition is most evident in his performances of regional favorites like "Shelvin' Rock," "Camp Chase," and "Jimmy Johnson," among others. In general, however, in the wake of fiddlers heard on radio and records, or encountered during travels through Texas and elsewhere, by 1947 Johnson's playing had become somewhat less localized. Elements of ragtime, blues, and "Texas" or "contest" style are all detectable in his music, which is typically fast and clean, and attests to his skillful manipulation of a long bow.

The general stylistic influence of Fiddlin' Arthur Smith is especially

MK: What about fiddle playing, John? I don't know if you're the best fiddle player in the world, but you're as good a fiddle player as I ever heard anywhere. And you told me you have never played the fiddle very much.

JJ: I doubt if all told in my whole life, if every hour that I played the fiddle, I doubt if it made six months. I don't know about fiddling. I can't figure out what kind of brain a fellow's got for to play a fiddle. I don't know. Probably something wrong with him.

MK: But anyway, as a young fiddler, you just started going around to different parts of the country? Where did you go?

JJ: Oh, I been everywhere. I been to all the states, I fiddled in all of them, from one side to the other, around and around and around and back again. There's really not very many fiddlers in West Virginia that I played with, but I played with a lot of good fiddlers in Texas, Ben Thommason and all them fiddlers down around Fort Worth and Dallas. I met a lot of good fiddlers in Houston, but I don't know any of their names. They're hard to beat down there. Good fiddlers down in that country.

MK: How'd you get to Texas to meet those guys?

JJ: Well, to begin with, I first went there when I was 14 years old. Hoboed down there. Had an uncle lived in El Paso then, the first time I went. I got to like Texas, and in later years I had a cousin lived in Arlington, Texas, so I went home with him one time. And then people got to knowing me down there. I worked around a lot. Have a cousin there now in Pecos, Texas, Bayard Johnson from over here at Frametown. He's bought a big ranch down there. One time I went down to Mena, Arkansas, and got in with these Ward boys, they were brothers. They build steel buildings of all kinds in Houston, and they wanted me to go over and work with them down there. But instead of getting a job, they put me to cooking. I didn't like that.

One day I went in the B&B Music store there to get a guitar string. I was looking at these fiddles and this fellow Bill come around to ask me what I wanted, could he help me? I told him I wanted a first string for a guitar. He says, "You interested in these fiddles? You play a fiddle?" "I play a little." "Let's hear you play one." And he hands me a fiddle. I hit a note or two and he says, "Let's hear that 'Sally Ann Johnson' on that thing." So I played it for him. That's how I got invited to a big party that night. This guy Bill whatever-his-name-was picked me up that evening about 7:30 and we went way out in the country to this fellow's house. He was a state roads superintendent and he had about nine fiddlers there, didn't hire anything but fiddlers. We played there all night. Played 'til 5:00 the next morning and they had to go to work. He had fiddlers from everywhere around there, and I don't know any of their names. We took turns about playing there, and they recorded all the tunes we played. We had a pretty good time that night. I learned a couple of tunes, but I don't

noticeable. Not only is this apparent in Johnson's version of "Forked Deer," but also in numerous other cases, particularly in his selection and renditions of old Smith tunes like "Dickson County Blues" and "Cheatham County Breakdown" (Bluebird Records 6369, 7351) as well as "Listen to the Mockingbird" (Bluebird 5843). Johnson's "Hell Among the Yearlings" also bears notable similarities to Smith's version on Folkways FA2379, particularly in the performance of syncopated chords in the low strain. A similar passage, played strummento, occurs in the second part of Johnson's "Garfield March." A real tour de force, this piece contains streams of slurred parallel thirds and sixths alternating with fast clean runs which provide ample evidence of the fiddler's adept coordination between bowing and noting.

As a rule Johnson's up-tempo tunes are fast-paced and permeated with crisp and even scale passages. Double-stops are employed sparingly, not generally as drones, but for color and accentuation at structurally important points. In slower pieces, though, where the emphasis is on harmony and intonation, successions of melodic double-stops frequently create a lush two-part texture.

Johnson's playing exhibits many characteristics of progressive old-time fiddling, and indeed, he readily admits his predilection for Benny Thomasson and others, yet variation and development, which are fundamentals to that style of playing, are by and large absent from the 1947 recordings. Johnson's and Kessinger's (County 747) renditions of "Under the Double Eagle" begin essentially the same. Kessinger's successive repetitions are in reality variations; Johnson's are not.

Nevertheless, Johnson's playing is far from dry. Monotony is never a problem to a fiddler with his dexterity and sense of musicality. In many ways his music is a reflection of himself: restless, fast moving, and diverse—an outgrowth of an extraordinary life and an extraordinary man.

EDITOR'S NOTE: This article first appeared in the winter 1981 issue of *Goldenseal* (vol. 7, no. 4).

remember what they was, but we sure did hear some good fiddling there that night.

MK: What is it about Texas style fiddling that's different, do you think?

JJ: I don't know. That Ben Thomasson, almost all those fiddlers, played something near the same pattern. They have a different style from most everybody else. I don't know just what you'd call it. I just play the way I learned myself, don't know anything else. Yeah, I pull a long bow. Some people uses a shorter bow. But I never did see but one bow that was long enough for me, really. I found it in a dresser drawer in Massachusetts. It was just the length of that dresser drawer. I had that bow a long time—had an ivory frog on it—before somebody stole it and fiddle and all off me. Never did see it no more.

But I fiddled everywhere. Fiddled my way out of jail one time. Dr. Lockheart was sheriff in Clay and he had an old fiddle. I stayed in jail all one night and the next morning he comes down. "What are you doing in here?" "Well, just like the rest of them." "Well," he says, he opened up the door and said, "come on, I'm glad you're in here. Been wanting to hear you play the fiddle." He lived upstairs there, the same place where I was born. He took me upstairs and let me eat my breakfast and handed me the fiddle. When I got through playing he said, "Go on down the road. You don't have to be in jail." Got me loose. That was one time the fiddle done me good.

And then another time I got in jail down there in the same place, Clay. And the jailer was Joe Carte, that Ferryman Joe's son. When I come out in front of the magistrate she says, "John, as many times as you've been here, I think I oughta give you 10 days." I said, "Whatever you say." Then Joe Carte says, "You ain't gonna give John 10 days. I'm gonna pay his fine! He wrote a poem about my dad, and it's every word the truth. And I've got it right here in my shirt pocket. Read that." And she read the poem and says, "Just let him go." And that was twice I got out, once for poetry and the other for fiddling.

But I've been everywhere, practically, married all these women. I've been looking for another now, just mailed a letter out this morning. I might get her, she lives in California. I met her on a Greyhound bus, a real nice woman. I might pick her up later. Of course, she'd have to learn to eat groundhog if she lived up here. About all they've got to eat in West Virginia is groundhog and poke greens.

MK: Did you play the fiddle for her?

JJ: No, I didn't play, she don't even know I can play a fiddle. Probably be a good thing not to tell her 'til after we're married. Then they'd be a sure divorce right there. Quick as they find out you're a fiddler, that's the end of it. But all these marriages was well worth it. Yeah, they was all good women, but out of the whole bunch there wasn't a one could play a tune or anything. I think maybe one could play a flute. I never heard her play, but I heard she could. And the last one I married, she took every dud of clothes I ever had. Never left me with a pair of socks, not a pair of shorts, nor a sheet of paper to write on. And a brand new three-quarter ton truck, four-wheel drive, she loaded everything there was in it and down the road she went, and I haven't seen her since.

MK: Do you think you'll do better with this next one in California?

JJ: I ain't sure whether I'll get her or not. Merritt is her name. I been trying to think of a poem I might make on her. Merritt, she ought to rhyme good with that there snuff, you know that Garrett snuff? But after you've been married five times and half the time you can't remember your wives' names, I think maybe it's time to quit.

MK: Why did they all object to your fiddle playing?

JJ: When a fiddler starts out to go play somewhere, the average woman thinks he's got 40 other women around his neck, just because he can play the fiddle. Back, oh, about '52, I was playing at the U.S. Grill in Charleston through the week. We got through playing one night and I started to count our tips, I had it divided up, about $4 apiece, laying on the bar, when somebody tapped me on the shoulder. I looked around. Nice looking girl standing there. "Are you going with me?" I says, "Well, if you wait 'til I divide this money up I'll be right with you." She took her hand and swiped all that money off the bar. Then she reached down her dress and pulled out a roll of $50 bills about like that. I said, "You fellows pick up the chicken feed, boys. I'm going!"

Out the door we went, right around the corner on the Boulevard there. She says, "I live right up there. The old landlady is cranky. If she notices who you are, just keep going. Here's the key. When you get to the top of the stairs turn left, the second door on your left." So I went. I got inside before she got there. About that time she come up. I could hear the landlady. "That's not the same man you had up here last night." "Yes it is. That's my husband." "The man you had in here last night wasn't that tall. He didn't have no fiddle, either." "Well," she says, "it's my husband, it's the same one I had."

Anyway, we got by with it for three nights. So she says to me next morning, "I want to go down to Capitol Street and buy you some new clothes." We went down to Capitol Street and she got me a new outfit from one end to the other: shoes, socks, clothes, underclothes, shirts, belt, and brought them back up to the apartment. "Now, I want you to change clothes. Get them clothes off you." I said, "What do you want me to get my clothes off for? These are the new clothes I have on. Ain't nothing the matter with my clothes." "Yes, there is. I don't want you to have anything on that any other woman ever touched." Right there I knew I was full in the hands of the Devil himself.

Well, three days was up and the old woman threw us out. We went down Lee Street, went into the Lee Hotel. Couldn't play music, she wouldn't let me go nowhere and play. Lost my job. Had my fiddle setting in the corner. I didn't even smoke cigarettes, but I said, "I'm gonna run down and get a pack of cigarettes." "You ain't going after no cigarettes, you don't even smoke cigarettes." "Yeah, I smoke cigarettes, I'm going down to get a pack." She grabbed my fiddle and says, "I'll hold this 'til you get back." That made me mad, and I grabbed the fiddle right out of her hand and walked out the door. Just a few days after that they picked that girl up. She was on parole from Atlanta for killing a man with a high-heeled shoe. She went back to Atlanta. That was one of the best I ever had on my rounds. I could tell you about some more. Probably be better not to. I may want to get married again, and if they hear all these things, I may never find a woman.

MK: None of them ever liked your fiddle playing?

JJ: One of them liked my fiddle playing, but I had to secretly play it for her when nobody else was around. Couldn't play it for the public, that was out.

MK: What is it about fiddle playing anyway?

JJ: It's not the fiddle, it's the way you play the fiddle. Why if some fiddlers sit there and play it from now on no woman would pay attention to it. It's the fiddler, ain't the fiddle.

MK: Do you think sometimes people are more interested in your fiddling than they are in you as a person?

JJ: Yeah. One hundred percent. Because for sure I don't have any personality at all. I'm no showman, can't put on a show. I can't get on stage and put on a big smile when there's nothing to smile about. They tried that with me in television. I wouldn't even begin to laugh. I just throwed the fiddle down and quit. When they told me I had to smile I walked out. When I'm really playing the fiddle I probably have a frown on my face. That's the way my Grandpa Hamrick was. My mother said she'd never seen him smile when he was playing the fiddle. If you're going to play the fiddle you have to put your whole heart into it. But if the fiddle means more to you than anything else, it's time to quit. I never did make anything with a fiddle in my whole life. What little dab I did make didn't do me a bit of good, not one bit.

One time in Roosevelt, Utah, I played all day long until midnight. Went in there with 15 cents and when I come out I had 73 silver dollars. And I was playing every tune they asked me to play, never missed a tune. Right at the end of the evening, a man throwed five silver dollars down and says, "There's $5 says you can't play 'Green Grow the Lilacs.'" Well, I couldn't think of it. And the crowd hollered, "Hey, fiddler, you didn't let that five silver dollars scare that tune out of you, did you?" I said, "No, I didn't let $5 scare it out of me, but I can't think of how it goes." "Well, you can't play it. We got you stumped now!" I just shoved back a dollar of

his money and said, "Here's a dollar says you can't whistle or hum it." He couldn't whistle it nor could he hum it. They turned on him. "Hey, you wouldn't know that tune if you heard it!" "Yes, I would," he said, "I know that tune, I just can't think of how it goes." "Well," I said, "it's the same way with me." But just about that time I thought of Tex Ritter and one of Tex's old tunes. I said, "Wait a minute," and I raked them five back. I said, "I've got it!"

So I played him "Green Grow the Lilacs." I come to find out he owned the hotel across the street and he gave me a room that night. The next morning at 8:00 he pecked on my door. "Come on, we'll go eat breakfast." I was going on to Price, Utah, and he took me out of town and offered to take me plum to Price, if I wanted him to. I says, "No, I can catch a ride across that hill." That was one streak of luck, if you can call it luck, with a fiddle. That helped me out. But other times I probably played the same tunes and got nothing, and wind up worse off.

One night I was playing there in Price when an Indian come in. "You want a job herding sheep?" "Sure." "You play fiddle good, I hire good fiddler." That fellow never saw a sheep, I don't think. He was one of them Ute Indians. I went with him all the way to Goshen, Utah. There was a beer joint over there they called the Dog House. Glass was at least six inches deep around the building where they'd broke up all kinds of bottles. And I was right there for one month playing the fiddle, sitting up on the bar. There wasn't a chair in the place or a table. Sit up on the bar or stand up, or any way you could get to play the fiddle—for a month—with not one bite to eat. Slept in a little back room there. For a month.

Old man Jim Eskelson lived right next door. He owned the building and rented it to these Indians. So old Jim says one day, "You know, these Indians will keep you over there 'til you die, playing the fiddle, and they won't give you nothing?" I says, "I don't care, this is my body I've got, this is mine. I don't care how long. I'm the one staying over there, they ain't keeping me over there." "They're giving you beer, ain't they?" I say, "Yeah, I get beer. I don't have to drink it if I don't want it." "Well, what are you staying over there for?" I says, "What's it any of your business what I'm staying over there for? I'm playing the fiddle for these Indians."

Well, about the end of the month, this guy, Ronnie Young was his name, that was running the beer joint, he says, "If I buy you a change of clothes would you go out to my place and fix a little fence for me? How long would you work if I bought you a change of clothes?" I said, "I'll work 'til I pay for the clothes." "Come on." He took me to Roosevelt, bought me a $40 hat, a pair of boots, two pair of Lee riders, everything. Took me out to his ranch and showed me the fence. It was a good fence, but he wanted willows wove through the wire. I wove willow all that day. That evening he come back, him and another guy. "By George," he said, "I

As with other artists, John Johnson's creativity takes a variety of forms, including mural painting. He also writes verse. Photograph by Doug Yarrow.

wish I'd a had you here long ago." I'd put about a half mile of them things in the fence, and me without anything to eat. Well, they fixed me a couple of bologna sandwiches and they left. I wove willows the rest of the week. I finished up that string of fence and he hadn't come back yet. So I hitchhiked out of there, walked four miles to the highway, caught a ride, went back to the Dog House, and he wasn't there. He'd closed her down. Old Jim Eskelson said, "You may never see them fellows again." I hitched out of that place, finally got out of there with nothing but the clothes I wore. So that's what the fiddle got me into that time.

Then another time there was an Indian wanted me to go home with him. He composed all kinds of songs and he could really play the piano. So I went home to see him. He took a case of beer. And hundred and twenty miles out in the mountains up in there to his house at the end of the road, and next morning there wasn't any beer. I got up early and went out looking around. Nothing but pine and cedar trees. There was some brush piled up against the fence. Then I seen a couple of bones laying around there. I pulled back the brush and there was a skeleton of a man laying there, or a woman one. He probably ate that one 'cause there wasn't a bite of food in the house. I figured my bones was going to be there next in a brush pile. A hundred and twenty miles out there. No beer.

I says, "Well buddy, I got to hit the road." "You can't walk out of here, don't you know it's a hundred and twenty miles across that desert?" "I don't care if it's 500," I says. "I'm going across it." Down the road I went. "Hey, come back here." I just kept going. I got a couple of miles down the

road and I heard that old truck a-going. I had it right in my mind: Mister you just make one move like you're going to harm me and you're a dead man. It'll be your bones instead of mine. He stopped. "Get in, I'll take you back." So he did. He took me back over there. And from that time on I never went—yeah, I did. I went with one other Indian.

He had a brand-new Pontiac and a sheep ranch. He had a lot of money. He said we'd go out on the sheep ranch. These sheep herders never seen nobody year round. Said they'd like to hear that fiddle. We started down the highway. There was about I'd say 40 or 50 ring-necked pheasants along the ditch, just thick way down through there. He said, "Hang on." He just whirled her to the right, down over that bank, him a-doing 60 miles an hour! Don't know how in the world he kept from turning over. And, buddy, them feathers flew, the air was full of them. Then we got out and gathered up the pheasants, 17 or 18 we got out of that bunch. We went on. On the left-hand side was another gang. "Hang on." Whew-man, he plowed the ditch as we were going down through there and we got another big load of pheasants. We took them out to the sheep herders to cook. I played the fiddle, we drunk whiskey, beer, and wine, and we had pheasant to eat. That was the last Indian I went home with.

And then one time I was going to Canada. Had 20 cents in my pocket. It was the fall of the year and real cold. I got up in the woods, and cutting brush, made me a bed. I laid down there and like to froze to death that night.

The next morning my knees was just a-cracking. I went down and there was a beer joint there, just opening it up. Went in that beer joint, it was good and warm in there, my

John Johnson with his granddaughter Heidi. Photograph by Doug Yarrow.

teeth was a-cracking, my knees was popping together. This drunk there got a six-pack, and I got a cup of coffee, 10 cents. I drunk that coffee, what I didn't shake out I drunk, and drunk another one. And I said, "That's the last of the money that I've got."

"Where are you going?" he asked. I says, "Well, I'm going up in Canada. I thought I'd go up there and see if I could find some work, in the timber or something." "Well, you can get all the timber work you want right over here in New Jersey." Just shows how an old sot drunk can help a feller out— undoubtedly God Almighty set that drunk there, brought him right up the road and put him right there.

Drunk says, "Ever work on a sawmill?" I says, "I can do anything on a sawmill." "Well," he says, "a man has got a sawmill not very far from here and he was wanting me yesterday to work for him, but I can't work because I drink too much. And I don't like to work on a sawmill anyway." So he took me right over there—the whole side was out of his truck—and I like to froze to death, wind blowing through that truck. Two men was working there on the mill. One was an Indian and the other was an off-bearer. "I come over here to see about a job," I said. "I'm needing a man, but I never

did have a drifter that was worth much." I says, "You can have your own judgment, but you'll never know whether I can't work 'til you hire me. You ain't got nothing there I can't do." "Can you saw and grade lumber?" I says, "Yes, sir." "I'm going to hire you."

Well, I only had a pair of dress shoes on because when I left Worcester, Massachusetts, I took my car with all my clothes and over a hundred dollars worth of fishing tackle and pulled it down through the woods and parked it by the lake and left it set there with a note on the steering wheel to my brother for a gift. Left a full tank of gas in the car and hit the road a-hitchhiking. They found that car three months later and thought I'd jumped in the lake and drowned, that's all they could figure out. And my brother like to never got the car. But the police finally gave it to him months after. But anyhow, I says, "I ain't got no work shoes." He says, "I think I've got a pair, a brand new pair here if they fit you." He was a big man, weighed around 300 pounds and strong as an ox, too. He went and got a pair of brand new loggers boots, fit me to a hair, exactly my size. "You can have them for $10." "All right." Then I ate supper with him.

I met him the next morning at Bill's Cafe. He sent them

other two guys home. Me and him run that sawmill. I done the off-bearing, the edging, and stacked the lumber by myself. Had big Hyster there, about a six-foot fork on it. I pulled her up there, tilted her back a little, and throwed the slabs on. And when the Hyster was full I jumped on and dumped the slabs and brought back a load of logs and put on the carriage. When we sawed out all the logs we had, we headed for the mountains the next day. I cut timber. He had a bulldozer and made roads. He skidded the logs, had a truck with a loader right on it. That evening at quitting time we had it loaded, ready to go. Me and him run that sawmill, nobody else helped. I worked way up 'til the winter and I left there in the wintertime. Smoke blowing down the chimney, you see. Bad weather a-coming.

Anyway, I took the flu and there was a liquor store close to the hotel where I was staying. I went in and bought a pint of brandy. That liquor fellow said, "Buddy, you're sick, ain't you?" He put his hand on my head. It was real hot. So he give me a bottle of lemon juice and said, "You get in your room and pour you a glass full of whiskey and fill her up with that. Drink it, and get in bed and cover up." Well, I did. Gulped down a pint and got into bed, just like he said. After a half hour I began to feel pretty good. I crawled right out of that bed and went down to get another pint and a bottle of lemon juice. He says, "I'm telling you, you ought to have stayed in bed, you'd have been well in the morning."

Well, I got me another pint and another bottle of lemon juice and back to my room I went again. Gulped down the whiskey and lemon juice and started playing a Gibson guitar I had there. Several people in the hotel come in and listened. I had my door left open on purpose so they could hear. I was singing some songs in my room when a fellow from the bar downstairs said, "Well, buddy, I guess you'd better put it away for the night." "Okay." So they all left. I throwed a few duds in my suitcase, left that guitar sitting right there—2:00 in the morning—and down the highway I went. In a blizzard, buddy, in a blizzard! Wasn't no buses run on that road at all. I walked three miles. There was a truck stop on the left, a tractor and trailer setting there. I walked in just almost froze to death. Man says, "Good Lord, you know you'll freeze to death like that. It's 20 below zero out there." I says, "Well, I can't help that. I've got to go." I told him I was going to Baltimore. "Well," he says, "you get in that truck out there and I can put you in Albany." I got the Greyhound from Albany to Baltimore. That was one of my good luck times when I hit that place. I could tell you a lot of things that happened when you'd think the next minute was death. I could tell you a lot of them.

MK: Do you like being in situations like that?

JJ: Don't bother me a bit. One time I was drifting through Akron. There was a circus there, and I went loafing around that circus. They was tearing down a small sideshow tent, and I went over and asked the guy for a job. Never had worked in a circus in my life. He says, "Yeah, I need a man steady." I said, "I got a suitcase. Is there any place I could put it?" "There in that trailer." So I got my suitcase and put it in this trailer with all these monkeys. There was a fellow stayed in there and he kept a hoot owl in there and a buzzard, and I don't know what else. A monkey or two. It stunk. There wasn't nothing to sleep on but tents and tentpoles, them great big ones. We went through Cleveland, Ohio, and all the towns going west. Got over to Clay, Ohio, right out of Toledo, there. I said to the guy, "When am I supposed to get paid?" He says, "You can get paid any time right over there in that tent." But the man in the tent says, "You'll have to have an order." The other man said, "You don't need an order." So I was getting in a pretty good mess of it, being two weeks with no money.

So then he says, "Say, did you ever sell any peanuts?" "No," I said, "I never." "Well," he says, "Try your luck. Buy a carton of peanuts for five cents a bag and sell them for 15 cents. You give me half of what's left. You make $36 on the whole thing." So I went to selling peanuts and sold out for $36 and hit the road with what money I had. I got about half a mile down the road and a car pulled up. "Hey, buddy, going into town?" Some old guy driving a Chevrolet. I got in the car and he said, "You been working for that circus? Ain't it a shame, them poor animals, they never feed them." I says, "They don't feed anything else, either, and they don't pay." Well, he took me into Toledo and gave me a $10 bill.

I was there two days and went down to Manpower to see if I could get a job. It was surrounded with gays and blacks and whites of every sort. I couldn't go in there, so I left. I just got around the corner and a pickup truck pulled up, two men in it. "Hey buddy, were you down at Manpower just now looking for a job?" I said yeah. "Come on, get in." I got in and went to work for them at $4 an hour pointing up chimneys. That pulled me out of that ditch. And I could tell you similar ones like that. Probably take me the rest of the day to tell them all. Things like that happened to me, where I was pulled right out of the hands of death, where I'd have starved to death or been killed.

But I've been everywhere, practically, in the United States, in Canada and Mexico. Played the fiddle, worked here and yonder, worked everywhere. Work a while, go somewhere else. Went when I pleased and come back when I pleased. That's the way a person ought to live. It's a pretty good thing all the way around.

EDITOR'S NOTE: This article first appeared in the winter 1981 issue of *Goldenseal* (vol. 7, no. 4). "Fiddlin' John" Johnson died on June 12, 1996, in Cowen, West Virginia, at the age of 79. He spent his final years in Craigsville with his daughter's family.

Robert Byrd

MOUNTAIN FIDDLER

Dave Wilbur

THE year, as Robert Byrd remembers it, was his 10th. It was a year for heroes like Charles Lindbergh and Babe Ruth. One of my musical heroes, Bill Monroe, was just starting his professional career in the mill towns of northern Indiana. A train rather than a car more likely than not got you in and out of the hollows of Raleigh County. There was no New Deal yet, no welfare state. John L. Lewis had been president of the United Mine Workers for seven years already. No doubt many fathers in those West Virginia coal towns spent their Sunday afternoons pitching baseball with their sons and pitched coal the rest of the week. It was the height of normalcy. The year was 1927 and that is when the persistent youngster who would become a U.S. Representative, Senator, and Senate Majority Leader prevailed upon his foster father to travel 10 miles up to Beckley to get him a violin.

It was no small gift. Senator Byrd told me the violin, case, and bow cost somewhere between 20 and 30 dollars, more than most miners made in a week. Titus Byrd, himself a coal miner, must have been convinced that his son would stick with the fiddle once he had it.

There was plenty of reason to think young Robert would stick with the fiddle. Musicians were plentiful around the coal camp of Stotesbury where the Byrd family lived at the time. The man who one day would be his father-in-law inspired Byrd with his violin playing. Another fiddler, who was left-handed, played a version of "Old Joe Clark" that the young boy just had to learn. A banjo picker by the name of Dana Blevins was a prominent influence. There was also the wife of the principal at Mark Twain High School. "Mrs. Cormandy taught me classical violin from the 7th grade through the 12th grade at Mark Twain," the senator remarked in a recent interview. "I played first violin in the school orchestra."

Though Mrs. Cormandy might not have approved of it, the first violinist in her orchestra kept right on listening to the local musicians and began to hear musicians who lived far from Stotesbury. "The 'Grand Ole Opry' was our kind of Saturday night entertainment. I particularly recall it in the Depression years, '33, '34, and I thought Arthur Smith was the best fiddler I ever heard." Through phonograph records, the teenage fiddler became acquainted with the most famous West Virginia fiddler of that era, Clark Kessinger.

Relatively few mountain musicians were professional in

Fiddling Senator Robert C. Byrd in 1979. Photograph by Blanton Owen.

the '30s compared to the enormous numbers of so-called amateurs who entertained themselves and delighted those within earshot of their string music. Senator Byrd said he never dreamed of playing on the "Grand Ole Opry" or making a record in those days. In his formative years as a fiddler, he learned to play in the relative isolation and thorough directness of his Appalachian heritage. The boarders who stayed with his foster mother were mountain people from Tennessee, Virginia, and Kentucky. Songs like "Cumberland Gap" were learned by the young West Virginian from folks who came from that area. The traditions of learning music directly and making your own music for entertainment or for use in worship were an integral part of the environment that Byrd grew up in.

As a young man, Robert Byrd worked hard as a butcher and, for a time, as a welder, before setting up a grocery store in Crab Orchard. His favorite recreation in the late '30s and early '40s was to play at square dances. One of his foster mother's boarders, Ed Milsap, played his guitar, and a coal miner named Jess Childers got together with him on many a Saturday night to entertain at the dance halls of Raleigh County. My wife's mother remembers Byrd playing at a family reunion. At the time Mr. Byrd first entered politics in 1946 he was undoubtedly better known as a fiddler than as a politician among his future constituents.

As the course of that '46 campaign unfolded, being known as a fiddler turned out to be much more of a blessing than a liability. As the senator now recalls it, "I had no connections then, no political ties through my family. In a field of 13 candidates for three Democratic nominations for the House of Delegates, I had to do something to become known." A Beckley lawyer, Opey Hedrick, is the person Byrd credits with suggesting to him that he use the fiddle in his campaign. "Now, Mr. Hedrick was a Republican but he convinced me nonetheless to take the fiddle wherever I spoke. He told me, 'Take the fiddle and make it your briefcase.' The idea was to play a tune, show people you were down-to-earth like them, give your speech and play some more."

A quick perusal of back copies of the *Raleigh Register*, the pro-Democrat Beckley daily paper, reveals what happened. When the Democratic Women's Club hosted a Candidates Night prior to the August primary, the sub-headline of the story read "Byrd Fiddles While Democrat Opponent Jigs." This opponent was one of the three incumbents Byrd beat out for the nomination a few days later. As the general election in November approached, a young Democrat named Hulett Smith organized a rally that included the top Democrats of that era, like Governor Meadows and Senator Kilgore. He also announced to the paper that entertainment at

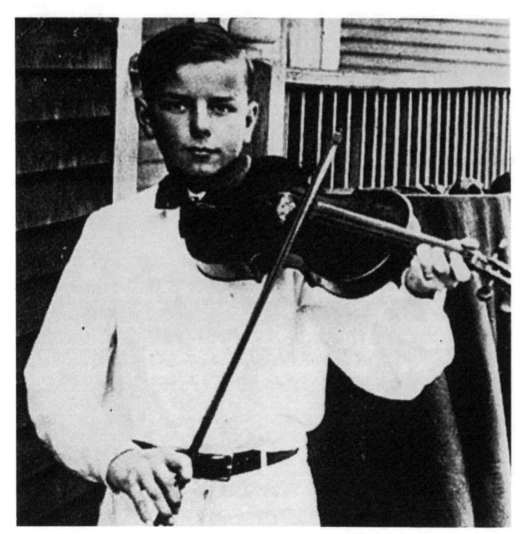

Robert Byrd as a 12-year-old fiddler. Photographer unknown.

Robert Byrd performs on the Opry stage on March 3, 1979. Other performers are James Bailey (banjo), "Spider" Gilliam (bass), Bonnie Gilliam (vocals), and Norman Wright (guitar). Photograph by Blanton Owen.

the rally would "feature the fiddling of Robert Byrd of Crab Orchard, candidate for House of Delegates, as well as 'Lost John' and his Allied Kentuckians." Numerous other, smaller rallies in that month of October 1946 were headlined "Demos to Conduct Rally at Lester," "Demos to Conduct Rally at Rhodell." These were organized by candidate Byrd, and it was invariably stated that "the program will include string music under the direction of Byrd." Nothing distinguished the young politician from the rest of his opponents as much as identifying him as the fiddler. His ads in the *Register* highlighted it to the public: "Come and see this candidate who campaigns in the true style of the old-fashioned South with his trusty fiddle and the bow."

The fiddle and the bow are not new to American politics, and Robert Byrd would be the first to tell you. Thomas Jefferson played the instrument and once remarked to his friend, Nicholas Trist, "I suppose that during at least a dozen years of my life, I played no less than three hours a day." Jefferson is supposed to have played the fiddle on horseback, while making his rounds as a young lawyer in colonial Virginia. The *Dictionary of American Biography* states that Robert L. Taylor (1850–1912), former populist governor and U.S. Senator from Tennessee, was known as "Fiddlin' Bob" to his constituents for his prowess with the fiddle on the campaign trail. He also conducted a lyceum tour in 1895 with his lecture "The Fiddle and the Bow" and is said to have reaped $40,000 in seven months. Although depicted as "a shallow fiddler" by his political enemies, he was immensely pop-

ular with the common people and is credited with saving Tennessee from the excesses of the agrarian revolt in the 1890s.

Anyone who has heard Robert Byrd play a fiddle could not depict him as "a shallow fiddler." His style and repertoire abundantly demonstrate his depth as a musician. What is noteworthy in the story of Robert Byrd the fiddler, though, is that he went into some long periods of not playing his fiddle at all.

Following his successful campaign for the West Virginia House of Delegates in 1946, he continued using the fiddle until he won a seat in the U.S. House of Representatives in 1952. From 1953 until 1963, as he recalls it, he seldom played the fiddle because he seldom had the time. This was a period in which he forged his political career while doggedly pursuing a law degree at night, a degree which he finally earned in 1963 at the age of 45.

He picked the fiddle up again but did not play it with the intensity of interest he'd shown in his earlier years until about 1974 or '75. He found it to be a hobby that complemented the pressures and responsibilities of his duties on Capitol Hill. "It gave me a great release," he told me, "and it gave me an outlet for my creative energies." Besides the pleasure of redeveloping a skill, he found playing was "tremendous therapy" and a political asset once again. "Any senator who invites me to speak in their home insists that I bring the fiddle along. People tap their feet in the North the same way they do in the South." Indeed, last June he quipped to a

Newsweek reporter, "My colleagues have discovered they like my fiddling better than my speaking."

This resurgence of fiddling led to a solo recording session at the Library of Congress in December of 1977. Alan Jabbour, Director of the American Folklife Center in Washington, D.C., had arranged for these tapings and made a further suggestion to the Majority Leader that he consider making an album. Jabbour contacted record producer Barry Poss of North Carolina and let him hear the Library of Congress tapes. "Poss assured me he could get the right kind of musicians to back me up on an album," said the senator. In mid-1978, Poss recruited Doyle Lawson and Jim Bailey from the prestigious bluegrass band, the Country Gentlemen, and Spider Gilliam, a Washington, D.C., bass fiddler, to make the album with Senator Byrd. Released in October 1978 by County Records of Floyd, Virginia, one of the most distinguished companies in bluegrass and old-time music, *Mountain Fiddler—U.S. Senator Robert Byrd* has been doing brisk business ever since, particularly in West Virginia.

Robert Byrd's name, of course, is by no means a sales handicap, especially in the Mountain State. However, to cynics who scoff that *Mountain Fiddler* was made only because a prominent person wanted to do it, it should be said that this album fully justifies Mr. Jabbour's and Mr. Poss's contention that the senator fiddles well enough to be recorded. Bluegrass giant and banjoist J.D. Crowe once remarked to me that "all too many bluegrass records are being made these days, and there's many that don't merit being made." Unfortunately that's true, but whether Bob Byrd was still a grocer in Crab Orchard rather than where he is now, his first album of bluegrass music would be enjoyable listening. It is distinguished by the energy and style of his fiddle playing and the authentic lyrics of the songs he learned fifty years ago.

The senator told me he would like to broaden his repertoire, especially in traditional (as opposed to "progressive") bluegrass, and in Scottish tunes. Recently he received an album from Scottish fiddle champion Ron Gonala and is attempting to learn the tunes by his own unique method. He says he listens to the tune, then transcribes it in his own tablature on paper, and practices it until he can throw the paper away and play it by ear. The Scottish tunes appeal to him because they constitute the origins of much of the Appalachian music he learned as a boy. "They have a plaintive, haunting tone that just follows you," he remarked.

There are always new worlds to conquer in the live playing of his music as well. After numerous performances at political rallies over the past few years, Byrd went to Nashville on March 3, 1979, for, as he puts it, "one of the most enjoyable times of my life." It wasn't just playing on the "Grand Ole Opry" show that he enjoyed so much. Meeting Roy Acuff and Howdy Forrester and jamming with the greats of country music backstage was a lot of fun, too. "I don't know how

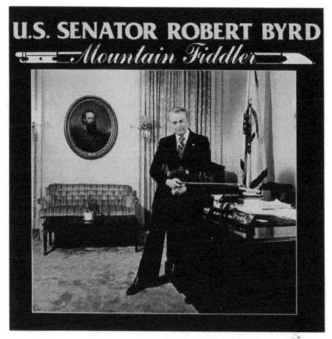

U.S. Senator Robert Byrd's 1978 album, released as County 769.

many times I heard Roy Acuff sing 'The Great Speckled Bird' when I was a young man," he said. He mentioned that Acuff felt the Opry hasn't had, in recent years, the kind of old-time fiddling that Robert Byrd does, the music that helped make the Opry the popular institution it is today. The senator expressed his own concern that the Opry may be getting away from its unique role in our culture.

I'm not so sure. If the Opry would invite more guests like Robert Byrd, people whose roots verify their authenticity as musicians, it might again strike a musical chord in the American people. Even though our participation in Senator Byrd's Opry performance came through the electronic media of radio and television, the point of his performance was to reinforce an invaluable folk tradition: You don't have to be a "professional" to make your own music, nor do you necessarily have to turn to the professionals to gain pleasure from music. No real fan of bluegrass music just sits and listens to other people doing it. It was clear that night that there has always been something worthwhile to Senator Byrd playing "Will the Circle Be Unbroken" simply for the pleasure it brings him. That it also brought pleasure to millions of others is relevant only in connection with keeping alive the idea that a folk art like fiddling is an art that is still made by the folk as well as by professionals.

EDITOR'S NOTE: This article first appeared in the April–June 1979 issue of *Goldenseal* (vol. 5, no. 1). Robert Byrd continues to serve as West Virginia's senior senator and still enjoys traditional music, although his fiddling has slowed down in recent years.

Ernie Carpenter

TALES OF THE ELK RIVER COUNTRY

Gerald Milnes and Michael Kline

WHEN you get to know Ernie Carpenter you learn a lot about the early history of Elk River. Ernie is descended from four generations of fiddle players on the upper Elk. His family home on the river was inundated after the construction of the Sutton Dam in 1955. Ernie "refugeed" to a small place just north of Sutton, the nearest piece of land he could buy to the old homeplace. He built a new house using lumber from the old, but has never gotten over his sense of loss. The old place near Sutton was his physical connection to his family's past.

Our early friendship with Ernie had to do with sharing the wonderful old fiddle tunes he knows. As we played music with him, we began to hear family stories associated with the tunes. At first it was hard to keep generations straight, since the tales took us back to Ernie's great-great-grandfather, Jeremiah Carpenter. Through the unfolding of the stories and tunes from Ernie's forebears, we have been treated to a rich musical lore from the early settlement along the waters of the Elk River. We began recording our conversations with Ernie in 1981, and the material presented here is edited from those tapes.

Sometimes the stories have seemed at odds with written history. In other cases family lore has amplified the established record. Historians have written about the Carpenter family in central West Virginia for seven decades or more, and the chronicles and the oral history have had that long to interplay with one another. Many versions of the stories have survived. It has been established that there were two Jeremiah Carpenters, contemporary cousins, who played strong roles in the early settlement of central West Virginia. The Jeremiah who dominates the following stories may be a composite of both.

If the precise history is not always clear, the lore provides a rich context for the Carpenter family music we have come to love.

∽

Ernie Carpenter: My grandfather is where I got most of my information, what I know, what happened. He would set and talk to me by the hour and tell me those things. I was just a youngster, just a kid then. Because I would set and listen to that kind of stuff it made him interested in it, made him want to tell me all these things. The most of the kids at

Ernie Carpenter in 1986, amid the apple blossoms. He says that the 150-tree orchard is his workplace, keeping him busy much of the year. Photograph by Michael Keller.

that age, you know, would be out doing something else. They wouldn't have the time to sit and listen to Grandpa talk, or Grandma. They'd have other things to do, something foolish or some play.

If you had seen the country around the mouth of Laurel

Creek before they built the dam that changed the whole situation—if you had seen that country at the time my people came in there! Before I was big enough to remember anything about it, there was already a railroad and they were already timbering back in there and coal mining, and so forth. But there was a lot of it that hadn't been changed too awful much, especially the lay of the mountains. The big timber was gone off it and second growth timber was growing up, but as far as the mountains was concerned and the valley there, it was the same.

If you'd have ever saw that back years ago before the backwater was up there from the dam, you could have easily understood why they picked that spot when they come in there. That's as far as they went. They settled right there. There were fish, game, bear, deer, there were elk, and they didn't only have Elk River to fish in but they had Laurel Creek. It was a paradise for them at that time, because there was everything there that they needed to live. You got your living out of the woods and out of the river. If you didn't get it there, you didn't eat.

All they had to do was build a cabin with a roof on it to keep them dry. They didn't even have that for a while. They stayed under rocks until they could get something built.

When they did build cabins they was log and the roof on them was old clapboards. They went out and cut down a tree and split out clapboards. My father learnt me how to make clapboards. He'd use his hand for a wedge to hold the board open when he'd split it. He'd follow up that froe with his hand, so he could push the froe on up as he split the board.

About the year 1760, Benjamin and Jeremiah Carpenter were young boys growing up on the outer fringes of the frontier in West Virginia. The Indians, by then pushed west of the Blue Ridge, were nervous about the advancing whites, and peace between the two peoples was unreliable and at times nonexistent. Ernie tells his family's story of how his great-great-grandfather, Jeremiah, and a neighbor boy adventured too far into the wildwoods one day and were jumped by an Indian hunting party.

EC: The Indians captured him when he was 12 years old, and a boy friend of his. It was a Holcomb boy, but I never did know his first name. They took them to kill them. That's what they captured them for. They took them into the vil-

Shelt Carpenter, Ernie's father, was descended from a long line of Elk River men. Photographer unknown, c. 1932.

lage. They had this Indian girl there that cried and went on and begged for them to spare their lives, not to kill them. They went ahead and killed the Holcomb boy anyway, and was going to kill Jeremiah. But she begged and cried and they told her they'd keep him for a few days. After they kept him for a few days they kind of took a liking to him—he was sort of Indian-minded himself. He liked to hunt and liked to do about all the things that they did, so they would take him out hunting with them. But they watched him every move that he made. And he said that they never, never let him get out of their sight or hardly out of their reach for six years that they had him. They had him until he was 18 years old. During that time he and this Indian girl had fallen in love and he told her that he was going to try to escape and get back to his people, but he would return and get her.

One day this one Indian took him out, and he figured he could run as fast, if not a little faster than that Indian could run. So he decided that he was going to give it a try that day. He kept working his way a step or two away from the Indian until he had a little lead. And he took off. And the Indian after him. They ran quite a ways and he knew of this rock ledge and he thought he would run and jump over that rock ledge and maybe he could get a little better start of the Indian. When he got to the rock ledge, he discovered that large tree had fell below this rock. Well, he knew he couldn't slow down and go around or the Indian would catch him. He thought his only chance was to jump the tree, so he jumped. He cleared the tree and didn't get hurt, and the Indian tried to do the same thing and he didn't make it. He fell down in the branches of the tree and got tangled up, and while he was a-getting out Jeremiah escaped and went back to his people. Soon after that he went back and stole this Indian girl away and they were married.

~

The family stories say that two brothers, Benjamin and Jeremiah, and their families came from Old Virginia in the late 1700s, carrying their belongings on the backs of oxen. They followed creeks and valley paths through the wilderness until they reached what is now Centralia, near the Braxton-Webster county line. They thought it was the prettiest place they had ever seen, with clear rushing waters and tall trees. They became substantial landholders in this part of the Elk Valley and on nearby Holly River. "My great-great-grandfather and his family once owned just about all of Holly River," Ernie relates. "He traded it off for a horse and saddle, a mountain rifle, and a bear dog."

First, however, the Carpenters had to build new homes and to establish their right to be where no white settlers had been before.

~

EC: When they was out there cleaning up some ground, getting ready to have a crop, there was some chips from their axes fell in the Elk River and floated down. Some Indians was a-crossing the river down next to Charleston somewhere and saw those chips floating in the river. And they said, there's white settlers upstream. So they took off up the river.

This big Indian—and I suppose the little Indian with him was a boy—continued the trip up the river, hunting for the white settlers. When they got up there to Centralia at the mouth of Laurel Creek and discovered Benjamin's cabin, he and his wife was out cleaning up ground. The Indians had learnt that the white man kept his rifle laying over his front door, where he could just reach up and get his gun. So the big Indian told the young Indian, said, "You shoot at him, and in case you miss I'll go around. You give me time to get to the cabin. I'll get his gun and hide back in the room. When he comes and reaches for his gun I'll shoot him." So that's exactly what they did. The young Indian shot and missed. Benjamin knew what it was. It was an Indian attack. So he run for his gun. When he opened the door and reached up to get his gun, the big Indian was hid back in the corner and shot him. And killed him. Then they went out and captured Benjamin's wife and scalped her.

When Jeremiah came home and found out what had happened, why, he took his wife—and she was expecting a baby then—because he figured they would come back that night. They went up Laurel Creek. They had to wade so the Indians couldn't track them. They had to wade the water after night. He had been there long enough that he knew that country so well he was able to do that. They waded the water up Laurel Creek about two mile to the mouth of Camp Run. It didn't have no name at that time. They went up Camp Run about another mile and there was this big rock there that just hung over, just a big ledge, you know, a shelf rock. They made camp under that rock, hid out until the Indians left out of the area. The next day my great-grandfather, Solly Carpenter, was born under that rock.

Jeremiah was on a hunting trip [on another occasion] and his wife was at home by herself. It come time to milk, get the cows in. She couldn't leave the kids and go hunt the cows because she was afraid the Indians might come along and stop in and maybe kill the kids. She didn't know what to do. The evening went on and she finally told the kids she was going to hide them in the house. She took up a piece of flooring in the cabin and hid them down under the house. She told them to stay there and not make a sound until she returned. And she went on the hunt of the cows.

While she was hunting the cows—they was on the opposite side of Laurel Creek from the side that the cabin was on—there came a downpour of rain, just a cloudburst. She hid under a rock to shelter until the storm was over. By the

One of Ernie Carpenter's best-known tunes is "Shelvin' Rock," commemorating the birth of his great-grandfather, Sol Carpenter, under this remote cliff. Photograph by Michael Keller.

time the storm was over the creek was out of its banks. All kinds of trash and tree limbs floating down the creek. She knew there was no way she could cross that creek without drowning. She could swim, but not in that kind of water. So she ran the cows and the bull into the creek and made them swim across, and when they did she grabbed the bull by the tail and they swam the creek with her hanging onto his tail, and got across safe. She came home and the kids was all right and when Jeremiah came in she told him what all had happened.

They hunted and they fished. Jeremiah was out one morning and he run on to this elk track. It had apparently headed down Elk River and he went back to the house and told the family that he had found an awful large elk track out there and he was going to follow it. He didn't know whether he would catch up with it or not. If he did, he'd try to get it. If he was gone all night, not to worry about him.

So he went out and picked up the track and started down Elk River. Getting dark that evening, he found where the elk had gone in the river. He looked across to the point of a large island there on Elk River. He saw the bulk of him laying on the point of that island. Of course, he had an old mountain rifle and one shot and he knowed he had a good chance of missing because it was getting dark, but he tried it anyway. After he shot, it kicked around there and couldn't get up, so he knowed that he'd got him. He waded the river over to the island and stayed there till morning, because it was too dark to try to do anything with it.

He stayed there until it got daylight. He managed to get the elk rolled into the river and got him across to a little river bar there, and he got him out on that bar enough that he could skin it and cut it up. He knowed that's the only way he had of doing it. He couldn't handle the elk the way it was by himself, and he couldn't go back home to get help because there was a chance of wild animals eating it up while he was gone. Maybe even Indians come along and steal it, or hide out and kill them when they came back to get the elk.

So he went out and cut hickory poles and split them so they would bend. He made a canoe-like frame with them bows and tied them with bark, and stretched the hide of the elk around that frame to make him a canoe-shaped boat. And he piled the meat of that elk there in that canoe. He waded and pulled that, because he didn't want to make no sign that the Indians could follow in case they happened to come along. He waded the water and took that canoe with that elk meat in it back to the mouth of Laurel Creek, which was about 20 miles from where he killed it. That's the way he got it home.

When my great-grandfather, Solly Carpenter, was a young boy, his father Jeremiah decided to have a Christmas tree for him. They knew about Christmas trees, but they had never had one in that village there where the Carpenters settled.

They began to make preparations. They built this cross, put it together and put tallow on it, beef tallow, to make it burn fast and bigger. They took this cross to the top of a very huge pine tree that stood just down on the bank below the cabin, and tied it in the top of that pine tree. They got all ready to light that cross that night. The families gathered in around, that lived there in the village.

Now, there was a bunch of Indians that had come across through the head of Elk River and they thought it was worth exploring. They'd go down that river a ways and see what it looked like. So they started down the river and they came to where Jeremiah's cabin was. When they discovered several cabins in that area they decided they'd hide out until night and attack and kill them all. Peace had been halfway made between the Indians and whites, but they still had some trouble. So they hid out until dark. When it got to be dark they began to move in, move up the hillside where they could rush in and attack before the people there knew anything about what was going on.

About dark, Jeremiah went out and clumb the pine tree and lit that cross. The cross just blazed up all of a sudden. The Indians didn't know where it came from. They didn't know what it was. But when it blazed up there so big and so bright and started to burn, they all got excited about it. Just in a little bit, it burnt down enough to burn the rawhide that they had the cross tied to the tree with, and let the cross loose. It rolled down over the limbs of the pine tree and the tops of the smaller trees, right down the mountain toward where this band of Indians was hid out ready to attack. They thought it was something that had come from the sky. They all got scared and took off. Clear left the neighborhood, that part of the country.

A good many years after, after Solly Carpenter had got to be a man, he was a-hunting one day and heard some screaming. As far as he knowed there wasn't anyone in the woods there but him, but he run to this noise. When he got there, this Indian was a-laying on the ground. He had killed a small deer, had shouldered it up and was carrying it in. A panther had smelt that blood and had jumped out of the brush and attacked him. It cut him all up with his claws. He was a-bleeding and in bad shape. Solly shot the panther as the panther run dragging the deer over in the brush. He shot the panther and killed it. He took the Indian, shouldered him up and carried him home to his own cabin. He started doctoring him up to see what he could do for him. The Indian got well enough to talk. He told Solly that he was one of the Indians that planned to attack their cabin that night and kill them all. But the Indian never got well. He died. My great-grandfather, of course, took him out and buried him.

As far as the Indian people were concerned, they weren't all as bad as what the white man thought they were. No wonder the Indians fought. It was their country. It wasn't ours. We was the invaders, not the Indians. If any country would invade us today, we'd fight just like the Indians did. They was only fighting for their territory, their home.

I've often been up in the area where my foreparents settled, Jeremiah and his wife and Benjamin and his wife. I've often just stood and looked north, south, east, and west. It's the most beautiful territory that you'll find anywhere on earth, that country right in there where they settled. No wonder the poor Indian fought so hard to keep what he had.

I have great respect for the Indian people. My people are kind of turned like the Indians. They like to live out where it's quiet, off to themselves where they got privacy. That was the nature of the Indian, you know. He wanted to be out in the woods. If you just turned him loose in the woods and he lived under a rock, he was happy. That's a good bit the way my foreparents was. It's my idea of real living. That [fiddle tune] "Shelvin' Rock" come from the camp rock that my great-grandfather Solly was borned under.

∽

Later on when the country was more settled, Solly Carpenter once witnessed the death of a raftsman on Elk River.

∽

EC: They used to hew out what they called gunwales. They were gunwales for barges. They would hew them out of very large trees and they'd just hew two sides of them flat, you know, like hewing a cross tie. They would hew them things out 30, 40, 50, 60 feet long and would float them into Charleston. When they put a couple of them together, they made a good-sized raft. Usually two men would man them to Charleston. They sold them down there. They made barge gunwales out of them for freight barges.

There was a fellow by the name of Gibson had made a couple of those gunwales, and he was going to float them to Charleston. He was coming down the river, it was late one evening, and my great-grandfather was out on the riverbank when he come floating along. He was on these gunwales by himself.

My great-grandfather knew that it took two men to handle a set of those gunwales, a man to handle the front and rear both. They usually put a big oar on each end. My great-grandfather told him, "You ain't got enough manpower on the gunwales to handle them." He said, "I'd like to tell you a little something about this next shoal down here that you're going through." It was a short shoal, but it was very rough. The name of the shoal was Breechclout, and it was the next little shoal below Stony Creek. He said back to my great-grandfather, "I don't thank God Almighty for advice on this river, I know all about it." He said, "I'll eat my supper in Sutton, or in hell!" That's just the words he repeated to my great-grandfather.

Well, he didn't say nothing more. There was an enormous big rock that laid right out there in the middle of that shoal, and it was tricky to get around that rock without hitting it. He went down there and hit that rock, tore his gunwales apart, and throwed him off in the river and he was drowned. Several days later, after the water went down, they found him on down the river. From that time on, they told all kind of spook stories about the place there.

I have heard spook stories all my life. Never believed in them, because sooner or later they prove to be something that you knowed about. But one thing in my life that I saw with my own eyes, that I never did know what it was. I was pretty small, but it's funny how some things will stand out in your memory, so real, so plain, just like the instant that it happened, for as long as you live, while other things will go away. This is one of the things in my life I've thought about so many times. I've studied about it a lot.

My grandfather and his brother, my great-uncle, went fishing, and they took me along with them. Mostly to catch bait. They went up there to the mouth of Stony Creek, where all them spook stories have been told about, to fish. My grandfather told my uncle and I, "You fellows go up the creek there and catch some crawcrabs and hellgrammites. I've got a few bait here and I'll be fishing while you fellows find some more."

We started up that creek and we got to where there were two very large rocks, laid a little piece apart, over on the left-hand side of the creek. Up the creek, I'd say approximately 100 yards, was straight, and the bed of the creek was just like pavement. Just little puddles of water in it. It was summertime.

Just before we got up to those rocks, my uncle saw some bees, honey bees, watering there in a little puddle of water. He said, "There's a bee tree here somewhere close. We might just be able to find it." He had found hundreds of bee trees in his life. A bee will water and go in a winding shape up so high, and then he goes right level to where he's going. He knew all that stuff. He said, "Well, we'll walk up here a little ways and look."

We walked up almost to those rocks, maybe 150 feet from those rocks. Out of nowhere, like something magic, I saw a man and he looked like he had on long underwear. He was just moving like slow motion towards us, coming down that creek. My uncle was standing right there by me, looking up that creek, and he never did see that! He never saw that at all. I was afraid to say anything, because I thought he saw it and was scared, and if I didn't say anything it wouldn't scare me as bad, you know. Being with him I wasn't too much scared.

I kept trying to delay him, but he said, "Well, let's go and get back down to the boat and fish some." I delayed him by telling him this and that, until I doubt if that thing was 50 feet from us. There was nobody lived in there, and if it had been anybody, they would have said something and wouldn't have been looking like that. Finally my uncle said, "Let's go," and took me and went on back towards the river. He never did see that thing.

We went on to the river and I was so worked up I didn't know what to do. I was afraid to say anything then, for fear he'd say I was seeing things. I knowed they wouldn't believe it. We fooled around there a little bit, and he told my grandfather about seeing the bee and where it was at. My grandfather said, "Well, we'll just walk back up there." That just tickled me to death. I thought sure we'd find out what that mysterious object was.

We went back up there to that same spot, and my grandfather or my uncle either one wouldn't go a step further. Ordinarily, they would have gone up that creek to the head of it, to find that bee tree. But neither one of them would go a step beyond where my uncle was in the first place. Just looked around a little bit and said they'd come back some other time and look. But that thing was gone. I didn't see it anymore. No sign.

❧

Ernie recalls the time his uncle Jake "Squack" Carpenter

got spooked into getting a dunking near this same place on the river.

❧

It was a good fishing territory. My grandfather and my two uncles went up there late in the fall to hunt and fish a little bit. My one uncle said, "While you fellows go squirrel hunting, I'm going to go fishing." They said, "It's too cold to fish. Fish ain't going to bite in this kind of weather." "Oh," he said, "it's a good time to catch pike." There was a ledge of rocks that ran along just a little above where that fellow had drowned. It was just smooth like concrete. It was about 100 feet long and there was a regular thicket along the back of it. You couldn't hardly crawl through it.

My uncle took his fishing tackle, and he went down there and caught a pike about a couple of feet long. Pretty good-sized pike. He just took it off his hook and put it down in the back of his hunting coat, and was fishing in that deep water. He was a-thinking about all them spook stories he'd been told about that place, and all the things that had been saw there. Just now, he rubbed his coat a little agin that brush, and caused the pike to start flopping in his coat. When that fish started flopping he said the first thing he thought was a

Thinking about Music

Ernie Carpenter

Music is a great gift, one of the greatest anybody can have, because it's something nobody can take away from you. No way can they touch it. They can't take a note away. It don't make no difference if you're a tramp or how low down you are, if you play music you can still keep it. That's about the only thing left that the politicians can't get in on! Money can't buy it. You can't even give it away yourself. You can learn somebody but you can't give it to them as a gift. It's a very precious thing, I think, very precious.

I think the old-fashioned music is the greatest music that's played. A lot of the stuff they're playing today is stuff that's come along in late years. It might suit the younger generation because they

live different, they see things different, and of course they play different from the old style. But I think that the old tunes and the old style of playing them are still the best. Nothing will ever change me from that. I don't like bluegrass music. I think bluegrass is kind of artificial. It's not the real thing. Many young people you run onto who play bluegrass will tell you they wish they had learnt the old-time music.

The old-time musicians are getting fewer and fewer. If they don't start trying to teach it and learn it to younger people, the old style of music is going to be a thing of the past. We're not going to have it. It'll be gone. The old style of music is what was handed down to us by our foreparents. If it was

"Music is a great gift," Ernie Carpenter says. A major concern now is to pass the old music to a younger generation. Photograph by Michael Keller.

ghost had him, and he jumped as far as he could jump right out in that river there! He lost his fishing tackle, but of course he was a good swimmer and he swam to the other side of the river. He couldn't get up on the side he was on. Then he went to camp and got some dry clothes on as quick as he could. The ones he had on had ice in them when he got there. The pike stayed right there in his coat, it never got away.

Ernie's grandfather William "Squirrelly Bill" Carpenter and his exploits are legendary around Braxton County. Brady Randolph, octogenarian and longtime county newspaper editor, said of William, "Elk River and its surrounding streams, fields, and woods were his transportation, his livelihood, and his playground." Ernie's fondness for his grandfather is evident whenever his name comes up. He remembers that he never wore shoes, but stuck to moccasins in the style of the old settlers. Author William Byrne wrote in *Tale of the Elk* that, "Squirrelly was an all-around fisherman, a canoe builder and operator, flatboat builder, and steersman, raftsman and general waterdog and fisherman; he was the most inveterate, persistent, and uncompromising fisherman ever known in the valley of Elk."

The canoes that William built were log dugouts, made from a single tree, Ernie recalls.

EC: My grandfather made canoes and sold them. They got a dollar a foot. If it was a 30-foot canoe, they got $30 for it. Fifty foot, $50. Sixty foot, $60. One time he had completed two canoes, and he had one old canoe, and they took all three canoes with them on this one trip to Charleston. They sold one new canoe and the one old one to two brothers, just up the river a little ways from Charleston. The brothers had a freight line of their own, and that's what they wanted them for. They paid $50 for the new canoe and I think my grandfather said $20 for the old one. The brothers got in an argument about which one was going to get the new canoe and finally got into a fight over them. A few days later, my grandfather came back up the river and saw the canoe setting there cut in two down the middle. He got to inquiring what happened, and found out those two boys had got into a fight and the one sawed it in two. There it was, not worth a cent to nobody.

Sutton was just a village, but there were two or three general stores there and they would give my grandfather an order

good enough for them, it's good enough for me. That's the style they had, and that's the style I have and that's the way I'll continue to play.

There's some young people who are interested in the old tunes and would like to learn them. They're going back and digging up these old records of the old fiddle tunes, like Fiddlin' John Carson, Eldon Browning, Clark Kessinger, and French Carpenter. They're scraping for those old records to get those old tunes. Those real old-timers back there like Jack McElwain, Edden Hammons, Tom Dillon, Bill Stutler, Reese Morris, Harry Scott, there's many a tune they played that when they died, they're forever gone. They didn't have no recording machines in that day and time. They didn't have the opportunity to record their music and pass it on to somebody else. There's more of

the old-time music being recorded now than ever before. That'll be a help to the younger musicians that's interested in it.

I think if we could get more of the younger generation playing the old-time music it would bring it back. There would be more of it. When you go to a contest you hear very little of it. Most of the music played at these contests is bluegrass. Oh, I think bluegrass is all right to a point, but when I sit down and want to hear real music, it's the old-time music I want to hear.

I love music. I'm a music lover. I'll stop and listen to anybody play music, if he's playing old-time music. I've gotten an awful lot of enjoyment out of playing the fiddle. When my brother and sister and I were playing together, it meant a lot to me. I never was too particular about playing for dances, but I never was at a dance in my life that they had any trouble.

I like to play with other people. I don't care if they play good or bad, I can learn something from them. You can learn something from anybody. I've always been glad to show other people if it was any benefit to them. I really think I've learned a little something from every fiddler I've ever heard play.

It takes a long time to learn to play music. Some people take longer than others. Some people don't never learn to play very much but anybody can learn to play some, just like any trade.

I don't care about mixing anything else with old-time music. I'll just play it as it is. If they call me old-fashioned, if they call me out-of-date, okay, that's all right. I'm out. But, I'll stick to it.

EDITOR'S NOTE: This article first appeared in the summer 1986 issue of *Goldenseal* (vol. 12, no. 2).

for what they wanted. Every time they wanted so many barrels of flour, and so many barrels of salt, and so many barrels of sugar, and coffee, my grandfather would take those orders and go down to Charleston. They would usually go down the river when there was a little extra water. It'd go faster. They would aim to catch a little extra water to go down. Elk River would come up quick, and it would go down quick.

By the time they got down there and got loaded up it would take a couple days, and in that time the river would go back down to almost normal stage. Then they would start up the river, three of them or sometimes four, because those big 60-foot-long canoes took a lot of manpower to push them upstream with poles. They didn't have no motors; they had manpower, that's all. When they would come to those shoals, it took a lot of power. A couple of them would get out, or maybe all of them, and they would wade. Even in the wintertime, when the water was pretty cold, they would hit times they would have to get out.

They would be several days making the trip to Charleston and back to Sutton. In the summertime, they would camp along the river. In the wintertime, when it was real bad weather, they had certain houses where they had engaged rooms to stay and eat. They would finally make their way back to Sutton with their load of goods and unload them. There would be a few weeks in between times and they would go back and do the same thing over. They did that for years and years!

My grandfather was quite a character. He had an instinct. It just seemed like he knew nature, and he knew what nature was a-going to do. He was just that type of person. One time my father, Shelt Carpenter, Jehu Carpenter, my uncle, and Jake Carpenter, another uncle, and my grandfather went fishing. They always took along a special friend of theirs whose name was Bill Thomas. Bill was an extra good cook and they took Bill along to do the cooking for them, while they did the fishing and hunting. I was a very small boy. I don't know how come they did it, because they seldom ever took me out like that, but my father took me and one of my uncles had his boy. Seven of us in the party. We was supposed to meet at what was called Bee Run Bar. The dam has got it covered up now.

When we got there that evening, my grandfather and one of my uncles had come up to this bar earlier in the day and already had a nice string of bass caught. My grandfather said, "Well, Jehu and I'll fish a little longer. The rest of you fellows take the boat and go up the eddy." We called them eddies and shoals—an eddy is the still water between the shoals. We went about halfway up the eddy, and we found this nice level spot and we put our camp there. We'd unloaded all our stuff, built a fire, and we was ready to start frying fish when my grandfather and my uncle came.

Right at the back side of this nice level spot was a huge

Grandfather William "Squirrelly Bill" Carpenter was a legendary Elk River hunter and fisherman. Photographer unknown, c. 1915.

chestnut tree up on the bank. This chestnut tree was dead, still a lot of dead limbs on it. My grandfather went straight to that tree when he got out of the boat. He made a circle around that tree and he looked up the tree and he said, "Get this stuff loaded in the boats and get out of here. That tree's liable to fall any minute!"

"Aw," the boys said, "that tree's been here a lot longer than we have. There ain't no danger. That tree's perfectly sound." He said, "Get this stuff in the boat." They put up a little argument, but they usually did what my grandfather said. We loaded everything back in the boat and moved up the river a couple hundred yards and found another camping spot under a beech grove. Nice level ground.

Well, we unloaded all our stuff, and got a fire built up and some of them started cleaning fish. That's all we had, fish and bread, but that was a fine supper. We was sitting there eating, not more than two hours at the very most from the time we left that tree, when we heard the awfulest crash you ever heard. Somebody said, "My God, what in the world was that?"

My grandfather set there, just as calm as a cucumber. He said, "That was that chestnut tree that I just got you out from under down there." "Aw," they said, "it couldn't be that." He said, "That's just what it was." Well, one of my uncles said, "I'll just check and see." He went down to the boat landing and went out on the end of the boat where he could see where the chestnut tree was. Sure enough, the water was a-floating thick with dead limbs, and the chestnut tree had fell right square down across where we had our camp fire built. If we'd stayed there, chances are every one of us would have been killed.

We camped that night. My grandfather had a gallon bucket almost full of dirt and fish worms. Fish worms was a prize, boy, in them days. That was your bait. He had this gallon bucket all fixed up to keep them fish worms for four or five days that we was a-going to camp. In taking the stuff out of the boat, somebody got a-hold of that and brought it up and set it down with the camping stuff.

Well, we made coffee in an open bucket. You just dipped you up a bucket of water out of Elk River. It was a lot cleaner than the purest of city water is today. You set it on an open fire and put you whatever coffee you wanted in there, and you boiled it. The next morning, Bill Thomas got up to get breakfast, and in fumbling around with an old oil lantern he got hold of the fish worm bucket, put coffee in it, more water, and set it on the fire. When we set down to breakfast somebody said, "Pour the coffee." Then somebody took a look at it and said, "What in the world's in the coffee?" My grandfather just raised up and said, "My God, you've got my fish worm bucket and boiled my fish worms!" Everybody was excited about it for a little bit, but it ended up with a big laugh. But we lost all our fish worms!

My grandfather learned to play the fiddle very young. They'd send horses for miles, when they'd have one of these log rollings, and get him to play for that log rolling and dance. The boy that brought the horse would walk, and he would ride the horse. The next day they brought him back the same way. A man that played the music in that day and time was really something special.

That fiddle I have was my grandfather's. It went from one to another in the family. Uncles and cousins and so forth and so on, and finally my father got a-hold of it. He had the fiddle from that time on. He was a good old-time fiddler. He used to keep that fiddle in a large safe that we had, the safe was never locked. He kept that fiddle on the top shelf. Just kept it laying in there on a cloth, never had a case for it. Not a kid on the place ever touched that fiddle or ever even went close to it. I was the first one to take any interest in it when I got big enough. As soon as I hit my first note on the fiddle, he said, "The fiddle is yours. I'm through. I won't be a-playing no more. You're going to do the playing from now on." It's a very fine instrument. Who it will fall to when I'm gone, I don't know.

My father worked in the lumber woods about all his life. We farmed, too. We had horses, hogs, milk cows, just the usual stuff you would keep on a farm. I was borned on Elk River, about three miles above Sutton. My mother died when I was about 10 years old, something like that. My father always had his own timber job. He never owned his sawmill, but he would buy a tract of timber and he had a fellow that did his sawing for him all the time. He hewed cross

Ernie Carpenter is a man with a deep attachment to the past and misgivings about what has been lost to the faster pace of modern times. "It was a paradise," he says of early times on Elk River. Photograph by Michael Keller.

ties and he sold them to the B&O. At one time, he cut about all the poles in this area for Monongahela Power and Bell Telephone. They were chestnut only, and when the chestnut timber all died they could get no more poles in this part of the country, so they started getting those creosoted pine poles. He also cut pulpwood and suchlike.

He took me in the woods when I was 10 years old. He would put me on the lower side of the log, so he could pull the saw back to him and it would almost go by itself downhill, you know. About all I had to do was keep it straight. When he cut the log down to where there was danger of it dropping off, he'd tell me to get on the upper side. Then he'd take the handle off my end of the saw and he would saw it the rest of the way off with one handle. The first time he put me on the lower side of a log I was scared to death, because I had watched them cut timber and I knew what the logs did when they were sawed off. They'd roll down the hill. Of course, they knew all that, too. When we'd get down to where it might break off, he'd tell me to get on the upper side.

We were going to log one day. We had a marker in the river that, if it was covered, there was too much water to ford the river with the horses. So this morning the water was just barely over that limb and he said that he just pretty well had to get a certain amount of work done, he was behind, and we'd try to ford it anyway. Where we had to ford, we had to go kind of slaunchways across, and we got about middleways and our horse, the one me and my brother was on, fell. My father was a-leading on the other horse, and he threw his axe as far as he could throw it beyond the horse. He always kept his axe razor sharp. Then he jumped off the horse and came to us.

When our horse fell, we floated off like a couple of light bulbs. I grabbed my brother. I was a little bit taller than he was and I could just touch the bottom with the tips of my toes, just enough to keep me from going under. I held him up, but I didn't have no power against the water to go anywhere. We was going down the river and there was a big swirl hole at the foot of the shoals, downstream. My father got to us. He was a tall man, over six foot, and he waded and got us to shore.

The horse that we was on was floating downstream, and he would have gone in the swirl hole and drowned. My father thought maybe he might be tangled in the harness some way, and he called to him and the horse got up on his feet and came out to the bank. The one that he was a-riding just stood in the middle of the river and nickered and pawed the water. When he got us straightened out, he called to him and he came out to the bank. So nobody actually got hurt, but that evening when we quit work my father put me and my brother on the two horses, and he said, "You fellows go around by Sutton." That was about a five-mile trip down to Sutton and back up our side of the river.

He didn't try to ford it any more when the water was at that stage.

☙

Although Ernie had to give up his education at an early age to work with his father, he accepts the fact that it was necessary to help support the family after his mother's death. The six children cared for one another and stayed together as a family until they were old enough to get married and go on their own. After Ernie married Mabel in 1930, his father Shelt lived with them on the old homeplace until his death in 1937.

Ernie worked for the Pittsburgh Plate Glass Company in Clarksburg for 38 years before retiring back in Braxton County in 1972. During his years in Clarksburg, he made regular weekend stays at the homeplace on Elk River. It was during this period that Ernie witnessed the planning and building of the Sutton Dam by the U.S. Army Corps of Engineers. This flooding of his old home and boyhood surroundings was a bitter experience.

☙

EC: They started in '55 and they finished in '60. They talked about it for quite some time. They had been doing some checking on it just about the time the Korean War broke out, and when the war broke out they dropped it. Everybody who was going to lose their places was in hopes, of course, that that would be the end of it. But it wasn't. Just as soon as the Korean War was over, they was going right back there in full force. We got a group together, and we hired a lawyer and sent him to Washington to talk to that committee down there that ruled on dam building. He went there and talked to them, and he came back and said, "Fellows, there's nothing that you can do about it. They've already got the promise of the money, and there's no way you can fight the government on something like that." We wasn't satisfied so we sent him back the second time, and he came back with the same story.

It wasn't very long after that till they started surveying, and it wasn't very long after that till they was taking people's property. They come down to my place and said, "We'll give you $25 an acre for your ground." I had a good small orchard, apple orchard. And I had a barn, outbuildings, and a frame house. The house wasn't anything fancy, but it was livable. We lived there. They didn't allow me nothing for that orchard. They didn't allow me a cent for my barn. They didn't allow me anything for the house. They just gave me $25 an acre for my land. They allowed me $2 an acre for my oil and gas. They allowed me $10 an acre for my coal and they allowed me $10 a thousand for my timber. You imagine! You can't buy stove wood for that kind of price. I told them they was robbing me, they was stealing me blind. No way

Dog Lucky knows all about Ernie Carpenter's comings and goings. Here they share a moment in the yard after a musical foray. Photograph by Michael Keller.

they would give me a cent more, so I took it to court. I gained quite a little by taking it to court, but I had my lawyer fees to come out of that.

Well, they sent word that if I wasn't out by a certain time, they'd set me out. "You tell them that the men that come up here to set me out won't be going back on their own. Somebody will have to come and get them." And I meant that. I got to the place that I was just hoping that they would start something and give me an excuse. Thank God I got out of it without getting in trouble. You can drive a man so far and he's liable to do something bad, and I was to that point.

They'd already started building the dam, and I was still going down to my homeplace. They cut the road off this side of the river, so I would go down Bee Hill and up the river to the homeplace. They found that out and they came up and cut that road off. So, I went over to Hyre then, over through Newville, and down the river. When they cut that off, I figured I could drive out to the top of the hill and walk down the hill through my own place. Everybody else was gone. I was the last person out of there. I went ahead then and tore the old place down and brought it up there. Part of it's in this house.

❧

Through the generations, music has always had an important place in the Carpenter family. As a teenager, Ernie played at home with his brother Carl and his sister Goldie. As they became proficient, they started playing at dances and parties around their community, limited by the distance they could walk. Carl played the guitar, Goldie banjo, and Ernie the fiddle. Ernie's fiddling was influenced by whomever he could hear. In the beginning that was his father, and grandfather William. Their music is still cherished by Ernie, tunes such as "Betty Baker," "Yew Piney Mountain," "Old Sledge," "Shelvin' Rock," and one he calls "Camp Run."

Another contributor of these older, special tunes was "Uncle Jack" McElwain, who Ernie states "was the best fiddle player I ever heard." Wallace Pritchard, a neighbor and family friend, also taught Ernie tunes as a boy. The wood alcohol plant near Sutton drew people to the area to supply wood. Ernie remembers many Calhoun County musicians stopping by the house to play music while working there. One old gentleman, George Hammons, would stay with the family and play the fiddle for a week or so in the spring and fall. Ernie recalls that he used to walk from Clay County, where he tended a cattle farm for someone in the winter, to the mountains at the headwaters of Elk River, staying with the Carpenter family coming and going. He carried all of his possessions with him, which included a fiddle.

There was a stretch of time, beginning when he went into the service and lasting for 20 years, when Ernie Carpenter hardly played music at all. He tells about what got him started again.

∽

EC: I'd come up home and they was having music down here at this little country store at Laurel Fork. Well, I'd stop there to hear them, and as soon as I went in, there'd be somebody in there that knowed that I used to play. They'd start hollering for me to come over and play. I wouldn't do it. Finally, they did get me to pick up the fiddle one night, and my goodness, I couldn't do nothing with it. It kind of worried me.

I had my fiddle up on a shelf in a clothes closet. One day I went and got it and took it out of the case, and there was white mold all over it from one end to the other end. It scared me to death. I was just sure it would fall apart. I cleaned it up and checked it over and didn't see any places it was loose. Then I heard a Propst boy, a real good fiddler, stop in and play music for them people down there. He played "Golden Slippers" awful good and I was determined I was going to play it something like he did. So, I went to work on the doggone thing, and put in quite a bit of time on it and that's the way I got started back.

EDITOR'S NOTE: This article first appeared in the summer 1986 issue of *Goldenseal* (vol. 12, no. 2). Ernie Carpenter received the prestigious Vandalia Award in 1988 for his old-time fiddling. He passed away January 23, 1997, in Clarksburg, West Virginia, at the age of 89.

PART 2

Banjo Players

Clarence Tross

HARDY COUNTY BANJOIST

Kip Lornell Jr. and J. Roderick Moore

B ETWEEN Moorefield and Petersburg lies Durgon, a small settlement shown only on the most detailed map of West Virginia. The village consists of a small variety store and a small church. At the variety store you need to stop and pick up a key which unlocks the gate that guards the small dirt road leading to Clarence Tross's home. The lock is placed on the gate to safeguard against poachers, Mr. Tross has said.

There is nothing unusual about the way this 92-year-old banjoist lives—with a grandson, off the main road in a small wooden house in rural northeastern West Virginia. What makes him such a unique figure is that he is very likely the oldest black man in America who remains a vital performer on the banjo, an instrument of Afro-American origin.

When most people think of the banjo, they probably think of bluegrass pickers like Earl Scruggs or Eric Weissberg. If they are interested in old-timey banjo playing, then performers like Uncle Dave Macon, Wade Ward, or Fred Cockerham will more than likely be mentioned. The music played by Clarence Tross is the antecedent of both of these styles, although it is linked most directly with the "clawhammer" playing practiced by the old-timey banjoist. Indeed, since the banjo was brought over to this country by a slave, it can be safely stated that blacks were the first people in this country to play the instrument. Because Mr. Tross began playing banjo in about 1895 and learned most of his tunes from his father, Andy Tross (born c. 1850), we believe he represents the oldest tradition of banjo playing to be found in this part of the country.

Clarence Tross was born on December 12, 1884, within

Clarence Tross in 1975. Photograph by Carl Fleischhauer.

sight of the home where he now lives. His parents, Lucy and Andy Tross, were both slaves. They had been owned by Ned Baker until emancipation and lived in a house near the large Baker house. Lucy Tross came to West Virginia from her birthplace in Jamestown, Virginia, but her son remembers very little of her, as she died when he was a child. Andy Tross lived until about 1910 and was the person who inspired young Clarence to begin picking the banjo.

One of the most interesting of Tross's remembrances concerns the black musical activity found around Durgon 75 years ago. He made a revealing statement concerning accordion players.

Clarence says, "I just don't know about the white people playing accordion much. They did, though. I know of one white fellow, Mr. Billy Baker, he used to play accordion. He's dead now. I think there were a couple of other white people, way back, who used to play accordion, too. There wasn't much of them playing accordion, it was mostly colored men playing accordion. They played for dances around here. Fiddle, banjo, accordion—all used to play together for dances."

Except for the accordion playing of black Cajuns in southwestern Louisiana, a black accordion tradition has never

Clarence Tross was 90 years old when this photograph was taken in 1975 by Carl Fleischhauer.

Clarence Tross at home with his son Sonny. Photograph by Carl Fleischhauer.

This photograph was taken "about 30 years ago." Left to right: Clarence Tross's son, Robert Andrew; his wife, Sally Duffy Tross; and Clarence. Photographer unknown.

Clarence Tross's home in Hardy County. Photograph by Carl Fleischhauer.

flourished, as far as we know, so it was surprising at first to hear of one in West Virginia. The explanation for its existence might be the pattern of settlement in the northern and eastern parts of the state. The immigrant groups that came to the area where Mr. Tross lives were primarily German and probably settled in the region in the 1830s and 1840s. Most likely the accordion was a popular instrument brought over from Europe. At some point, for an unknown reason, it became an instrument of the black musician, and by the 1880s or 1890s it had fallen out of favor with the German immigrants.

A second item of interest was Mr. Tross's description of how banjos were made when he was young. Nowadays, of course, store-bought banjos are common, but in the 1890s when you were poor and lived far away from general or variety stores you made your own banjo with materials found at hand. At the age of about eight, Clarence made his own instrument.

"I went out and caught a groundhog, set a trap and caught a groundhog, took off the hide and put it in the ashes. I let it sit here for several days, then took my knife and slit the hair off it. We used to buy cheese in a hoop, a round hoop. We took carpet tacks and tacked it [the hide] around. Then we would take an old piece of oak wood. I was just learning to play, and they wouldn't let me have theirs. Went to a horse's tail, took my knife out and took the hair off. We stretched them out and used banjo strings out of them. Went clump, clump. That gives you some idea what we had to do. Always put five strings on my banjo."

Naturally the banjo had no frets on it. Most old-timers remember when fretless banjos were the rule, and it was roughly World War I before the commercial fretted banjos were commonly found in the rural enclaves of the Southern Mountains.

Mr. Tross also explained the process his uncle, Mose Tross, went through in order to construct a fiddle.

"He went out and got him a piece of poplar wood and planed it real thin. Then he put it in hot water. Then he got this here wood glue. Then he went out into the woods and got him one of these here white oak saplings. Took and shaved it off nice. It was green then. The poplar was for the top and the bottom. It was catgut strings he used. It looked pretty much like fiddles today."

According to Tross, his Uncle Mose was a fine fiddler and played with his father on many occasions. The tunes he can remember his uncle playing are "Soldier's Joy," "Arkansas Traveler," and "Leather Britches."

Finally, Mr. Tross remembers his father playing bones to accompany people dancing. The use of percussive instruments is a strong one in the Afro-American heritage. In some rural areas of the Deep South, Dave Evans and other researchers have turned up small groups of black musicians

Clarence Tross preserved a unique style of black rural music with his banjo playing and singing. Photograph by Carl Fleischhauer, 1975.

who feature a homemade fife and two or three drums to set up a complex polyrhythm. Reports on slave music indicate that bones were often used by blacks to accompany dancing. We have never before met a musician who could actually remember a black man practicing this technique; certainly it was not commonplace after the turn of this century. Andy Tross took four beef bones and placed two in each hand (one between his thumb and forefinger, the other between his forefinger and middle finger) and kept time for dancing while a fiddler and banjoist played the tune. Mr. Tross, not surprisingly, calls this technique "beating the bones" and makes the interesting analogy that its role was much like that of a drum. A descendant of this device is the spoons, which people often play today at informal musical get-togethers.

Mr. Tross's repertoire is quite wide in range. We believe there are three distinct streams of music at work in his playing. First, there are the songs which at one time were popular tunes. These amply demonstrate George Foster's theory that "folk" and popular cultures work in a symbiotic relationship, feeding off one another. These particular songs of Tross's are ones that have passed from popular culture into a stage in which they are now part of his "folk" repertoire. They are picked rather than played clawhammer style. His

renditions of these songs are not nearly as dynamic as his playing of the older, more traditional tunes. He is not as confident playing them as he is with the pieces he learned from his father. These songs include "You Are My Sunshine," associated with Jimmie Davis, a governor of Louisiana; "Casey Jones," which Mr. Tross learned after hearing it played on a steam organ of the traveling Sun Brothers Show, a carnival, presumably; and "Roundtown Gals."

Two unexpected songs from this group, "Oh, Susannah" and "Carry Me Back to Old Virginny," were written by Stephen Foster in the mid-1840s. They are quite uncommon items in the folk repertoire of rural black musicians, and in our several years of collecting, recording, and studying black folk music this is our first encounter with songs like them. Stereotypically they have been associated with a lazy black man sitting on a fence strumming his old banjo while a Mississippi steamboat slowly rolls by. This is one throwback to a foolishly romantic conception of black life in the Old South and should have disappeared along with the notion that all blacks ate watermelon. As far as we know these so-called "coon" songs were never a strong part of the repertoire of black folk musicians and may have been transmitted through the medicine or minstrel shows.

Secondly, Tross plays tunes that have been vehicles for

old-time musicians for many, many years. They are picked clawhammer style, which he terms "beating it out" or "beating the banjo," and are fairly universally known. "John Henry" heads this group, which also includes "Soldier's Joy" and "Turkey in the Straw."

Finally, we come to the most important segment of his repertoire, those songs that are unique to Mr. Tross or unusual variants of better-known songs. Our guess is that they reflect the older black banjo tradition in general. For the most part, they are songs he learned from his father, and, like most black banjo tunes, they have very little melodic content. The emphasis is instead on the rhythmic complexities of a piece, and they become intense, stark statements. An analogy might be the guitar patterns of the Mississippi bluesman, Charlie Patton, whose song "Mississippi Boweavil Blues" contains some of the same qualities.

There are several songs unique to either Clarence Tross or to West Virginia. One is "Old Man Can I Have Your Daughter?" which is the first tune he learned some 80 years ago from his father. It has a simple AB tune, and he picks it with his thumb and forefinger. Another West Virginian has recorded a version of this song; Burl Hammons performs it on the Rounder Records LP, *Shaking Down the Acorns*. Mr. Tross can remember only a few words to this song. Also he plays two quite pleasing instrumentals. "Pretty Little Girl Get Your Foot Out of the Sand" is similar to the A part of "Sally Ann." The other he calls "Hipple Creek," and is nearly equal to "Pretty Little Girl."

Actually, his titling to "Hipple Creek" is confusing. When he performs it with words, the song is clearly the well known piece, "Cripple Creek." This interesting titling could be considered an understandable mistake, except Tross clearly states he also performs a piece he calls "Cripple Creek." He insists "Hipple Creek" and "Cripple Creek" are two separate songs, although he declined on our visit to play his version of "Cripple Creek."

There were three songs he played which had rather complete texts. One is clearly a version of "Cindy." He first heard it as "Miss Lucy Neal Down in the Cotton Field," and he commented that he heard the song as "Cindy" much later, after he heard his father play it. In searching through the Folklore Archives at the University of North Carolina—Chapel Hill, we could not locate one version of "Cindy" with lyrics like his:

Old Miss Lucy Neal down in the cotton field,
If I had her by my side how happy I would feel.
Ain't I gone, ain't I gone, down to Arkansas.

Today I might get married, tomorrow might be gone.
Next day might be sitting down in old Arkansas.

REFRAIN

If I had a needle and thread so that I could sew,
Sew Miss Lucy to my side and down the road I'd go.

REFRAIN

Old Jim Thorne courting that girl. I was courting her too.
The only way to get that girl was to put on my long tail blue.

REFRAIN

Kneebone had the coffee pot and Henry had the spout;
Every time Kneebone wanted coffee, Henry poured it out.

REFRAIN

A second song that had both a banjo part and lyrics unfamiliar to us was "Going Back to Baltimore." The text is:

Fare you well, Miss Dandelion.
Fare you well, Miss Dandelion.

I'm going back to Baltimore, pick this tune and pick no more.
I'm going back to Baltimore, hop light ladies on the floor.

Hop light ladies on the floor, that's what makes my banjo roar.
Fare you well, Miss Dandelion, I'm going back to Baltimore.

Charleston ladies get mighty bold, pass by the gate and pay no toll.
Fare you well, Miss Dandelion, I'm going back to Baltimore.

I've got a gal in Baltimore, streetcar run right by her door.
Fare you well, Miss Dandelion, I'm going back to Baltimore.

Finally, he performs a song with a tune similar to "Georgie Buck" but with lyrics that are almost totally different. He calls this "Sorry I Left My Father's Home." Like the two previous songs, it was sung by his father.

Oh, me, oh, my, sorry I left my father's home.
The day I left my father's house, that's the day I left my home.

Oh, John Brown is dead, last word he said, never let a
  woman have her way.
If you let her have her way, she lead you astray. Never
  let a woman have her way.

It's rock, darling, rock, rock, oh, rock, Lord knows.
Going on this rock, hound tree'd a fox. Hunt when I ready,
  Lord knows.

Going down the street, catch the first girl I meet.
Nobody's business but my own. Nobody's business but
  my own.

Bloodhound on my track, sheriff on my back.
Get to the shanty, Lord knows. Get to the shanty, Lord
  knows.

The second verse of this song is commonly found in
"Georgie Buck," while the last verse has been sung by a
number of blues musicians, including John Hurt in his song,
"Payday," and the Mississippi Sheiks' version of "Bootlegger's Blues." Tross plays "Sorry I Left My Father's Home" in
his "beating out" style, and there are strength and vitality in
it, as well as in his performances of the other older pieces.
Surely in his performances of these there is more spirit than
there is when he plays more recently acquired songs. Indeed,
it is the older, "blacker" portion of his repertoire that is the
most exciting music.

In Clarence Tross's words and music we capture a unique
glimpse into black rural music as it has existed in one section of West Virginia since the turn of the century. He
affords us a singular opportunity to record and preserve the
Afro-American banjo style that ultimately serves as the pre-
cursor for the intricate banjo styles of today.

EDITOR'S NOTE: This article first appeared in the July–September
1976 issue of *Goldenseal* (vol. 2, no. 3). Clarence Tross was well
known for his performances at Hardy County Heritage Weekend
each year. He died on September 22, 1977, in Petersburg, West
Virginia, a day before that year's festival began. A song entitled
"Clarence C. Tross" was written in his memory by West Virginia
politician Clyde M. See Jr.

Sylvia O'Brien

"WE LIVED GOOD BACK THEN"

Ken Sullivan

SYLVIA O'Brien makes a home for herself in an out-of-the-way part of Clay County, with a million-dollar view and a rough road out. She has lived on the family farm there all her life, leaving only for a spell of war work in Baltimore and a brief marriage. Widowed early, she ripened into old age with bachelor brother Jenes Cottrell back at the homeplace. Sylvia and her brother grew up before the modern conveniences and developed no affection for them when they did become available in rural Clay County. The house today is just as it was built at the turn of the century, without electricity, central heat, or running water. It is a matter of personal choice, not poverty, for the Cottrells are independent landholders and have been for generations.

Jenes has been gone for several years now, and Sylvia carries on alone. She remains true to the pre-industrial lifestyle her family chose, cooking on a wood stove and drawing water from a hand-dug well by the kitchen door. For thus preserving a glimpse of early mountain ways and for sharing her music and wisdom at fairs and festivals, Sylvia received the 1989 Vandalia Award, West Virginia's highest folklife honor. This interview was conducted at her home soon afterward.

∽

Ken Sullivan: Sylvia, tell me about your life here on the mountain.

Sylvia O'Brien: Well, I'll do the best I can. I was born down there in the bottom in a little white house. Daddy and Mommy wanted a house up here on the point. They had timber and they had the timber cut, and the logs hauled to a mill down here in this same bottom, and cut this house pattern that we're in right now. My brother, Jenes, and a car-

Sylvia O'Brien in 1989.
Photograph by Michael Keller.

Many of Sylvia O'Brien's fondest memories involve good times with her brother Jenes Cottrell, now deceased. In this picture she plays for Jenes's stomper doll. Photograph by Richard Gross.

penter and my father, they put this house up. I drove the team that hauled the lumber up the hill when I was seven years old.

This land was all owned by the Tidewater Lumber Company at one time. They come in here and they took the best of the timber. Dad come down in here and worked for them. When the Tidewater sold this property, they sold it for $5 an acre. And Daddy bought this farm here from the lumber company.

KS: Do you know about when he bought it?

SO: I'm 80 now, so it's been every bit of 85 years ago.

KS: Where was he from originally?

SO: Well, in a way I can tell you. As far back as we can get the Cottrell race traced, they was a colony of Cottrell people lived in Ohio, way back in the Indian time. And the Indians went in there and they destroyed all these people but one little girl. The chief took her and kept her for his squaw, like a wife would be today. And she raised a baby and it was a boy.

She watched her chance and she swum the Ohio River by the help of a horse and made her way back through this

country to Hackers Valley, where there was a settlement of white people. Of course, that baby growed up under the name of Cottrell, and he drifted down this way. That's all we know about it.

KS: By the time your dad grew up, where was the family living?

SO: Way back in Braxton County, back in Braxton and partly Pocahontas. They come down when the Tidewater was coming here, come to work. He bought this place and he met Mother over here on the West Fork, Calhoun County. She was a Metheney, Melindy Metheney. And they married and settled here and lived here 'til they both died.

KS: What was your father's name?

SO: Andrew Cottrell.

KS: Why do you think your folks decided to leave the bottom and come back up on the hill here and build a place?

SO: Well, it was more convenient. You can see around. There was other people lived in this holler at the time, and they just wanted to be up here. They owned cattle and horses and they wanted up here where it'd be more convenient

The O'Brien home is a solid cabin of a sort once common in the mountains. The T-shaped floor plan includes three rooms across the front, a rear kitchen with small side porches, and a full half-story above. Photograph by Michael Keller.

Sylvia O'Brien traces her background through the ancient family Bible and through recollections handed down to her. The Cottrells were among the first white settlers of central West Virginia. Photograph by Michael Keller.

for raising them and taking care of them. And up there in Braxton and Pocahontas, most people lived on the hills. Way back up, you know, on the level-top mountains. So my father just wanted to be up here.

KS: What kind of farming did your family do?

SO: They raised corn and oats and wheat. They had to raise their living. They had to mill corn for their meal, take the wheat to the mills and get flour, and they raised cattle and hogs. We had horses and chickens. They had to raise the feed for them. We kept Hereford cows and sold the calves when they was six months old.

KS: Did you grow any kind of crops for market?

SO: We got to raising tobacco. They raised tobacco for several year and sold it at 25 cents a pound. Handed-off tobacco, dry and ready for market, or ready for to chew or smoke.

KS: How did you get the tobacco crop out of here?

SO: People come and bought it. I've knowed four and five people to ride their horses up out there and hitch them and come in and buy five and six pound of tobacco and take it off to their homes. They would stem that tobacco, take the stems out of it, then they'd twist it and make these tobacco twists. They bought that tobacco the year 'round. And [when] one growing season was over, the old tobacco was gone, and we was ready to go in on a new crop.

KS: Did your father take any of it off to a market or warehouse?

SO: No. He never done that. But we'd raise four and five thousand plants at a time. This big Roanoke, Sweet Roanoke. It growed, oh, it growed over my head and I'd work in

Sylvia O'Brien, the ninth winner of the prestigious Vandalia Award, had this portrait made at Vandalia in 1986 by Michael Keller.

that tobacco a whole summer through, as did Jenes and my daddy. If everbody knowed as much about tobacco as I do, nobody would chew nor smoke it. I'd have to pull tobacco worms off of that stuff as big as my finger. Just reach up and take a-hold of them and pull them off and throw them on the ground. Stuck my foot on them, never looked down, go ahead looking for another one.

KS: I bet you were barefoot?

SO: No, they kept me shoes. The ground was rough. And I had to sucker that tobacco, pull the suckers off. And I had to reach up there and pull the top down and break that seed stalk off. Then when cutting time come, Dad and Jenes, they had knives. They'd go and they'd split them stalks plumb down to about two foot of the ground. Then they reached down there and they'd cut them plants off and lay them on the ground. And I'd harness the team, put the tobacco in the sled, and haul it out. They'd help me load it. I could reach down and take two of them big plants and lay them up across my shoulders, but that's all I could pack.

KS: When you took it to the barn that way, how did you hang it? Did you say they split the stalk?

SO: They split the stalk down to about, I expect, a foot and a half or maybe two feet. And then they had tobacco poles at the barn, some of 'em's at the barn yet. They'd take the tobacco stalks and they'd hold them apart and they'd reach up and they'd put them over them tobacco poles and push them back. They'd just keep that up 'til they could get a whole tobacco pole full of tobacco.

KS: So you didn't put the plants on sticks in the field?
SO: No, no.

KS: Did you use the sled for all your hauling on the farm?
SO: Yeah. It's out here now, hanging up under the building. They didn't use wagons to amount to anything. It was too steep and rough. If the wagon would get started down the hill with a team, why, the horses couldn't hold it back.

KS: Where did you go when you needed to go to the store?
SO: There was some little old stores down around the mouth of the holler. That was pretty handy. But I rode a horse four and a half miles to get corn meal ground up so we could eat it. There was always one or two millers there and they'd come out and take the grist off from the horse. I'd get off and they'd take the horse and tie it up 'til they got the

meal ground. Then they'd put it back on the saddle and I'd get on the horse and go back home. The wheat, they had to send it further. There wasn't too many wheat mills in the country.

KS: What about your garden? What kind of vegetables did people grow at that time?

SO: They growed most anything they could get to grow. They raised sweet corn, and they raised beans, they raised taters, and cabbage, lettuce, and onions. Just most like gardens now, but they raised more of each vegetable, had to save them up for winter. We done a lot of canning. We'd can beans, we'd can apples, we'd can tomatoes, and most anything we could keep in cans. And what wouldn't save in cans, we dried. We dried beans and we dried apples. And we would also keep apples in our cellar, dig taters and put in our cellar, and put all stuff like that in our cellar.

We had two good orchards. After we'd get done picking, why, we'd let other people come in and gather apples, to keep them from going to waste.

KS: Where were your orchards?

SO: Back here on the hill. It's prettier back there on the hill than it is around here.

KS: Seems like people generally put their orchards back on top.

SO: They did. It's cooler back there and it kept them from coming out longer. If they was late about coming out in the spring, the frost didn't kill the blossom. It would be colder back up there, and it'd keep the bloom from coming out as soon as it would down here. Mother had big jars, 10- and 20-gallon crocks, stone, I reckon it was, that they done their pickling in. I got one in here yet, a 20-gallon one. They made pickles, they pickled corn, and they pickled beans.

KS: Did you pickle in vinegar or salt?

SO: We pickled in salt.

KS: What kind of meat did you generally eat?

SO: Well, we mostly lived on hog meat. We'd fatten two or three big hogs that we'd smoke and keep, you know, and pickle a lot of it for summer. Keep meat down under salt brine—take it out and it's just like fresh meat. We'd can the ribs, and make sausage and can that. We lived good back then.

KS: Did your family do any hunting?

SO: No. Never was no hunting. They didn't like hunting, and they didn't like anybody else to hunt. My family just didn't like to take the life of something they didn't help to live. And they didn't like the meat of the wildlife. They just let stuff live and raised and put up their own meat. And we had meat the whole year 'round, we never lacked for any kind of meat. We had chicken and hogs and stuff.

KS: What would have been a typical meal? What would you have eaten, say for breakfast, back then?

SO: Well, we liked corn bread for breakfast, and cow but-

ter. We made our own butter. They liked a good, hot pan of corn bread, mixed up good and baked. Quarter that and eat butter over it, and coffee and meat and eggs and other stuff like that. That was mostly our breakfasts.

KS: What about the midday meal? Is that what you called dinner?

SO: Yeah. That'd be called dinner. We'd cook beans, we'd cook taters and we always had meat, milk, and butter, just pretty near any kind of stuff like that. We'd cook it up and have dinner. That was our biggest meal, was dinner. And then for supper, if there was no bread left over, we'd bake bread and we'd eat bread and milk. And whatever else was left, you know, from the dinner table that we wanted to eat.

KS: Did your eating habits change at different seasons of the year?

SO: Not too much. Of course, we couldn't get green stuff like tomatoes and cucumbers, only in the summer season. But in the winter, we had pickles canned and we had tomatoes canned. They wasn't fresh like getting them out of the garden, but we had them anyhow.

KS: What were the first fresh greens you had in the spring?

SO: It'd be creasy, dandelion, and wild beet and wild lettuce, something like that. We'd just gather it wherever we wanted. It'd grow wild, you know. And people would raise beds of lettuce and they'd go and pick that and they'd fix it up. They'd cut it up good and fine, then they'd pour milk over it, and pepper and vinegar. And they'd mix that all up together and they'd put it in a skillet and they'd kind of wilt that down a little bit. Then they'd put it back in the dish. Now, it was good eating.

KS: Where did you go to school?

SO: I went to school a little, not too much, down here at a school that was called Otterville. Nettie Chapman was my school teacher. Outside of that, I got my education here at home.

KS: Was that down on Big Otter Creek?

SO: Right down here on Big Otter Creek, then up the creek a little bit. There was no state road then. Nettie lived across the hill and she rode a horse to the schoolhouse. I'd walk down and then up to the schoolhouse. Kids had 'til nine o'clock to get there. They give them a hour's rest and play at noon, and then turned them out at four in time to get home before it'd get dark.

KS: Did your family go to church?

SO: Well, there wasn't no church, only in the schoolhouses. They'd have Sunday school in the schoolhouse and they'd have church and sometimes a protracted meeting in the schoolhouse.

KS: A protracted meeting was something like a revival?

SO: Revival meeting. They'd call it a protracted meeting at that time. A preacher would come, he'd preach, and people gathered in.

KS: Was Jenes the only brother that you had?

SO: The only brother that I had. Me and my brother was the only children. Just Mother and Dad and me and Jenes. He was seven years older than I was.

KS: As a young woman, after you came up a little later in life, did you ever work outside the home anywhere?

SO: No. I never worked. Well, too, I went to Baltimore and kept a boardinghouse during the Second World War. One of Dad's brothers and his wife come through and they wanted to go out there. He wanted to work in the shipyard and she wanted to work at something else. And there wasn't no place to stay. So they got this boardinghouse and wanted me to come and do the cooking. Well, I went and I took the boardinghouse over and kept it there for over a year. I was about 40 at the time, maybe not quite that much.

KS: How did you travel to Baltimore?

SO: On the train and the bus. I catched the bus down there at Ivydale, rode the bus to Clarksburg, and changed there to the train that went on in to Baltimore, Maryland. Where the train stopped it wasn't very far from the boardinghouse, and I walked from the train to the boardinghouse.

KS: How did you like the big city?

SO: I didn't like it. Most of my life was right there in that building. I had, let's see, 17 boarders to cook for and take care of. Some of them went out at about six, and some of them come in about four and it just kept me busy.

KS: You were married at one time, weren't you?

SO: Yeah, I married a man that come from Montana. That was shortly after I quit the Baltimore job. And he lived three year and died, right here on this bench where I'm a-sitting. He just took a heart attack. We were going to travel, was planning on going back to Montana and back in that country. I just took up where I'd left off and have been here ever since. He had come from Montana. A lot of people went to Baltimore for that big work, and they was froze to their job. Pretty near had to stay there until the war ended. I met him in Baltimore.

KS: Did you ever live in the West yourself, in Montana?

SO: I went there and stayed two year, among his people. But he was gone. They wanted me to stay longer, but Jenes got sick. Murray Smith [of the Clay County Bank] sent me a telegram, to come home and help Jenes fix up his business. I knowed what that meant, and I come home. And I've been here ever since.

KS: And your husband died here?

SO: He died here. During the three year that he lived, I got acquainted with his folks and all like that. And I liked Montana. I'd rather be in Montana right now as to be here. But that's over, too far back, I can't go there now.

KS: Were you here on the farm during the Depression?

SO: Yeah. That's when we was selling that tobacco. We never wanted for nothing. We had tobacco, you know, that

This log barn has stood on the Cottrell place since early in the 20th century. It is a classic "double-pen" design, with one of the log pens shown. The bottoms of the two pens were used as livestock stalls, and the open breezeway between them offered easy access to the building. Sylvia O'Brien says the barn was hung full of curing tobacco in season. Photograph by Michael Keller.

Once upon a time, a wood-burning range was the center of most West Virginia homes. Sylvia O'Brien keeps it that way on Deadfall Mountain. Photograph by Michael Keller.

they'd come and buy. But now, there was people that just almost perished. We were able to go through it without want of much of anything.

KS: When did your mother and father die?

SO: Well, I don't know just exactly the date. But Daddy's been gone 30 year or over. And Mother's been gone, I expect 10 or 12 year. She lived right here and she fell in there in her room and broke her hip. She died down at Charleston in the hospital. She lived seven days. She was right around 90 when she died.

KS: Where were her people from originally, the Metheneys?

SO: They were originally Dutch, Holland Dutch or something like that. It took them a long time to come across the water. I think it took 17 months or something. They come in a sail ship and they said that some days they could travel far, and that there was other days the wind would maybe take them back further than they had traveled the way they wanted to come.

KS: So you were still hearing stories about that when you were growing up?

SO: Yeah. I have heard that from Mother and Daddy, about Mother's people. And when we'd ask Granny, Mother's mother, she would sing in Dutch.

KS: Was there much music in your family when you were coming up?

SO: Nothing, nowhere. No music.

KS: Well, then, where did it come from? Where did Jenes learn to play music? Where did you learn?

SO: I don't know, unless it was just a gift of talent. Now, Jenes could pick up a banjo, play most anything he wanted to and he didn't know a note in a songbook nor a chord in a music book. And I'm the same way. I don't know a note in a music book and I don't know a chord, nothing like that.

KS: Did he associate with other musicians where he might learn?

SO: Mostly, it was French Carpenter. French Carpenter's gone now. French Carpenter had no home and he come here and stayed quite a bit. French could play, and he could sing. And he done a lot to help Jenes, but I think Jenes's music mostly was his gift of talent. I know my talent was gifted. French'd stay for pretty near a month at a time, maybe longer. He'd help them around. He didn't have no home. And he just pretty near had to grow up staying with other people. He was about the same age as Jenes. He'd help around the place.

KS: I've heard you talk, Sylvia, about the midnight suppers that you used to have here.

SO: Well, that was quite a while back, not too long Jenes was a-living then. I expect it's been 15, 20 years. That started back when we first got to getting together traveling, going on these trips, French Carpenter was a-living then. The musicians would gather up, sometimes they'd come here and sometimes they'd go up to French's. We'd all take something for to make a midnight supper. The music players would gather in, the Morrises, and most all of them around. They'd play music 'til midnight and us women would go in the kitchen and we'd cook a meal and have it sitting on the table. And when the clock would strike midnight, we'd go and tell them that the midnight supper was ready. Well, they'd all lay their music down, they'd come in, they'd go around that table and they'd eat. And then they could play as long as they wanted to. Some of them would stay and play, and some of them would go home. People liked it very well. Other people would come, you know, sit and listen.

KS: Was there any particular reason that you had the supper at midnight?

SO: No. Only they wanted a night session of playing. Some of them would play from when dark had almost set in, and when they'd play right on through about half a night they was wanting something. And we just fixed up a supper for them. No special reason, we just done that.

KS: What kind of things would people eat for a special meal like that?

SO: I usually would take fried chicken and I baked pies and stuff like that. And I always had a lot of good pickled beans, so I'd take a cooker of pickled beans. The rest of them would all fetch something, and they'd bake fresh bread and have hot coffee. If there was meat, they'd fry meat up and fix it good. It was a delicious meal.

KS: I want to hear you play a tune, if you will, before I leave here. And I want to ask you about two or three tunes. "Minner on the Hook"—where did you learn that, for example?

SO: Well, I'd heard Jenes play and sometimes I'd just play it to suit myself. "I fished all summer and I fished all spring, I catched one minner—poor little thing!"

KS: And you also play "John Brown."

SO: I don't know too much about that tune. But I read a book one time about John Brown. They hung him in Old Virginia. He was coming across over to Harpers Ferry. I thought that they treated him bad, that he didn't need that kind of treatment, for the slave man was set free, anyhow. And I just kind of worked that up myself.

KS: Jenes was known as an outstanding craftsman as well as musician. When did he begin doing craftwork, woodwork?

SO: Well, he always had that idea. When he was just a little feller, he was making sleds, he was making wagons. They had to watch him to keep him from driving nails in the house. And [when he got older] he about put up this house. He done pretty near all of this work. After the carpenter quit and left, he put up the ceilings and he laid the floors and he just worked and worked. He was 17 years old. He made these chairs here. He first started by making chairs and cabinets and tables. And he made them for several years and then he got to making this craftwork to go to these craft fairs. And he got to making banjos. He started off in making chairs, but first he made a banjo out of a holler gum tree. It played pretty good, but he sold it and I reckon it was destroyed. I wished that I had it now, but I don't have.

KS: Did he sell the chairs that he made?

SO: Oh, my goodness, they'd come here with wagons and take off wagonloads of them. Took them to their houses, to sit in.

KS: He had his shop set up with hand-powered tools, a full setup. Do you know where he got the idea for that, was there somebody else that had such a shop?

SO: Yes, one of his uncles had a turning shop, and he learned how to make that from him. You know, a turning lathe [powered by an overhead pole] that would come down and go back up. And it has to be a poplar pole. They'll come down, they'll go back. But a hickory pole or anything else, it'll come down and stay down. It won't go back.

KS: So you want something that's got a pretty good spring in it?

SO: Yeah. You have to.

KS: You say Jenes started making craftwork to take to the festivals. Where did he go?

SO: Cedar Lakes is the first craft festival he went to. And from then, he went on to other places. He went to Glenville. I went to Glenville with him, different times. We both went together [to the festivals]. It took us both. See, we'd have a booth and when he would have to go to his meals or somewhere, why, I had to stay there. So many people, somebody had to be in the booth the whole time.

KS: Jenes was kind of famous for the banjos he made out of auto transmissions.

SO: Yeah, I've got two of them in there yet that he made. It was made out of a Buick transmission, a '56 model. And that's been back quite a way. They quit making them kind of models before he quit making banjos. And then the transmission was hard to find.

KS: How did he ever get the idea of making a banjo from part of a Buick transmission?

SO: He was down here at Everett Drake's one time. Everett Drake is a junkman and he had one of them a-laying out. Jenes picked it up and looked at it. You know, he was craft minded. And he told Everett, said he believed he could make a banjo out of that. Everett looked at him, he said, "Well, if you can make a banjo out of that, I'll give it to you!" And Jenes fetched it home and he made as good a banjo as he ever made out of it. Then he got to buying them, but they got so scarce he couldn't get them.

KS: Now, what he was using was actually just a ring out of that transmission, wasn't it?

The banjo Sylvia O'Brien plays is one of many made by her late brother Jenes Cottrell. The prized instruments represent an ironic blend of fine handicraft work and instrumental technology, incorporating the aluminum torque converter ring from 1956 Buick transmissions as the banjo tone ring. Photograph by Pamela Hutton.

SO: Yeah, the inside. It was something on the inside of that transmission.

KS: What was his best seller around the fairs and the festivals?

SO: Canes. There's one a-hanging up here yet.

KS: I think I bought a rolling pin from him somewhere, years ago.

SO: Yeah. He's been gone nine year.

KS: Jenes has been dead nine years? I bet that changed this place, didn't it?

SO: Changed it, my goodness. But still, he seems near.

KS: Are you doing any gardening up here now?

SO: No, not any more. I rent my bottoms to this woman down here, she raises them. She gives me what I want. Of course, I don't need much.

KS: Do you remember any superstitions about living in the country back when you were young? Any kind of ghost stories, things on that line?

SO: I can remember, we had a house over here on the point, for renters. And the night their little baby died, I heared something out among the chickens and I walked out that-a-way and I seen something come down, just looked like a big white pillow and laid there on the ground. I was too afraid of it to walk down closer. And I stood there a little bit and that, whatever it was, just disappeared. Then in a little bit, why, that little kid's brother come over and told me that the baby had died. And if that wasn't a token or something, I wouldn't know anything.

KS: Do you know of other tokens?

SO: Well, on the night that Homer died, that's my husband, why, I thought I heared a woman a-hollering back here on the hill and she just hollered and hollered. I even answered her and asked her what she wanted. And she quit. That next morning about seven o'clock, why, Homer died. I thought right on that it was the woman across the hill that got up in there and maybe got lost. But I asked her if she done that hollering and she said she hadn't.

KS: Did you ever hear about anybody finding a feather cross in a pillow where an infant had died?

SO: Oh my, yeah. I've found them, just a crown of feathers, just works together. And you can pick them up and you can't hardly pull them apart. But I don't know that it's somebody dying or whether it's just the feathers work together like that, sleeping on them so much. I've seen crowns of feathers in pillows but as far as why they was there, I don't know.

KS: Did you ever know any witch stories, anything like that, in the early times?

SO: Ah, I don't know. I've heared some talk about witch-es taking milk from cows. And I think they did do that. [The victims] would put a 50-cent piece in their churn and churn it, and they wouldn't be bothered no more. The 50 cents always had "In God We Trust." And they'd churn a 50 cents in their churn and whatever was bothering them would quit.

KS: Did it have anything to do with the silver in the coin, or was it just the motto?

SO: What was on the silver.

KS: Sylvia, you showed me a picture of your dog a while ago.

SO: He was a Johnson black wolver. They had them out there in Montana [when I was visiting] and I liked them. They had no pups at the time but about two years afterwards, I found this dog out here in the yard and a note that told me where he was from and who fetched him. And says, "I hope he survives 'til you get back home." He was sent from some of Homer's relatives in Montana. We was over there at Cedar Lakes at the time. Well, I took him in and raised him. That dog had a 500-pound grip in his jaws, and I couldn't lift him, only one end at a time. I wasn't afraid of man nor beast while that dog was with me. But there was some people had some gip dogs down here on the creek and he was lovesick and, of course, he went down there and got out on the hard road and a man in a truck or a car hit him. They said he was killed instantly. That's been about a year ago and I don't want no other dogs. That's the only dog that ever I want to claim, is Buster.

KS: You've got a beautiful, beautiful place here on this point.

SO: In a way I'm happy, and in a way I ain't. I get lonesome and I have most all of my memories back behind me.

EDITOR'S NOTE: This article first appeared in the fall 1989 issue of *Goldenseal* (vol. 15, no. 3). Sylvia O'Brien continues to live on her own in a remote area of Clay County, West Virginia, and appears each year at the Vandalia Gathering in Charleston. She won the Vandalia Award in 1989.

Elmer Bird

THE BANJO MAN FROM TURKEY CREEK

Paul Gartner

Now Turkey Creek's sure runnin' wild,
From here to the mill is about three miles.
Wadin' that creek to the other side,
Sack o' corn on my shoulder to keep it dry.
Turkey Creek's way out of its banks,
Come on Fred, got to take a chance.
Swim that creek, keep your head up high.
Mama needs meal that's nice and dry . . .
  —*from "Turkey Creek" by Elmer and Beulah Bird (© 1987, John Hartford Music BMI)*

LIFE on Turkey Creek has changed since the late 1920s when Elmer Bird lived the words to his song, "Turkey Creek." A paved road now winds along the quiet valley in rural Putnam County, and the grist mill to which Elmer rode his mule is long gone.

Many residents there know Elmer Bird as a neighbor, a farmer who raises Black Angus cattle. Others know him as a former co-worker or fellow retiree from Union Carbide.

But old-time music fans everywhere have heard of "The Banjo Man from Turkey Creek." The Banjo Man plays a driving, "double drop-thumb" clawhammer style. And since the late 1970s, Elmer and his wife Beulah have taken his music across the United States and Canada, entertaining audiences with his brand of old-time music, which has its roots right there on Turkey Creek.

Elmer's branch of the Bird family has lived there since the Civil War, when they migrated from Virginia. "They came from Franklin, Virginia," Elmer says. "The one which would have been my great-granddad I guess, he got into it with his brothers. They were gonna sic the army on them. They sort of took up for the slaves. They left probably on account of fear of being harmed.

"They came into Narrows, Virginia, [and on to] Flat Top and Jumping Branch. They came looking for land."

After some time the Birds arrived in Putnam County. "Some of them walked through first and they found this land way up this holler here. That's where my grandpa settled. He was just real young then. They walked right up Turkey Creek."

That little boy who walked up Turkey Creek, Joseph, grew up to marry a woman named Elizabeth, and they had 11 children. Elmer was born May 28, 1920.

While Elmer doesn't think those original Birds played any music, three of Elizabeth's children were "the ones that picked the music up": Winifred, John, and Andrew Bird.

Elmer's parents were Andrew Jackson Bird and Lottie Johnson Bird. Andrew learned to play the banjo from his brother Winifred. Elmer later taught himself to play by watching and listening to his father.

"They called him Andy Bird. We farmed on a little hillside farm here on Turkey Creek," Elmer says. "We'd be working in the fields, and he'd come in every day at noon. We worked pretty hard, hoeing tobacco and corn and stuff. We'd eat dinner then he would grab the old banjo and start playing it. I'd lay down on the floor and rest. I was tired.

"See, all the time I'm listening to him playing [while I'm] relaxing on the floor. I'm trying to figure out what he's doing. And every evening he'd play the banjo.

"And I'd say, 'Aren't you tired? I'm tired.'

"He'd say, 'Yeah, but it relaxes me.'

"He was one of the best drop-thumb clawhammer players. He was smooth, real smooth. He never took his music nowhere. When he was a youngster they played for square dances within five or 10 miles of where they lived. Back then, people didn't have automobiles or anything like that. This would have been back in 1915, back in there."

His father and uncles learned their music in picking sessions at the home of an older man named "Daner" Bowles,

Elmer Bird in 1997. This banjo, which belonged to his father, Andrew Bird, was recently restored by Early Vermillion. Photograph by Michael Keller.

who lived past the head of Turkey Creek, up on a ridge which shared his last name.

"Bowles Ridge was traveled a lot back then," Elmer remembers. "We went to the mill at Griffithsville. We had to raise wheat and have it threshed. That's where we got our wheat made into flour over there, at Griffithsville."

Daner was a farmer and good friend of the Bird family. "That's who had this banjo that I have now, that my uncle learned to play on, and my dad learned to play on. I learned to play on the same banjo. You know, I can barely remember Daner Bowles when I was a kid. I can remember seeing him when I was eight or 10 years old. He played a lot of different instruments. I would say he was probably responsible for old-time music getting started here."

When Elmer took up playing the banjo, he was at least the third generation to play music on Turkey Creek.

Elmer started out with a two-finger style of banjo playing, but all along he wanted to play drop-thumb clawhammer like his father. Drop-thumb clawhammer playing uses the thumb and first or second finger—held in a clawlike manner—to strike down or brush on the strings. The thumb

pulls the fifth string and is also used to cross down to the second, hence the term drop-thumb. "I picked two-finger, you know. For three or four years there that was all I could do. I wanted to play drop-thumb. I got about seven years old I could do pretty good, two-finger, I could play about any tune my daddy was playing. I couldn't do drop-thumb.

"I set down on the porch and tried to get daddy to show me how. I was about ready to give up on the banjo. One day I was sitting out there and it came to me just as natural. I sounded just like my daddy. Tickled me to death. So I really put in a lot of time on the banjo then, after I got so I could drop-thumb."

One uncle who helped to shape Elmer's music was Addison Bird. But he didn't play an instrument. He danced. "I'd take my banjo up to his house. He lived off Turkey Creek up a holler. I'd be playing the banjo for him to dance. It was funny to me how good he danced and I'd just ease off on that banjo and he'd still be playing the tune [with his feet]. If I could dance like that now, I'd be John Hartford."

Addison didn't clog, exactly. "He called it the backstep, the double-shuffle backstep. His head didn't even hardly move, feet just moved and he literally played a tune with them feet. I mean he played a tune like you play it on the banjo."

But the biggest influence on Elmer's music was his cousin, George Bird. They were boyhood friends and learned the family music together. For many years, the boys would get together on weekends at Uncle John's house on Clymers Creek. With his Uncle John on fiddle, George on banjo, and Elmer on guitar, they played music into the wee hours.

Of course, life was more than music back then. Elmer was also exposed to his share of hard work. The Birds were farmers and raised corn, wheat, and tobacco, plus their food. Elmer attended school until the fourth grade, but that was his choice, he says. He wanted to farm.

"I started working cattle when I was just five or six years old. My dad gave me a calf and we made a steer out of him. Got him from a fellow named Tom, and that's what we called him. Called the other one Low. My dad made me a little yoke. Anyway, I started working the cattle. The longer I worked, I wanted to stay home and work. I scraped their horns so they looked like Texas longhorns. One weighed 1,750 and the other weighed 1,800 pounds. I did everything there was to do on a farm.

"Later on, I sawlogged with them. People found out I had that real stout yolk of cattle and I could go over any bluff with them; people hired me to do their logging."

This was by the time he was 12, "and I wasn't big as a minute."

In those early days, Elmer was hearing more than just fiddle and banjo music at home. There was another sound reaching the mountains—radio. More specifically, the "Grand Ole Opry."

In the 1920s, radios were few and far between, but Beulah, then Beulah Edwards, had an older sister who owned a radio. While Beulah is a bit younger than Elmer, she has known him all her life. Eight-year-old Elmer and other youngsters in the area would troop way out to her house on Thornton Ridge to listen to WSM from Nashville.

"We sure would enjoy the 'Grand Ole Opry,'" Elmer says. "That was back when they had the Crook Brothers, the Possum Hunters, Dave Macon, and all those guys like that."

The "Old Farm Hour" was another popular radio show, broadcast over Charleston's WCHS. When he could, Elmer would travel to the Middleburg Auditorium and catch the show. "When George and I were just kids [teenagers] we played on WCHS and WSAZ. The Future Farmers of America had programs and they would always want us to come and play."

Elmer and George continued listening to the "Grand Ole Opry" and around 1939, with local radio performances under their belts—and maybe some stars in their eyes—they set out for Nashville and the "Grand Ole Opry." Walking.

Brother Hamon (left) and baby brother Verland (center) with Elmer Bird. Photographer unknown.

"I was about 19. George was 16 or 17. We didn't have money. I had about $18. He didn't have a cent. I had sold my tomato crop. We were walking and hitchhiking. We got to Ashland, Kentucky, and we played in a couple of beer joints and picked up a quarter or two here and yonder."

In Ashland, the boys found a room at the Southern Hotel on Carter Avenue. "This lady, she rented us a room for a dollar. It was a big old hotel, had about 40 rooms in it." Soon Elmer was helping to clean the hotel in exchange for the room, and George had a job at a local grocery store. "Pretty good deal," Elmer says. "Didn't interfere with our music."

The landlady told the boys they ought to see if they could audition for Asa Martin, who hosted a show on radio station WCMI in Ashland.

When they saw Mr. Martin at the station, he asked the boys to play a fiddle tune, then he asked for a song. Then he said, "Yeah, you can sing, too. I'll just put you down for those two numbers on the show today."

"That was the end of our audition," Elmer says. Asa

Martin's radio show was called "The Morning Roundup," and it went on the air about 6:00 A.M. "We had to walk about nine blocks every morning to the first show on WCMI and we were late most mornings and we would have to run that nine blocks," Elmer says.

As part of the "Morning Roundup Gang," they played two shows a day: a 15-minute show in the morning and a 30-minute show at noon. "We had been there just a little while and we started getting a lot of requests for our songs, especially out of Ohio. So we told them our names were 'George and Elmer,' but part of the time they called us 'The Bird Brothers.' We played 'Columbus Stockade Blues,' 'Echoes from the Hills,' 'Beautiful, Beautiful Brown Eyes,' and a lot of fiddle and banjo tunes. That's what Mr. Martin really wanted us to do."

The Roundup Gang also played on Asa Martin's live Saturday night broadcast from the Cliffside Casino. "It was a big theater back north towards Huntington from Ashland. They had square dances and prizes for the best square dance group. They had fiddle contests."

Elmer and George showed up for the fiddle contest and made a big impression. "The first night we were there George said, 'We want to sign up for the fiddle contest.'

"I said, 'No, we don't know nobody here yet.'

"He said, 'Well, we can play better than they can.'"

George approached the judges, and they asked where his guitar player was. The usual format was fiddle with guitar back-up.

George told them he only had a banjo player. The judges were skeptical. "He kept arguing with them," Elmer says. "Then one of the judges said, 'Let him go ahead. The banjo won't carry him no way. Even if he can play the fiddle, he'll lose anyway.'"

George replied, "We'll take our chances on that."

"If you miss a string on that banjo," George said to Elmer, "I'm gonna kill you. We're gonna win this." And they did.

"I'll never forget what tune we played. We just played one tune. We played 'Arkansas Traveler.' I can see the rosin standing up on that fiddle. I was driving that 'Arkansas Traveler' right on down the road," Elmer says.

George and Elmer had been in Ashland for six months when it was time to return home. George had to finish high school at Hurricane, and Elmer went back to the farm.

"That walk to Nashville was the end of us playing together," Elmer says. It wasn't too long until World War II broke out, and Elmer was in the service. "I got called in the Army in the first of '42," Elmer says, but "George didn't go in the service for a while. He went to Pittsburgh and got married."

Elmer saw action in North Africa and on through Sicily. He was in a staging area for the D-Day invasion when he got the news that George had been killed in the invasion of France. Elmer came home in October 1945. "I don't try to remember anything from the war. I was just real glad to get home."

After the war, with his musical partner now deceased, Elmer figured his music days were over. He and Beulah married on December 4, 1945, and started to raise a family. They built the house they live in on Turkey Creek, and farmed, while Elmer drove a truck and did hauling for people. In 1954, he was hired at Union Carbide in South Charleston.

That same year, a local bluegrass band—Eck Gibson and The Mountaineer Ramblers—had a daily radio show and needed a banjo player at the last minute. "They had six radio shows on WHTN," Elmer says. "Eastern Food Market sponsored them. They played a 15-minute show five days a week and on Saturday they had a 30-minute show.

"So he asked me if I'd go down and talk to that guy, he wanted me to play banjo and I said, 'Well, I'm not bluegrass.' So I showed him, I did clawhammer. I could pick two-finger, but I wasn't a bluegrass player. So they put a set of picks on me and told me to play three-finger. Never had nobody show me or nothing. They told me if I could help them out a week, they would get another banjo player.

"I played banjo with them for 15 years."

Elmer and the Mountaineer Ramblers continued the daily radio show through 1955. Every Monday evening they recorded shows for the whole week.

"It wasn't bluegrass I was playing, it was old-time three-finger is what it was," Elmer says. "I kicked off anything they wanted to play. But I never was bluegrass. People told me 'You're not a bluegrass banjo player.' I said, 'I'm not trying to be. I'm just filling in till they get somebody!'"

This wouldn't be the last time Elmer's music would invite such comparisons. Years in a bluegrass band brought with it a reputation as a bluegrass player. As a result, he met some resistance at old-time banjo contests.

Once a contest judge in Harpers Ferry warned him, "'Now don't you "grass it,"'" Elmer says. "I played 'Red Wing' and 'Under the Double Eagle,'" Elmer recalls. "Just as slow as you could play them and still get in all the notes. I couldn't see no bluegrass.

"They said, 'If you "grass it," we'll have to disqualify you.' So they disqualified me. They said it was too slick.

"Since then, I've judged a lot of contests. You don't judge a guy by what he is wearing or who he is, or whether they are male or female. You judge his instrument. They judged me just as soon as I walked up there."

Elmer doesn't see anything wrong with playing a bluegrass standard like "Orange Blossom Special" in the clawhammer style. "I just use their tune. They use ours. That's where bluegrass started from."

By the early '70s, Elmer wanted a change. It was at the Art and Craft Fair in Ripley that he met a fretless banjo maker named Gene Dickerson.

Eck Gibson and the Mountaineer Ramblers: Dewey Thacker (left) and Leonard Thornton (right) on fiddles, Elmer Bird on banjo, and Eck Gibson on guitar. They asked Elmer to play with them for one week and he stayed for 15 years. Photographer unknown.

Elmer Bird and John Hartford at Hartford's home on the banks of the Cumberland River in Tennessee. John and Elmer met in 1975. "Elmer is one of the strongest people I've ever met in my life," John says. "He has an incredible sense of willpower and determination, in all aspects of his life and particularly in his music." Photographer unknown.

Elmer remembers that he picked up one of Dickerson's banjos at his booth, and Dickerson asked, "Where did you ever learn to play like that?"

Dickerson asked if Elmer played in a band, and Elmer explained it was a bluegrass band and they didn't have much use for clawhammer. "He said, 'You need to leave that band immediately.' He started sending me to where there were gonna be old-time shows and contests. He actually got me started doing my single act."

So by 1974, Elmer knew it was time to move on. He told Beulah he wanted to go solo, and play what he wanted. "If I want to play fast, I'll play fast. If I want to sneak in a country song every now and then—I do 'Momma Tried'—a few country songs like that. I found out after I got to doing a lot of different jobs, I could play to a lot wider audience."

That "wider audience" is what led Elmer to develop his "double drop-thumb" style.

As Elmer explains it, straight clawhammer "sounded too draggy and the audience didn't pay attention to me, because I was playing like my dad played. The audience didn't like it, it wasn't good enough, they wanted something more lively," Elmer says. "I doubled my speed just about. That's when I came up with double drop-thumb clawhammer. I still pick the drop-thumb, fifth and second, but I'm getting *all* those strings at one time or another—wherever it needs it. Only thing I'm getting on the way back up is the fifth string with my thumb. Everybody thinks I'm catching [notes on the way back up], but I'm not."

Elmer played a lot of jobs for free the first year, but with the understanding that the following year, he wanted paid. It was at one of those early gigs that he picked up his "handle."

A promoter in Ohio had listed him as "The King of Clawhammer Banjo Players," but Elmer wasn't comfortable with it. Sometime later, "Dave Morris was putting on a show out at Rippling Waters," Elmer says. "He wanted me to play on it. He couldn't remember what I called myself, so he said, 'We'll just call him "The Banjo Man from Turkey Creek."'"

It was at the 1975 Skyline Bluegrass Festival in Ronceverte that he met his future collaborator and producer, John Hartford.

One of the scheduled bands didn't show up and Elmer was asked to fill in at the last minute. "So I ran up the hill and got the banjo and got up on the stage," Elmer says. "I got my breath and I told the audience I would try to do this for them.

"John Hartford was down under the stage and I didn't know that." After Elmer's set, the Grammy Award-winning songwriter had some advice for him.

Elmer remembers Hartford said, "'You're the best old-time banjo player that I have ever seen, but sit down and let me tell you, don't ever apologize to an audience again, even

if they don't like you. Let them be the judge and don't ever tell nobody again that you're gonna "try" to do something.

"'You just play that banjo like you're capable of playing it. Let them make up their mind what they think of it.'

"It was actually good training for me," Elmer says. Elmer already had two albums out at this time, starting with *Elmer's Greatest Licks* in 1979, and *Home Sweet Home* in 1982.

This chance meeting with Hartford led to a friendship and musical collaboration—the internationally acclaimed musician wound up producing and playing fiddle on Elmer's next three albums: *Bumble Bee Waltz* in 1985, *Turkey Creek* in 1987, and *George How I Miss You* in 1992. The latter album was a tribute to George Bird.

In the two decades he has been a solo act, Elmer's music has taken him across the United States and Canada. He has performed at the 1982 World's Fair, the Renfro Valley Barn Dance, Berea College, Midnight Jamboree in Nashville, Silver Dollar City in Missouri, Burbank Center for the Arts in California, at the Winnipeg Festival in Manitoba, and many other places.

And he is known at home, too. Elmer has appeared on "Mountain Stage," at the West Virginia State Folk Festival in Glenville, and at the Pumpkin Festival in Milton. Elmer is a regular at the Appalachian String Band Festival at Clifftop and the Vandalia Gathering in Charleston. He was honored with the Vandalia Award at the 1996 Gathering. And he is also a six-time, first-place winner at Vandalia.

The Society for the Preservation of Bluegrass Music in America respected his banjo prowess, too. The group awarded him "Best Old-Time Banjo Player" in 1984, 1985, 1986, and 1990.

And he hasn't lost touch with his radio roots, either. He is a cast member at "Jamboree U.S.A." in Wheeling.

Elmer's best moment on stage? It was last November in Cincinnati, in that city's brand-new Paramount Theater. "The promoter knew I wasn't up to par. I went out there and hit the banjo one time and said, 'I'm just a clodhopper from Turkey Creek.'"

Elmer asked the crowd to sing along with him. "I let the crowd do about half of it—I pulled a John Hartford trick on them."

The crowd gave him a standing ovation and called him out for an encore. He obliged with the "Orange Blossom Special." "Man, I just burned it down," Elmer says.

"I don't think there was ever any more people to come backstage after a show," Beulah says.

"That was probably the best show I ever did in my life."

In 1985, a woman in Shreveport, Louisiana, was watching the Nashville Network's "Nashville Now" show on television when she heard country star Charlie Louvin announce that "The Banjo Man from Turkey Creek—Elmer Bird" would be at his upcoming bluegrass festival. The woman went next

Elmer and Beulah Bird in 1997 at home on Turkey Creek. Photograph by Michael Keller.

door and asked her neighbor, Vedious, if this might be the same Elmer Bird who used to play music with Vedious's late husband, George Bird.

Vedious called directory assistance and found Elmer's number. They became reacquainted, and later she asked Elmer if he wanted George's old banjo. Soon it was back on Turkey Creek.

It wasn't in the best shape, so Elmer had it restored by his friend, luthier Early Vermillion. The beautiful turn-of-the-century, open-back banjo, with mother-of-pearl inlay and fine carved heel, is a prized possession.

In 1992, Elmer was diagnosed with a rare blood cancer. While it has meant frequent trips to hospitals for treatments, his spirits are good and he is anxious to play again.

Last fall, he completed another recording, *My Most Requested*. Fans and fellow musicians asked him to record an all-instrumental tape. "I'm glad I did it, because I sure couldn't do it right now," Elmer says.

Last December, Elmer and Beulah celebrated 51 years of marriage. They are the parents of three children—Jane, Elmer Robinson Bird Jr., and Craig. They also have six grandchildren and four great-grandchildren.

"I worked at Carbide for 27 years and 10 months. At one time I had 100 head of registered Angus cattle and played music every weekend. People would ask me, 'Doesn't that make you nervous?'

"I'd say, 'I don't have time to be nervous.'"

EDITOR'S NOTE: This article first appeared in the summer 1997 issue of *Goldenseal* (vol. 23, no. 2). Elmer Bird received numerous honors and awards for his unique "double drop-thumb" banjo style, including the 1996 Vandalia Award. He died on July 29, 1997, at the age of 77 at his home on Turkey Creek in Putnam County, West Virginia.

Aunt Jennie Wilson

"I GREW UP WITH MUSIC"

Robert Spence

HOLDING her "banjer" under the television lights in the center of Southern Community College in Logan, Jennie Wilson began telling her young audience about a different and older way of living. She told of growing up in Logan County when it was still a farming area, of learning to play mountain music, of her pleasure when her songs became popular long after they were thought of as antiques, and of the need to preserve the old style of playing Appalachian instruments.

As the audience listened she began strumming a tune in her familiar clawhammer style. Aunt Jennie smiled when she caught the eye of a friend among the listeners, delighted with both the reception from the crowd and with the knowledge that she has helped save the music of her time and place. The smile stayed on her wonderfully lined face long after she turned her attention back to the audience.

Virginia Myrtle Wilson will be 85 years old next February. She is a survivor, having lived through the arrival of the coal industry in southern West Virginia and the gradual fading away of the manner of living that her preindustrial parents knew. She has known many of the sorrows and joys of the region. Her husband, Jim Wilson, was killed by a slate fall in the mines when he was a young man. Jennie finished raising their children alone in the 1940s, a time when the economy of the area was showing the serious weaknesses that have become intense in recent years.

Yet it is through playing her music that Jennie has been most typical of the strong-willed and poetic women of Appalachia. She began making music as a child, abandoned it to have a home and family, and then returned to it nearly 30 years ago when younger Americans began rediscovering the beauty of old ballads and instrumental music.

"When I was growing up, nobody knew how to read music, but we really made music," she said. "If it wasn't at one person's house, it would be at another one's. If it was in the summertime, we'd get out in a big barn some place and play music until the wee hours of the morning. That was the way we played music and that was the way I like it. I don't like to play in buildings. I think it is more authentic to be out and play under the trees."

Jennie Wilson was born an Ellis, on her family's farm on Little Buffalo Creek near the town of Henlawson in February 1900. In Logan County then the farming families all knew

Aunt Jennie Wilson in 1983. Photograph by Rick Lee.

each other well and appreciated the differences in individuals. Many of the Ellis clan were picturesque and eccentric and nearly all of Jennie's line could pick out songs on a guitar, a banjo, a dulcimer, or a fiddle.

"I grew up with music on our old farm down there," she said. "My father was Hughie Ellis, but he always went by the name of Dock. My mother was Cinderella Lockard. And my brothers and sisters were Lewis Webster, Mandeville Warren, Genevia Ann, Jesse Wilmer, Eliza Catherine, William Hughie, Isaac Calvin, Leotas Richmond, Cora Belle, Biddie Adeline, and I was the youngest, Virginia Myrtle. Now isn't that a collection?"

She remembers their lives together as a cooperative way of doing things. "Children then," she said, "went to school for six months, then they would let them go home and farm. Everybody farmed, you know. My father and my brothers, they were timbermen. They worked at sawlog jobs and at sawmills, but they farmed in the summer.

"The work was all done by hand because we had no machinery. We just used mules and horses to plow with and we didn't have tractors or things like that. And then we had just plain old broad hoes to hoe out the crops."

Yet if the work was difficult it also was done in a way that let young people enjoy their free time. "If we had a lot of corn to hoe out there would be gangs of young people to come in and help hoe that whole field of corn," Jennie said. "It was the same way when the fall of the year would come. We had bean-stringings and apple-peelings and would get all those things ready to dry. Then after that was all over, we'd all dance. Just so the work came first, that was all that was necessary. That's the way we grew up."

It was during those evenings when the crowds of young women and men played their old-fashioned songs and shared their tall tales that Jennie Ellis fell in love with music. In 1909, when she was nine years old, she met in that setting the first person who inspired her to learn to play an instrument.

In many ways it is a shame that not very much is known about Delpha Maynard, who must have been a personable and charming woman, and whose way of playing the banjo eventually was considered pure enough to be preserved by the Library of Congress through Jennie's playing. Aunt Jennie herself remembers Delpha as one of the liveliest women she has known.

"One summer my brother Hughie started dating a girl named Delpha Maynard who could play the banjer and dance just like anything and I wanted to be just like her," she said. "So I started learning how to play the clawhammer style when I was nine years old. My fingers were too small then to reach around the neck of the banjer, but I would pretend that I was playing like Delpha until I got to be 10 and could reach the chords."

Delpha was born, most likely in the 1880s, in the area that became Mingo County and died at about 75 in the early 1960s. "She was a real pretty-made woman," Aunt Jennie said. "She was about five-feet-three and weighed about 130 pounds and had kind of a round face with a pretty smile. She usually wore blue clothes and she had long strawberry blonde hair that she wore in a bun.

"She was about 21 or 22 years old when she met my brother while he was playing at a dance somewhere and they dated for about a year. She loved children and she took to me because it pleased her that I wanted to be so much like her. I liked for her to come to the house and I would sit on her lap and, you know, she'd pay attention to what I'd say.

"Most women then didn't play the banjer and she wanted me to learn how to do it. Delpha never told me who taught her to play, but I always thought she must have learned it from her family or from some older person who lived near

Jennie Wilson in 1939, the year her husband was killed in the mines. Photographer unknown.

her and she passed it along to me. I wish now that I'd had a picture of her and kept it all these years."

Jennie's father and her brothers Jesse and Hughie were glad that she wanted to play the banjo and they, too, taught her something about it. Dock Ellis told his young daughter that he would buy her a banjo of her own the next time he made a pushboat trip to Huntington. He did, and Jennie began learning music much faster. The songs were learned in a way that later was seen as an authentic folk process.

"The songs," Aunt Jennie said, "were the same folk songs that they sing today. About the way we'd do those songs, see, we'd all be sitting around to play and sing and maybe you'd know a song that I didn't know. I'd like that song and I'd say,

Writer Robert Spence, a
Logan County friend and fan
of Aunt Jennie Wilson, joins
her for a laugh. Photograph
by Rick Lee.

'Write me the ballad to that.' So you'd do it and the song
would just pass around like that. That's how we all learned
our songs.

"We didn't have songbooks or anything. Oh, there were
some Christian songbooks but the love songs and the old
ballads were songs that somebody would learn someplace
and just pass it on. If someone did know music it was someone like a preacher who learned it out of a songbook."

Another way that mountain music was learned was in the
informal setting of a country square dance. Social life for
young people in Logan County then was centered around
hunting and fishing, the town's annual Christmas get-togethers, church meetings, and square dances. Older persons
often disapproved of waltzing. The square dances were mor-
ally acceptable, but were spirited in their own way.

"When I began playing and going to square dances I was
about 14 years old," Jennie recalled. "I would go along with
my brothers and they would fix me a box or something to sit
on and I would get up on that box and play my banjer so it
would blend with their fiddles and guitars. And we'd have
the best time there ever was.

"Sometimes, of course, it wouldn't be too good. They
would get into a fight like they do today, but not as often as
they do now. I've really seen some skirmishes at dances, I'll
tell you. Today that would scare me to death, but then it
didn't scare me the least bit. One night someone fired a pistol and the shot went through my banjer and I thought for
sure I was shot. I remember many a time I would go to a
dance carrying a pistol when I was just a girl. If you didn't
take care of yourself, nobody would take care of you.

"But still," she added, "we always enjoyed ourselves. Each

Aunt Jennie Wilson making music with her grandson Roger
Bryant at the 1983 Vandalia Gathering. Photograph by Rick Lee.

one would see just how much fun they could be. If somebody was a kind of still-turned person, well, they weren't too popular. But the meaner they were and the 'all for a good time,' why, they were the most popular."

Yet if the county was rowdy in Jennie's younger days, there were still many old-style customs that affected the way younger people behaved. She has vivid memories of the old practice of family members telling each other ghost stories and tall tales. She also remembers the courting customs of the time.

"When a boy had a date with his girl, he would ride his horse to her house and then go in," Jennie said. "She'd meet him at the door and take his hat and coat and then tell him to sit down, or else her parents would, and just treat him the very best. If there was another boy and girl there all of you would sit and talk or play games like checkers or dominos—something like that. The parents would go on about their business.

"When the boy would go to leave, usually around 10:00, his girl would walk out on the porch with him and bid him goodnight, but they didn't sit and talk out there. If they did the parents would tell them to come in the house. They were just that strict, but you didn't see so many divorces. Sometimes on Sunday the boy would have dinner with all of them, but usually that was when things were getting serious."

Jennie's own courtship was, typically, very different from that. "I met Jim Wilson when his family moved to Henlawson. Some of my girlfriends met him and were telling me what a good-looking boy he was. I asked the Wilson girls—they weren't any of his relations—to introduce me to him. They said he was already engaged, but I laughed and said, 'Well, I can out-talk her!' One day they came up to the house and he was with them. He was the nicest looking boy I ever saw but he was one of the stillest people I ever met. The next time I saw him it was at a party and I walked right over and started a conversation and we really had a great time. Then one day I went to the post office and he was there and he walked me home.

"All the Henlawson girls were stuck on him but I didn't think I was, because he was so quiet and he wasn't musically inclined. But then he was at a party once when I was playing the banjer and he asked to take me home and then asked

"A Real Fine Looking Man"

AUNT JENNIE REMEMBERS FRANK HUTCHISON

Robert Spence

Aunt Jennie Wilson has crossed paths with a lot of musicians. This is in part a natural outgrowth of her recent prominence as a folk musician, as she travels around and people come to Peach Creek to see her, but the interaction goes back to her youth. In 84 years she has influenced, and been influenced by, a host of musicians.

One of the first was Frank Hutchison. Though his work is not widely known in West Virginia today, this Raleigh County native was one of the most influential Appalachian musicians. His use of the blues in his music was one of the factors that shaped modern country music, and at least one of his tunes entered the country mainstream, although under an-

other name than the one he gave it.

Hutchison, who was born in 1897 and died in 1945, lived in Logan County much of his life. Reliable information about his life is hard to come by, so I was delighted when Aunt Jennie told me she had not only known Frank Hutchison but had once been engaged to marry him. Her memories of the man and his music follow.

∾

Robert Spence: Aunt Jennie, how did you meet Frank Hutchison?

Jennie Wilson: When I first met him he was at Slagle on Rum Creek. He was working on a timbering job; he was a right young man. Then at different times I would go to dances and parties and

things and he would be there. So eventually I got to dating Frank and I dated him I guess for two years. Frank and I got engaged after we had gone out for a couple of years, but we didn't get married.

RS: What can you tell me about the way Frank played his music?

JW: Frank had a unique way of playing. I remember he had a kind of steel bar, and he would hold his guitar on his lap and play it like you would a steel guitar. He could make it sound just like a steel guitar.

He also played a mouth organ—what we call a harmonica today. He had kind of a contraption that he put around his neck and held the organ on it. I have heard different people sing the song "Coney Isle," but Frank wrote it and he would me for a date. We went to a circus in Logan together. His girl heard about it and gave him his ring back and eight months later we were married. That was on December 16, 1918, when I wasn't quite 19 years old."

Where the coal was working was sometimes hard to find, for the industry was in decline. The first and most hopeful era for Logan mining had occurred during the years from 1904 to 1918, when new operations were being opened almost daily and the future looked wonderful. The second era of that history took the years 1919 to 1946 when the industry's hopes were shattered and men and women became aware of how difficult it would be to live and work in the coalfields. Aunt Jennie's memories of the nightmare of the Great Depression in the coalfields are a story of their own, to be told another time. For now it is enough to know that as the Depression was ending she experienced a more personal sorrow, when Jim Wilson's life became one of those lost to the production demands of coal mining.

"Jim was killed in the mines here on Peach Creek," she said. "He was hurt in a slate fall on August 9, 1939, and died on November 2 that year. To get along I took $300 of the insurance money that I got and paid for the house that I'm living in now. I figured that if I had a roof over the children's heads we could get along. I got $35 a month in compensation and took in washing and did whatever I had to do, so we'd make ends meet. Two of my children were grown, but Evelyn was in grade school. Willard went in the service and Virginia did housework and we did all right until Evelyn was grown."

In those few spare sentences Jennie Wilson tells the story of how many widow women found ways to live during the 1940s and 1950s, when at times it looked as though the coal industry was dying in southern West Virginia. Other people, perhaps less hardy, despaired and moved away. As men and women left Appalachia to find work in other states, many of them took along the music their parents had made.

The heart of the music remained in the mountains but the sound traveled well, adapting to far-off places as the mountain people themselves adapted. Enough survived in mainstream country music and through the efforts of collectors to show the coming generation the value of the style. By the 1950s there was more interest in saving the tradition-

Frank Hutchison's album on Rounder Records. Photographer unknown.

really play it with his guitar and that mouth organ.

RS: What about Frank himself?

JW: Oh, he was real outgoing—a real friendly fellow. And he was a real fine looking man.

RS: Was Frank very much interested in the old ballads, the English and Scottish songs?

JW: That was a strong interest that he had. Everybody around loved those songs like "Barbary Allen," and he could really play them. He sang those songs as well as the ones he wrote. He loved those songs.

RS: Did he ever tell you who taught him to play the guitar?

JW: No, I don't believe he ever did, but I thought that he just taught himself how to play, like so many people did, by just practicing and fooling around with it himself.

RS: Frank is supposed to have been one of the first white musicians who started working the al songs than there had been for decades. Among those in West Virginia who knew the value of that revival was the late Dr. Patrick Gainer. He is credited with "discovering" Aunt Jennie Wilson, and she remembers him well.

"In 1955," she said, "Dr. Gainer of West Virginia University taught a class in folklore over at Logan High School. He told his students that they had to bring someone who could tell the class about how things were done here when I was growing.

"My son-in-law, Clyde Bryant, told one of our neighbors who was taking the class that if she could talk me into going with her and playing the banjer she would have it made. Now I hadn't played the banjer in about 35 years, but I went to that class and it came back to me right away."

She added that that was about the time when the arts and crafts fairs and folk festivals were being started all over West Virginia. People soon heard about Aunt Jennie Wilson of Logan County, and she has been in demand ever since. She has played often at the Mountain State Art and Craft Fair at Ripley, and at the Vandalia Gathering in Charleston nearly every summer.

Yet there is more to Aunt Jennie's story than her popularity at folk festivals. Dr. Gainer, a serious student of Appalachian music, was so impressed with Jennie's clawhammer style that he made arrangements for her to go to Washington, D.C., to make recordings for the Library of Congress. Another close friend, Billy Edd Wheeler, arranged for her to record her songs for *A Portrait of Aunt Jennie*.

In that way her music was recognized as one of the most perfect gifts that Appalachia has given to American culture. Among those who agree and who appreciate that gift is musician Karen McKay of Lewisburg, who has been learning the clawhammer style from Aunt Jennie. She has shown that appreciation by dedicating an album to Jennie for sharing "... her courage, strength, wisdom, and wit ... the birthright of mountain women everywhere."

Aunt Jennie Wilson is now famous in certain circles. Her reaction is modest, yet in character. Thinking back on her times she said, "It was a hard life, but it was a good life. I'm grazing 84 now. The woman who has had more trouble or more pleasure than I've had is just a bigger woman that I am."

EDITOR'S NOTE: This article first appeared in the spring 1984 issue of *Goldenseal* (vol. 10, no. 1). Folk legend Aunt Jennie Wilson died on March 2, 1992, at the age of 92 in Logan County, West Virginia. A recipient of the Lifetime Achievement Award from the West Virginia Department of Culture and History and the 1984 Vandalia Award, she had a folk festival named in her honor that takes place each October at Chief Logan State Park.

---

sounds of black songs into his music.

JW: I think that was probably true. Both Frank and his friend Dick Justice loved the blues, though Frank probably didn't love them as much as Dick did.

I knew Dick right well. He worked in the mines down at Kitchen and up at Ethel and Mac-Beth. He played the guitar like Frank did, and the fiddle. They'd go to dances together and play half the night. Chet Atkins couldn't do anything with the guitar that Dick Justice couldn't do.

They went down to Cincinnati once. That was the place where a lot of musicians went to record, like Nashville is today. A representative of a company told them he would pay their expenses to come and make a recording there. I never knew exactly what happened, but they never made a dime off the recordings.

RS: Did Frank ever tell you about the trips he made to record for the OKeh Company in New York?

JW: Yes. When he came back I asked him how it went, and he laughed and said he messed up the first sessions because he tapped his foot too hard. I used to have a lot of their records on the old 78s, but through the years they all got lost or broken.

RS: Do you remember anything about the shows Frank put on in the 1920s?

JW: He'd play a lot of songs, of course, and tell stories in a very funny way. He always told one about a cross-eyed man and a near-sighted man who bumped into each other. The cross-eyed man said, "Why don't you watch where you're going?" And the near-sighted man answered, "Why don't you go where you're watching?" It would be so funny the way he'd tell it.

I never knew much about him after he married. He married Minnie Garrett and they had two children. But I heard that Frank took to drinking. Then they left here and I didn't know his children. I heard that he kept a store down at Lake and for a while kept the post office, too. I can tell you where he is buried—it's over on Hewitt's Creek.

Frank was very original. I've heard any number of people since his time use the guitar like he did, but Frank was the first one I knew who played like that. I think it is a good thing that people are getting interested in music again.

EDITOR'S NOTE: This article first appeared in the spring 1984 issue of *Goldenseal* (vol. 10, no. 1).

Andrew F. Boarman

THE BANJO MAN FROM BERKELEY COUNTY

Peggy Jarvis and Dick Kimmel

THE Hedgesville barber shop, painted a quiet pink with white trim, is misleading. The man in charge, Andrew F. Boarman, called Andy by most, no longer trims sideburns. He fixes banjos. The animated barber always did play music and work on instruments in between haircuts, but in 1974 he moved the barber chair out and devoted his time exclusively to music.

The walls of the shop are a pale green, over which are scrawled names and phone numbers of past visitors searching for a guitar or mandolin. Pictures of bands and singers are taped here and there. Only the fluorescent lights, the porcelain sink, and the wide mirror attest to the previous status of the workshop. A cabinet contains dentistry tools with which Andy does the intricate work on his handcrafted banjos he calls Dixie Grands.

Above the sink, next to the diploma from West Virginia Barbers College, is a clock advertising Samsell's Watch Repair. On the adjacent wall in large print is the warning: "Not responsible for instruments left over 90 days."

The rack of old banjo necks and the scattered mandolins, fiddles, and banjos suggest the small shop's current purpose. The lively musician who used to cut hair is proud of being the personal repairman for musicians the caliber of Don Reno. Since he opened the shop in 1962, it has been a gathering place for traditional musicians and novices, as well as the center for Andy's instrument repairs.

Andy's shop and his playing have attracted a great number of people to his home near Spring Mills in Berkeley County. U.S. Senator Robert Byrd spent one afternoon playing music and chatting with Andy. Earl Scruggs and other professionals have listened to Andy's unique arrangement for tunes such as "Home Sweet Home." The native West Virginian has been featured in the Winchester *Evening Star;* the Hagerstown, Maryland, *Morning Herald;* and *Grit.* An article in the magazine *Bluegrass Unlimited* referred to Andy as "the guru of the five-string banjo."

The alert 68-year-old man tells of the conflicts that grew from barbering and repairing in the same place. "There was a [health] inspector from Charleston and I was outside. I had instruments strung all over that shop. I come out and locked the door and there he was. I knowed what he was. I says, 'I don't know whether to leave you in there or not.' He says, 'You have to leave me in.' I says, 'I tell you what I'm

Andy Boarman in May 1975 showing off the banjo he made. The back of the resonator, neck, and peghead are inlaid with cut pearl and abalone. Photograph by Dick Kimmel.

going to do. I'm going to take a shot at you. I'm going to let you in that door, but you're going to find the biggest surprise you ever found in barber inspecting.' He says, 'O.K.' I opened the door. He looked around and seen them music instruments. He says, 'I've found one guy in West Virginia who wants to work. Just keep it up.'"

Andy did keep on working as a successful barber. "Some days I had as many as 26 setting out there waiting for me and, boy, that's awful." He has lived most of his life in the apple orchard country around Falling Waters and remembers living along the Potomac River.

"I used to barber when the bush bobs come out in 1928. They was famous for the girls," he remembers. "I used to barber over along the river. No shop, just set on a chair over along the river. I was the one who cut the hair. There is nine boys up in that family and five down in this one and somebody had to learn to cut hair." He said when he started barbering, no one had money. "I was barbering and I'd get so many eggs—you couldn't sell that at the store—that I had to dump them over the river bed.

"The house burned down. We were living in a toolshed over there, my wife and I, when we first got married. There were big wide cracks in the building and you'd get up in the morning and shake the snow off the blanket."

As successful as he was as a barber, Andy is even better known for his music. His banjo playing is unique. Lloyd Longacre, a well-known classical banjo player, describes Andy's style on the five-string banjo as a "blending of early classical banjo and folk music of his youth with the bluegrass music of today."

"I like my own style and classical," Andy says. "If it don't suit my sound, I like to change it. I blend my chords and make it fit in." He plays his own arrangements of familiar tunes such as "Buffalo Gals," but also plays traditional tunes like "Soldier's Joy," which he can play four or five different ways. He performs difficult classical arrangements of tunes like "Darktown Dandies" and "Dancing Waves Schottische."

Andy admits there is never an end to what anyone can learn about playing music, although he has been working at it for almost 60 years. "There is never no way. You can't learn it all. You can't learn all about music—it and religion," he says with the energy and freshness of a beginner. The banjo expert can switch effortlessly to the fiddle, guitar, or Autoharp. He does not read music. "I started out but I got away from it. Notes look like a bunch of blackbirds sitting on telegraph wires to me."

He disappears into a room off the kitchen of his house and brings out a Martin guitar made in 1952. He begins to discuss the guitar, but starts playing instead, as though he would rather play than talk. The concentration shows on Andy's face, but his hands are relaxed. Andy plays the guitar in the alternating finger and thumb style. "That's old-time playing," he says. His picking is even and the broad fingers with flat tipped nails move loosely along the neck.

As a rule, classical banjoists have always used nylon strings. Andy prefers to play in the classical style without finger picks, but has opted for the more modern steel strings on a crisp sounding banjo, a setup similar to that used by many of today's bluegrass stars.

"These nylon strings is fine but they drive me about wild, I can't get them to note out true for me. I don't know whether my ear's too keen or I'm too dumb. A lot of people likes them. I can't get along with finger picks as well as I can

with just the balls of my fingers. My uncle learned me to play with the balls of my fingers.

"I like a good solid tone. You can tell a good solid tone whether the sound is blowing up on your face or whether it carries and leaves you. Like throwing a little pebble in a still puddle of water and you can see them little waves leaving where you throwed that. The music leaves practically the same way." He makes a fluttering motion with his arms, opening them wide to indicate the ripples.

Andy is always on the lookout for quality woods for constructing banjos. Necks are made of mahogany or sometimes walnut with a fingerboard of choice ebony. The resonator and neck of one of his special Dixie Grand banjos are decorated with designs of pearl and abalone. The fifth Dixie Grand Andy made has an eagle on the resonator. The banjo he is now completing has an intricate design of West Virginia on the back.

"I named my banjos after the Southern states for the simple reason that's where the five-string banjo really started from—Lynchburg, Virginia. Joel Sweeny built the first one in 18 and 43, I think," says the craftsman.

The pearl position markers between frets of a Dixie Grand are distinctive. With a jeweler's saw and a small file, Andy cuts the pearl to his own designs. He explains where the ideas for the designs come from. "Just in my mind. That's just imaginary markers. I'd look at frost on the window. I've been in old houses where it's cold. I look at the frost. You watch them sometime. You watch them formations that ice makes. I get them in my head." The outcome of what he translates from those sources is detailed and most attractive.

One of his more recent Dixie Grands has metal parts of gold plate engraved with a Kentucky fern pattern. At the top of the banjo, above the tuning pegs, three letters, "A.F.B." are inlaid. Andy once said that represented "A Fine Banjo," but it could also indicate the skilled craftsman, Andrew Forrest Boarman.

Although the instruments are valued at thousands of dollars, Andy is not interested in making great profits. "When I was in the hospital, I promised the good Lord I'd help people out and that's what I've done." Andy does not state the exact amount of time he puts into one of his Dixie Grands. "I made it between haircuts and hunting and fishing. I didn't hunt and fish but I was thinking about it."

In addition to the skilled work he does on these banjos, Andy also repairs instruments. He makes special spruce and ebony banjo bridges which have been used by such well-known bluegrass pickers as Sonny Osborne, J.D. Crowe, and Little Roy Lewis. Andy cuts a bridge out of wood with the grain of the wood extending the height of the bridge so it runs perpendicular to the strings on the instrument to improve their sound. He sets up and adjusts banjos for Bill

Andy Boarman in his shop in November 1973. Photograph by Dick Kimmel.

Runkle, Jim Steptoe, and Darrell Sanders. It's been said that at one concert intermission, Andy set up a banjo for Little Roy Lewis and people thought the musician had a new banjo during the second half of the concert. Andy responds to that story unaffectedly. "Yes, maybe Little Roy would back that up and maybe he wouldn't." Bill Harrell, a popular singer and guitarist, wrote to thank Andy for his repair work, saying, "You're the Rolls Royce of repairmen when it comes to instruments."

Andy feels that instrument repair work is demanding. "A good repairman is better than the man who builds them. You take a man who builds them, he's got a mock to build them in, everything cut out ready to put together, but you take one and set it under an automobile wheel and let somebody run over top of it and then let the repairman put it back together, and that separates the men from the boys."

Andy has had a lot of experience with instruments, and got started at an early age. He was born October 11, 1911, to William McGary Boarman and Ada Lee Stump Boarman. His uncle Charles Cleveland Stump was an expert classical banjo player. "I started making banjos with my uncle. He got to showing me a lot of things. Started me working on them back in 1928, tinkering around with one, before that. My uncle, he showed me a lot. And there's a fellow by the name of Vizelle; he was a painter by trade and a [wood-] grainer. Graining is like putting grain in a door, wood grain . . .

"I get a lot of my wood ideas from this violin maker. He'd made violins all his life. His name is Art Velardo over there at Hagerstown, Maryland. He's made about 15 upright basses, 30 or 40 violas, a couple of cellos, and about 65 violins.

"We had five in our family, two girls and three boys. All of the Stumps on my mother's side and the Stokes from my grandmother is where the music part of it was. None of the Boarmans that I knowed of played music. My uncle, Charlie Stump, and Uncle John Stump and Uncle Harry Stump and my Aunt Suzie and Aunt Mary and my mother Ada had a band. My mother played a five-string banjo, clawhammer style. She played upright bass and the organ. Uncle Charlie Stump played a five-string banjo only. Uncle Harry Stump, he played a violin and guitar. And they played for a lot of church doings and square dances.

"Getting back to me, I was 11 years old that I can remember of when I used to sneak my brother Bill's five-string banjo that my mother bought for him. They would go to town with the horse and buggy. When they would, I'd take the ladder and put it up to the window and get in his bedroom and play the banjo."

Andy also says that he started scratching around an old Autoharp when he was about six and that he would play just about anything he could get his hands on. "Every opportunity I got, I'd go out with the boys around Falling Waters. My mother died when I was about 11. I left home when I was 16 or 17, and went on construction work. I was playing the five-string banjo and the fiddle for square dances down around Canowing and Peachbottom, Maryland. I was playing with a boy by the name of Andy Jones. He played the ukelele most of the time. After we got through paying our board and working 55 hours a week, we had $11 left. Well, they'd come off the job—we worked there a year back in '29 and '30. We'd go back up in them mountains, and they was really rough people. A lot of moonshine and whiskey up in there, and I got to work out just playing the banjo by myself, or the fiddle. Sometimes they'd take a collection up down there. Wasn't much money floating around then, but they'd take a collection up. I've got as much as $65 for one night."

In 1930 Andy moved to Virginia to live with his uncle C.C. Stump. "When I came back from construction work I went to Vinton, Virginia, six miles out of Roanoke, and was up there and learned more about the five-string banjo from my Uncle Charlie Stump and old Fiddlin' Arthur Smith. He was up there with my uncle in the starting of the '30s. Things got a little tough there, and Arthur wanted my uncle to leave and go to North Carolina with him but my uncle wouldn't go. So Arthur went on down there and he was playing the fiddle advertising for that checkerboard feed, Purina, or something like that. I never did get to see him any more after that."

While in Virginia, Andy had the opportunity to hear and play with other string musicians including two important classical banjo players, Bacon and Van Epps. Andy played with Billie Edwards and the Neighbors family. "The boys' names was Roy and Tad. Mr. Neighbors was also a fine clawhammer banjo player. That's where I really fell in love with clawhammer playing even though I was up there with my uncle and Arthur Smith playing classical music and ragtime music."

Andy moved back to Berkeley County with his uncle in 1931. He played in a band with his cousins. James Boarman played the fiddle, Joseph the plectrum banjo, Harry the guitar, with Andy on the five-string banjo and Autoharp. "I played some old-time music at home. There was a bunch of us Boarman boys. They was seven boys in one family and three boys in the other one, and we picked enough out of the both families to have a band. We called ourselves the "All Night Ramblers" and we played for square dances. These barn dances we used to go to, we'd take lanterns for lights, and sometimes we'd get outside of the barn and play if it was pretty nice.

"When we played for them square dances we drove a Model T Ford sometimes 15 miles. You would end up playing for a ham sandwich probably, and a couple cups of black coffee. We'd have house dances, old-time house dances, and we'd have great big pots; we'd take one of these lard cans, and make black coffee in there . . . And sure, there was a lot of moonshine floating around then. Home brew beer. We played, we traveled in snow two and three feet deep to get to play for a square dance. We'd play and drink a lot of hard cider. We'd have a bunch at a farm; a farmer would come up and say, 'We want you boys to play over at my place this coming Saturday night.' And over there we'd set another place for the next Saturday night. It was always on a Saturday night, so if anybody had a big head, he had all day Sunday to try to get rid of it." When he was asked why people no longer have the local house and square dances that were once so popular, he explained, "People's got too fast a way to travel. Everybody's trying to go too fast."

Andy remembers how the town of Falling Waters used to look. He can point out where houses have replaced the old post office and the two dance halls. With enthusiasm he points to the wood left from the wheel of Sherer's Mill that began operation in 1775. Water from the spring runs into the Potomac a few hundred feet away where the Boarman boys used to play on a river boat from 1931 to 1933.

"We had square dances right on a boat. The *White Swan*, it was 38 feet wide and I believe 80 feet long. We played on there for two years. Every Saturday night, we'd get on the boat at Falling Waters, and go down the river 12 miles to Dam Number Four and back, which we'd get off maybe five or six o'clock in the morning. We'd play down and back. There were about 30 or 40 couples on there. We'd have a figure caller: 'Up the river and around the bend / Six legs up and going again,' or 'Swing Ma, swing Pa, swing the old man from Arkansas.'" Andy changes from conversation to quoting calls as quickly as he can change a chord on his banjo. "This big freeze come up and the river froze over. It got to raining a whole lot, and ice raised up in there and it took our boat down over the dam and busted it all up."

Andy says his aunt Mary's son taught him a lot about the Autoharp. "Charles Boarman, he's the one that I really learned my Autoharp playing off of. He was one of the finest fiddle players that's in the country, but he'd only play with me. He was shy." Andy also learned from Conley Hoover of Falling Waters.

In November 1933 Andy married Lois Tyson from Sleepy Creek. "When we first got married I learned her to pick a couple of schottisches on the banjo but after the first boy was born she give up." The Boarmans had four sons and a daughter: Vincent, Forrest, Donald, Robert, and Beverly. "We got hit in hard times in the Depression time and I was living three miles from work, walking to work in the orchard for 11 cents an hour. Not only me but a lot of us, and I worked many a day in the Depression just for my dinner and supper. There was plenty of work around but no money."

After working in the orchard, Andy worked on structural ironwork. He was a journeyman rodsman and worked in Altoona, Pennsylvania, while his wife maintained their home

Andy Boarman with his wife, Lois Tyson Boarman, at a bluegrass festival near Indian Springs, Maryland, in September 1976. Photograph by Dick Kimmel.

in West Virginia. In 1947 he began working at the Fairchild plant in Hagerstown, Maryland, where he worked until he had a heart attack in 1958. When he recovered, he began work as a barber in the shop behind his home.

"I give the banjo up for a long, long while, some 20 years, back in the Depression time. Things got tough. I just lost interest some way or another in the banjo, but when these bluegrass festivals started up down at Watermelon Park, I forget what year, I went down there, and the first time I ever seen Bill Monroe, him and I ate watermelon together up under a big sycamore tree. After I seen how the music was blooming I said to him, 'Mr. Monroe, it's really a fine thing you did to get the five-string banjo back to life again.' You got to give Earl Scruggs and Bill Monroe a whole lot of credit for bringing the banjo back."

Andy is doing much on his own to promote five-string banjo playing. "I've seen it leave and the tenor take over. In them days when you was learning to pick a five-string banjo you had to learn on your own. But my style that I play is partly my own. I guess God gave it. I know God gave it to me."

What natural talent he had, Andy has developed, and he is quick to encourage others. He has taught several hundred young people to play the fiddle, Autoharp, banjo, and guitar, but he is modest about his accomplishments. "I can give them a big push and they take it from there," he says, emphasizing the vowel in "push." Andy started Darrell Sanders on banjo, and he is now playing with Bill Harrell. Andy taught Blaine Sprouse, who has fiddled with the Monroe bands. He has received many sincere letters of thanks from people he has met and helped at various festivals. One letter came from a beginner on the Autoharp who pledged to pass on what she learned. These kinds of letters are numerous but Andy doesn't dwell on them. "Oh, I've bushels and bushels and bushels of them."

In 1978 Andy gave concerts in Berkeley and Morgan county public schools with the help of a grant from the West Virginia Arts and Humanities Commission. After his performances the children asked for autographs and advice. "They'd ask you, 'How long did it take you to learn to play this fiddle?' I'd tell them, 'Well it just depends on how much talent you got. It takes maybe three months or three years to pick something up. The other guy can pick it up in four or five hours.'"

He recommends quality instruments even for beginners. "Anybody that's going to start their kid to play a guitar, they should not have no cheap junk, because you're whipping them to start with. If you get a good brand of guitar, if they decide they don't need it, they can still sell it for what they've got in it."

Andy has a bright and lively manner, but he is serious about learning to play an instrument. "If you want to play one, I'd tell them when they started, you just didn't buy it across the counter like you would a Coca-Cola. You really had to work for it. It's like a fellow said to me—Paul Chaney was in my shop playing the banjo and I was cutting this guy's hair. He says, 'I'd give anything if I could play a banjo like that.' I asked Paul how long he'd been playing the banjo. He said he's been fighting the banjo for 20 years. The fellow said, 'I wouldn't want no part of that.' I said, 'Well, that's what the man had to do.'"

Andy thinks it is easier to learn to play a banjo today than when he began, because there are more musicians around. "Maybe that's helping them out. I imagine it would because they can steal licks off of each other and learn different ways of doing it."

His uncle C.C. Stump taught classical banjo in Vinton, Virginia. "He had a studio and a blackboard and as many as 68 students and he'd teach them all at one time. He'd mark it down on the blackboard and after he give them a half-hour lecture, he'd have 68 or 69 chairs and he'd set them all down and let them get fooling with their instruments and after a while one would look over and say 'How did you get that,' and he'd get them to teach each other."

Although the musical influence in Andy's life came from the Stump side of the family, the Boarman side has its own legends. The house next to Andy's is a stone one called Rosebud where his grandfather John Boarman lived. A family legend says Stonewall Jackson stayed in the home for several days during the Civil War. Andy's great-grandfather was Rear Admiral Charles Boarman who served in the Navy for over 60 years. He served on Lake Ontario during the War of 1812 and commanded a frigate in the Brazil Squadron for 11 years. From 1861 to 1865 he was on special duty, and retired in 1876.

Andy has inherited more than a rich family history. The banjo he plays is a Clifford Essex Concert Grand made in London in the early 1900s. It was one of the banjos his uncle played. "My uncle bought it from Harry Bowman in Martinsburg. Harry got it from the Banjo Fraternity in Lewistown, Pennsylvania. I like it because I've played it so much and because it's got a good, deep sound."

Impatient to play, it seems, Andy lifts the instrument out of the case he was given by Don Reno and begins to play. The head has the faded signatures of most musicians he has played with. He picks with his thumb and two fingers, accentuating the notes clearly. He has a smooth rhythm he maintains, even as he double picks. He usually plays different styles and his pieces are remarkably complex. In some of his arrangements he chooses to drop or add a beat; the "before and after notes," as he calls them, are regular features of his versions of tunes.

Andy has performed for innumerable informal audiences but also for the Heritage Arts Festival in Harpers Ferry and H.L. Wilson's festivals in Moorefield. He keeps a letter from Governor Rockefeller that thanks him for contributing to the Vandalia Gathering at the Cultural Center in Charleston in 1978.

Dr. William J. Canady of West Virginia University recorded Andy's first album, *Mountain State Music—Andrew F. Boarman* (June Appal 027). It features his Autoharp and banjo playing. He arranged most of the tunes, and they represent his uncle's influence. One song is his original composition, "Somewhere in West Virginia." He recorded this tune for a television segment with former reporter Carl Fleischhauer for the "Mountain Scene Tonight" shown on WWVU-TV on September 29 and October 3, 1975.

Traditional and bluegrass musicians regularly fill Andy's shop. They return to practice and to hear his engaging stories. He takes a personal interest in all musicians who visit. "The Southern Sounds of Grass," a group formed at the barber shop, has made its own record. Andy cautions his musician friends, saying, "A band is like a baseball team anymore, they're hard to keep together."

Andy has a way of bringing people together and delighting them with his music and his talk. "I love music and I love people," he says. "I love bluegrass, but I don't go to them festivals just to hear bluegrass. I go there to meet people. You meet some of the best people in the world at the festivals. Fine, fine people, fine musicians."

There seems to be a lot of Andy Boarman reflected in what he says of others. He is a master craftsman and musician with a genuine and ebullient personality. With the barber chair now gone from his shop, by all signs Andy is more "The Banjo Man" these days than he ever was.

EDITOR'S NOTE: This article first appeared in the January–March 1979 issue of *Goldenseal* (vol. 5, no. 1). Andrew Boarman was the 1991 Vandalia Award winner and continues to "tinker around" playing, repairing, and making banjos. He is the subject of the documentary film *Catching Up with Yesterday,* which explores his life as an active bearer of folk traditions in the state.

Charlie Blevins at the Red Robin Inn

THE COON DOG TRUTH

Michael Kline

THE Red Robin Inn at Borderland, just eight miles north of Williamson on old U.S. 52, has long been a gathering place for lonesome, weary travelers in search of refreshment, a good tale, and plenty of old mountain music. Charlie Blevins, the proprietor, loves to expound on "our old mountain ways" with his songs and lore, and his inn doubles as a museum. Every imaginable artifact from hand-loading days of coal mining can be seen hanging on the wall behind the bar, along with various other assorted antiques. Charlie has a story for every item, including his favorite tale sparked by a photograph of a 12-toed moonshiner, about whom he has written a song. His Blevins forebears were some of the early long hunters who ventured through the Cumberland Gap in the mid-18th century. His grandfathers were among the first men to go to work in the coal mines of Mingo County. Charlie himself, now 57, has subsisted by coal mining and farming. His present livelihood, the Red Robin Inn, is threatened by the construction of Corridor G highway, about which he has also written a song to a familiar John Prine tune.

The interview took place in the Red Robin Inn last year under a grant from the Humanities Foundation of West Virginia and Davis and Elkins College. A radio program called "The Red Robin Inn," highlighting Charlie's music, was produced as a part of "The Home Place," a 13-part series about West Virginia stories and music. Charlie's song, "Corridor G Highway," was featured on the program:

When I was a child I was raised in the old coal camps,
Down by that old Tug River on the Borderland shore.
There's a backwards old tavern I've often remembered,
So many times that my memory is worn.
And Daddy won't you take me back to Mingo County,
Down by the Tug River where the Red Robin stays,
I'm sorry little Charlie, too late in the asking.
Old "Corridor G" has dozed it away.

∽

Charlie Blevins: See, there's a highway supposed to come through this area here and wipe out a lot of our heritage. They call it the Corridor G highway. And it's already supposed to have been here, but they run a little low on funds and things. This tavern is kind of a landmark where these people gather in here to meet with friends and listen to a little of this here old country music, and their old ways of life. It's kind of passing on and getting away from us, and I try to hold it together through history just the best I can. The people still enjoy it. They get away from it, you see, they go plumb off to these other states, and when they come back, they'll get right in here and hear the old-fashioned stuff they heard way back when they was young. They still want to stay with their heritage. But this modernization thing, it's whupping a lot of our heritage out, they're taking it out fast. We're trying our best to hold some of it together, to preserve it. So I kind of made this song here about when I was a kid raised in these old coal camps.

I run my own history back, all the way through my generations, and they came into this country from Scotland there, back in the 1600s. Dr. Daniel Blevins was one of them, and I believe his brother's name was William. William and Daniel. They came from Scotland down into England, which was the embarkation point back in them days for anybody coming into America. They embarked from England, then, and came into Virginia. They got an Indian land grant and settled in there for a while. And then they came out of Virginia, I'd say 1680 or so, and settled in North Carolina. Then through the Cumberland Gap and scattered out all over Kentucky. Yes, William and Daniel. From them two brothers the Blevinses started springing up just like stick weeds all over the country, and yet today they still stand out true to form. They're still Blevinses.

On my dad's side I was pretty well Scotch on both sides. They was Blevinses, and Puckets, and Comptons, and Poes. And then on my mother's side you come down into German there, you get that Hager in there, and then you come right back to Scotch again. She was a Hager on her mother's side. Wyatt or Watt, that's strictly a Scotch name.

All of my family come into Mingo County from out of Johnson City, Kentucky, over there around White House and Paintsville, Kentucky. I've got a picture of all of them old-timers hanging right over here on the wall, my grandpap, my great-uncles there. By the turn of the century Johnson County was still a backward place. The mines over there hadn't ever got built like these mined right in here. The C&O Railroad hadn't made it up there then. It was all just farming and timber, and it was even pretty hard to get your timber

Charlie Blevins at the Red
Robin Inn in 1982. Photo-
graph by Doug Yarrow.

The Blevins brothers of Johnson County, Kentucky. Charlie's grandfather, Marshal (far right), moved to West Virginia in 1909, about the time this photograph was made. Photographer unknown.

out of there at the time. They cut this here timber through the winter and they'd have to wait until the spring raises come to raft the logs out of there. They'd make log rafts and bring them down the creeks to the Big Sandy River, on into Catlettsburg, Kentucky. That was the lumber center for the whole eastern part of Kentucky. So everybody out there was a-cutting timber and there was a lot of competition. It was awful hard work, too. Most of them didn't mind hard work, but they figured they could better themselves coming in here and getting on this railroad that was coming through, or working these mines. There was a few that worked the road for a while, but I guess they had that there mining in their blood. Most every one of them went right to the mines as quick as the mines got started.

I heard Pap tell about when he come in here, he was a little old boy, said he wasn't over five or six year old. He's got a memory like an elephant, he can go back there and pick it up! He said one of his older sisters, Mandy, and her husband, Boyd Adams, come in here first, and Boyd worked as a guard at the Williamson tunnel. They had just put the N&W train tunnel through the mountain at Williamson. Pap said he'd go up to the guard shack and stay with his Uncle Boyd. Mostly what they watched for, you see, they hadn't ever walled the tunnel up on the inside. Loose rocks,

maybe, or something would come down on the track. He'd have to go in there and remove them rocks, or get the crew if it was a big rock, to keep the train from hitting it. Later they got the tunnel all walled up with stone and cemented it.

I heard Pap tell about coming here when he was just a little old kid. Pap said they moved in here on a wagon and team away back there about the turn of the century. Pap and his oldest brother had to drive the milk cow through. Said they drove her from Paintsville, Kentucky, into Nolan, West Virginia—it's about two miles down the road here—and they settled at Nolan, back up in the head of one of them hollows. Grandpap bought a little old farm and they settled in there.

And I said, "Did you drive that milk cow all the way from Johnson County on foot, Pap?"

He said, "That's what we had to do, had no other transportation." It was just a little old wagon road through there at the time, all there was.

I said, "What in the world did you do when you got hungry?"

"Well, we just milked the old cow. She had to be milked, so we just milked the cow and drank the milk."

"How long did it take you to drive that cow from Paintsville?" I said.

"About three days and three nights."

"What did you do when nighttime come?"

"We just milked the old cow. We'd just tie her up and lay out and go to sleep. Morning time come, we milked, drank the milk, and hit the trail again. We made it in here."

I said, "You fellers had it pretty tough, didn't you?"

He said, "Getting here was just the start of it. When we went to cleaning up these hillsides to farm it, that's when the rough part come in."

They was seven brothers, and about the turn of the century they all come in this territory but one, my Uncle Tom. He stayed in Morgan County. See, this had just started to open up in here. The N&W Railroad come through here. I reckon it got in operation about 1892. At first Grandpap went to work on the railroad, then he went to work in the mines. As his boys got older he got them jobs in the mines. 'Course, they went to mining back then at 12, 13, 14 year old. Pap went in when he was 14, went to this old mine right over here at Borderland, on the Kentucky side. He said he went to trapping for 10 cents an hour. You've got these trap doors in the mines for motors pulling out the coal on the main lines. When the motor (it's like a little train; in the old days the cars were pulled by mules) comes through there you have to open a door, which held your air up at the work face. It was your ventilation back in them days. After the motor passed through, you'd shut the door, you see, so that the air'd stay up in the face where the miners were working. I've got an old cloth bank cap, got an old oil light on it, and that's what Pap used when he went in the mines. I said, "Pap, that didn't make much light. How'd you see with that rascal there?"

"Well, Charlie," he said, "you put yourself in my position. Back in them days that's the only thing we had. We thought we had it made," he said. "You could see good with it."

He said you could use about any kind of fuel in it, you could take kerosene or coal oil and burn that, or you could take "Sunshine Wax"—I can remember that whenever I was a boy that they still had it, it come in a little old box just like a candle. You could take that wax and stick it right down in that light there. The lamp has got a little old catcher on the side there that catches your wax as it come down and run around the spout. You could buy that wax for a nickel a box, and it would last you a week. And he said if you run out of money, didn't have enough to buy coal oil with, he said you could take this here old fat, just like when you killed your hogs and things, render that fat down into lard oil, he said, and burn that lard oil in your lamp. And he said that's all they had.

Pap had another cap—I've got it over here—that was a little bigger, but about the same difference. They called it a chore torch, and they burned oil or lard in it when they'd go out to do their chores. I can remember they didn't have no electricity or nothing in here until about 1941, and you had

to use a chore torch to do your chores with of a night. A lot of times, after you'd worked these fields and things, you'd be after dark and you'd have to have something to milk by. But now, they made their preparations, and they come through it pretty good there, but they had everything, and what they didn't have they'd make it. And that's one way you'd come through and the way you survived.

And back in the tail end of the Depression, in '42 there, just when the war was getting started, we lived in these old coal camps, and they'd run you from one house to another. As the mines played out they'd sell the houses right out from under you. They'd come in then and just tear most of them down and sell them for what they could get out of them, maybe salvage five or six hundred dollars worth of lumber. They'd give us boys about a dollar a day to tear them down. They just kept a-running us there, and we run out of places to go. We was over on the West Virginia side here when we got sold out again. My Pap, he said, "Damn if I ain't tired of being pushed around these here places. They've run me all my life and I'm getting tired of being run. I'm going to buy me a damn place!" I wondered what in the hell he's going to buy with. He's just worked these old mines in here like everybody else has. He ain't got nothing to buy with. Why, everyone in here is poor.

Old man, he kind of fooled us. He always was kind of shifty, and he come up with a little money, enough to pay a down payment on a little farm in Martin County. And he went down there and bought it off an old-timer. Twenty-four acres of land and a two-story house, one of these here pre–Civil War houses, way it was built. It was an awful fine place, nice barn, good pasture land, everything on it. We fixed everything up and got it rolling pretty good. That's the first home we could ever really call our own.

From then on after Pap got his start, that kind of set us all up. We had a place we could go. And once we got settled in I seemed like I had more time for things like music. I never could seem to get enough of that when I was a little old kid.

Most of the Blevinses could sing pretty good, but the real talent come from my mother's side, it was on the Wyatt and Hager side of the family. My mother could play just about anything she picked up, she was just gifted to it. She was real good on a piano, and she could play a handsaw, or blow one of these old jugs, or play an accordion, or just anything she played.

I remember one time whenever I was a boy, about 12 or 13 years old, didn't have nothing but an old big dommer hen. An old feller had an old handmade banjo. It had a ground-hog hide on it. I fell in love with that thing when I heard it, and I says, Lord, I'd like to have that banjo there. I asked him what he'd take for it and he said a dollar. I said, hot dog, a dollar was as big as a wagon wheel back then. I said, there's no way in the world I could get a-hold of a dollar. I happened to think, I had that old dommer hen, and I said, "You wouldn't take a big fat hen for that rascal, would you?"

He said, "What kind of a hen you got?"

I said, "I got an old big dommer hen!" I went and got it, took it over there.

"Yeah, yeah, I believe I'll trade you for that hen there, boy," he said, "except for one thing. Them strings cost a quarter a set. I'll have to take them strings off."

I said, "Well, that dad-burned banjo ain't no good without the strings!"

"I'll tell you," he said, "what I'll do. You go pick me a gallon of blackberries and I'll give you the strings." Well, I cut loose and got my old eight-pound lard bucket and filled it full of blackberries and hustled it back to him there.

And I said, "You tune that thing up for me." Well, he tuned it up, and I was so dad-burned tickled with it I knocked it out of tune before I got it to the house. I didn't know nothing about it nohow too much. I'd seen a banjo before but had never had a-hold of one, never was that fortunate. So I got it in and my mother looked at it.

"What have you got there, Charlie?"

"I got an old handmade banjo."

She said, "Where'd you get that?" And I told her what I had done.

"Let me see it." I reached it to her and she just sat down. It had them old wooden keys and things there, and she tuned that rascal up there and went to playing it. I got to listening. She was playing that "Groundhog" so plain you could smell him a-cooking.

"Where in the world did you learn to play banjo like that, Ma?"

"Well," she said, "I played one when I was a little girl, been several years since I picked one." She just played the daylights out of that thing. So I kind of picked it up from her.

I got kind of tickled at my pa there. I'd peck and bang on the old banjo and just raise all kinds of sand. And he'd say "Charlie!"

"What, Pa?"

"Get down over the riverbank and pick that thing, you're just aggravating me to death!" He'd run me over the riverbank, and I'd get down there where I wouldn't aggravate nobody and I'd just thump and raise sand with it. I got to where I would pick it a little bit, and got to coming in on that "John Henry" there. The old man was standing on top of the riverbank one day and heard me.

"Hey, Charlie!"

"What, Pa?"

"Come up here and play me one."

"Hell with you! You want to hear me, come down over the riverbank. That's where you run me to."

I asked him one day after I got grown, I said, "Hey, Pap, it don't seem like none of your people ever liked the five-string banjo too good. What was the matter?" About everybody in the country loved to hear the banjo back in them days. It was the leading entertainment. And I said to Pap, "You take an old banjo picker, he always got by when no one else did."

"Now," he said, "I like to hear one, but I'll tell you the reason, Charlie, that none of our people ever did like the five-string banjo. Way back there your grandpa, my dad, always told me, said if you see an old boy coming through the country, and he's got a five-string banjo strapped over his back and got a rooster under his arm, said you watch that rascal, said he's up to no good. He'll have your woman and be gone by dark. Said he'd pick, pick, pick around that woman, said she'd get struck on that banjo picking. Said, and he got that rooster, and he'd have your woman gone."

"Oh, foot, there ain't nothing to that."

He said, "Now Charlie, you watch him." And I did. And, by day, there was a whole lot of truth in it. Now the way we do it here, when we tell the truth now, we say it's a "coon dog" truth. 'Cause you can swear by your coon dog. That old coon dog, if he lies, we'll shoot him. So when we say it's a "coon dog" truth, then it's true.

Back in those days you'd see them old banjo pickers coming through the country, them old gals, they'd kind of fall for them, you know. And that rooster, well, that was his status. That let them know he had more than just that five-string banjo, he had a rooster, too.

About three years ago I went over to Jenkins, Kentucky, over to a Blevins family reunion they had over there at Laurel Lake every year. Me and my brother Bob always pick and grin a little bit for them there, and they get a big kick out of it. Well, that year one of my great-uncles, old man Hamilton Blevins, was there—he was around a hundred years old and an old Baptist preacher—and I seed him standing there. So whenever I got up there and hit down on that old banjo I seen that old man take off at a little trot. He shook his head and he left. That was my grandpa's brother. That belief is still held there. It come right back to him that an old banjo picker wasn't no 'count. So I just rared back and played that thing as loud as I could and he got way over there in the tall timbers and stood there shaking his head.

But mostly back in the old days the biggest majority of people could pick an old five-string banjo. They were about their only entertainment. That's the way I picked up my old tunes. If I found out a feller picked, if he lived up this hollow over here, well foot, I'd go up there. Just a little boy. If he had a little time on his hands, I'd just sit there and listen as long as he'd play. If it ended up where he'd get tired, I'd go hit up the next way. Maybe the next one would have a different tune or a different key or something, and I'd get me something a little different. I watched and watched. Back in them days there wasn't no such thing as a three-fingered roll, or picks. They had what they called a clawhammer style, but I

Beer was a quarter a bottle on opening day at the Red Robin in 1955. Pictured from left to right are Charlie Blevins's sister-in-law Tina Ruther, Charlie, his cousin Ford Blevins, and his father, Arthur. Photographer unknown.

Like any tavern keeper, Charlie Blevins dispenses free advice and good counsel. Photograph by Doug Yarrow.

Night is the time for the old music at the Red Robin. Charlie Blevins performs regularly, as do other musicians.
Photograph by Doug Yarrow.

never could get that down pat. So I just come through and got my own patent on my style. I got what you call kind of a loping style. I keep my time in it just like an old horse a-trotting. I could do a little of that clawhammer, but I was more comfortable with my own style.

I've got an old banjo here with a cat hide on it—I traded an old preacher out of it—I've traced it back, and I'd say that banjo is around 115 or 116 years old, been around this country for generations. It's got wooden keys on it, it's fretless. Back in our day we just called it a "slick-neck" banjo. We didn't know what a fret was, anyhow.

We'd see one of these here store-bought banjos, which in them days only cost you about 15 or 20 dollars. I seen this Sears and Roebuck catalog dated 1902 and you get one for $2.75. Now a set of strings costs $4.50. So it just tickled us to death even just to get a look at one back then. We didn't get to touch it, we just looked at it. Back then they would value them by the brackets, the more brackets you had on it to tighten that hide down much tighter, the more tone you could get out of it. With the modern plastic heads you never

hear much about brackets anymore. I've got three: a German one, an old Gibson RB 100, and I got one of these here whatchacallit Silver Eagle Keys that I like pretty good. They just run in dollar value today, but back then if you had a banjo you just made the best of it. There wasn't anything around sounded much better, 'cause about everybody had about the same thing. They all sounded good to me.

I've got another old instrument here, it's our old Appalachian plucking dulcimer. Now this old instrument here, it's been in these mountains for years and years. There's more of these went out of these mountains than ever came into them. This plucked dulcimer, I guess you could call it a cousin to your hammered dulcimer, one of the oldest instruments on record. It's mentioned in the Bible in the Book of Daniel, third and 10th chapters. The plucked dulcimers were brought in here from Scotland and Ireland and all over Europe. Most of them around here was made around Huntington, and I've run them all through these hills, down through Kentucky and Tennessee.

I run this dulcimer back. It was made during the Civil

War, about 1863. An old gentleman up here in Chatteroy made it, and I used to work with his nephew, Mose Alley, way back—he'd be up in his 90s now, so I know it's an old dulcimer. He said his uncle made two of them, he hadn't ever strung this one. An old preacher happened to get a-hold of this dulcimer and I traded him out of it. I traded him an old shotgun. That thing could shoot and throw rocks for 30 minutes and just kill from both ends. You know, I ain't heard from that preacher since? I don't know whether the shotgun got him, or what. But I still got the dulcimer. If he's gone, may his soul rest in peace, 'cause he sure left me a good piece.

I could play you a lot of different tunes on it, but back in these mountains, if you don't know the "Wildwood Flower" you ain't considered a mountaineer. We call that the West Virginia national anthem, and when you're off somewhere playing music, that's the first thing they'll ask for. "Hey, buddy, play that 'Wildwood Flower.'" Then you can play it and they'll turn around and say, "Buddy, do you know that 'Wildwood Flower'?"

This here was a good, soft music, and these old mountain people enjoyed it in here. Well, that's what it is, "dulcimer" in Latin, I believe it's "sweet, soft music."

I have a lot of old pictures here, old photographs. Here's one, John Fleming was his name in this country, but it was Mullens to start with. I knowed that old rascal. He died back in the '50s and he had 12 toes, six on each foot. He was what you'd call our king bootlegger, from down on Kenny's Creek at the Wayne-Mingo county border. He come in this country from Kentucky where he had to leave—I was reading where he had 37 charges agin him over there. He was supposed to have killed a man over there, and according to legend he called himself half-bear, half-cat, or half-wolf. He was something else! His feet was so big he couldn't get his shoes on and he went barefooted. I've got another picture of him setting in an old cane-bottom chair at his home on Kenny's Creek after he got older. He looks about the same in that picture, them old feet spreaded all over the porch, and his old britchy legs rolled up there. He kept the judges pretty well supplied with moonshine. There was Judge Ferguson. They'd catch old John and take him down there once in a while. Judge'd ask him, said, "John, is that moonshine any good?"

He'd say, "You ought to know, you've drunk enough of it!" And old judge just look at him and grin. He'd let him off kind of light. So he kept the judge supplied down there.

One day the judge was a-holding court there, and old John tried to get a gallon to him. He got him an old big pumpkin and cut the top off it, and took the stuffin's out of it. Then he put a gallon jug of 'shine down in that old big pumpkin. He went in the courthouse then, old judge was a-holding court, you know, he seed John come in, kinda

"Now the way we do it here, when we tell the truth, we say it's a 'coon dog' truth," Charlie Blevins says, "'cause you can swear by your coon dog." Photograph by Doug Yarrow.

winked at old John and grinned a little bit. So old John says, "Judge, I brought you a pumpkin."

"Yeah, John," he says. "Just bring it up here and roll it back under my desk." So old John walked up there, and them 12 big toes all over that courthouse floor, carrying that pumpkin. He got up to the judge's bench and just laid that pumpkin there and took them old big toes, and went to pushing that pumpkin back towards the desk where the judge was holding court. Rolled it back and says, "There you are judge." Old judge had him a gallon sitting right there between his feet in that pumpkin, and John walked out of there just a-grinning. He knew what he'd done for the old judge.

And he sold it to the high sheriff over here in Logan County. And there was a bunch caught him one time, he was going down there with a wagonload of it. This bunch of deputies didn't know him, and they captured old John, had his load and everything. Well, the sheriff had already paid for that load of white lightning that John had on the wagon. When they brought him in and the sheriff found out who he was he hollered, "What in the hell did you fellers do with that damn wagon?"

"We got it confiscated, Sheriff."

"Let's go get that wagon!"

They went and got the wagon, and the sheriff turned old John loose. "That's my damn liquor, I've paid for it," he said. That old John had a time. He's got descendants all over the country.

All these pictures and things reminds me of when this country was young and wild, and of how my family come here to help settle it. What they went through has helped us younger fellers—'course, I'm not that young anymore, right at 56 years old—but it taught us a whole lot, learned us how to kind of survive on our own. Today, now, they agitate the people pretty bad right through this recession, inflation, and everything. But you take these old-timers around my age. They know what it was back then. We can look back and think, well foot, people now got it made to what we had it. I mean, you could make out just fine on the bare necessities.

People get used to having a lot of stuff they don't need. That's what they look forward to all the time. You deprive them of it and they think they're suffering. There ain't no suffering to that. The way we was raised kind of made us self-sufficient, the way we come through. 'Course now, we're having a time with this younger generation. A lot of it, I guess, is our own fault, 'cause we kind of made it a little too easy on them, which everybody wants to make it easy for their kids. But I try to keep mine in line and let them know where it come from. I know they got it a lot easier than what we had but I like to make them where they're self-sufficient and where they know they can survive without being on this or that. That's one thing my family never did do, we always was proud. We never did accept no hand-outs, no relief, or nothing else. We didn't care how low we got, we'd always dig for ourselves. We'd help our neighbor if we could, if he was down and out, we'd help him. That's the way we worked back in these mountains. And my family come through like that, like these old pioneer settlers. And most of them are hanging like that right today. I know I've got some brothers just about like I am, independent as a hog on ice. We always just stayed right with it.

EDITOR'S NOTE: This article first appeared in the winter 1982 issue of *Goldenseal* (vol. 8, no. 4). In 1992 Charlie Blevins moved the contents of his Red Robin Inn across the river when the business was closed to make way for the Corridor G highway project. His museum of relics and antiques, including dulcimers, banjos, mining gear, and other Appalachian memorabilia, sits about six miles north of Williamson on Rt. 292 in Kentucky. He still plays music and says he's "booked into several places" on a regular basis. One of his favorites is a yearly appearance at the Augusta Heritage Arts Workshops in Elkins, West Virginia.

PART 3

Dulcimer Players

Russell Fluharty

THE DULCIMER MAN

Ken Sullivan

"I was born on the head of Dudley Fork, that's a fork of Flat Run." Thus Russell Fluharty begins the story of his 80 years, speaking of the Marion County countryside he loves. Both of the streams he mentions are among the smaller tributaries of the Monongahela River, as is nearby Mahans Run, the most important landmark of his life. The three head up in neighboring hollows in the rolling hills north of Mannington.

This country has always been home to Russell. He has left it many times, ranging far and wide to promote his favorite musical instrument, the ancient hammered dulcimer. But he has always returned. The big move of his life came when he was still a toddler, and it was from one of the creeks to another. "We moved here to Mahans Run when I was two years old," he reports. "And believe it or not, I can remember that move just as well as I can remember anything. A lot of people will say they can't remember when they was five years old or something like that, but I remember that."

Russell has a story to prove the point, as he often does. "I had a little pet groundhog. My dad made a wooden box for me, to keep him in and to move him in. It was made out of heavy, rough, inch lumber, and this old belting they got around the oil wells was the hinges. When the lid opened back, it still had a little pressure on it, wanting to come shut. This little groundhog was maybe a third grown. I was getting him ready to move and he hopped up on the edge of the box and that lid just flapped down there and crushed the little fellow. And of course, that crushed my moving day, too.

"We come from the head of Dudley and a little over halfway up Mahans Run, about eight miles," Russell continues. "It was in the fall of the year, just after corn-cutting time. My dad, as he moved us with the horses and sled, would also bring a load of fodder. That way, he killed two birds with one stone."

On Dudley Fork the Fluhartys had lived at the homeplace of Russell's mother, looking after Grandmother Efaw. "The Efaws had always lived on that side of the hill," he says of his mother's people, "and the Fluhartys on this side." Both families go back a long way in this part of West Virginia, and Russell has traced the Fluharty side to its European origins. "My people were originally Norsemen," he explains. "They came down into Ireland. The first name I could ever get track of was Flaitbait. When they got into Ireland, they became

Russell Fluharty at home in his music room in 1986. Photograph by Michael Keller.

O'Flahertys, and later on just Flahertys. They got over here and they become Fluhartys."

In America, the Fluhartys headed west early and then worked their way back to the Appalachian region. "When they first landed on this shore, they went west," according to Russell. "I remember my grandfather telling many times about them coming from Iowa back this way.

"In the old days, it seemed like people got around any-

The Marion County home of Russell Fluharty, The Dulcimer Man. Photograph by Michael Keller.

how, whether they walked or rode horseback or thumbed on a freight train," Russell muses. "My mother's brother, when he was a young man, 19 years old, went west to get a job. His name was Solomon Efaw. He landed in St. Louis, farmer boy, you know, walking down the street. Guy come along, looked at him and said, 'Stranger in town, ain't you, Mister?' And Uncle said yes, he was. He said, 'I'm looking for work.' The man said, 'You're lucky. You just found the right man.' He said, 'You come go along with me.'

"He went along with him a little ways, and a few blocks down there that man pulled a gun out, just shot a man, throwed the gun down and run. So Uncle, in a brand-new town and didn't know which way to go, he was just whirling 'round and 'round. The cops got him—the gun laid there, see—and they sent him up. He was 38 years old when he got out of there. The man that did this, on his deathbed confessed.

"I remember my uncle coming in, walking from Mannington over. He had on a suit of clothes that the shoulders come down to his elbows, and he had one dollar. They give him a train ticket, a new suit of clothes and one dollar. And that was the way he come back home. The thing that impressed me was how fast he eat. Amazing, how much he could eat in a minute or thereabouts."

Solomon Efaw exerted an early musical influence on his young nephew. "While he was in prison, he learned to play the fiddle," Russell relates. "He taught me to play a tune, 'Pop Goes the Weasel.' He was a pretty good fiddler. The only

thing I couldn't hardly stand was that he made a horrible face when he played. He rolled his eyes and twisted his face till it looked like it was killing him. But he seemed to enjoy it.

"Of course, most of Mother's brothers played the fiddle," Russell elaborates. "That might have been what got me going." But he recalls that his Uncle Solomon brought back an unusual style from his stay in prison, and also the trait of singing while he fiddled. Russell later adapted the latter habit to his playing of the hammered dulcimer, another instrument generally not accompanied by voice.

Meanwhile, the family had settled into its new home on Mahans Run. Father Arlie Fluharty had been born on the head of the run and moving back was a homecoming to him. He established his family at the old Lewis Cook place, one of the early farms on Mahans. Russell recalls Mr. Cook cautioning his father on the proper care of the old place. "'Arlie,' he said, 'take good care of her. Remember she's over a hundred years old.' He was talking about the house, you know. It was just an old log house, walls about 18 inches thick. You made two steps before you'd get through the door."

The old house continues in use today, although now in other hands. Russell occupies another place, but he is still nearby and still on Mahans Run. He and his wife live in retirement in a small house on the stream's bottomland. Russell busies himself around the place, getting out to make dulcimer music from time to time. The West Augusta Historical Society is a special interest, particularly the spectacular Mannington Round Barn, which Russell and the Society

David Frost put two of West Virginia's leading folk figures on his national TV show in 1970. Here Frost (second from the right) talks with New Martinsville toymaker Dick Schnacke while Russell Fluharty (holding the dulcimer) looks on with football player Alex Karras. Photographer unknown.

were instrumental in restoring. The folk strategy game, Fox and Geese, is another pet project, as Russell works to propagate the old board game among modern youngsters. In between, he will sometimes make time to answer questions about the past, as he did at this interview last September.

Life on the Fluharty farm was one of simple abundance but few frills, he recalls. Food was plentiful and money scarce. "For a long time we didn't have any money," Russell comments. "I mean, any money. We took butter and eggs and produce to the store, and got a due bill and traded that out. Then we'd take some cabbage, corn or something, and trade it. It didn't seem like we needed money like you do now. You could go out and earn a little money and be happy with it. But anymore, you just can't do any good with a little money. You got to have a lot."

Everyone worked. "Either work or starve, that was the way it was," Russell says today. He considers himself fortunate to have had a father who taught him to work and made the learning fun. "I learned to do most everything. It so happened that my father was a very congenial sort of somebody. Lots of times, I would rather work with him than go out with kids to play. He made a hard job easy by causing us to enjoy it."

Russell remembers doing the sort of things that other farm boys did. He worked with oxen and other stock, in the hay field and in the woods. His formal education through the first eight years came at the little schoolhouse on Mahans Run, the same school his daughters later attended. Religious

training was taken care of at the local Evangelical United Brethren chapel, later affiliated with the United Methodists. The church was the spiritual bedrock of the Fluharty world. Russell's father and grandfather helped build the church, using the wood of two great poplar trees according to family lore, and grandfather Conrad Fluharty was the first superintendent.

Marion County was changing as Russell grew through boyhood. Industry edged out family farming as the economy matured. Oil had been discovered more than 15 years before Russell's birth, sparking growth in lumbering through the demand for oil well timbers. The two extractive industries, plus a local sanitary pottery, offered exciting possibilities to a boy coming of age. Russell's memory of timbering goes back to his early days.

"When I was a boy, there was big timber in here," he says. "There was virgin timber, a lot of it at that time. I've seen them chop the sides off of logs so that the road wagon wheels wouldn't rub. They'd take the front wheels off a road wagon, and just stand the tongue up like so and drive them dogs in there. When they pulled the tongue down, it loaded right there between the wheels and the truck." Russell pauses to ponder human inventiveness, especially the principle of leverage that allows a slender wagon tongue to raise a massive log off the ground. "The man that invented the pry did something great, because you know yourself a very small man can move a big something if he can get a pry on the thing, the right kind. The front end of the log rode the front

Grandson Jerry Taylor worked public appearances with Russell Fluharty two decades ago. Here they are ready for a job in October 1964. Photographer unknown.

wheels and the back end just drug on the ground and went pretty easy.

"At that time, they used oxen, lots of oxen. When we first moved on Mahans Run, the schoolhouse was on up above my father's house. Moving it down here, they got stuck fast between some apple trees right close to the yard fence at home, right up agin the fence and couldn't go any further. They took off four or five pairs of horses and put one yoke of oxen on there and pulled her right through that place."

Russell also has vivid memories of the oil and gas boom, which lured able-bodied farmers into industrial work. "After the oil boom come, many a time we'd be putting up hay or something, and they'd come and want a string of tools moved from one well to another, real important," he says. "Dad would just unhook from the hay rig and say, 'I'll be back in a couple of hours.' Man, when he began to work them horses out there and get two or three dollars a day out of them, then we was in the money!"

The drilling tools were pulled up for moving to the next well site, Russell explains. "My father had a road wagon," he says. "He would come by and they would load what they had. Maybe they just had a bit and a stem, a bailer and a rope. They used a big rope cable which was about two or three inches through." Sometimes the cable could be dragged from one well to the next. "I've seen them hook onto the end of a cable with horses and they'd run it off the bull wheels and take it to the other well and hook it onto the

wheels over there and start their engine up. As they run it off of this one they put it on that one, see. Didn't even load it on the wagon."

It turns out that Russell knows a lot about early drilling, a subject of which he likes to talk. "When I first knew about drilling they just used rope cables to drill with. There's a stem on there, sometimes 25, 30 feet long. You could use a certain size stem on maybe two or three bits. If the drilling got tough, they put a set of jars on. After the bit hit on the bottom, that was just like hitting it with a hammer again, you know. There was so much give, so much stretch in the rope cable, and when they was down pretty deep they'd run that down there and stop it real sudden with the brakes on the bull wheels. When they did that, the rope would stretch out and you'd see the bit hit the bottom. You could feel it if you'd hold to the cable, the stretch of the rope. You had to know just exactly how to do that to make it drill. Those old drillers'd go over there and they'd stand in the hole with that rope.

"They started out with a 13-inch hole, 13-inch bit," Russell continues. "Then about the next step from that was a 10-inch bit. And the further down they went, the smaller it got, till they used a six-inch bit. It depended on how deep they went and where they located the oil and all like that. Lots of times they'd hit real solid, hard rock and drill two or three days, it wouldn't hardly go down a bit.

"A driller had to know his soils, whatever was in there,

rocks and the slate and the coal and everything, and know what to do with it when he got to it, see. There was places there was sand and that'd cave in and just muck up the tools till they wouldn't work. I've seen them spend maybe a day or two just a-jerking on a set of tools to get them out of the hole. Sometimes, they couldn't do it. They'd have to run a rope cutter down there, cut the rope in two, drill back down to it and then hook onto it with something and pull it out. And I've seen the time they never got whatever was in there out. They moved the rig."

The drilling rigs were driven by stationary steam engines, requiring a complicated power linkage. "They had the engine in the engine house and then they had a belt house with a big wheel in that," Russell explains, his hands moving through the air. "That gave it extra power, the small wheel on the engine and the big belt wheel here, see. It had an arm on the side of it, called the pitman, and this was what they hooked their beam onto. I remember one man kind of stuttered a little bit. He'd say, 'Charlie, pppp-put the pitman on.'"

Russell chuckles at the thought, and goes on to explain that the pitman was a connecting arm that worked similar to those on railroad locomotives. "Same way, see, only this one on the beam hung down on the front end of it and the back end went back in the derrick and was over the hole. The bull wheel sits on behind that, further back. And the cable goes up and over the crown pulley on top of the derrick and comes back down in the middle."

It is an impressive explanation from a man who spent most of his own career in other lines of work. Russell worked some for the oil companies, digging tank grades and such, but mostly his is the intuitive knowledge gained by growing up in the oil fields. Marion County youngsters got to know the oil and gas business early, he says, taking the opportunity to tell about another aspect of the industry. After the wells were drilled they were set to pumping, he explains, with steam passing from a central boiler house through steam boxes to the wellhead pump engines. Children found the industrial maze a made-to-order playground. "Us kids would run barefooted in the wintertime on them boxes, because the steam went through there and they was warm, you know. You couldn't hang onto it very good with snow-covered, slick shoes, but you could take your shoes off and barefoot you could run on them warm boxes. Sometimes it would go 25, 30 feet across the holler, big scaffolds underneath."

It was a natural progression from such robust play to the hard labor of a man's work. Russell Fluharty made the transition at a young age. He took his first serious job, carrying water to workers building the road to Rachel, while still a schoolboy of about 10 years old. "Bought my first bicycle working on that road, carrying water," he says. "Every bit of work that was done out there was hand work. They just dug her out with a mattock, put her in the wheelbarrow and hauled it away someplace."

Soon he was doing heavier work, carrying slabs away from the saw at the sawmill where his father worked at the

Russell Fluharty and Jim Meade play a double mountain dulcimer—a so-called courting dulcimer—at the 1973 West Virginia State Folk Festival in Glenville. Photographer unknown.

time. "I drawed the same wages as my dad did when I was 13 years old," he recalls. "Buddy, I worked, though—13 years old and off-bearing on a sawmill. Some of them big slabs were two feet wide on the butt and eight inches deep, anywhere from 12 to 32 feet long." The biggest timbers cut at the mill were beams for oil rigs, Russell says. "Made me feel pretty good, making as much money as my dad," he adds.

Such industriousness brought its rewards, as Russell explains. "When I was 16 years old, I bought my first automobile," he notes. "I paid $409.17 for a brand-new car in 1922, and I paid cash for it. Model T Ford Roadster, and it was a beauty. I mean, I knew it was a beauty!"

Russell's voice crackles as he recalls that car and what it took to get it. "I had to work some to get it, you know, selling potatoes and whatever I'd raise. Sometimes my dad would tell me, 'Now, pick you out a sheep and it'll be yours. If you happen to get a ewe, you can raise you some sheep next year.' A lot of boys didn't want to work, but I enjoyed working, really I did. Why, I'd still rather work than be sitting here talking." That pops out before he thinks about it. "Not that I'm against talking to you."

By the time he acquired the new Ford, Russell had taken his first steady adult job, at the Bowers Pottery, with the company shaving the child labor law a little to get him in before he was quite 16. He would spend the coming years mostly alternating between the pottery and local coal mines. "I worked between Rachel mines and the pottery, whichever one was working better than the other," he explains. "Mine superintendent Rosie Fletcher finally got till he'd say, 'Now, you won't leave me this time, will you?' They knew they could depend on me working. Even though I'd move on sometimes, I could still get a job whenever I went back and asked."

In his heart, however, Russell would have preferred to work outdoors. It suited him better and there were health considerations as well. "I liked the best to be out farming or in the oil fields, where you was out into the good fresh air," he says. "The coal mines had the dust and black lung, and silicosis for the pottery. In 1944, the superintendent at the mines said that he could get us deferred from the draft on account of we was doing special work. None of us wanted that, but when I was taking the examination they X-rayed my lungs and said, 'Your lungs is 50 percent gone.' Said, 'You wouldn't be able to retreat as fast as you ought to.'"

Russell enjoys talking of work, but it is clear that there are only two great loves in his life. The first, music, has been with him as long as he can remember. "Every once in a while somebody'll ask me, 'How did you learn to play all these instruments?' I tell them I just growed up knowing how. That's really the way it was. I played the fiddle and the banjo and guitar early-like in life."

Russell's other love is Marjory Ice Fluharty. "We've been married a hundred years," the proud husband tells visitors, "50 for her and 50 for me." Those years have set lightly on Margie. She is a chipper, vivacious woman whose eyes glitter when Russell is around. Her family is of German extraction with an impeccable West Virginia lineage. Patriarch Adam Ice was the first white child born in the Monongahela Valley, in 1767, and Andrew Ice started Western Virginia's first authorized ferry in 1785. Russell reports that there is Shawnee blood in the family, as well.

It won't do to call Margie his second love, but the fact is that Russell discovered her as a direct result of his music making. Their meeting was almost an accident, as he tells the story. "It used to be, we had Indian medicine shows that went up and down this little valley from Fairmont to Littleton, and also the old summer stock shows that were too old to play around New York," he says. "I kind of sneaked around and got acquainted with one of the fellows. He knew I played some music, so he asked me to come and play for them. A friend of mine was the draftsman for the South Penn Oil Company and he played with me, then I did a few things by myself, just solo. We kind of got off our main route and went out to Joetown one time. And out there's where I met Margie.

"The amazing thing is," he adds with a chuckle, "the first night I met her, I took her cousin home. Then the next time I saw her, she had come into Mannington to go to high school. I run across her there the first day of school. I was looking for her." Russell himself was out of school at the time, working for the pottery.

By the time he met Margie, Russell had already begun a lifelong association with another old friend, the antique hammered dulcimer that shares the couple's home. There is a story to that meeting, too, one he tells with glee. "I had an uncle, Ezry Fluharty, that was a game hunter," he says. The introduction seems a long way from dulcimer playing, but Russell Fluharty always comes around to the point. "During the early part of my life, I game hunted with him quite a bit. After I got interested in music he kept telling me, 'I have an old dulcimer at home in the grainhouse loft that I would like for you to learn to play.' Said, 'It makes beautiful music.' But I'd never heard tell of a dulcimer, never had seen one, and it didn't interest me a bit, you know. But he continued to talk about it.

"One night we'd went to Highland, over where I had originally moved from, on the head of Dudley. We'd walked out there and it was nine miles. We took turnabout taking the game, and this night we caught a big raccoon out around the Highland Church. When we got back to my uncle's home, I'm wore out, five o'clock in the morning in January. I'm so cold, so hungry, so tired, so sleepy, that when he said, 'Now, about that old dulcimer,' I just says, 'Uh-huh, I'll take it.' So he went up into the grainhouse loft and he ruffled around there for about half an hour, and finally he come down with this old fellow that I'm playing now.

"As I come down the valley, I thought to myself, 'Golly, I'm glad it's dark. If anybody would see me with this raccoon and a dulcimer on my back, they'd think I'm crazy.' But you know, that old fellow became a part of me, really just a part of me. I didn't go anywhere without him."

Russell doesn't know the full history of his instrument, but figures he has it pretty well documented for a century and a half. "I've got it tracked down to where it's 144 years old now," he reports. "My uncle told me that a man named Ira Phillips had owned it. When I went and talked to Ira Phillips, he said, 'I got it off of Johnny Koon down toward Farmington, the miller.' So I went to Johnny Koon and I asked him about it. 'Yeah,' he said, 'I owned that thing. Got if off my brother, Charlie.' I took it to Charlie Koon, asked him where he got it and he said, 'Don't know. Just seemed like it was always here.' He said, 'The thing I do know is that they played it at Sissie's wedding.' Sissie's wedding was in January 1842, and come this January this instrument will be 145 years old, for sure. But it could be older than that."

Coming from his uncle's grainhouse, Russell's dulcimer was full of mud wasp nests and in bad need of repair. Upon taking it apart, he made another discovery which helped to trace the history of the instrument. "I took the wasps' nests out of it and found a piece of what Mother said was foolscap paper, kind of a brown ruled paper. And on this paper it says, 'Repaired by William Varner in 1878.' I threw that away, just wanted to get the junk out of it. Wish now that I'd saved it." Varner was an instrument maker of the time, and Russell theorizes that he may have built the dulcimer in the first place.

Whatever its exact life story, the old dulcimer was Russell's to keep only if he could get music out of it. "My uncle gave it to me under a condition," he recalls. "If I'd learn to play one tune on it, he'd give it to me.

"I let it go for a year or two after I got it and one night we was game hunting again. 'About that old dulcimer,' he said, 'have you learned to play it yet?' I said, 'No, I haven't.' He said, 'Now, if you don't learn to play that thing, I'm going to come and get it.' So I thought, 'Well, I'll do something with it.'" There was no one around who knew anything about the instrument, so the young musician had to figure it out as he went along. "I just tuned him like a piano would be, Do Re Me Fa So La Ti Do, see, until I run out of strings," he says with a grin.

Fluharty's inability to find anyone to help proved typical for several years to come. He agrees that the hammered dulcimer was nearly a "lost" instrument, one which had been out of favor for nearly a generation when he picked it up and which would be preserved for coming generations by only a handful of people such as himself. The present popularity of the instrument was unforeseeable at the time.

Russell Fluharty received the 1986 Vandalia Award. Photograph by Michael Keller.

"For 40 years I played that thing and I would say, 'As far as I know, I'm the only person playing this kind of an instrument,'" he reports of this period. "I played the Newport Folk Festival, the Philadelphia Folk Festival, the Smithsonian Folklife Festival in D.C., and the National Folk Festival and oodles of places for the Commerce Department of West Virginia, as far away as Charlotte, Indianapolis, and up to Cedar Point, Ohio, and Harrisburg, New York, Baltimore. No way did anybody ever confront me with another dulcimer player.

"The Smithsonian has a picture of Henry Ford carrying a dulcimer down the streets of Detroit, back in the early 1900s. I was thinking that he might have been trying to revive the dulcimer and come up with the Model T Ford! But from that time on, from the early 1900s, seemed like it just disappeared. I found some when I first began. But when I would go back maybe four, five or 10 years after, they'd say, 'Oh, the kids throwed that away, they burnt it up, did away with it, I don't know what become of it.'"

Russell Fluharty says he and his wife, Margie, have been married for 100 years—50 years for him and 50 years for her. Here, Margie joins him in a favorite song. Photograph by Michael Keller.

Russell was delighted to find out that his mother was one of the older people who could tell him something about the hammered dulcimer. "Come to find out, my mother had played a dulcimer when she was a girl," he says. "She told me about how they used to play it for square dances and house warmings, and wood gatherings and cuttings, and bean stringings and so on like that." The dulcimer was generally played by itself, unaccompanied by other instruments or singing, Russell learned. "It at one time was real popular," he says.

That popularity was a thing of the past by the time Russell started researching the instrument. "I found probably dozens of instruments and four or five players, but at that time they were all old people," he reports. One of the few knowledgeable people close to his own age was the late Patrick Ward Gainer, West Virginia University's legendary folklorist. "Dr. Gainer played the mountain dulcimer, the Appalachian dulcimer," Russell says, speaking of the unrelated three- or four-

stringed lap dulcimer. "Sometimes we would both be at the same place. He is the first person I ever heard call mine a hammered dulcimer."

Pat Gainer founded the State Folk Festival at Glenville, West Virginia's most venerable music festival. Fluharty was there from the early days, finding Glenville a useful place to continue his search for old-time dulcimer players. One he recalls in particular. "There was an old man named Ira Mayfield," he remembers. "He lived up about Moundsville and he came to Glenville to the State Folk Festival. The last time I heard the man play, I helped him, kind of steadied him as he came out on the stage. Most of the old people soon was gone and that left nobody in this section that knew anything about a dulcimer."

Nobody, that is, except Russell Fluharty himself. By then he was as much an authority on the instrument as anyone around and he set out to spread the word. These were his busiest performing years as he and the old dulcimer traveled everywhere they were welcome. "I played for practically everything," he says today. "I played for colleges, grade schools, churches, nursing homes, all kind of festivals. Sometimes I'd do two or three in one day—play here in the morning, someplace else in the afternoon, someplace else at night. And I never went anyplace, only where I was invited."

Grandson Jerry Taylor joined him for a while in the 1960s, before moving on to military service and several years as a house musician at WWVA's "Wheeling Jamboree." After Jerry left, Russell organized the Mountaineer Dulcimer Club in 1971, to put the promotion of the old music on a more formal footing. The club has been successful from the first, attracting interest far beyond the Mountain State. "A lot of times we'll have eight, 10 states represented at one of our meetings," the founder reports. "One time we had a member in Tokyo, Japan, two in England, and one in Mexico."

Sometimes invitations came to play for the high and mighty. Russell tells of one such occasion. "When Governor Moore was governor before, I was doing travel shows for the Commerce Department and seems as though he asked about me to come to the Greenbrier Hotel and play for the Republican Governors Conference. There was about three or four of us. They called us 'resource people'—me and Frank George and Dr. Maggie Ballard and Aunt Jennie Wilson. Our audience was the governors and their wives, including Governor Nelson Rockefeller and his wife and the governor of California, Ronald Reagan, and his wife. So, I've played for a vice president of these United States and the president and his wife." Russell's eyes sparkle at the recollection.

The governors got the same Russell Fluharty that thousands of ordinary West Virginians have been treated to over the years. The act is low-key, consisting of an energetic playing of hymns, patriotic tunes, and other familiar numbers. Russell departs from tradition in considering the hammered dulcimer an instrument to sing to, and his high-pitched voice joins in on favorite songs. Audiences can count on some bashful commentary on the ancient instrument, the

music and the musician's philosophy of life. As much as anything, Russell's show is a visual treat, the sight of a sprightly man in a plaid shirt and vintage picking hat fussing over a table-height instrument from another age. West Virginia and American flags stand guard at the front corners of his dulcimer.

It was for all these things—for the music and the singing and the enthusiasm, and for the sheer persistence in clinging to an almost-forgotten folk instrument until it could be handed safely into the hands of a new generation—that Russell Fluharty was given the 1986 Vandalia Award, West Virginia's highest folklife honor. At the Cultural Center south garden his name joins that of his old friend Aunt Jennie, enshrined among their peers in our state's pantheon of human treasures.

Maybe Russell sneaks a look at the big bronze plaque when he is in Charleston, but at home on Mahans Run things are kept in perspective. The Vandalia certificate holds a place of honor among other awards in the Fluharty music room, but a place secondary to that occupied by the battered dulcimer he carried home from a coon hunt long ago. Russell holds matters in similar perspective in his heart. Looking back, he is not able to sum up a long life in a few words. Work, family, and the 50-year love story with Margie crowd each other in his recollections. But it is clear that his contribution to saving the hammered dulcimer ranks among his proudest accomplishments. "I think I had something to do with preserving the dulcimer as it is now," he modestly concludes.

EDITOR'S NOTE: This article first appeared in the winter 1986 issue of *Goldenseal* (vol. 12, no. 4). The organizer and president of the Mountaineer Dulcimer Club and a charter member of the West Augusta Historical Society, Russell Fluharty received the Vandalia Award in 1986. He died at the age of 82 on March 29, 1989, in Fairmont, West Virginia.

Worley Gardner

MOUNTAIN MUSIC, DANCE, AND DULCIMERS

Mark Crabtree

"THAT old man who played the dulcimer would come to your house and play all day if you gave him a meal. If you had moonshine to drink, he'd play better and stay longer."

That old man, Simon Meyers, and his hammered dulcimer playing started a lifelong love of the instrument for Worley Gardner.

It doesn't take a free meal or moonshine to get Gardner to play music. You're likely to find him playing dulcimer, mandolin, fiddle, or banjo at most any gathering of old-time musicians anywhere near his Morgantown home, at festivals around the state, and, of course, at the Winter Music Festival he directs.

Playing what he calls "mountain music" started early for Gardner, but it wasn't until many years later that he learned to play dulcimer, on an instrument that had been played by Simon Meyers himself. It's a long story, and a good one.

Worley was born February 19, 1919, in rural Monongalia County. "I grew up on a typical West Virginia farm—it was hilly as the devil! It was halfway between Blacksville and Daybrook, four miles to either place. All the work was done with horses. We didn't have a tractor back then. We raised cattle and grew our own food.

"The paying crop on the farm was cattle. We didn't take them to auction in those days. Buyers would come around every fall. They'd make you an offer by the pound. You'd either take it or hope someone would come by with a better offer. When you did sell, they'd take your cattle off and weigh them, then you'd get your payment. That was the farm's earnings for the year. We also had a gas well on the farm. We got a royalty check for that every three months.

"There was a gas boom then. My dad, William Gardner, worked a team of horses in the oil fields when he could. What he did was put the casing in the wells. Sometimes he'd be gone for a week at a time making the rounds of the wells in the territory."

Music was the main pastime at the Gardner farm. "We didn't have a radio, except for a crystal set, so we played our own music. My dad and my grandfather played fiddle. Most of my brothers and sisters played an instrument." Worley was the youngest of 12 children, so there was quite a lot of music. "We would play at the house, whoever was there and wanted to play. We played a good bit. I learned some songs

Worley Gardner on his music porch in 1992 with a hammered dulcimer of his own creation. Photograph by Mark Crabtree.

from my dad, like 'Bull Pup,' that I've never heard anywhere else."

Worley played guitar first, but it wasn't long before he picked up mandolin and banjo. Banjo was the only instrument he ever took lessons on. "I play two-finger picking," Worley says. "It's the old type that was out in the country around that time. You use your thumb and index finger. It's not a style you find much anymore. This fellow in the neighborhood, Elva Foley, came and tried to teach me lessons. Practically his whole family played banjo."

It wasn't long before Worley started playing guitar for square dances. He remembers, "I helped play for dances up there. I don't know how old I was, but my sisters would have to carry my guitar, because it was too much for me to carry that distance.

"In those days they had dances in people's houses. They'd empty up a room in the house. Sometimes they'd have two adjoining rooms and we'd play music in the doorway between the two rooms. They always had a caller for each set of four couples. He'd dance within the set and call while he was dancing. It was up to each caller what dance he wanted to do. When you'd look out over the sets there'd be four or five different figures going on at the same time.

"That went on for a long time because there wasn't all these mikes and power equipment. I played dances in '42 in Fairview at a great big dance hall. They had 10 or 12 sets in there and every one of them had a caller within the set."

Worley played regularly for dances, but the first time he danced himself was in 1936 at the Fox Hunters Reunion in Daybrook. "Even after I wouldn't dance. I thought it was crazy. I couldn't remember all that stuff."

Margaret Tennant remembers that as her first dance, too,

but evidently her future husband failed to make an impression. She says, "I knew Worley but I don't recall seeing him there. We grew up about six miles apart as the crow flies over the hills, but that would be a long walk following the roads. I didn't know him at all until we started high school together." Margaret started dating Worley when he came home for weekends while attending West Virginia University. They celebrated their 50th wedding anniversary in January.

The Gardners had the first of four daughters before Worley left for the war in 1943. He spent 22 months with the Second Division Artillery as a high speed radio operator, leaving the service as a T4 Technical Sergeant.

When he returned from World War II, Gardner went back to his job with Monongahela Power Company. "After the war I wasn't involved with music or dancing in any way, shape, or form for a number of years. I was concentrating all my energies into making a living for my family. I didn't think I had time for anything else."

It was about 10 years before Gardner was drawn back to playing music. "The company was going to have a square dance. They got me to come and help play music. Then I played for years at square dances, but I didn't call and I didn't dance."

Margaret remembers that it was in the '60s they started dancing and Worley got interested in calling. "We went to Waynesburg, Pennsylvania, to dances in the firehall," she

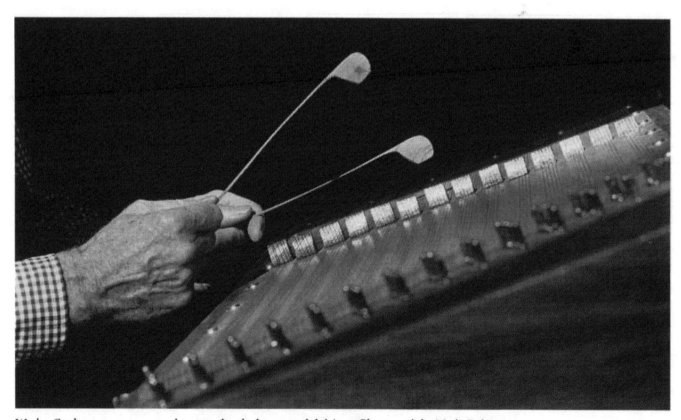

Worley Gardner says anyone can learn to play the hammered dulcimer. Photograph by Mark Crabtree.

CLASS *of* 1936
DAYBROOK HIGH SCHOOL
FAIRVIEW W.VA.

Margaret and Worley Gardner met at Daybrook High School and appear side-by-side in this yearbook photo of the class of 1936. Photographer unknown.

says. "Buckwheat Lemley from Blacksville called. Worley liked him so well that he took a tape recorder and taped Buckwheat's calls."

Worley says, "I thought he was the best caller I'd ever heard. He had almost perfect timing. He made his calls go with the music, but it was also in perfect time with your motion on the floor. That's what I liked about Buckwheat's calls. It wasn't just standing up there yelling words at different times. I call it singing calls. Maybe he had different words for it."

With singing calls each dance fits a particular tune, Worley explains. "You sing the calls to the melody. Buckwheat was the one that introduced me to that. I used those tapes I made to learn the figures, then I started calling them myself.

"I picked up dances from other callers, too. I used to think that was a real hard job, but it's not that hard to learn if you break it down. The only thing you have to do is learn to take one couple through.

"I called at the Big Country Ranch in West Finley, Pennsylvania, every Saturday night for two and a half years. But it just got to be too much. It tied up every weekend. Dancing is a lot more fun than calling, I'll tell you that right now. Now, playing for a dance is work. Calling figures is work. It's nice to know how to do it, but the enjoyment is out there on the floor."

Worley obviously enjoys the work, though. In 1972 he

started calling for a monthly square dance at the Marilla Recreation Center in Morgantown. After a time it got to be every two weeks, and it continued for nearly 18 years.

The Marilla dances were featured in *West Virginia Square Dances,* a book by Robert G. Dalsemer, published in 1982 by the Country Dance and Song Society of America. Worley taught at the society's summer camp near Plymouth, Massachusetts, in 1982.

Gardner does one thing a little differently than other callers. He explains, "They always used to line up the set a certain way. Your head couples was always facing you or had their back to you. They did it traditionally that way, and people still do it that way. Well, that's just not necessary. It doesn't matter who starts off. Then, the others just follow in turn. That really puzzled them up in Massachusetts. They thought it was funny how we started dancing and it didn't make no difference who was head couples."

About the time Gardner started calling dances, he heard that a childhood neighbor, Dora Foley, had died and a hammered dulcimer was going to be for sale in the estate auction. Dora was the brother of Elva Foley, Worley's banjo teacher in the 1920s, and the nephew of Simon Meyers, the dulcimer player who had visited the Gardner farm when Worley was a boy.

"I always did like the sound of the dulcimer, and I wanted to learn to play it. I had gone to the sale when Simon Meyers died, but there wasn't any dulcimer there. I heard that Simon's dulcimer had burned up in a fire at his house, and that the dulcimer he played in later years was owned by his nephew Dora Foley.

"I went to the sale and bought that dulcimer for 30-some dollars. It was a match to the one Simon Meyers played in the '20s. They'd both been made in the Foley family. The one I bought is over 100 years old.

"I didn't know anything about a dulcimer then. My neighbor in Morgantown was a professor of music at the university and he helped me figure it out and restore it. That's the one I learned to play on.

"Learning to play was just trial and error. It really isn't hard. I could pick out 'Red River Valley' right off. Then I was hooked."

Worley's style of playing isn't like that of most dulcimer players. "Most of them play notes with this hand, then that hand. What I'm doing is beating time with my left hand. I play the tune with my right hand, and my left keeps time while playing notes in the chord.

"That old man must have played something like that. I think I just had the memory of the sound of it, and copied that when I was learning. You really don't know what makes you do it a certain way."

Worley's brother Asel retired and moved from Washington, D.C., to Kingwood, Marion County, about this time.

Margaret and Worley Gardner, who celebrated their 50th anniversary in 1992, have made music together for a long time. Photograph by Mark Crabtree.

"His first year there he almost went stir crazy," Worley says. "He was interested in dulcimers, so I said we should try to make one. The first one we made just fell apart. It wasn't strong enough and the string tension buckled it up. The next one we made I kept to play myself. Then we started selling them."

The first few dulcimers the Gardner brothers built were copied after the old dulcimer Worley owned. Then Worley started experimenting. "I designed them and Asel built them. I had been playing dulcimer with square dance bands. They let me play, but you could tell the musicians didn't give a damn for the sound of that dulcimer. The strings were real short and they were just too high pitched. They didn't blend with the other instruments. What we did then was lengthen the strings to bring them lower on the scale. When you lengthen the strings, you end up with a bigger box. All of that made for a more pleasant sound.

"Another thing we experimented with a good deal was the number of strings to a group," Worley adds. The Gardners' dulcimers have up to 27 groups of strings. Each group is tuned to the same note. "When you add more strings to a group, you get more resonance. We tried from two to eight to a group. The quality of sound was improved by up to five strings in a group, but from five to eight I didn't really hear much difference."

Another problem with the original dulcimers was that they were hard to carry. "They were trapezoid-shaped and you had to cover them up with something to carry them. We just decided that if it's a box, let's make it a box and put a lid on it. Putting it in its own case was our own idea, but when I went to the Smithsonian I found out it was nothing new. They had dulcimers like that in their collection made in France in the last century."

Worley's visit to the Smithsonian Institution was in October of 1977. He was there as a featured performer at the museum's Festival of American Folklife. Four hammered dulcimer players from around the country were brought in to demonstrate their craft each day at the Museum of History and Technology.

"Two things were really special that week," he recalls. "We played for a luncheon that Mrs. Mondale, the vice president's wife, was giving for the foreign ambassadors and their

Worley Gardner, well known as a dance caller, is shown here calling at the 1992 Winter Music Festival in Morgantown with fiddler
Blackie Lemley behind him. Photograph by Mark Crabtree.

wives. The other thing was a square dance. I told them,
'Forget it! You can't have a square dance here. Nobody will
pay attention to it.' Well, I was surprised, but we had a good
square dance. Those people could really dance. So, that was
fun. These things just happen to you as you go along."

Something else that just happened to Worley was a feature on CBS Radio. "Well, this fellow called and said he was
from CBS. I thought he was just trying to put one over on
me." But Rob Armstrong flew in the next day to record
Worley and some friends playing and talking about their
mountain music. That was broadcast August 2, 1985, on
CBS's "Newsmark Magazine."

By this time the Gardners's dulcimers were selling well. A
lot of people saw and heard them at the Mountain State Art
and Craft Fair in Ripley.

"Our first year at Ripley was 1969," Worley recalls. "We
didn't sell a single dulcimer. Then they took off. Word got
out we were doing this. We shipped them all over the country. Asel was making them year-round. My brother Willis
wanted to learn to play the dulcimer, so we built him one.
He played with me until his death in 1979."

Then Asel died in 1983. "We'd been partners for 18 or 19
years," Worley says. "We'd had a good relationship.

"I thought about getting someone else to build dulcimers
for me, but I never did. After all, this was a hobby for me. I
just wanted to see what we could do with it. I figure we made
between 400 and 500 dulcimers altogether.

"I didn't go to Ripley that next year, since I didn't have
any dulcimers to sell."

But Worley found out that he was in demand at festivals
whether he sold dulcimers or not. Now he performs at
Ripley, the Vandalia Gathering in Charleston, and the Stonewall Jackson Jubilee at Jackson's Mill every year.

He puts on his own festival, too. It started one winter when
he had driven to an old hotel in Burlington, Mineral County,
to play music with his friend, banjo player Sloan Staggs.
"There wasn't all these things going on like now," Worley
recalls. "I told Sloan we ought to have a regular get-together
so musicians would have something to do in the winter."
Worley sent invitations to his friends and acquaintances, and
hosted his first Winter Music Festival that same winter.

This past March 140 musicians from six states joined
Worley in Morgantown for a weekend of non-stop music at
the 14th annual Winter Music Festival. Now the festival is
sponsored by the Board of Park and Recreation Commis-
sioners of Morgantown, but Worley Gardner still runs the
show. He's often too busy to play much music himself, but
always makes time to call for a traditional square dance on
Saturday night.

Does he have any more projects in the works? "Man, I'm
73 years old," he says. "I just want to play music and enjoy
myself. But, I tell you, I would like to see somebody building
the dulcimer I designed. I think we made a good dulcimer."

EDITOR'S NOTE: This article first appeared in the summer 1992
issue of *Goldenseal* (vol. 18, no. 2). Worley Gardner died in November 1992, but his annual Winter Music Festival continues each February in Morgantown, West Virginia.

Patty Looman

CARRYING ON THE MUSIC

Danny Williams

FRIENDS of West Virginia music and heritage are fortunate. Most of our musical traditions live on in rich variety. Our hills were once full of fiddlers, singers, and banjo pickers, and they still are. We have dozens of musicians who are preserving the music of the legendary old-timers.

But hammered dulcimer players are scarcer. Mainly there are Patty Looman and a handful of others.

The hammered dulcimer was never as common or widespread in our state as some of the other instruments. The recent history of the hammered dulcimer in West Virginia is dominated by two men—Russell Fluharty and Worley Gardner. Both of these gentlemen have passed on, but the spirit and music of each of them lives on in Patty.

There are actually two unrelated instruments named "dulcimer." The hammered dulcimer of this article descends from an ancient Middle Eastern instrument which has infiltrated many of the world's folk traditions. It consists of many strings stretched across a shallow box. The player strikes the strings with small beaters or hammers.

The "mountain" or "fretted" dulcimer is an Appalachian invention, and has never spread far beyond our mountains. It's a long, narrow, three-stringed instrument which is usually held on the lap and strummed with a flexible pick.

Confusion over the name has drawn these two separate instruments together, and now they frequently appear at the same events. Patty is an accomplished performer and active teacher on both dulcimers, but her first love and her great mission is the hammered dulcimer.

She enlivens the West Virginia dulcimer scene in every way—as a performer, tune collector, teacher, and promoter. She even owns the largest collection of historical instruments in the state. To hear Patty tell the story now, it sounds almost like it had to happen.

Patty was born 70-ish years ago in Mannington. She recalls that music was an important part of her community and her early family life.

"My parents were very insistent that I would be a professional musician," she says. "It's real interesting, because my dad was not a person who had a lot of education; I know he didn't get any farther than seventh grade. He had been taking piano lessons—which surprised me, because he was pretty wild. But he loved music. When Georgie Moore, the

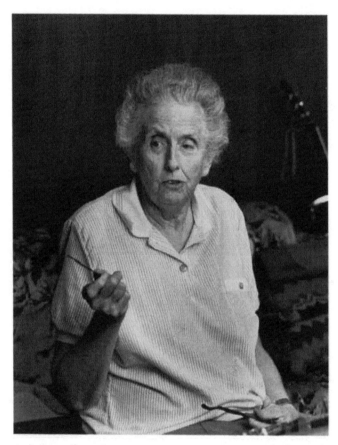

Dulcimer player Patty Looman in 1995. Photograph by Mark Crabtree.

pianist for the silent movies at the Mannington Theater, would get sick, she'd call on Dad to take over. He would play from sheet music, you know, the chase scene, or the burning scene. I still have all of that sheet music.

"Mom tried to play," Patty continues. "For a while she was fairly decent on the violin, but she developed arthritis at an early age, and that took care of her. Mom liked to sing.

"And so I was supposed to be a professional musician. They really went out of their way. For two years, I was excused from school every Wednesday, and I rode the train up to Wheeling to take organ lessons. It was a two-hour ride, and I took my lesson and stayed up there and practiced, and caught the evening train back.

"And they gave me private piano lessons here in Mannington. Piano was quite important for kids at that time here; we all had to take piano lessons. We were all scared to death of her—Miss Baker. Lovely lady. And everybody that took lessons, you practiced! She had a ruler, boy, she'd hit you!

"So then I had all these lessons, played in the high school band, went to All-State Orchestra on the cello, went to All-State Band on the trumpet, then went to Fairmont State College and took music courses."

While Patty was growing up in Mannington, her neighbor Russell Fluharty was waging a vigorous campaign to popularize the hammered dulcimer. Fluharty was a fine musician, but was even more well-known as a performer, a personality, and a gentleman. His mixture of music, banter, and sincere corniness made him a familiar figure across West Virginia. The current popularity of the instrument is largely a tribute to the energy and persistence of Russell Fluharty. Patty Looman recalls that converts were not easily won.

"We had to listen to Russell," she says. "He always played at the Mannington District Fair, and we were expected to go because my parents knew Russell and Marge very well. And so we'd go over to the fair, and we just hated it. We didn't like the music, and we didn't like the instrument. It was the '30s, [with] the development of swing music and that sort of thing, [and I was] a teenager.

"Then at the end of my sophomore year at Fairmont State, in 1945, I went to Central Michigan University, and up there I liked speech and drama so much that I ended up with a triple major—speech, drama, and music."

Patty's degree was in education. After graduation, she worked in Michigan as a high school teacher for 35 years. That's hammered dulcimer country, as it happens. The instrument occupies only a small place in traditional Appalachian music, but it is very important in the folklore of the Midwest. So as Patty's musical tastes matured beyond the pop music of her youth, the corny old dulcimer was right there waiting for her.

"I taught speech and drama, and did a lot of work on musicals. I came home to Mannington summers and all holidays during that time, and came to have great respect for Russell Fluharty as the years went on.

"It was in the early '60s I really began to think about the instrument as being maybe something worthwhile to consider. I'd gone over to Russell's house, even in the '40s, because I was interested in the instrument just as something different, and he would try to show me how to play. But in the '60s it was really Worley Gardner that got me going."

The late Worley Gardner of Morgantown is the second major figure in the hammered dulcimer's history in this state. An accomplished musician on several instruments, Gardner extended the range of the dulcimer beyond the folksy simplicity of Fluharty's style. With his brother Asel, Worley Gardner designed and built dulcimers more com-

Dutch Looman's children, ready to roll for their father's hauling business. Brothers Joe and Jack joined sister Patty in this playful 1920s picture. Photographer unknown.

plex than Fluharty's, and he was the first in West Virginia to show that the dulcimer could be played alongside guitars, mandolins, fiddles, and banjos. Sitting at her own Gardner dulcimer, Patty explains how Gardner's designs removed so many of the instrument's limitations.

"You could take the instrument and fool around with it, but to really get definite, that's what Worley did.

"Most of the time Russell never tuned to a tuner or anything; he just tuned to whatever sounded good, and the people who played with him adjusted to Russell's playing. Russell had only nine strings on his dulcimer. [Modern dulcimers commonly have 23 or more groups of strings.—ed.] And he played mostly, as he said, 'by hear.' He played in two keys, C and F, or C and G, depending on the tuning. Sometimes I'd tune up one of his old ones to the key of D, so he could play with some of the fiddlers around here.

"But now, Worley's dulcimer was different," Patty adds. "The key of A was good, the key of D was good. Worley played a lot in the key of G, and he could always manage to hit that F-sharp up there. Here at the bottom you could move one of the bridges and play in the key of C, after a fashion."

So Gardner's instrument design carried the dulcimer beyond its role as a solo curiosity. Now it could be played in the wider circle of string music, and appealed to more ambitious musicians. Patty notes also that the Gardner brothers' fine woodwork improved the tone of the instrument. "The earliest dulcimers around here were very, very tinny sounding. They used to say that a man could take just any piece of seasoned wood, and whatever wire he had, and that he would get a hammered dulcimer built. Now, the idea seems to be to make them as mellow as possible."

Once Patty had developed an interest in the hammered dulcimer, she didn't have to look far to find an instrument of her own. Her mother, Edith Looman, had long been West Virginia's most active collector of folk instruments. Patty chose an antique instrument decorated with a pokeberry-juice design and took it back to Michigan. Soon she was performing and teaching everywhere—in the Michigan area during the school year, and home in West Virginia during summers and holidays.

After her retirement from the classroom in 1982, Patty hurried back to West Virginia and threw her considerable energy and enthusiasm into promoting her instrument. She found a variety of opportunities to spread the word.

Russell Fluharty, the original grand old gentleman of the dulcimer, had organized a dulcimer club in Mannington in 1971; five players attended the first meeting. As Russell's energies declined, Patty began to organize and conduct the twice-yearly conventions. Now the meetings usually attract about 100 musicians and friends to Mannington, and Patty conducts the affair with charming authority.

The take-charge manner developed during 35 years in the classroom still serves her well. Patty remembers everyone's name, and introduces each in turn for an opportunity to perform. At this event, master musicians and beginners are treated equally. When it's time for a group tune, Patty's "one, two, three, play!" gets everyone off at the same speed. The Mountaineer Dulcimer Convention is the largest dulcimer gathering in the state, and it's one of the most comfortable anywhere. Patty is especially proud that so many closet musicians have felt safe enough to play their first public tunes in this group.

As a stage performer, Patty trusts her audience and her tunes. "Most people would rather hear 'Golden Slippers' and 'Redwing' than hear some really complicated piece of music that they can't follow," she says.

Patty does let her listeners hear a few of the obscure tunes she learned from Fluharty and Gardner, but she always plays plenty of familiar hoedowns, smooth waltzes, gospel tunes,

Patty Looman carries on Russell Fluharty's work at the Mountaineer Dulcimer Club. She is shown here presiding over a 1994 meeting. Photograph by Mark Crabtree.

Always read to go, Patty Looman sits by a Marion County roadside with the old family feed store in the background. Photograph by Mark Crabtree.

and Carter Family material. She believes that these tunes work on their own, and don't need a lot of help or improvement from the musician. She performs them with grace and rhythm, and without distracting embellishments or showy techniques. Patty's approach to performance is summarized in the title of her recording, *Nothing Fancy: Old Favorites for the Hammered Dulcimer.*

Besides her musical ability, Patty possesses a charm and sincerity which easily cross the gap between the stage and the audience. She has become the most active hammered dulcimer performer in West Virginia. Any time you talk to her, she has just played somewhere and is on her way to play somewhere else, and she always reports that she is "enjoying it enormously."

Patty is also the busiest dulcimer teacher in the state, currently seeing about 40 private students. She teaches at home in Morgantown, and drives to Fairmont, Clarksburg, Oakland, Maryland, or wherever someone is willing to learn. Often she can't be persuaded to take any payment for her teaching. By emphasizing her music's origin in Russell Fluharty and Worley Gardner, Patty makes her students aware that this is a tradition, a document of a past time which today's musicians need to understand and preserve. Patty is now teaching Worley Gardner's music to Gardner's grandson, and living around the corner from Worley's widow Margaret.

Patty regularly teaches group classes at Garrett Community College in Maryland and at the Augusta Heritage Arts Workshops in Elkins. These events offer a special opportunity for her to preach her music to students from outside the Appalachian region. Patty says there are plenty of non-teaching performances as well. "We do clubs, weddings, festivals, nursing homes, or wherever we're wanted."

Like any great teacher, Patty commissions all her students to go and teach others. As soon as one of her beginners learns a few tunes, Patty brings them onto the stage or into the classroom. Several of her former students are now quite active themselves, playing and teaching like Patty herself, anywhere they're wanted.

On a recent recording from the West Virginia State Folk Festival, there are two hammered dulcimer performances. Patty plays "West Virginia Waltz," one of Russell Fluharty's signature tunes. Her young student, Eric Cox, performs "Redwing" with his fiddling granddad, Frank George. Listeners who remember Worley Gardner will recognize that master's style in Eric's playing.

Once again, Patty has combined good music with a little lesson in the history of her instrument. Practically all the hammered dulcimer music in the state points back to these two men. "I am trying to keep Russell and Worley's music alive," she says. "Their contribution to West Virginia's heritage is enormous." Now that list has expanded by one, adding Patty Looman's name to those of past masters.

EDITOR'S NOTE: This article first appeared in the winter 1995 issue of *Goldenseal* (vol. 21, no. 4). Patty Looman remains very active as a dulcimer teacher and performer. She is a Master Artist in the West Virginia Folk Arts Apprenticeship Program, chairs the Mountaineer Dulcimer Convention of West Virginia, and performs with the band Hammers and Strings.

PART 4

Guitarists

Doc Williams

A HALF CENTURY AT THE "WHEELING JAMBOREE"

Ivan Tribe

WEST Virginia country music will reach a milestone this May, when Doc Williams celebrates his golden anniversary with the "Wheeling Jamboree" and radio station WWVA. There have been dark periods when Doc's appearances have been relatively few, but his heart has never been far from the big stage and the WWVA microphone. Like Roy Acuff and the "Grand Ole Opry," Doc and the Jamboree are linked together in the minds of longtime country fans—and, for the record, Doc has been at Wheeling nearly a year longer than Acuff has been at Nashville.

Before "Doc Williams" existed there was Andrew John Smik Jr. He was born of immigrant parents in Cleveland, Ohio, on June 26, 1914. Doc calls himself "the only hillbilly who ever came out of Cleveland," and he is surely one of the few country musicians of Slovak origins. Doc's father and mother had both been born in what is now Czechoslovakia, in those days part of the Hapsburg Empire. The elder Andrew Smik came to America at the age of 20 about 1906, and Doc's mother, Susie Parobeck, came at age 12. The couple eventually had five children. Younger brother Milo (known professionally as Cy Williams) would work with Doc as a fiddler and occasional duet partner for some 20 years.

When Doc was two, his parents relocated to the small community of Tarrtown, in the coalfields near Kittanning in Armstrong County, Pennsylvania. Coal camps offer an unusual mixture of rural and urban and the Cleveland boy soon learned something of country living and Appalachian music. His dad played several musical instruments, preferring the traditional fiddle tunes of East Central Europe. Doc's playing eventually came to reflect a mixture of traditional American country music as it was commercially evolving in the late '20s, with just a touch of East European ethnic stylings. The latter mirrored his own background as well as the tastes of audiences in northern West Virginia, eastern Ohio, and western Pennsylvania.

Oddly enough, Doc's first musical instrument was the cornet. From there he went to the accordion, the harmonica, and finally the guitar. The latter was favored by Jack and Jerry Foy, his earliest country radio influences, and by Jimmie Rodgers, whose recordings had considerable impact on Doc from about 1928. Cy learned to play fiddle from their father and the two brothers worked square dances around Kittanning.

Doc Williams celebrated a 50-year association with his favorite radio show, WWVA's "Jamboree U.S.A.," in May 1987. Photograph by Michael Keller.

Aside from this, Doc gained his first performing experience back in Cleveland where he periodically went to live with his grandmother. He and neighbor Joe Stoetzer "teamed up to play beer gardens," Doc says today. Doc played guitar and harmonica, while Joe played a kazoo with an attached horn and also the mandolin. Both sang and together

The Border Riders were the hot new band in Wheeling when this publicity photo was taken in 1937. Next to the unidentified "gunman" on the left is fiddler Cy Williams, then Curley Sims, and Doc Williams. Seated are newcomers Sunflower and Rawhide. Photographer unknown.

they called themselves the Mississippi Clowns. They auditioned for radio and went on a show called "The Barn Busters" at WJAY in Cleveland, hosted by Morey Amsterdam of later TV fame. The Clowns appeared on this program once a week for about six months. They then found themselves absorbed into a larger unit called the Kansas Clodhoppers, led by Doc McCaulley, a fiddler from Belington.

About 1935, Doc returned to Pennsylvania when his dad asked him to help support the family by working with him in the coal mines. It wasn't long, however, until he returned to radio, teaming up with his brother Cy on fiddle and an Ohio mandolin player named Leonard "Curley" Sims. With the addition of a bass fiddle, this band took the name Allegheny Ramblers and worked at radio station KQV in Pittsburgh. Doc describes their sound as almost "bluegrass at the time, but we didn't know it."

Pittsburgh was no center of hillbilly culture, but the Steel City's varied population did support some early country musicians. Among them were Jack and Jerry Foy, and a band called the Tennessee Ramblers that had been put together by West Virginians Dick Hartman and Harry Blair. The Ramblers later included Cecil Campbell, the group's eventual leader, and West Virginian Harry McAuliffe, whom Hartman gave the sobriquet "Big Slim, the Lone Cowboy." When Doc Williams arrived on Pittsburgh radio, the Tennessee Ramblers had moved on to Rochester. Big Slim, however, remained to play a role not only in Doc's career, but also at WWVA.

Doc's Allegheny Ramblers soon became the band for girl singer Billie Walker, taking the new name Texas Longhorns. At the end of 1936, Walker took an opportunity to go to WWL in New Orleans. Doc, Cy, Curley, and Big Slim chose

The historic Capitol Theater in Wheeling, built in 1926, is the undisputed mother church of country music in West Virginia. It is known to music lovers as the Capitol Music Hall. On January 7, 1933, the "World's Original Jamboree" was born here before a crowd of 3,266 people. Photograph by Michael Keller.

to remain at KQV. By now, the four were known as the Cherokee Hillbillies and were also being carried on two other local stations. It was about this time that young Andy Smik became Doc Williams. He had already been called "Doc," as had his father before him, both being health food advocates, and people tended to confuse Smik with Smith. Billie Walker had suggested Williams, since it was a common last name not likely to be confused with Smith. An autographed picture from about 1936 bears the signature "Cowboy Doc."

In May 1937, Doc and his group changed places with performer Tex Harrison. Tex came to Pittsburgh and Doc went to WWVA in Wheeling. This was when Doc's band took the name Border Riders. The group now consisted of Doc, Cy, Curley, and two new members. One newcomer, show business veteran Hamilton "Rawhide" Fincher, was a 26-year-old Alabama native who had worked at times with his brother Shorty Fincher and as part of the duo of Rawhide and Sue. The other was the not-quite-18 Mary Calvas, a Davis native

of Italian background known as Sunflower. She would marry Cy Williams and work for several years as the band's female vocalist.

The Border Riders achieved almost instant popularity at WWVA and in 1938 were acclaimed the station's most popular act. Each Saturday night they performed on the "World's Original Jamboree," as it was then called. Broadcast from the Wheeling Market Auditorium before a crowd of 1,200 or more people, the program had been a favorite since its inauguration before a live audience on January 7, 1933. The Border Riders also performed on a daily show from the WWVA studio in the Hawley Building. Each day they greeted their listeners with a theme song that Doc had recomposed from "Riding Down That Old Texas Trail":

We are the happy Border Riders,
Who ride down that old border trail.
We are here to bring you cheer,
And to sing you songs so dear,
That will tell you of that old border trail.

Ridin' down that old border trail,
Ridin' down that old border trail.
We'll try hard to make you smile,
And to make it worth your while,
If you'll tune us in for just a little while.

In addition to their radio broadcasts, Doc and the band began playing show dates almost nightly in nearby parts of Ohio, Pennsylvania, and West Virginia. Since all their programs were done live in the studio, they could never go farther than a hundred miles or so from the station and get back in time for the next broadcast. Most of their stage shows were sponsored by community organizations, fundraising concerts in the schools, theaters, and public auditoriums of small to medium-sized towns.

In December 1937, Rawhide Fincher was injured at a fire in his apartment and missed several weeks of shows. Doc brought Big Slim McAuliffe to Wheeling to help out. Slim remained at WWVA and became one of the all-time Jamboree favorites. Soon after returning, Rawhide left to join his brother Shorty, who brought his Prairie Pals to WWVA. Doc, a firm believer in keeping a comedian in his show, hired James J. "Froggie" Cortez in his place. A native of Pennsylvania, the bass-playing Cortez sang old country comedy songs like "Courtin' in the Rain" and added a trained monkey named Jo-Jo to the usual bucolic humor of the country clown. The music of the Border Riders continued to be built around the fiddle and mandolin, and Doc's solid rhythm guitar and vocal leads, with other members singing on certain numbers. This band remained together until 1942, when the war brought changes.

During this period, the Border Riders usually took several weeks off in the summer. On one occasion, Doc and Froggie Cortez went to Texas and California. Snapshots from their adventure show a pair of fun-loving country boys enjoying themselves, somewhat awestruck by actually experiencing for the first time the West they sang about. The Texas border, ranches, horses, cowboys, and the wide-open spaces made an impression later conveyed to fans via their souvenir booklets.

Doc courted and married the one true love of his life during those early years at WWVA. Jessie "Chickie" Crupe was a West Virginian, born in Bethany on February 13, 1919. Her father, Fred Crupe, was a renowned old-time fiddler. He had been contacted to record for Columbia, but death intervened and the family moved to Washington County, Pennsylvania, where Chickie finished high school in 1938. She had once written a fan letter to Doc when he was still at KQV, erroneously addressed to Buck Williams. The two met at a dance in Washington County and following a pleasant courtship were married on October 9, 1939.

The first of their three daughters, Barbara Diane ("Peeper") arrived on December 22, 1940. Madeline Dawn ("Poochie") came on April 11, 1943, and finally Karen Dolores ("Punkin") on June 10, 1944. The girls all performed on special occasions with the Border Riders from an early age, although only Karen ever made any real efforts at a career in music.

The year after Doc and Chickie's marriage, the Border Riders turned their summer vacation into a work break. With Doc's first child on the way and some of the band members also with increased family responsibilities, the musicians worked at WREC in Memphis. On the way home, Doc received an offer from WSM, home of the "Grand Ole Opry" in Nashville. He had sent Chickie back to Wheeling early and was driving his band and their families through Tennessee when he stopped to see Harry Stone, the most powerful behind-the-scenes figure at the Nashville program. After hearing the Border Riders, the WSM manager offered them a daily show and Opry spot. Doc, thinking more of his expectant wife in Wheeling and the other band members' squalling babies in the car, asked Stone for a rain check. He never followed up on this offer.

To place this missed opportunity in better perspective, recall that Nashville had not yet attained its "Music City U.S.A." status. Doc Williams and the Border Riders might have become as famous as Roy Acuff, Bill Monroe, Pee Wee King, or Ernest Tubb.

On the other hand, they might have stayed a while and then moved on, as did folks like Fiddlin' Arthur Smith, Asher Sizemore, Zeke Clement, and the Milo Twins. Nashville's reputation would soon receive such boosts as the Republic film *Grand Ole Opry* and an NBC slot for the Opry. But in 1940 Wheeling ranked only a little below Nashville in music

Souvenir booklets were important money-makers during the heyday of live radio. Shown here are a Border Riders family album, a listener "scrap book," and the 15th anniversary booklet of WWVA's Jamboree. Photograph by Michael Keller.

prestige. In fact, WWVA officials passed up a chance for the Jamboree to go on the NBC Blue Network at about that time.

Back in Wheeling, the Border Riders continued as they had in the past. The Jamboree, daily radio programs, and almost nightly live shows kept Doc, Cy, Sunflower, Curley, and Froggie busy. The group first sold photos and a little souvenir scrapbook over the air, and about April 1940 they came out with a more elaborate *Doc Williams Border Riders Family Album*, including 39 pictures and 14 songs. They weren't making phonograph records, but neither had any other WWVA acts since the Hugh and Shug's Radio Pals session for Decca in July 1937.

Among the WSM acts, only Acuff and Monroe were recording at the time. After Christmas of 1940, Chickie stayed home with little Peeper and Doc indulged his spare moments in a fascination with aviation. He learned to pilot planes and later even managed an airport for a time.

After Pearl Harbor, the world of country music went through many changes. Gasoline rationing curtailed personal appearances and also reduced the number of fans who could come to Wheeling to see the "World's Original Jamboree." Many musicians entered the armed forces or were called into defense work. At the same time, people depended as much or even more upon radio for entertainment and the popularity of country music increased a great deal. Performances tended to be confined to the studios and from December 1942 until July 1946, the WWVA Jamboree was not broadcast before live stage audiences. The musicians who remained with the station, disproportionately women, got more opportunities to sing over the air than ever before.

The effects of the war came gradually for Doc. The service took Cortez and Sims and eventually only he and Cy were left. Chickie was singing with them often by this point. In 1943, Cy entered the military and Doc acquired other musicians. Marion Martin (Marion Keyoski), the blind accordionist, had his first association with the Border Riders during this period. So, too, did steel guitarist Tex King.

It was during the war that Doc began to put together the guitar instruction course which became one of his trademarks. With financial help from the WWVA management, he succeeded in getting his *Simplified By Ear System of Guitar Chords* printed in June 1943. The 42-page booklet proved an instant success as a mail-order item. By 1966 it had sold more than 125,000 copies. The course went through six printings by the end of 1944 and in those months when travel was limited it provided a major source of income.

By early 1945, Doc began producing transcribed radio programs for airplay in various sections of the country. He bought time on other stations, sent off the large disc recordings, and made some profit. In the latter part of 1944, Doc, along with Chickie and Tex King, left Wheeling and went to WFMD in Frederick, Maryland. This station had excellent facilities for cutting transcriptions and it was here that many of the early programs advertising the guitar course were made. Doc recalls that when not playing live from the studio, he, Chickie, and Tex would be in the transcription room recording programs for broadcast elsewhere. Other entertainers at WFMD included Mac Wiseman and folk singer Ed McCurdy.

This situation came to a sudden end early in 1945 when Andrew J. Smik Jr. found himself drafted into the U.S. Navy. Doc had registered for Selective Service back at Memphis in the summer of 1940. Despite one bad eye, he now memorized the eye charts and got into Navy flight school. The weakness soon became apparent and on April 12, 1945, Doc received his discharge. President Franklin Roosevelt died the same day and the final Allied victory was less than five months away.

When the war was over, Doc returned to Wheeling. Still much under the influence of the romance of aviation, he operated an airport at nearby Martin's Ferry, Ohio, with a friend and also organized a contracting firm, the Cook and Smik Company. An article in the July–August 1945 *National Hillbilly News* reported that "Doc isn't doing any broadcasting in person," but had transcriptions on a station in North Carolina and one in Ohio. Soon he added two more North Carolina stations. Doc recalls one Sunday afternoon at the airport, when an old fan pleaded with him to get back into live music on a regular basis. By then he had already resumed solo appearances on the Saturday night Jamboree. A little later, he got his band back together for three-a-week daytime shows at WWVA as well.

Late in 1945, Doc Williams and his reassembled Border Riders gave a show in Newcomerstown, Ohio. That happened to be the residence of *Mountain Broadcast and Prairie Recorder* columnist Mary Jean Shurtz, who reported that Doc "really packed them in." Her review of the concert provides a glimpse of the Border Riders in their prime:

Like most musicians, Doc Williams and his band spent a great deal of time on the road. Left to right in this 1947 photograph are comedian Hiram Hayseed, Marion Martin, Cy Williams, Doc Williams, and Chickie Crupe Williams at the WWVA broadcast tower. Photographer unknown.

"What an act! Flannels Miller . . . is just about the cutest thing. . . . Flannels plays the fiddle, banjo, bass, guitar, and almost any musical instrument in the old-time band. . . . Then there's Doc's wife, sweet little Chickie. She's called the Girl with the Lullaby Voice. . . . Chickie plays bass, and is one swell radio personality. The next Border Rider is Curley Sims. . . . Curley is doing quite a bit of comedy . . . along with the rest of his entertaining features.

"Now we come to that fellow every WWVA listener has admired . . . for years—Doc Williams! . . . Congratulations, Doc, for working at it until you have the Border Riders where they belong—at the top of the world in old-time musical entertainment."

Flannels Miller fiddled for the Border Riders until Cy Williams returned from the service. Froggie Cortez and Sunflower had gone off to New Castle, Pennsylvania, to work with Curley Miller's Ploughboys, since Cy and Sunflower's marriage had become a casualty of the war. Cy was back with the Border Riders by 1946, and a later article by Mary Jean Shurtz praised his fiddling on "Orange Blossom Special" and his singing on the recent Spade Cooley hit, "Shame On You." Cy continued to work with Doc until October 1956, when he left show business for a job with the U.S. Post Office.

Doc hired William Henry Godwin, an old-time vaudeville performer, to replace Froggie as comedian. A native of Georgia by way of Texas, Godwin had recorded for Columbia in 1929 as Shorty Godwin. By the time he came to West Virginia in 1938 with Mack Jeffers and his Fiddlin' Farmers, Godwin had developed his comic character, "Hiram Hayseed." Specializing in novelty fiddling, dancing, comedy, and singing, he remained a Border Rider from 1946 until his death in 1959. When Curley Sims left in 1947, Marion Martin renewed what became perhaps the longest association of any musician with Doc, outside his own family. If the Sims mandolin had been the outstanding feature of the Border Riders sound in the earlier years, Marion's accordion would provide the main characteristic for the next quarter-century. The three Williams daughters often performed, too. Doc made his first record in 1947. The WWVA management had not encouraged phonograph recording by their artists earlier, and Doc had not concerned himself much with this aspect of entertainment. But the increasing importance of records for radio airplay made the post-war situation different. Chickie had come into her own following Sunflower's exodus, and Doc decided to feature her on the record as well. Both did their initial recording in Cleveland in December. Chickie's first release was "Beyond the Sunset," a single, with "Silver Bell" on the flip side. "Beyond the Sunset," including a recitation of the Rosey Rosewell poem, "Should You Go First," was the hit of the session. The sentimental performance spread the lovely 28-year-old brunette's fame far and wide.

Other numbers from that first session also had some im-pact. Doc's original "Willy Roy," a ballad about a little boy with a terminal illness, went on to become a bluegrass standard, although Wilma Lee and Stoney Cooper's 1949 recording would have more influence than Doc's own. "Silver Bell," an old song about an Indian maid by Percy Weinruch, became one of Doc's best-known numbers, while "Merry Maiden Polka" showcased the sound that made Doc Williams and Marion Martin popular with ethnic audiences.

This 1947 recording session was a promising beginning for Doc's new enterprise, the Wheeling Record Company. Between them, Doc and Chickie would wax more than 200 masters for the label, which was releasing discs as late as 1985. Wheeling Records has never had any million sellers or adequate distribution, but it still has records in print and much of its catalog remains available on cassette. In the meantime, the Williamses passed up a chance to record for Mercury.

Through 1947, 1948, and 1949, Doc operated a summer country music park at Musselman's Grove near Altoona. Parks of this nature, with weekend afternoon family entertainment, had become quite popular through the tri-state area, especially in Pennsylvania. Jake Taylor's Radio Ranch near Grafton was West Virginia's best-known park. Doc and his group played often with big-name talent from Hollywood, such as singing cowboys Tex Ritter and Jimmy Wakeley. Doc promoted Chicago "National Barn Dance" stars like Lulu Belle and Scotty, and such Opry heroes as Roy Acuff, Bill Monroe, and Ernest Tubb. Jamboree performers like Big Slim and Hank Snow also appeared at Musselman's Grove.

By 1950, Doc, Chickie, and the Border Riders were doing far better than most country acts. Few performers enjoyed much security at the time. One contemporary recalls that when he came to WWVA in late 1950, folks said that Doc Williams was the only entertainer at the station prosperous enough to pay cash for a suit of clothes. Doc hardly felt rich, however. In 1950, he finally let the WWVA management excuse him from broadcasts long enough to do more road shows. He says that he had only "$87 in the bank" when he left for an extended tour in the East and Canada. On this and later trips he drew good crowds in eastern Pennsylvania, upstate New York, rural New England, Ontario, Quebec, and the Maritime Provinces. Doc's several tours of Newfoundland proved especially rewarding. WWVA had been a powerful 50,000-watt station since October 1942, and its artists found that they had an eager audience waiting in eastern Canada. Daily live shows began to be phased out during the '50s, but WWVA entertainers now could play personal appearances in a much larger hinterland.

Doc left WWVA a second time in the fall of 1956, buying a 37½ percent interest in radio station WMOD in Moundsville. One-time Jamboree artist Jake Taylor was the other principal owner. Brother Cy had remarried and quit music.

Show business trappings were put away for this 1953 family portrait of Doc Williams and his wife, Chickie, with daughters Barbara (standing), Karen (left), and Madeline (right). Photographer unknown; courtesy of Stanford Hankinson.

His replacement, Buddy Spicher, later left to go with Johnnie and Jack and Kitty Wells in Nashville. Doc decided to get off the road for a while. He did 55 minutes of deejay work daily and spent most of his remaining time in the business end of things. He didn't play at the Jamboree, because WMOD gave WWVA a lot of competition for the daytime audience. He didn't play many live shows either, but did do a three-month television stint at WTRF in Wheeling.

By 1958, Doc had sold his interest in WMOD and returned to his true calling. His love for music, for the Jamboree, and for performing proved stronger than the attraction of radio as a business. During this WMOD interlude, Doc

did his first Nashville record session on October 8, 1956, with Chet Atkins among the accompanying musicians. The results were not especially satisfying and he did not return to Nashville to record until 1963.

For another 20 years, Doc Williams and the Border Riders remained on the road much of the time, entertaining at school auditoriums, parks, clubs, fairs, and other such locales. Doc branched out into live television, hosting a very successful show for two years at WJAC in Johnstown, Pennsylvania, and earlier at WFBG Altoona. The Williams girls grew up and went to college. Peeper and Poochie both obtained degrees, but Punkin came back to pursue a musical career as Karen McKenzie. Paul Cohen, who had produced Patsy Cline's hit recordings, chose Karen as a replacement after Cline's tragic death in 1963. Cohen produced Karen's session for ABC Paramount Records, but then his own death intervened and the releases never went anywhere. Nonetheless, she remains a fine contemporary country singer.

After Hiram Hayseed died, Smokey Pleacher worked for more than a decade as Border Rider comedian, until his own death in 1971. Pleacher and Marion Martin recorded a pair of albums for Wheeling Records. During the 1960s, he and Martin became as well known as Cy Williams and Shorty Godwin had been earlier. Other sidemen came and went during those later years, with Dean McNett, Curt Dillie, Gary Boggs, Fred Johnson, Jack Jackson, and Bill Barton among the more memorable. Sometimes older WWVA figures like Toby Stroud, Roy Scott, and the armless musician Ray Myers worked tours with Doc.

By 1966, Doc was playing the Saturday night show now known as "Jamboree U.S.A." only about once a month. Much of the rest of the time, the Doc Williams Show remained on the road. Crowds mostly were large and the Border Riders continued to please their fans. But with the increasing conformity in musical styles associated with the bland "Nashville Sound," Doc and Chickie found themselves the survivors of a vanishing breed. Still, Doc recalls the middle and late '60s as among the most lucrative times of his career.

The 1970s proved to be a time of transition. At the beginning Doc and Chickie continued as before, but then their careers began to wind down. They eased away from constant touring and began playing just now and then. By the end of the decade, their Jamboree appearances were down to one or two per year, and sometimes then for old-timer reunions or other special occasions. Although Doc and Chickie had connections with the Jamboree as solid as Roy Acuff or Minnie Pearl had with the Opry, the Wheeling management never seemed to appreciate them in the same way, often choosing to favor some special guest from Nashville. Jamboree management has not had the continuity of that at WSM, and perhaps that was a reason. Doc, for his part, became increasingly a spokesman for regional distinctiveness and the endangered notion of country music as clean family entertainment. He became a critic of today's complex and expensive recording arrangements, which, together with emphasis on the top-40 formats by country radio stations, forced many musicians far younger than himself into near obscurity.

Doc also opened his Country Store across the street from WWVA's Capitol Music Hall. Stocked with a goodly selection of Wheeling and music souvenirs, western clothes, and traditional country recordings and publications, the store has become a gathering spot for the music's traditionalists and long-term Jamboree fans. Daughter Peeper manages the

Doc Williams takes a stand outside his Country Store on Main Street near the Capitol Music Hall. He believes in the traditional sound, in appreciation for the past, and in country music as clean family entertainment. Photograph by Michael Keller.

store and Doc and Chickie often can be seen helping serve the customers who crowd in on Saturdays.

Doc has not fully retired. He and Chickie still play several show dates yearly. From 1979 until 1984, he organized a yearly reunion concert which featured his own family, former Border Riders, and West Virginia show business veterans like Lee Moore, Blaine Smith, Curley Miller, Bonnie Baldwin, and Roy Scott. Beginning in 1974, Doc, Chickie, and the band taped several programs for the public TV station in Morgantown. One, featuring an in-depth interview by folklorist Carl Fleischhauer, later was aired on 200 Public Broadcasting System stations nationally. In 1982 a crew from the British Broadcasting Corporation came to call, filming Doc for an overseas special on West Virginia music. In August 1985, he and Chickie appeared on the Jamboree with Grandpa Jones and the Sunshine Boys. In February 1986, the couple headed a group of Jamboree veterans in a show that included such old favorites as Shirley Barker and Lloyd Carter, and younger performers like Jimmy Stephens and Junior Norman. In 1983, Doc was probably the major symbol of continuity when "Jamboree U.S.A." celebrated its 50th anniversary as a live radio barn dance.

Although Chickie is content in semi-retirement, Doc has recently announced that he will book appearances with Jay Kirk, a veteran comedian with whom he has worked over the years. Plans are under way for a big special at the Capitol Music Hall on May 19, 1987. Honored as a Distinguished West Virginian and as West Virginia's Country Music Ambassador by Arch Moore during his first term as governor,

and as a 1984 inductee of the Wheeling Hall of Fame (along with opera singer Eleanor Steber), Doc has more than made his mark on the state's musical history. He stands with Craigsville's Buddy Starcher and those West Virginia symbols of tradition on the "Grand Ole Opry," Wilma Lee Cooper and Little Jimmy Dickens, in professional careers that go back to the early days of country radio. They were not only country when it wasn't cool, but before today's stars were born.

EDITOR'S NOTE: This article first appeared in the spring 1987 issue of *Goldenseal* (vol. 13, no. 1). Doc Williams still appears as an occasional guest artist on the WWVA Jamboree and does live performances throughout the region. Doc's Country Store closed in 1998, although Doc still maintains an active mail-order business selling recordings and memorabilia.

Blackie Cool

"WHOOP IT UP A LITTLE BIT"

Sam Rizzetta

Sam Rizzetta: I've heard conflicting stories about how you got your nickname. I know your real name is William Cool.

Blackie Cool: Actually, it started way back when I was just a kid. See, my mother and father are mixed with some Indians, got a little Indian in them, you know. On my dad's side is Cherokee and Blackfoot, and on my mother's Seneca Indian. When we'd be playing cowboys and Indians way back in young days I was the chief Blackheart, and it just stuck. Someone was telling about me working on a tipple, lot of coal dust around there and I got black like that, started calling me Blackie there. But actually it happened when we was playing cowboys and Indians when we was just young kids and that name stuck. Even my mother called me Blackie. That's the only name I know. I get mail from my own relations that way.

SR: Were there still Indians in the area when you grew up?

BC: No, but my grandfather could remember them, my grandmother and grandfather. I had a cousin, Jesse Cool, up in Webster County, he traced our ancestors back. And he went back way beyond the Civil War, way back when we had relations in covered wagons go west, you know. But he run out of money and didn't finish it so I don't how it happened. I guess they just got mixed up somewhere or other. You know, there isn't many Cools around, the law and disease thinned us out.

I had one of the wonderfulest grandfathers there ever was, he was a lawman back in them days. J.D. Cool, he was named after Jefferson Davis. Jefferson Davis Cool was his name. My mother's father, my other grandfather, he was a Clifton, he lived about eight mile below Diana and he was six or seven years old when the Civil War was going on. They was raided down there. I've heard him tell it many times. He was standing in the log cabin door looking down at the barn where his brother went down to save the calves and horses and things. They killed his brother. He stood right at his cabin door and watched it.

SR: And your grandfather Cool was a lawman for a long time.

BC: I never knew when he wasn't.

SR: Was this around Diana?

BC: Yeah, Webster County. He was constable there at Diana for many years. He died in 1926.

SR: We're talking together up here on Ware's Ridge above Valley Head. This isn't too far from where you grew up. Is that right?

BC: Not too far, 'course I grew up in two different states, Pennsylvania and West Virginia.

SR: Well, I know you were born in Diana. How long did you spend there?

BC: Well, when I was six years old my father moved out, he was a coal miner, moved down to [the town of] Carolina, south from Fairmont. And he worked for Consolidation Coal Company there two or three years. Then he moved down into Uniontown, Pennsylvania. Went to Collier, Pennsylvania, at first and I sort of grew up down there till teenage. Spent my first years down in there.

SR: That's where you started working in the mines?

BC: Yeah, 13 years old, I worked for Pittsburgh Coal Company. If you was big enough, you know, and dumb enough, why, you was all right to work. That was before child labor law. If you was big enough, you was old enough.

SR: You decided not to go to school but to work?

BC: Yeah, I quit in the fifth grade and went to work the coal mines.

SR: You were telling me about doing the kinds of things that men do even when you were 13.

BC: Oh, yeah, when I was 13 years old I drank, gambled, I was on my own.

SR: Were there many young people working in the mines like that?

BC: Not too many, not too many. I guess they had better sense. They went to school like my brother who was two years older than myself. Why, he kept going to school and he became a federal mine inspector in later life. So I guess it does help to go to school a little bit.

SR: When did you start playing music, was it about that time?

BC: Well, no, I loved music ever since I can remember. See, my father used to play the five-string banjo, that old thumping style like Uncle Dave Macon. And he was good, he didn't know what key he was playing in but he played it good, and I just loved it, loved music.

When I was about nine years old he got me an old guitar that I tuned up like a banjo. Tuned up what I call Spanish. Not natural, but Spanish. Open tuning, open G. And I

William "Blackie" Cool in 1981. Photograph by Sam Rizzetta.

learned to play with a bar, with the guitar down on my lap. And you bar the fifth fret you got C, you bar the seventh fret you got D, open is G. I was quite a while like that, playing like that, I got so I could make sevenths, ninths, or anything like that, slant the bar. You know there's quite a lot of people in the '30s come on the "Grand Ole Opry" playing that way. With the guitar strung over their neck and holding the guitar like a Dobro now, and that's the way they played. You can play some beautiful pieces that way, you know. "Marching Through Georgia" is a beautiful piece to play on that.

SR: Did you play with your father?

BC: Sometimes. And I got to learning what key we was playing in and I'd try to teach him and show him, and he don't want to learn, didn't want to remember it. He could tune up whatever he'd play in A or G or whatever, and then all the pieces he'd play like that. But he was good, while he played it. He was good.

SR: Did anyone else in your family play music besides your father?

BC: I had an uncle was a pretty good fiddler and guitar player, he was my dad's brother. He played old-time stuff, you know. He played fiddle and guitar pretty good.

SR: Did you ever all get together and play?

BC: Not my uncle and my dad and me, but I played with my uncle in different times. Dad, he just played the banjo, but he had a style all of his own, too, you know. He used his thumb up here for that fifth string, and he had a way of going up and coming down on it. It was actually nice. And he learned hisself, he just learned to play hisself.

SR: Do you still play any of the pieces that your father played?

BC: I can remember some that he played. There's old pieces like "Barbara Allen." Then there was another old song that my dad used to sing and play on his banjo, "Wake up, wake up, little Lulu, what makes you sleep so sound, the Indians are a-comin' to tear your building down." Did you ever hear of that one? That's an old song he used to play and thump on the banjo, and I always liked to hear it. And all them old songs that Uncle Dave Macon played—I just can't remember names of them now, I got away from them.

SR: Did he play dance music too?

BC: Yeah, you could square dance with it, now he played "Goin' Up Cripple Creek," he played pieces like that. He was a pretty good thumper. That's what you call thumpin' on the banjo.

SR: What were guitars like then, where did you get a guitar?

BC: I don't remember where my father got that guitar, but it was a red one and I forget the name. I don't know whether Stella made them guitars or not. You remember Stella? I know I had a Stella at one time but I can't remember if that was it or not. Later on I got a Kaycraft, a Kay guitar.

SR: Did you play Spanish style when you started to play for dances?

BC: I'd already learned chords. After we moved back into West Virginia then I really did get into playing.

SR: How old were you then?

BC: Well, let's see, I was about 17, I guess.

SR: Did you come back to the Webster Springs area?

BC: Well, there was a little town called Parcoal, it's about a mile, maybe a mile and a half, from Webster Springs. A new coal mine went in, their head office was in Pennsylvania, you see, and my father came up there in 1929 and we moved back into West Virginia. Lived in Parcoal till it worked out and then my father moved over here to Randolph County when Hickory Lick opened. See, this Hickory Lick mines is the same mines, same company, just another opening. When they worked that one out they opened this one up. Then my father moved over to Monterville, where I live now.

SR: Did you work in the mines and then play dances at night?

BC: Yeah, I worked on the tipple. I worked outside most of the time then. We had dances going everywhere. They was anywhere from Richwood, around Summersville—anywhere, you know. There was dances going on all the time, they was hollering for musicians. Me and Aretus Hamrick played for a lot of them. He was a good fiddler. And Dewey Hamrick was one of the best.

We played a lot of music there in Webster County. That was in the '30s. We played there at the Oakland Hotel, and Ella Gregory's Restaurant on Main Street in Webster Springs. She may still be living, she was an elderly-like lady then. That was when Aretus Hamrick and I played a lot. I played a lot with Dewey Hamrick, too. Dewey came over from Randolph County into Webster County because there was a lot of work there. He run the monitors at Curtin. So I got with him again at Parcoal and we got to playing a lot together. But Aretus was the one that done most of the fiddling for square dances around there then.

SR: I remember Dewey telling me that he was the one who taught you how to play the guitar.

BC: Well, Dewey showed me a lot on the guitar and I'd been playing quite a little bit of his style. I learned a lot from Dewey. And he was one of the best fiddlers West Virginia had back in them days. I'd rank him up with Clark Kessinger and Natchee the Indian, and Brownie [Ross]. Brownie, from around Philippi, was a good fiddler.

SR: When was it that they had that big contest in Charleston?

BC: That was back in the early '30s. I can't remember the year, it may have been '32. I think it was.

SR: You and Dewey went and played against Clark Kessinger?

Blackie and His Melody Girls—cousins Louise and Dorothy Cool—in the late 1930s. Photographer unknown.

BC: Yeah, and Natchee the Indian. Dewey come up second, but he wasn't advertised or nothing. Cowboy Copas played the guitar for Natchee the Indian and I played for Dewey. Dewey was just as good back then. He had to be if ranked up with them, because they were hot fiddlers.

SR: When did you get started playing the fiddle too? Was it about that time?

BC: Well, back in the '30s I played quite a lot, just around, playing square dances.

SR: Did you know Woody Simmons?

BC: I met Woody in 1932. I was playing with a band called the Sunset Ramblers. We broadcast at Fairmont, once a week, WMMN. In between, we had little shows for these towns. So we was doing a show way over here at Junior or one of them little towns over in there. I was still living in Webster County. And we went down through Mill Creek and we stopped and met Arnold VanPelt, good musician, great musician. We got to playing a little music and talking and the first thing I knew there's somebody come a-walking up, had a pullover white sweater with his sleeves rolled up.

It was Woody Simmons and he played the banjo beautiful. That's the first recollection I have of seeing him after that. Then later on, I guess in the '40s, we played some together.

SR: He had started out playing on the banjo and it wasn't till later that he worked on the fiddle?

BC: Yeah, he was really a beautiful banjo player. I can even remember one of the pieces he played, "Home, Sweet Home." I'll never forget it, 1932. It was real beautiful the way he done it. And Arnold VanPelt was a good guitar player. He played Riley Puckett runs and that's what interested me. Because I had a lot of Riley's records and I was learning a lot of his stuff, too. And them licks that he was getting like on the "A Rag," that's the way I was playing back in them days. That suited me, you know.

SR: I've heard a lot about Arnold's playing. Did he play other instruments besides guitar?

BC: Well, now his brother played the fiddle. And I imagine Arnold could play anything, he was just a good musician. But his brother played a good fiddle and Arnold was real good on the guitar.

Dewey Hamrick and I played a lot of music together back in them days. In 1937 Dewey Hamrick and I went down and played at the [Mountain State] Forest Festival. We won first prize there, and old man Charlie Bell was one of the judges.

Another time I remember playing down there, me and Dewey played against Edden Hammons. Edden won first prize that time. When he goes to put his fiddle away, he opened his violin case. I was standing pretty close to him, and looked over and in there was a great big fifth of whiskey, red whiskey, you know. They made moonshine back in them days a lot, but they'd color it. They'd take sugar and scorch it and color it, and that was the color that whiskey was, so I know that was moonshine. And old Edden looked up, and the lid of the case slapped down real quick. He put the violin case under his arm and took the fiddle in his hand and carried it without a case. He kept the whiskey in the case. I guess that was the last time I saw Edden.

SR: Did you play fiddle for dances, too, besides guitar?

BC: Yeah, I used to fiddle quite a lot over at Webster County and have here in Randolph County. Back in the '40s I played some.

SR: That's about the time that you met Woody Simmons, too, or started to play with him?

BC: Yeah. At one time Woody and I had a program worked up. We put twin fiddles together and we had one of the beautifulest programs you ever heard. We just had it down perfect.

Now, when I'd go play somewhere, I wouldn't drink anything. Of course, I don't drink at all now, but back in them days I liked to whoop it up a little bit, you know. So, we was going to play at the Strawberry Festival in Buckhannon, and we left and Woody picked up a guy to play with us, bass fiddle player or guitar player. Well, when he got in the back seat with me, he had a fifth. I remember I never eat breakfast, so we started nipping that bottle. I don't know whether Woody knowed it, I don't guess he did. Well, when I got to Buckhannon, I didn't know where I was at, and I don't think the other guy did either. But it rained everything out, so I don't think it hurt anything. I can't even remember coming back. I got on a terrible tear that time.

SR: You mentioned earlier about having some of the Riley Puckett and Clayton McMichen records. How did you learn your music, was it mostly from the other musicians around or did you also have a lot of records and learn things off the radio?

BC: I had a lot of records, and radio, too. Back in them days, I liked Riley Puckett's style. But then there was Nick Lucas, the plectrum-style player. He played with a plectrum pick all the time. He was more what I'd call a classical guitar player, and Riley Puckett was right down into a dyed-in-the-wool runner. He was always running on the guitar, always running them basses.

SR: Your finger-picking style seems really distinctive and beautiful. Is that mainly what you played, or did you play with a flat pick too?

BC: I played a lot with a flat pick. When somebody wanted to hear me play just the guitar I'd start finger style. I learned that from Kirk and Sam McGee. And then I was developing another style, just my own way. People ask me where I learned that style. It just come to me.

SR: There weren't other people around that played that way?

BC: No, no.

SR: Well, when you played for dances did you mostly have to use a straight flat pick, or could you use a finger style or Spanish style too?

BC: Yeah, now a lot of times I would, and I have used thumb picks. Hit the bass and then the others. But I used the straight pick for a long time.

SR: But when people call for a guitar solo, then you do use the finger style?

BC: Yeah, when it's just by itself, like on the "Wildwood Flower." "Wildwood Flower" was a great piece back in the '30s, and anybody that played a guitar played that. That's finger style, you know. Of course, you can play it with a flat pick real good, but it just comes out better if you play it finger style.

SR: One of the other interesting things about your guitar playing is that you do do some Spanish-sounding things. You did say you'd been to Mexico. Was it the circus that got you out there?

BC: It got me started that way.

SR: Tell me about the circus.

BC: Well, there was a show come into Webster Springs there. Me and my brother Jim, we both joined up, and they needed a driver for the lion cage and a driver for the bear cage. So Jim, he took the bear cage and I took the lion cage and we followed that old Seneca Trail. Now, this was a group from Barnum and Bailey, "The Greatest Show on Earth." It was, what do you call it, an offspring of the main thing, you know. We'd show these little towns, then we'd meet the main train. They had their own train and cars, flat cars and everything. My brother, he came back. He went as far as Quinwood, I think, and he was trying to get me to come back home. And I said, "No, I'm going on." So I went down through the Southwest, seen all that country for the first time. That got me started then.

SR: How old were you then?

BC: Oh, let's see, I was in my 'teens.

SR: Was that after you'd worked in the mines in Pennsylvania?

BC: Oh, yeah, yeah, I was 13 there. I went over from El Paso, Texas, I went over to Juarez. And there's where I found them real beautiful guitar players. Seemed like everybody had a guitar, and little kids just played beautiful tunes on the guitar, some real nice. I got crazy about it and one of them played the "Cielito Lindo." It was so beautiful, and I tried to learn that. And while I was down there I was learning to speak Spanish a little bit, too, but it's so many years I forgot it. But I always did love the sound of Spanish music, they got their own way of playing. And it's beautiful.

SR: And it seems like some of that style comes through in some of your pieces.

BC: Yeah, I like to play stuff like that. I just never followed it up and that's where the 25 years that I quit playing hurt me. 'Cause I was playing a little bit more on the Spanish side, you know, and I've forgotten that.

I went back into Pennsylvania later on, in 1939 or '40. I worked a while in a mine down there, and I got with a group and we got to playing over the radio. Charleroi, Pennsylvania, station WESA, and we played there regular. We played for round dances, square, polka, for anything. We got to playing a lot of music then. We had a wonderful band there. There was seven of us all the time, and nine when we needed it.

SR: Did you have a name for the band?

BC: Yeah, Smokey Jack and the Saddle Pals. Smokey Jack was John White. Now he loved music, but he didn't play. He done all of our business, him and his son-in-law, done all of our business and kept the group together, got jobs for us. He wasn't one of the performers, he was a figure caller, a good figure caller, but he didn't play music. Smokey Jack, that was his nickname.

SR: How long did you play with them?

BC: I guess about five years. About every time I moved there would be a different group or something, you know. I

Blackie Cool in his music room. Photograph by Sam Rizzetta.

played around Morgantown for a while and we had a group there called Arizona Rangers. But I was just a while with them, that's when I left and went to Baltimore.

See, I've always held my job, I never tried to make a go of music, that was just a side line. After I left Morgantown I went to Baltimore. Well, first I went to Pittsburgh. See, this mine blew up at Osage and it just missed me, I was still in pit clothes when it went up and killed 56 miners there at Osage. That was in 1942. They sealed the mines off, had to leave one body in there, couldn't find it, you know. I helped go in and get all the bodies, all we could, you know, load them and bring them out. I stayed till it was sealed over and then I had to go look for another job. So I went to Pittsburgh and went to work for the Pennsylvania Railroad, as freight handler, because war was looming and everybody was wanting to work. I stayed there a while and that's when I left and went to Baltimore, and went to work as a welder in the shipyards.

SR: How did you get away from music?

BC: Well, I got married, you know, and the last I was playing was down at WESA, Charleroi, like I was telling you. We had a lot to play around there. After this mine quit up at

Osage, why, I'd left and went to Pittsburgh. I was waiting for it to open up again. I was intending to stay around 'cause I had a lot of friends there. I thought maybe I'd wait till it opened up. It takes six months to smother a mine fire out—the Osage mines was on fire, you know. But then I met Helen my wife, and we left and went to Baltimore and I went to work for Bethlehem Steel shipyard as a welder. After we got to raising a family, why, I got away from my musician friends and 25 years slipped by real fast.

SR: Did you play any music at all when you were in Baltimore?

BC: None at all, none at all.

SR: How did you get back to West Virginia? I know a lot of people want to come back and don't make it.

BC: I worked at that shipyard for quite a few years and they got to losing a lot of their contracts, the company did. Bethlehem Steel would get a contract to build a ship or repair one. But then if they lost a bid, they would bid real high on the next one, 'cause they had to make money. Now, a little company would underbid us. Well, we'd lose that job and there we'd be out of work for a while. So I just got disgusted with working a little bit like that and I come back to West Virginia and went to work back in the mines. And then like I said I met you fellows and got me started back. I guess I'd been a-strumming around on the guitar, maybe for six months or a year, and I met you fellows and got started back.

SR: It seems unusual to hear someone who's played old-time music way back the way you did and yet who knows so many different guitar styles. How did you ever put that many together? I hear you play polkas finger style on guitar and blues and ragtime and fiddle tunes.

BC: I just learned with different groups. With Smokey Jack and the Saddle Pals, I played a lot of polkas. I've forgotten a lot of them, but it's like Woody says. "How in the world," Woody Simmons asked me one time, "can you remember them old tunes?" But they just stuck with me, I've never forgot them. Like one time I started playing "Bye Bye Blues," Woody said he hadn't heard it in 40 years.

SR: He likes some of those Hawaiian ones that you play, too.

BC: Yeah, "Hawaiian Sunset," he likes that one.

SR: Do you still play any tunes that you used to play, you know, with the bar in the Spanish style?

BC: Well, I haven't fooled with that in a long time. Now "Jinks" Morris, I used to play music with him and he played a beautiful Hawaiian guitar. But he was a banjo player, he was a classical banjo player at that time.

SR: He's from around Cowen?

BC: Yeah. Him and I played quite a little bit. And we had one of the best dancers I think that ever been around here, Gandy Digman. Gandy Digman was our dancer, he just couldn't be beat. He started dancing down there in Elkins, one time we was all down there on the street. There was some good dancers around, standing watching him. So one of them got in there and started dancing, competing against him. And I remember he had an overcoat on, Gandy did, and was doing that Gandy dance, you know. So he seen that guy making it pretty hot for him, he just kept a-dancing and throwed his coat off. And I never seen such dancing in my life. Well, you know he had to be good, he was in Keith's Vaudeville. He was good.

SR: Well, he seems to be a legend around here.

BC: Yes, he was really good. Oh, Woody I guess has known him all his life. I met him back in the early '30s. A lot of times we had to go after him when we had a job to play, he may be down in Pennsylvania somewhere. He'd just take off and go.

SR: West Virginia seems to be known for its fiddle players and banjo players. I think maybe that's partly because there have been so many contests, that we've gotten to know who the fiddle and banjo players are. But were there many guitar players back then who played a lot of different guitar music like you?

BC: No, not too many of them. I spent a lot of time in the back room just by myself and things just come to me and I'd put them together. Like a lot of time I'll use all my fingers and call it the roll. Stuff like that just come to me, I never learned that from anybody. When I got first started I picked finger-picking like Sam and Kirk McGee. I heard that kind of playing and got interested in it and I just started playing like that then. Then the other just came to me, you know.

SR: Another thing that impresses me is that you're still making up many of your own original pieces, both in the old-time style and polkas and blues and rags and so on. Were there other musicians who were making up their own music in styles like that?

BC: No, not too many of them, not that I know of. Might be a few made a song up or something. See, I made up two songs, I thought I'd get them registers or whatever. I sent the one to U.S. School of Music, where you send your poems and songs, too, you know. So they wrote back and they liked it but they wanted me to let them change some things to it. But I never did write no more about it. It was personal, you know, it was about Irene Keaton. These two sisters sang, the Keaton sisters. And every Saturday we'd be there playing music, at their home, you know. They were lovely people, and Audie, the other sister, still lives over at Parcoal there yet. But Irene died. Well, I was in Pennsylvania and they'd send me the clippings about it. And later on I wrote and asked the mother if I could compose a song about it. After I wrote the song, I sent it to the Keatons and they kept it. And I never did get it copyrighted or nothing like that.

SR: I know that in some ways you're kind of a legend around Webster Springs and this end of Randolph County. Some of your early exploits are still remembered by people around here.

BC: Well, I used to be sort of wild way back in them days and I was known for fighting, seemed like I couldn't keep out of a fight. People even came all the way from Richwood. Back in them days it just seemed like what you hear of a gun fighter out west—they'd hear in one town of a gun fighter and they'd go to that town to see if they could outdraw him—that's the way it was back then fighting. They'd hear of you fighting and whipping everybody, why, somebody had to go whip you.

And me and the town cop didn't get on very well in Webster Springs. Every time he'd want to come up to arrest me for drinking or fighting, why, him and I'd have a fight. Jake Ferrell was the sheriff. He'd been lawman with my grandfather and he knew me and knew all of us. And he was one of the wonderfulest guys I ever saw in my life and I thought the world of him.

One time this town cop wanted to arrest me and I wouldn't let him do it. Lot of times he'd arrest me or try to arrest me and I hadn't even drank a beer or nothing. He told me later on, years later, he done that to keep me from getting in trouble. But it seemed to me like he was putting me in trouble and I'd fight him every step of the way. One time he got a handcuff on me there, you know, trying to get me up to the jail and I got the best of him, beating the dickens out of him, I guess. He hollered, "Hey, Jake!"—for Jake Ferrell, you know, the sheriff. We was right in where you walk up to the courthouse, and he hollered, "Hey, Jake!" So we'd take turns about hollering for Jake. I knew if Jake came, everything would be all right, you know.

I regretted all that, naturally, after I grew up. But you know what, I had a lot of friends back in them days, too. Back in them days a fight or drinking a little bit didn't matter, wasn't looked down on like it would be today. You see someone drinking and fighting today, you shun them, but that wasn't the case back then. Webster Springs was wild and woolly just like the Wild West. In fact, it looked like it, it had them false fronts and boardwalks, and a mud street up the center. Just looked like Tombstone or something.

SR: I heard some story about your first trip to Summersville. Someone told me you went into Summersville and told them you'd cleaned up everything in Webster Springs and asked if anyone wanted to start anything here in Summersville.

BC: There's a lot of tales told on me that wasn't true. There's a lot of them, too, that I guess was. I never was large, but back home I had a great big sandbag, and I'd practice fighting and I used to love to put on gloves. And I guess I got pretty good at that, you know. I was quick and small, and I never did fight a little man. Seemed like my luck was to get a great big one. So I guess I couldn't hardly talk it down, you know.

SR: Well, life around here was a little rougher in those days.

BC: Yeah, it was. At that time, the coal mines just begin to open up all around, you know. And there were wood hicks, too—I mean the loggers, you know. So you take them two groups of people, miners and wood hicks, they're different, and when they meet in a little town like Webster Springs splinters are going to fly. The next day, after you sober up and everything, you shake hands, you know. Meet again the next payday, and do the same thing.

There's a lot of people in Richwood who still remember Denver Mullens, he was an awful man, actually a strong man, just a young fellow, too. He sang and played guitar pretty good, that's how come me to get acquainted with him. We was good buddies, but he was an awful scrapper. I think he whipped everything over in Richwood, and then he come over in Webster Springs and we got together and had a wonderful time. So we went over to Camden-on-Gauley and we was drinking in a little place there. There was a little town cop there that we called Little Boy Blue, I believe it was. This cop knew Dan real well, and he didn't want him to get drunk.

Well, we was just drinking, having a nice time, so he comes in was going to arrest Denver and Denver squared off for a fight. The cop grabbed for his blackjack, and I grabbed him and told Denver to run. Now here I got my arm full of cop and Denver he run, so when I turned him loose he arrests me. So Denver got word to me not to worry, he went down to Hokey Selmen, who run the wood camp down there. In fact you know the banjo player over there at Cowen, Selmen, that's his uncle. Denver worked for him, he went down and got the money, come back and paid my fine and he went on.

He liked to show off his strength. He had a hundred pound sack of beans. He'd reach down and get it with his mouth, and he had a neck about that big, and he'd pull up that sack of beans with his teeth and throw them over his head. That's something, ain't it? He was a man, indeed he was.

SR: One of the other stories that I've heard is that if you got arrested, you always managed to break out of jail in time for the square dance.

BC: Oh, yeah, I didn't need them bars to keep me in. First time I was ever in jail in my life, I was in there for nothing. A girlfriend of mine brought me a hacksaw blade. I sawed out that night and was gone. They all know it in Webster Springs. I guess I tore that old jail up and they had to build a new one there.

You take a small town like Webster Springs, you break out five times, why, it's just unusual, you know. So it wasn't nothing to see an inch-and-a-half headline: "In Again, Out Again Blackie." Poor old Jack Ferrell, he beared it through with a smile, and every time I'd leave he'd smile. It became a game with us. A lot of times he knew where I was and let it go, you know. Of course, it'd be different nowadays. But back in the '30s, things was different. You done things then that you thought was all right. Drinking and fighting was a way of life for every young man in them days, you know, raised up like I was—I mean on your own ever since 13 years old.

SR: I've heard some stories about you and some of the musicians that passed through the Webster Springs area.

BC: There were groups traveling back in them days. One group had an old flatbed truck, the Tweedy Brothers. The redheaded Tweedy boys come up into Webster Springs and I got acquainted with them. Just as luck should have it we was having a square dance at Ella's that night. So Aretus and I liked them so well we asked them to play for the square dance as an honor for them. And they made a little extra money that way. We done that several times they was up.

Blind Alfred Reed, now I got acquainted with him down in Morgantown, he traveled quite a lot. He married a young girl and she was a fiddler. Once they were up in Webster Springs, at what we call Morton's Store, playing on the outside there. I went up, told them come down, we had a dance

"I learned a lot of blues from an old friend of mine in Pennsylvania, an old black guy," Blackie Cool recalls. "I just went crazy over that kind of playing." Photograph by Sam Rizzetta.

that night. "How about you playing for the dance, so everybody could meet and hear you?" We do things like that, different musicians come in, why, we let them play in our place. Blind Alfred Reed, I guess he's dead by now, it's been years. He was a good singer, he played and sang and then his wife played the violin, she was really good.

SR: Do you remember Clayton McMichen?

BC: Oh, yeah, I played some with Clayton McMichen in Webster Springs. I must have been pretty fair back in them days. He was making up the Georgia Wildcats, and I found out later Woody Simmons met him that same year. I didn't know that till Woody told me. But this year he was going around playing, because I remember he told me his next stop was Cincinnati, Ohio. He was making up the Georgia

Wildcats at that time. I played the guitar, what I guess you'd call trying out, and he give me the job right off. I was up to go. I wanted to go but I had a girlfriend, and she had other ideas, you know. And when he left, he left without me. If I'd went with him I could have been a good musician by now because his band became famous, the Georgia Wildcats.

SR: That might have changed your life.

BC: It might have, it might have.

SR: But you're still playing great music today.

BC: Well, you know I quit for 25 years. That hurt me a lot. I could have been good, probably.

SR: Well, you certainly are good now, it's good that you're back into it.

BC: You know I sort of got to give you credit for that, you and Gerry Milnes and Paul Reisler.

SR: Well, we just like to hear you play and to play music with you. One of the things that seems unusual around here is that you play the blues. I can't think of other guitar players that I've heard around here that play much blues.

BC: Well, now, when we used to live in Pennsylvania, I learned a lot from an old friend of mine, an old black guy. I forget his name. He was one of the prettiest players ever I saw, he had long fingers. He'd be playing down here and tremolo it and add this finger right up there and maybe reach seven frets maybe. And I'd never seen anything like it, and then he reaches up there and gets it, and I just went crazy over that kind of playing. He'd sit with me and I'd play with him and I sort of learned to get started like that. And then you improvise, he told me. That's the way he learned his own blues. Of course, you take the black race, they are actually blues oriented. They really love to play the blues.

SR: It seems like when you play the blues everyone wants to hear the blues, they really like that. Was it popular back then, too?

BC: Yes, it was.

SR: Did you get a lot of requests for blues?

BC: Yeah, and way back I used to play the "Saint Louis Blues." You may have heard me run over it a little bit. I used to get it in the key of G minor, but I've never tried to get back into that yet. I may do it later. After all, I'm only 68 years old, got a long time yet.

EDITOR'S NOTE: This article story first appeared in the fall 1981 issue of *Goldenseal* (vol. 7, no. 3). William "Blackie" Cool, a frequent guest artist of the Augusta Heritage Arts Workshops in Elkins and other statewide festivals, died on August 17, 1988, at the age of 75.

Carl Rutherford

MUSIC FROM THE COALFIELDS

Jim McGee

W HEN Carl Rutherford performed at the 1978 Vandalia Gathering in Charleston, the audience was
spellbound. "You are about to hear an incredible
guitar player, singer and songwriter who recently moved
back home to West Virginia," the master of ceremonies announced. "Straight from McDowell County, give a big welcome to Carl Rutherford."

Carl's guitar rang out with fancy finger-picking as he hyp-
notized the audience with his own instrumental, "West Virginia Breakdown." There wasn't a sound in the place until
the last note rang out—and then the audience roared. Later
on Carl did a set with Hazel Dickens, a nationally known
singer from West Virginia. With his deep resonating voice,
Carl put ineffable feeling into a country blues version of
"Amazing Grace." The emcee had to send Carl and Hazel
back on stage. They played five encores, and the audience
shouted, "More! More!"

After Carl Rutherford moved from California back home
to the McDowell community of Warriormine in 1975, he
brought back to the mountains a style of guitar picking that
people had virtually forgotten. Carl plays a finger-picking
style that was popular in the coalfields of southern West Virginia during the 1920s, a style which his family had preserved and passed on to him.

In 1950 Carl had moved from the coal mines of southern
West Virginia to the logging camps of northern California,
where he continued to develop his guitar playing and songwriting in the honky-tonks around Redding. When Carl
moved back home a quarter-century later, his song style was
a highly artistic blend of mountain ballads, old-time music,
big band tunes, bluegrass, country, honky-tonk, blues, and
gospel. Not only does Carl perform traditional songs with
deep pathos, but he writes new, innovative songs about coal
mining, his home in West Virginia, his faith, romance, and
love gone bad.

His songwriting reflects the inner conflict that people face
when they migrate out of West Virginia—a feeling of love
for home mixed with the necessity of finding steady work
out of state. When Carl moved away, he did not intend to
reject his mountain roots. To know why Carl left West
Virginia, you have to listen to his coal mining stories.

He recalls the pride he felt when he started to work at the
Olga Coal Company mine after earning his miner's certifi-

Guitarist Carl Rutherford in 1994 on the front porch of his home
in the southern McDowell County community of Warriormine.
Photograph by Michael Keller.

cate in 1948 at the age of 18. "Got me a job in the big mines,"
he says. "Got someone to pass the physical for me, because I
wasn't physically capable. Paid 'em to do it."

But after two weeks digging coal, Carl witnessed a disaster
that demolished his aspirations of being a miner. A string of
mine cars overloaded with rock, coal, and heavy batteries lost
its brakes and barreled down the track. Ahead of the runaway was a double-header mantrip carrying 60 men, putting
along at 12 miles an hour. Some distance from the bottom

West Virginia festival stages are Carl Rutherford's second home. This photograph was taken at the 1988 Vandalia Gathering in Charleston by Michael Keller.

the runaway caught up with the mantrip. Carl vividly recalls the collision: "All this acid and all this steel and all this rock, all this weight—rock and steel and acid—all this hit and went all over everybody," he says. "We went to funerals for a whole week."

Following that week of funeral services, Carl stood on the mine elevator cage ready to go back to work. But something made him stop and say, "I ain't going."

Carl's father was on the cage. He said, "Son, if you don't go down now, you never will be able to again." Carl stepped back on, and as they were about ready to go down, he hopped off again. He stepped on and off until everybody was fuming mad.

Finally he said to himself, "All right, I'm going to go back into this mine and I'm gonna work in this mine till I save up enough to leave here. And then I'm out of here. It took me about two or three years to do that." In July of 1950 Carl moved to California to seek his fortune.

Leaving was not easy. Some of Carl's buddies had left to find construction jobs in Virginia, but they always came straggling home to ride the cage back down into the black hole of the mine. Carl headed for the other side of the country to make a clean break. "I got far enough away," he explains, "that during a short financial depression I wouldn't head back to the coalfields. It would take a massive move to get back 3,000 miles."

So Carl told P.D. Turner, the general superintendent of the Olga Coal Company, that he was not coming back to work after his miner's vacation. "I'm going to California," he announced, "relocating and starting me a new life in a different kind of trade."

The super was not going to let a good worker go that easily.

"'If you get out there and get you a job, you drop me a card and let me know,'" Carl recalls him saying, "'and I'll give your job to somebody else permanently. Otherwise I'll keep your job open for ye one or two weeks extra.'" Carl said he appreciated that but didn't think he'd need it.

Three days after he arrived in Redding, Carl wrote a letter to Turner saying that he had a job making $2 an hour, the same wage that coal miners made, and that everything was beautiful. In actuality, Carl was out of work for six to seven weeks until he found a job making $1.25 an hour at the Knotly Box Factory. After six months, he received a raise to $1.30 an hour. Fortunately, he landed a better job for $2 an hour working as a logger, a choker setter—the man who fastens cables to logs—and running a D-8 Cat. He began to live his own life the way he wanted to.

Carl can tell you exactly why he left the coal mines. "Somewhere in that phase of time I learned that a mule was more valuable to a mining company than a human being," he told me. "Because when a human being gets killed, it costs you enough chalk to go out and write up on the board, 'Need another hand.' But if you lost a mule, you had to go pay the *money* to buy another mule. So I'd seen the value and worth of a human being in a job like that—wasn't quite my bag of apples. I count myself worth a little something, more than a mule anyway."

Carl was raised with a strong work ethic, and he is not afraid to protest practices that are degrading to workers. His "Coal Miner's Song" contains a subtle yet powerful tone of protest in the second verse:

No a man's life ain't nothing,
Lord that's how it seems,
They're just muscle and guts,
Down here working these machines.
And when the rock it starts falling,
The boss man says, "Son
You got to bring out my machine,
Don't you leave it and run."

To the boss in this verse, the mining machine is worth more than the life of the worker, just as in older times the mule was more important than a man. Some workers tolerated harsh working conditions because they were dependent on the company for their income, housing, and groceries. Carl Rutherford headed for California.

When Carl moved from Warriormine to Redding, he had keenly felt the conflicts and problems of the mining community. But he wasn't about to throw out the good with the bad. He preferred to retain his identity by playing the music he had learned from his family, which represents a deep and vital musical tradition.

As a boy in West Virginia, Carl learned to play guitar from his Uncle Will Muncey, who picked the guitar like a Dobro tuned to an open-E chord. Uncle Will used a knife handle to play slide guitar. Since the action on Carl's guitar was too high to let him press the strings down easily, he learned to play slide in an open tuning.

Earlier West Virginia guitar players in the coalfields had used the same open tuning that Carl learned. Among them was Frank Hutchison from Logan County, who recorded "The Train That Carried My Girl From Town" in 1927 and "Worried Blues" in the same year (now on Rounder Records 1007). From Beckley, the duo Roy Harvey and Leonard Copeland used the same open tuning in their recording "Weary Lonesome Blues" (County Records 523).

Though Carl never heard the music of Frank Hutchison or Roy Harvey, he picked up a similar style not only from Uncle Will but from his aunt's brother, Lee Altizer, who also played "The Train That Carried My Girl From Town." Some of Altizer's guitar licks, as Carl demonstrates them, resemble the guitar picking in "Brown Skin Blues" (County Records 511), which Dick Justice from Logan County recorded in the 1920s.

Carl also learned a lot of music from his Uncle Iser Muncey, who picked the banjo with two fingers and played finger-style guitar. Carl recalls seeing Iser pick his banjo after he came in from the mines, black all over except for white feet, white teeth, and white eyes.

Carl's mother, who played the banjo, taught him square dance tunes, mountain songs, and ballads such as "John Henry," "John Hardy," "Rovin' Gambler," and "In the Pines." His mother picked the banjo with her thumb and first finger, as did most of the banjo players where Carl grew up. Carl picks his guitar with his thumb and first finger. In California, when he was homesick, he would sit out on his front porch and sing songs he learned from his mother—songs that turned his fancy back to the beautiful hills of West Virginia.

Out there, he also remembered the popular tunes he had heard while growing up during the 1930s and '40s. At 17 years of age, Carl had worked in the Villa Vista Cafe in Abingdon, Virginia, where he listened to popular music on the jukebox. The pieces included mostly big band tunes like Glen Miller's "In the Mood" and Artie Shaw's "Summit Ridge Drive," which inspired a tune Carl later wrote in California. On the jukebox Carl also liked to hear Ernest Tubb's honky-tonk hit, "Walkin' the Floor Over You," and Eddie Arnold's "It's a Sin."

Carl took all of these musical influences to California, where he bought an amplifier and a National electric guitar made out of a two-by-twelve. In the logging camp, he perfected his guitar style in Uncle Will's open-E tuning, which allowed him to play lead and rhythm simultaneously. He applied, in other words, his two-finger mountain guitar style to honky-tonk music. He was playing in beer joints where people wanted to dance to the honky-tonk sound rather than the mountain songs of Bill Monroe.

Near Orick, California, Carl played guitar in honky-tonks four nights a week. He says that he ran a dance hall for a year in Pine Grove, where he lived, outside of Redding. During the winter, when logging work was slack, Carl would draw unemployment and pick up a little money in the joints and bars, playing music along with a steel guitar player and sometimes a bass and drums. Somewhere around 1954, he went totally blind because of an infection in his optic nerve. After overcoming the infection, he partially regained his vision two years later. During his blindness, he played for a year at a honky-tonk called the Green Derby for $20.92 a week.

The need for loud, rhythmic dance music in the honky-tonks inspired Carl to write many songs and instrumentals. Once while he and his steel guitar player were tuning up to play at the Green Derby, they composed a honky-tonk dance tune on the spot, based on Artie Shaw's tune "Summit Ridge Drive," which Carl remembered from the Villa Vista in Vir-

People familiar with the exuberance of Carl Rutherford's music won't be surprised to learn that the man is a dreamer as well, with schemes as wild and free as his mountain home country. Photograph by Michael Keller.

Carl Rutherford shows off a handcrafted sports car in a shed near his house. Photograph by Michael Keller.

ginia. They called the tune "Mr. Rhythm." When Carl recorded the song for the first time in 1991, he changed the name from "Mr. Rhythm" to "Blue Ridge Drive." Most of all, the tunes that inspired Carl's songwriting were the tunes that helped him feel connected to his home in the mountains. And the music he had learned as a young man helped him make a meager living in the honky-tonks.

Country music historian Bill Malone points out that honky-tonk music, which combines the rural sound of country music with the urban sound of the electric guitar, became popular in the 1940s among rural people who moved to the cities. That makes sense in Carl's case. Honky-tonk music allowed him to adapt to northern California while preserving his mountain heritage. Carl lived three miles north of Redding in a semi-rural community called Pine Grove. Situating himself between the country and the city, he could keep up his rural ways, yet still accommodate the culture of an urban area.

By keeping one foot in the country, Carl was carrying on a deep tradition in his family. All of his grandparents were farmers who stayed connected to the land instead of working in the coal mines. Riley Muncey, Carl's maternal grandfather, was born around Inez, Kentucky, close to the West Virginia line. Carl says that Riley was half Irish and half Cherokee. Somewhere during the 1890s Riley migrated to McDowell County, where he married Patsy Hagerman of Bradshaw. They had eight children, among them two sons, Will and Iser, and a daughter, Clara.

The Muncies leased land in Shop Hollow just north of Warriormine, where they grew corn and ground it in their mill to sell and trade. They also dug roots such as ginseng, poke root, lady slipper, yellowroot or goldenseal, and cohosh, which they sold to a medicine manufacturer in St. Louis, Missouri. Patsy made lye soap to trade and sell as well as for the family's use. Pap Riley, as Carl calls his grandfather, cut timber out of which he made mine props to sell to mining companies, but that was as close as he came to the mines. The Muncies had no reason to work underground.

Fred and Ruthie Rutherford, Carl's paternal grandparents, farmed throughout their lives and ran a boardinghouse for railroad workers near Coal Creek, Tennessee. Fred never worked in the mines. Carl's father, Robert Bruce Rutherford, hoboed on trains during his teenage years. He finally settled down in Warriormine, where he married Clara Muncey on April 11, 1926, and began working in the mines. After they were married, Robert and Clara rented a company house near the company store, but in 1939, they moved outside of town to Shop Hollow, just down from Pap Riley, on land that they leased from the Berwind Land Company. By leasing land, Carl's family enjoyed a degree of independence from the coal company, which could control residents of the town with the threat of eviction.

Carl carried on his own version of the family strategy in Pine Grove, California, by purchasing land cheaply and building a house out of wood scraps from a lumber yard where he worked. He adjusted by learning new ways, keeping the old ones, branching out while maintaining his roots, being rural and urban simultaneously.

All that showed in his music, especially. In California, Carl began writing innovative songs, not just singing old-time songs from the southern mountains. His big move encouraged Carl's songwriting by putting him in honky-tonk beer joints where he needed to compose instrumental tunes for people on the dance floor.

He wasn't the first mountaineer to find his creativity sparked by a change of scene. Sarah Ogan Gunning, a radical singer from eastern Kentucky, began writing her songs after leaving the coalfields and moving to New York City. Hazel Dickens, with whom Carl performed at the Smithsonian Folklife Festival in 1978 as well as at Vandalia that year, wrote a bundle of songs after she moved from West Virginia to Baltimore. Carl says that in California he wrote 20 to 25 new songs, though he has recorded only 12 of them. Before he left West Virginia in July of 1950, Carl only wrote one song, "All Because of You," composed in the spring of 1950.

Why hadn't he written more songs in West Virginia? Maybe the energy which had gone into escaping the mines now found a new outlet. After working himself out of the coal camp, Carl could channel his creativity into his music and his songwriting.

By moving to California Carl also gained new experiences which he could use for songwriting material. His writing blossomed when he got married and had a family. Many of Carl's songs are about the excitement of finding a woman companion, his eventual frustration in romance, and then finally bidding each other farewell. He married in 1957 and tried to make the relationship work until 1975, when he and his first wife were divorced.

Carl says that he wrote 85 percent of his songs as a way of dealing with problems with women. "That woman was rough on you," as his daughter Deb remarked on one occasion, "but she made you write some good songs."

By writing songs about the loss of love, Carl was able to put it behind him and to try again. "Gonna Let My Guitar Put You Out of My Mind," the title of one song suggests, while another is called "Gonna Give Love One More Fling." And after coming back to West Virginia, he did. In 1991, Carl married Frankie Patton, a native of Caretta, a coal camp north of War. They reside in Shop Hollow, on the leased land that Carl's family passed on to him.

Now Carl Rutherford uses his music to enrich the culture of his own community. In 1994, he did 18 performances for children in the Head Start program and at War junior high

Carl Rutherford (left) and writer Jim McGee had just taken part in the local Mountain Music Festival when this photograph was taken by Michael Keller.

and elementary schools, on top of his steady schedule of church revivals and family reunions. Carl is the founder and president of the Mountain Music Association in McDowell County, which sponsors a folk festival the second Saturday in July.

"The biggest thrill of my life," Carl recalls, "was to come back to West Virginia and play at folk festivals for whole families—parents and children." People enjoy hearing his music not only at Vandalia but also at the West Virginia State Folk Festival at Glenville, the Appalachian String Band Festival at Camp Washington-Carver near Clifftop, the Augusta Festival in Elkins, and the Stonewall Jackson Jubilee at Jackson's Mill. He has recorded four cassette tapes of original songs, which include a variety of blues, gospel, honky-tonk, country, and mountain guitar picking. In the summer of

1993, he entertained visitors at welcome centers on the West Virginia Turnpike.

Carl's music allowed him to keep his roots in the mountain soil of McDowell County while moving across the country and branching out in all directions. Perhaps the beauty of his music is in the way it speaks to everyone who tries to negotiate the transitions of life by making grand changes while hanging on to the best of tradition. Strong branches do grow from deep roots.

EDITOR'S NOTE: This article first appeared in the fall 1994 issue of *Goldenseal* (vol. 20, no. 3). Carl Rutherford still lives in southern West Virginia, works as a community organizer, produces the annual Mountain Music Festival in Coretta, and performs widely.

Nat Reese

SOMETHING TO GIVE

Michael Kline

I was introduced to Nat Reese 10 years ago by folklorist Joan Fenton, who researched black music in West Virginia during the 1970s. Nat and his wife Bessie have since opened their hearts and Mercer County home to me during several visits. I have always been impressed by how Bessie's warm practicality balances Nat's wandering, artistic nature, and by the wonderful ways they have kept each other going through difficult years.

Protracted conversations with Nat have revealed his strong grasp of local history, which he views without heavy judgments or bitterness. His story spans a period of great social and technological change, especially during the decades of the 1920s and '30s. This was the wide-open era of boom towns and labor camps, when Duke Ellington, Bessie Smith, and many others toured through the coalfields "meeting the paydays."

As a struggling young musician, Nat was in the thick of exciting changes and heart-breaking recessions. His music playing took him to every corner of southern West Virginia, from roadhouses and house parties to uptown "white only" clubs, where "you could play dance music for the people all night, and then the man would refuse to sell you a sandwich on the way out."

And though Nat describes the kind of inhibition that

Blues guitarist Nat Reese in 1987. Photograph by Michael Keller.

results from such abuses, he met the world around him undaunted, with courageous enthusiasm. You will feel here the warmth in which Nat wraps his stories, and sense his optimism as you smile at his wit and turn of phrase.

The recorded conversation from which this article grew occurred at Nat's home in Princeton in June 1981. That year I interviewed various West Virginia musicians under the joint support of Davis and Elkins College and the Humanities Foundation of West Virginia, to better understand the diversity of West Virginia's cultural make-up. A series of 13 eight-minute programs called "The Home Place" was the final product of the project. We called Nat Reese's program "Bird in the Hand." Also present at that visit were Bessie Reese and Doug Yarrow.

Here, Nat relives his experiences growing up in the coalfields and traces his development as a musician. He usually begins his narratives talking about his family, especially his enterprising father, Thomas.

❧

Nat Reese: I was born in Salem, Virginia, on Water Street, 1924. My dad was Thomas Reese Sr. My brother, he was Thomas Reese Jr. My sister is Barbara Lee Reese, which she's a McClanahan now, lives in Mullens. And old Nathaniel, me. Old Nat. N.H. Reese.

Michael Kline: Did your family come from the deep South?

NR: See, my father was born in Birmingham. Everybody was migrating, looking for work. He got as far as Salem, Virginia, and he started working for a coal and ice company in Roanoke. So he bought a home in Salem. He would do custodial work in the evening for the women's college there, Hollins College.

He started him a little restaurant there on Water Street, oh, about a block down the street from where we lived. He'd sell soft drinks and had two pool tables there. He paid a guy to run that while he would drive a truck for the coal and ice company.

And then he heard of all the money that people was making out here in the coalfields. You know how rumors go—you can shake money off the trees. So he decided he'd kind of like to shake a couple of these trees. He came out here and worked on the Virginia Railroad for about 58 years, and he still didn't find that money tree.

In '28 he moved us from Salem to Itmann, West Virginia, which is in Wyoming County, down below Mullens. Then we moved back up here to Princeton. And then we moved from here back to the coalfields, and then came back again.

At that time, you know, jobs were pretty plentiful. I'll tell you what was really good about the coalfields at that time: If you could play music or play baseball, you could get a job. They would make you a job. One of the workers, all he had to do was go to the bank boss and tell him, say, "There's a

An undated promotional photograph for the Starlight Gospel Singers of Itmann, in Wyoming County. Nat Reese (left) got his musical start singing gospel. Photographer unknown.

Nat Reese takes time out for a favorite pet. He says his cat is deaf, but they have no trouble understanding each other. Photograph by Michael Keller.

good ball player here needs a job." And they'd give him a job picking bone, or anything, just to keep him there to play, because the quartets and choirs and baseball teams were the main goal at that time. ["Bone" is the shale or other impurities in coal, which was removed by hand in the days before mechanical processing plants.—ed.]

All those mines wanted to keep the people happy. And they knew to let them sing and have a good time, play ball. They'd get a bulldozer to push the slate dump off and flatten that slate dump and make a ball field out of it. And on Sunday evening it'd be more people there than you could get into one of these parks you see around here, people all up the side of the hill looking at that baseball game.

And those guys played a whole lot better ball, some of them did, than the major leaguers now getting two and three million dollars a year. I'm not lying. Some of these players now couldn't hold a light to those players, boy! Those guys back there then would run a hundred-yard dash in, oh, 9.2, 9.3, 9.5. They were doing that here in 1935, '36. That's right. It was awful swift fellows, yeah boy. Awful swift.

MK: Did you play ball yourself?

NR: I played after I got up some size, after we came up here. I never played in the coalfields because I was too small then. I sang in a quartet with the grown guys then. They always needed a tenor and see, my voice hadn't changed and I had a soprano that they could use. I think that's how I got into that religious singing. They called it gospel music at that time.

Of course my dad, he played the guitar. My mother, she played the accordion. But after he got his fingers all mashed up working in the coal, he quit playing and didn't play any more. He just played long enough to show me a few chords, and I went from there on my own until I moved up here to Princeton. That was in early '36.

I met a fellow called Mitchell Gordon. He was young, too, about three years older than I, and he was just a natural, he was a born musician. He could write it, play it, any instrument. Well, he started me. And he said, "If you're going to play, you could play well by ear, but let's play by music." So we started burning a lot of midnight oil then. We'd work together at the Elks Club down here, and then after the club would close, we'd stay up and practice music until 4:30 and 5:00 in the morning. Then we'd sleep about three or four hours and then we'd open. We'd stay at that club all night long. It'd be in the wintertime a lot of times, and snow was on the ground. It was warm in there and so we'd just stay there. We had to clean the club up and open it up at 9:00 the next morning. Then he'd go home and change clothes and come back, and then I'd go home and change clothes and come back, and we kept the ball rolling.

MK: You're not talking much about hardship through the Depression in your own family. You seem like you got by.

NR: Well, I'll tell you, it was rough. It was rough. But it wasn't as hard on my family as it was on a lot of people. Now I remember my dad, he'd work eight to 10 hours, and he wasn't making but $2.64 a day. And he would take part of that and give people dinner and food, and buy food and pack them lunches when they were hoboing. If you came to the door he'd give you a meal and pack you a lunch to help you on your way.

I never can remember being barefooted in the wintertime. I had new shoes in the winter and I *wanted* to go barefooted in the summer. He'd always buy me a pair of shoes for Sunday school. If I didn't go to Sunday school there was no playing.

See, that was one of those things back there then. It wasn't so much what you had. It was what you did with what you had. Most of those people, they had a running account in the company store. You've heard the old Tennessee Ernie piece, "I Owe My Soul to the Company Store?" There's many a man never seen the light out of that deal. They were good workers and they worked for years and years. The company knew that they was good for the money because they prove themselves worthy of working, you know. You could get anything you wanted. And if you needed some money, it was always a way they could fix it so you could get the money, and you'd pay it back in payments. It's just one of those things.

When I came along they didn't have all this machinery and stuff in the mines. We had machines that cut coal in some mines, and in some mines you had to cut coal with a pick. And when you went into the mines the bank boss says, "Bring me a cut of coal or bring your tools." You know what that means. You clean up the whole cut, or you don't have any job. That's right. And he didn't pay for no rock. The time that you took to load that rock and carry it outside and dump it, you didn't get anything for. You just got paid for the coal.

MK: So how old were you when you first went in the mines?

NR: Oh, I first went in about 17 or 18, somewhere along in there. I would work a while and then I would go to school, and then I'd work a while and then go to the railroad. I guess I had about eight years in the mines, something like that. I worked in a lot of small mines up this way, you know, these little one- and two-horse mines up here in Matoaka.

Back, say, in the early '40s and back in there, boy, you had to do your own shooting. You'd blow your holes, cap up your own powder, and boy, that put out a smoke and a gas that was hard to inhale. And you'd have to get that out and move that rock. Oh, you'd have to go back on that powder. You shoot it and then you take your shovel, a No. 4 shovel, and fan the smoke, to go back in there so you can hurry up and start loading, set your timber and start loading, you see.

Nat Reese (center) makes music at a Rockwell company picnic. He played professionally with black bands but often sat in with white musicians, too. Photographer unknown.

And you had to do your own brattice work. Brattice is nothing but burlap, you've seen burlap bags. It was cut in great big sheets and you would nail it on the posts, on your timbers, and that's how you got air to the coal face where you worked. And it didn't work good. Now, I'll just tell you, it didn't work good.

Well, now they got a law, said you must have 10 years, or better, or you would have black lung. Well, two could be loading in a place, and that dust would be so bad till I couldn't see you over there. I know you're over there because I can hear you shoveling, but I can't see.

And, oh my God, you cough that stuff up. I bet you the last mine I worked in, it was three years afterwards that I was still coughing up black. And I don't know how many years that it was just brown, just like I was chewing tobacco, or something. Two or three years of that is black lung. Now I've got it. Now, I passed my test for it.

MK: I wanted to ask you a little more about the late '30s and early '40s. Were there a lot of black people from the South coming into southern West Virginia at that time?

NR: The biggest part of them was already here. I'll tell you what they were doing. The young ones was growing up and having more children, and they were just multiplying more. The biggest of the migration from the South in the late '30s went to Michigan, Chicago, and New York, places like that. You see, those people that run the foundries and steel mills

and things like that, would send buses all the way south and bring those people up, because they were hard workers, brother. Now, you take a man that's been working for 75 cents a day, and you give him $3.50 to $4 and $5 an hour, that man's going to really put out some work. You see my point?

Many of the black families here got pretty well established. Now what they did during that time, they would move around. You'd find them leaving, some leaving the coalfields and coming this way, some leaving here and going to the coalfields. Well, see, some younger ones would marry, they'd leave here to go to the coalfields and go to work, where some of the older heads had worked themselves out.

But a lot of them would drift in here because this is a border. This is the border part of our state, you see. You can just come right across the line from Virginia or Tennessee. I mean, because it's just a hop, skip, and a jump. They just easily drift into here. This was called for years the gateway into the coalfields.

It was a lot of people that come in and stayed 10, 15 years, and moved, just kept going, go somewhere else. They would maybe come in here and stay six or seven years and then go on down the line to Logan. And then, maybe seven years later, you'll run into him in Beckley, or somewhere, and he says, "I settled in Logan," or "I settled in Glen White on the other side of Beckley." Something like that.

But they were mostly musicians. I'll tell you what. We had

what they called a dance band, but we played jazz, and then we played polkas. We played blues. It wouldn't be the regular, what you call alley blues, or cotton field blues. It wasn't the regular Delta blues, see. There's a difference in Delta blues and, say, sentimental blues. The original blues did originate in the Delta bottom, between Louisiana and Georgia in different communities down there. When it began to travel through Chicago, different ones would leave from there and come this way. They'd come in here and begin to kind of modernize it a little. They'd make it smoother. Make a lull, or put more feeling in it.

MK: By the mid-'30s there was a whole class, I guess, of traveling professional musicians?

NR: It was. And they was the poorest bunch in the United States. Man, you didn't make a lot. People wanted to hear, but they didn't have the money. They didn't have the money to pay for the music. Oh, when you made $10 to $12 a night apiece, you have made a lot of money. You have made a lot of money.

MK: And yet the famous musicians did come into the coalfields, Bessie Smith and . . .

NR: They traveled all around. Now I seen a time when Duke Ellington came over here and played at the Hillbilly Barn, between here and Bluefield, for $500. Well, you couldn't get his band, several years before he died, under $50,000 or $100,000 for a night to save your life. And I think when he was getting the $500 he played better music, really, in a way, because he was in his prime then. Ah, that was Duke Ellington, Tiny Bradshaw, Count Basie, Jimmie Lunceford, the Woody Boys, and Gene Krupa. He was with Benny Goodman then.

They came over here to what they called dance halls then. They would come and have dances there, and it would be people all the way from Charleston come in here to hear it. You'd get people out of 18 or 20 counties. You'd see white in there mixed in it, yeah. Yes sir.

MK: What were some of the wide-open places in the coalfield then? People have talked to me a lot about McDowell County's Keystone, for example.

NR: Yeah, Keystone was open. Wide open. Cinder Bottom. That's where I was playing the night the guy shot through the guitar.

We were playing and the people were having a good time and dancing and somebody got to arguing, a sailor and some guy got to arguing, and somebody shot. I felt a tug and when I looked down it was a hole there, and in the back of it was a hole there. I got up and politely made it to the door and pointed to the guitar and told them, I says, "Someone has shot a hole in it and I won't be back!" I went out and got in the car and locked my door, and I didn't go back any more. That seemed to have been a warning to me. And I tried to heed it. Well, they stood around and tried to see if

anyone was hit, or anything. And then they went on and played the rest of the night.

MK: Tell us a little more about what people mean when they say Keystone was wide open.

NR: Well, someone was killed down there about every week. There was gambling, hustling, numbers playing, prostitution. You could buy whiskey, any kind you wanted: Scotch, bourbon, good moonshine, bad moonshine, almost-good moonshine. And home brew. Every other door, or every three or four doors there was a house you could buy whiskey, or something else. And if that's not wide open, I don't know what you would call it.

And see, the law at that time was ruled by the biggest company that's there. It was a politician deal. People had no say-so, much. The politicians say, "I'm getting money from that place and that place and that place, so don't you bother them. As long as nobody ain't hurt or nothing, just pass on by." Well, that went on.

There was a lot of places like that in the coalfields here. Lester was that way, over near Beckley. And of course, you know Charleston was that way for years and years and years. And, uh, Logan, Welch, Northfork, Keystone, Bramwell, Switchback. A lot of times, places like that gets a name only according to who's telling it, you know. Logan was as open as Keystone was, really.

MK: What kind of music was made in those places?

NR: Piano music, mandolin, guitar, and the small bands—three, four, five, and six pieces. And the blues, you would hear them at what they called house parties. On Friday nights one house would have beer, home brew, and whiskey, and they would hire someone to play, or two people to play guitar. And they'd have one of the biggest house dances ever was, boy! People'd be dancing everywhere. A man'd knock the paneling out of between two rooms and make one great big space. People would get in there and dance just the same as they was in a ballroom, boy, at the Holiday Inn! Yes, sir. And they would dance all night long, as long as the music was there.

Of course, when you seen one house party you seen them all. They were no different, wasn't nothing but a couple of walls knocked out, where you'd have enough room to jitterbug. That's what they called dancing back in that day, it was jitterbug. It was swing, and then jitterbug, and then they went to doing the "Big Apple," and "Susie Q," and all that, you know. And they started doing the shuffle, the slow drag. They did the two-step and they waltzed, and they just kept progressing. Somebody find out they could dance a little bit faster, and there you go.

Everybody knew who they were dancing with at that time. You disco now, and everybody's out there doing their own thing. I don't know who is with who, when you look out there. And I don't think they do, either, part of the time. I think they start with one and end up with another. It does look like that. Of course, I know who they come with, you know, but it does look awful far between.

People would sell fish, chicken, barbecue, chitlins, all such stuff [at the house parties]. You'd be surprised at the money people have made. People have made their living and got well-off doing that, because, you see, during that time they were building the railroads through Wyoming County and on to Virginia. And they had boxcar loads of people come from east Virginia, work on the railroad. They called them "extra gang men."

Biggest of those people were single, and they'd line those rails and ties and lay track. Those guys made that money, and they spent it just like they made it, brother! It was good money, because they made a little bit better than the average worker at that time, which was $5.18 for 10 hours. That was a lot of money then, because you could get a two-pound box of sugar for seven cents, eight cents. So that's what made the great difference in the economy at that time.

The first time I ever played anywhere out in my life, I was about nine years old. My father bought me an instrument, it was bigger than a ukelele, but smaller than a regular guitar. They called it a tiple and it had 10 strings. In Mullens, they gave some kind of shindig there. And one of the men who worked for the foreman on the railroad, a white fellow, heard me sitting on the porch singing and playing that tiple. He went down there and told. And they asked me to come down and play on that show and told me, said, "You don't have to play but one song." And I think I played 10 songs before they let me off that stage. I was nine years old then. Me and my little tiple. That's right. The first song was "Corrine, Corrine," because that was a popular piece back then. I can remember he said, "You won't have to play but one song."

My father started me off in the key of C, playing pieces like "Corrine." You remember that old piece. Years ago you heard people singing it. "The Preacher and the Bear," that type of thing, and "Shanghai Chicken," those pieces. Now they are real old pieces, and the biggest of them were played in the key of C.

But we don't play them now, a lot of these pieces, like the people played them originally, because those pieces were given from one person. Then another person got a little different style and he'll play it a little different. And it keeps a-bobbing, and after a while you got about nine different styles of that one song, and it's about that long, when it was about this long in the beginning. Of course, now, you take pieces like "Stardust," and "How High the Moon," and "Blue Moon," and stuff like that—"Mood Indigo," and "Solitude," and "September Song," and all those pieces—ain't too much variation you can put to them, you know. They really hold their own, because a lot of those pieces never die.

Oh, I'll say two centuries from now people will still be singing "Stardust." That's right! One of the beautifulest pieces ever wrote.

But at that time I played a whole gob of songs, you know. I'd keep setting around and go from one song to another. I'd learn a whole lot off the radio, see. Everybody had them old Philco radios. Well, on Saturday nights the only entertainment you had was to listen to the "Grand Ole Opry." And they'd have "Amos 'n' Andy" and "Ozzie and Harriet," Arthur Godfrey, and like that, you know.

And I always was waiting for the "Grand Ole Opry," see. DeFord Bailey blowing the "Fox Trot," or "Fox Hunt," or whatever he called it. Boy, that guy could blow a harp, one heck of a harp blower. You could almost see that fox running in front of them dogs. And Uncle Dave Macon, he played the old thumb-type banjo, you know, he played like Grandpa Jones do now. And of course, Minnie Pearl. Arthur Smith was a young man. He was playing on there then. And Homer and Jethro, they were going strong.

MK: What did you think about programs like "Amos 'n' Andy," about the way black people were portrayed?

NR: Didn't think anything about it. It was just something that went on and that was it.

MK: Did you think it was funny?

NR: Yeah, it *was* funny. It was funny. If I heard it now it would still be funny. But I'll tell you what. It was just like Santa Claus. When I first heard it I thought they was really colored. Really. But they were white, both of them. And, buddy, they had that dialect down 100 percent. If you didn't see them you'd never know. It surprised the heck out of me!

Really, I didn't believe it until they had a newsreel in the Royal Theater down here, and I seen them. I said, "Well, I'll be doggone." That was just one of them things. Now, those guys were showmen. They were really showmen. These people now call themselves show people, but back there you really had to have something to give, or else it didn't work.

MK: What instruments did you take up after the tiple?

NR: I went from the tiple to the guitar, and from the guitar to the piano, from the piano to the organ. From the organ I went to the bass viola, and from that to a standard string harp, concert harp.

MK: Where did you play that?

NR: Over WHIS, Bluefield. I picked it up, first time I'd seen one for years, when I was over there playing one night with Bill Harmer. He played piano with us for years. But every Saturday night from 10:00 to 10:30 Bill would play blues, sentimental music, jazz, and like that on the radio. So he asked me, said, "You ought to come on and play with me sometime." Said, "That would give me a great back-up." So I started going with him and I played with him for over two years, every Saturday night 10:00 to 10:30. They had a harp over there, and I asked the announcer one evening, I said, "Is

An artist as well as a musician, Nat Reese checks through his portfolio of paintings. Photograph by Michael Keller.

this thing in tune?" And he said, "I guess it is. Got too many stings on it for me, I don't know whether it's in tune or not."

And I started playing around with it, and I got so I could play bluesy on that thing, boy. Yes sir, and it just come natural. Just come natural. I could play anything, you could hum anything and I could play right along. Yes sir. I think that is really the beautifulest music you'd ever want to hear.

MK: Tell me about the band you played in.

NR: I'll start with the guitar, we had a guitar. We had two trumpets. The alto sax player, he would rotate backwards and forth, alternate. He would play the clarinet. And boy, he was some musician, too. We had the bass, the piano player, the drums, and we had a tenor saxophone player, and at one time we had two alto sax players.

We first started out with a stand-up bass, and then we tore a kitchen cabinet out, old kitchen cabinet, and got us some Elmer's Glue, took a long neck off a guitar and made us a lap bass. We went and bought us a DeArmond attachment amplifier [pick-up], you know, what you used to add to old flat-top guitars. And at that time you could buy a DeArmond amplifier for about six or seven dollars, and it was made better than the ones you buy now for 20-some dollars. And we hitched that up to the lap bass, and we had a lap bass instead of a stand-up bass. We finally ended up going back to the stand-up bass because it had more volume. That stand-up is really beautiful, boy.

Wasn't but nine people in that band. But now we played for the Elks Club, country club, and places like that. Now, these house parties, when they had their little bands they very seldom had a drummer. It would be maybe a mandolin and two guitars, or just two regular guitars and a tenor guitar. And you'd be surprised at the music those guys could make.

We had to sign a contract for most jobs. I'm not lying, they wanted contracts back there then. I know one time we had contracts for a dance hall in Christiansburg, Virginia. We started down there, and there was two carloads of us, and one of the cars broke down. We traveled together and we wouldn't leave the other. And the contract was for $360. That was on a Friday night, and it was hard to get anyone to work on your car. Everybody was out in them beer joints, and you couldn't get nobody to work on no car.

Finally we got a guy to come and pull it in. We was closer back this way than we were to Christiansburg, so we come on back. And we had to pawn our instruments downtown to get the money to pay that contract off. See, that man done sold all them tickets and things. He had to give them tickets back, and he wanted his money, boy! And we ended up paying that $360. Yes, we did. That was a lot of money back there at that time, but we all pooled together and made it. Then we played three or four places, and then it wasn't too hard on nobody, see, because we taken that money and just put it back in there, covered what we borrowed.

MK: Was that a totally black band?

NR: Yeah, at that time it was. But when we played for the Elks Club or over at the country club in Bluefield, there was a number of white would come up and play with us. A lot of the white ladies, if they wanted to play they come, say, "Let us sit in a little bit with you." We'd tell them to come on.

We played sheet music, we wasn't playing by ear. Back there then you couldn't fool the people. Now a lot of the guys out here, they don't know one side of the street from the other. But, you see, back there then you set up and you played for a dance. Somebody liable to come up and bring you a whole full illustration, got a part for everything in it. They'd say, "Play this piece for me, and I'll give you $50 or $75." Well, now, if you can't read, you don't play the piece, see. We would practice all during the week, at night, and in the evenings.

MK: Where'd you work during the day?

NR: Bartending here in town at the Elks Club. I was a cook and a bartender. Steaks, salads, chiffon pie, marble cakes, German chocolate cakes. And I was a second cook at the McArthur Hotel in Pearisburg, Virginia, for almost two years. That was years ago, though.

At that time we would practice a lot at the Elks Club because it was the availability of a piano there at all times, see. One man would take care of the barroom while the others practiced. Or a lot of the club members down there, they would say, "We'll take over for you for three hours or so." Because we played for their dances, too. So they was helping theirself when we practiced. The more we practiced, the better we were. It worked out real good.

Relaxing at home, Nat Reese reflects on a lifetime in southern West Virginia. He reports that the "bird in hand" philosophy was best during the days of segregation. Photograph by Michael Keller.

MK: Did you ever play any songs related to coal mines, or were you trying to forget about mining when you had a guitar in your hand?

NR: It never crossed my mind. Well, really, to tell you the truth, I was in another world, because when I was playing music nothing else was on my mind but music at that time. You could walk up and say something. You might have to speak to me three times before I'd know you were talking with me.

MK: Did you ever think of music as a way out of the coalfields?

NR: Well, I'll tell you. At the time I came along, it wasn't what you knew, it was who you knew. If you was at the right place at the right time, you had it made. And if you wasn't, shame on you! And then in your traveling, ah, where you really made your money was at the places frequented more by white people. There was a lot of people there would dance to your music all night long—and the owner of the restaurant wouldn't sell you a sandwich after you got through.

So if you had a place where you can make a living, you wouldn't turn that loose. See, I married young, and you don't just grab a wife and a couple of kids and tear off down the road, you know. It don't work like that.

And, see, it's a lot of rough stories, boy. It's not near like it is now. Transportation was bad. The old cars run good while they run, but they didn't last too long. You could take a piece of baling wire and a screwdriver and a pair of pliers and keep one on the road. But you didn't come by them too fast.

And so many places—where now you can go, you can get your foot in the door, or you can go talk to the manager— you wasn't allowed to walk in then. They had a WHITE ONLY sign up there and you couldn't go in there. So in fact you were, well, inhibited. Inhibited in the beginning. And so, you'd either have to know someone that's there to help you, or else you're better off staying in the coal mine. A bird in the hand is worth two in the bush. You mess around and don't have no bird at all!

EDITORS NOTE: This article first appeared in the winter 1987 issue of *Goldenseal* (vol. 13, no. 4). Nat Reese has been teaching and performing at the Augusta Heritage Arts Workshops for more than 20 years. He was presented the 1988 John Henry Award by the John Henry Memorial Foundation in Princeton and also received the Vandalia Award in 1995. A retired commercial artist and cabinet maker, he continues to play and perform his music. Bessie Reese passed away in 1991.

PART 5

Family Bands

The Lilly Brothers

"WE SING ABOUT LIFE AND WHAT IT MEANS TO US"

Carl Fleischhauer and Tom Screven

IN a recent interview Everett Lilly remembered the early '30s before he and his brother became professionals. He was nine or 10 and Bea was 12 or 13. The boys played in and around their home in Clear Creek, a Raleigh County community on the Clear fork of the Coal River, sometimes called the Little Coal River.

The dates and places that order the Lilly Brothers' biography are elucidated in articles like the one by James McDonald in the previous issue of *Goldenseal* ("Principal Influences on the Music of the Lilly Brothers of Clear Creek, West Virginia," April–June 1975) or in Ivan Tribe's thorough listing of the brothers' radio career in the July 1974 issue of *Bluegrass Unlimited*. This article offers certain of Everett Lilly's reminiscences and opinions selected from a conversation recorded at Lilly's home on March 22, 1975. The interview was conducted and later edited by Morgantown photographer Carl Fleischhauer and *Goldenseal*'s editor Tom Screven.

⌒

Everett Lilly: Now, our church here, Methodist Church, since back in my days we used an *Old Choice Collection* songbook. Well, I don't really know the name of the new book, but I notice now they have a new book and it has a lot of new songs in it. And of course they sing a lot of the new songs. They sound, the new songs sound very well, but, uh, if you're going to class 'em better than the old songs, I doubt if you can really do that. You take this old song, "Life Is Like a Mountain Railroad," these old numbers like that, uh, for instance, "This World Is Not My Home," they're all basically based on the Bible, they were wrote from the Bible's. You can sing a song, search the Word in the scriptures, you'll find it written there. So I don't see where we could better ourself with a new song. *Any* better. Except I think it's nice to learn a new song. I like to hear new songs. But, uh, I can't see they're better than the old one.

Carl Fleischhauer: Right.

Tom Screven: So you were in the Methodist church more than anything? Is that the main one?

The Lilly Brothers, Everett (left) and Bea, in 1972 at a festival in Berryville, Virginia. Photograph by Deborah Marks.

EL: Well, yes and no. Me and my brother and I—we're speaking of some of our beginning now—I'll explain some of the beginning. Probably when I was around 10 years old, which would have been in about 1934—by then we were getting well on our way to playing and singing in church, around through the neighborhood. We really started singing for the neighbors, and uh, the neighbors would brag on us. They'd say, "That is good!" Well, that was encouragement.

TS: No instruments, just singing?

EL: Oh yeah we'd have—my brother played a guitar, but I didn't have no instrument at that time. And he'd play the guitar and we'd sing together. The funny thing is—when I was in grade school—of course our singing really begin there, you know. That's of a morning we would always sing when books took up—at least three songs before we sat down. And at that time they had The Lord's Prayer in school. And that was the first thing you done when you went in school. They would say The Lord's Prayer, which got the day started off to a good thing. Then we sang at least three numbers. I can remember the old song, "Battle Hymn of the Republic," "The Spanish Cavalier." A lot of time we'd sing these of a morning before books took up. And, uh, to us that got the day started off with some kind of a good feeling, because the songs we sang there had a lot of facts in 'em. Some of it was sadness, some of it was good, and then The Lord's Prayer and these things—it just made a school kid feel like that they was something there for him, you know, instead of just books. To me it left sort of, you might call it a spirit, which we need. I believe we're all spiritual in some way, and I do believe that that had a lot to do with our music, our playing and singing.

∾

Everett Lilly in 1975. Photograph by Carl Fleischhauer.

The Lilly Brothers made the transition from amateur to professional in stages. Music in church and school led to other live, paid performances and finally to radio.

∾

EL: They would pay us $15 to come down about once a month and play between the movies. Now in those days we didn't have a band, just the two of us. And in between the movies we'd play about 15 or 20 minutes, the songs. Oh, we'd get a big hand, and to us that was really terrific, you know.

CF: Did you get paid anything?

EL: Yeah, they paid us about $15 plus we got to see a free movie. And we were just counted kids, you know, but yet that was good.

Then later in our days I guess probably we might have been 14 years old then or so—I'm just kindly guessing at these dates. One of our neighbors here, they had a thing in Charleston, they called the "Old Farm Hour"—WCHS. And they had such entertainers that used to come there as Nat-

chee the Indian, T. Texas Tyler, Cap, Andy and Flip. Indian Bill and Montana was there several times. So, uh, our neighbor here, he played the fiddle. He didn't really play much professional at all, he was a coal miner. His name was Brian Toney. He liked our playing and singing very much and he realized that it was more than just ordinary style of playing and singing, so he taken us down to the Farm Hour. The Farm Hour, they liked us so well there that they booked us back and paid us to come there on Friday nights. So that was good, too.

∾

From the late '30s to the early '50s the Lilly Brothers performed on radio stations in and near West Virginia. This was a particularly rich era for traditional music on the region's airwaves, but in the '50s stations began programming more and more rock 'n' roll music. For Lilly, this meant leaving behind the one form of music capable of dealing with the truths of life and death.

The Lilly Brothers on either side of Everett's son Everett Alan at a jam session in a small club during their 1973 Japanese tour, with banjoist Don Stover and bass player Jerry Tainaka. Photographer unknown.

Everett Lilly, to the right of a Japanese friend, holds some of the flowers presented to him on stage at the end of a performance during the Lilly Brothers' first tour of Japan in 1973. Photographer unknown.

∾

EL: I still say my music is a part of a human being's life. You live to die, we know that. We play about the song from the cradle to the grave, and every word in our songs are true. We live—we even feel when we sing our song expressing that-a-way—it ain't words, it's truth. What we sing about,

whether you believe it or not, you have to pass that way of life. Now I have somewhat agin' radio stations for that reason. Seem like they have forgot what a human being is . . .

They would only play rock 'n' roll, nothing else. So if that's all you're going to play and not allow nothing else, then nothing else gets a fair chance. The bluegrass and country music really didn't die out, they just stopped it from being heard on radio stations. Radio stations hasn't got me fooled by no means. I been in this business so long that I know what's going on. A radio station, when they stop all of the kind of music that they want to stop and play what they want to, the public will float along with that. Just same as they would if there was only one bar of soap that you could have in your house. They'd use that, if they couldn't get what they wanted. And the public is the same.

Then if you advertise in a big way, then the young kids'll fall for it while they can't hear nothing else, but then once they get the chance to hear what they want to hear you'll see 'em drifting one by one right back to it, because that's the way of life. Country—American folk music—country music—bluegrass *is* a foundation of the world's music. And every time you blot it out through not allowing it to be heard, when they get a loophole, they'll come right back to it.

∾

The Lilly Brothers moved to Boston in the '50s, and James McDonald's article describes their life there. McDonald, a friend who learned mandolin from Everett, mentions the role of the band in the folk revival of the '60s, a decade when all forms of country music emerged from the shadow of rock 'n' roll. Lilly related their college concerts to the war with rock, saying "For some reason Lilly Brothers in them colleges fit the battle right on through."

⌇

EL: I don't remember the date, but I can remember the first time when we played in their college over there. The first one, if I remember right, was there in Cambridge; and, uh, the way they sat around on the floor and watched us play and the way they admired us, uh, really got to us a little bit at first, because we couldn't believe anybody could be that interested in us. We begin to wonder, is this making fun or do you really like this music? But the funny part of it, it didn't matter what old sad song we got a hand on the end of it. It teached us one thing: these college kids has done passed the rock 'n' roll stage. They're interested in real stuff now. It come to us that plain, that college kids are interested no more in this shimmying and shaking; they're interested in real life, and they still are.

CF: Some of them are, but not everyone.

EL: Yeah, not everyone, but, uh, not everyone or nobody is interested in true life. Most people are—I'll put it this way, most of the world is interested in *nothing*.

CF: Well—

EL: How did that grab you?

CF: Well, I know what you mean. It seems often that most people don't really think very much about *things*, do they?

EL: That's right. They sure don't—I mean why not face facts like, it's in The Book there. The Bible says, man'll love pleasures of the world, and it says the pleasure—the lust of sin and the lust of the world will destroy the soul. Well, now, I believe that. I may not be like a lot of fanatics that'll say, "Hey, God hollered at me," or "I seen God." That Bible tells me that Jesus Christ said, "No man has ever seen God or heard His voice at any time." It also tells me that God is all in all. All the good that's in you and me come from Him—ever what and who He is, the Unseen.

What is God? We don't know, do we? All we know is He's *all* in all. Yeah, I like to go to church and I like to hear their view on it, but sometimes it aggravates me to hear people say they've heard a voice or seen a face that the Bible says no man has ever . . . If He didn't make into Heaven they won't none of us make it . . . So what are we going to do with, with these things? Destroy? It's a part of the songs we sing, these everyday songs we sing—it's a part of it.

⌇

Lilly finds McDonald's article generally accurate and he was appreciative of the respect paid his music by interviewers, saying, "If there wasn't no interest in it, they certainly wouldn't be any future in it, would there?" Still, reporters sometimes erred or at least saw things from a different per-

The two-story "Perry house" on Workman's Creek, just off Clear Creek in Raleigh County, where the Lilly Brothers were born. Photograph by Carl Fleischhauer.

spective. During the nearly 20 years the brothers played in a Boston tavern, their repertory featured more and more "honky-tonk" songs and fiddle playing. McDonald sees this as a "time of very gradual loss of enthusiasm and ability to perform well in the style they considered their forté" due in part to isolation from their cultural peers and constant interaction with northern, urban, working-class people, together with pressure to play radio and jukebox hits.

⌇

EL: Here's the part that McDonald didn't bring out on that. You see, in playing a night club, the type of music that Lilly Brothers play and sing you could not play seven nights a week in a place, 30 minutes off and 30 on until 1:00 at night. You couldn't exist and sing like that. Your lungs, your

Everett Lilly emerges from the family's mobile home near Clear Creek. Photograph by Carl Fleischhauer.

health, your body could not stand that. So Jim didn't get that across very plain. It wasn't that they wanted to hear something else, absolutely not. Lilly Brothers has never played anywhere that they wouldn't rather hear duet after duet, but you can't stand that; you cannot stand that. Your body just won't take it.

The type of music we play is that driving stuff, so I started playing a lot of fiddle to eliminate so much singing. And not only that, but the type of fiddle I play the people go wild after it, so that was—I mean they ain't no use to lie, it was encouragement to play a lot of fiddle. And the fiddle's nice and loud; they liked it. And that's why we did a lot of solo work, like I sang a lot of solos. Well, while I'm a-singing a solo, my brother's a-resting. His voice is resting. Well, when he sings my voice rests. When I play the fiddle all voices rest. So we had to figure out ways to not abuse our health and playing and singing.

A lot of music players didn't get to play as much as and sing as much as they wanted to, but we's musicians that got in positions that we had to figure out ways not to overdo yourself. And Jim didn't get that across at all. I believe he made it sound more like to the public that we lost out; maybe our style didn't fit the people any more or that's the reason, but that's not the reason. And we told McDonald that many times, you know, because he was a real good

friend of ours, hung around us all the time. But that, that's one note that he certainly didn't hit on the head.

༄

Two Japanese musicians, Robert and Jerry Tainaka, visited Boston in the early '60s and made friends with the Lillys. Subsequently, Everett Lilly sent them a tape of the band performing at Hillbilly Ranch, and it resulted in the release of their first Japanese record album. In 1973 the Lilly Brothers, banjo player Don Stover, and Everett's son Everett Alan toured Japan.

༄

EL: This album is what opened the gate to Japan. Now, a lot of people had went to Japan and played for the USO but the USO wasn't playing for the Japanese that couldn't understand American.

CF: Right.

EL: Our records went direct to Tokyo, Japan, and was teached to the Japanese. That's why the Japanese knows Lilly Brothers above everybody else, because they was taught our kind of music. So now in Japan, when we go to Japan, we can look for a crowd of people there . . .

CF: How many times have you been to Japan now?

EL: I've been there twice.

Everett Lilly (left) and other family members warm up in a dressing room before a 1977 concert on the steps of the West Virginia statehouse. Photograph by Carl Fleischhauer.

CF: Twice?

EL: Uh-huh. And the December coming will be the third time.

CF: Hm. Well, that's nice. Do you enjoy those trips? Is it fun for you to visit Japan?

EL: Yeah, I like to visit Japan and they're so nice to you over there, uh, the American people's heard so much about Japan that—if it was ever true it don't exist today. The Japanese moral standards, uh, I have to say, I believe's far above ours.

CF: Well, that could be.

EL: Ah—they're so polite, when you meet the people and speak to 'em. They're so polite to you that they don't do nothing to offend you in any way, and they try to make everything as comfortable and nice for you as possible. And their streets are clean, everything is clean. And when they do something, they do it quick; they don't decide all day. If we do it we do it. You would have to go there to, to really know what I mean. I had heard so much about Japan myself, you know, that when, the first trip I went over I was wondering if—just how everything was going to be when that plane was going in there, you know. This is Tokyo, Japan, we're going in. Then, we all think about the war between the United States and Japan—all of those things.

∾

For Lilly, it was no more surprising to see his music reach the Japanese than the Bostonians.

∾

EL: When we went to Boston it was sort of like going to a foreign country. It strikes me when I think of the first time I went to Boston and heard them people talk—there's not much difference in the feeling I had when I hit Boston and when I went to Japan, the same kind of feeling. To me they were all "Greeks." You hear that word—now, that's not slandering the Greeks, they're as good as me, you know, but "It's all Greek to me!"(laughter) Yeah. Yeah, those people that "pahk the cah," ("park the car") and we didn't know what they was saying. (Laughter) I'd have to look and say, "What?" And it didn't take 'em long to ask where you was from either—with our accent.

∾

There has been much discussion of proper definitions for "bluegrass" and "folk music"; disputes over these and related terms often become heated. Lilly is sometimes troubled by the way people categorize his music, but he is more concerned to stress the way his art connects with life.

EL: Lilly Brothers still play the same kind of music then, and today, as we did 35 years ago. We had a banjo player with us; they didn't call us bluegrass. But now every band that has a banjo in it—it's bluegrass; automatically they call it bluegrass.

CF: Well, do you think that's the right way to use the word or the wrong way to use the word?

EL: To use the word "bluegrass?"

CF: Does any band with a banjo in it—is that bluegrass to you?

EL: No. Not really.

CF: What's it take?

EL: It's still, to me, American folk and country music. What I play is still American folk-country music. We've even been called mountain music and hillbilly music.

CF: Do you mind the word "hillbilly"?

EL: Depends on how they say it.

CF: If they smile—?

TS: You don't like it too much, I take it. Uh, the term—Have to be pretty careful of, to use it around you, or you get—

EL: Well, to me, I think it's somebody wanting to dig your style and lower it. And I, I don't appreciate that, because I'll go back to my facts again. I believe in what I'm a-doing. I believe it's a foundation of the earth, and I believe when anybody forgets how to go out and plant a garden that they don't know much. I don't care how much education you know. If you know so little that you couldn't survive with—if something happened to the world—then you don't know

much. At least, you don't know what you're supposed to know. D'you get what I'm saying?

CF: Right.

EL: What you're supposed to know in this land is how to survive. If the power goes off, you gonna freeze to death? Are you gonna go out and use your nature, what God give you, to get some wood and get a fire? And if it comes starve to death or pay across the counter, are you gonna starve or should you go out and raise you something to eat? Now, this music is based that I'm doing and that's why I uphold it in the biggest way. We *sing* about *life* and what it *means* to us.

We sing songs, tragedies, that's warning, that's songs of warning, for *you.* If you listen to the words and you can gather the feelings and the thought. Don't *let* this happen to you! This song's sad, remember what you hear! We sing gospel songs, songs of the Bible. They're to be obeyed, respected in that way. In other words, when you're singing about a song of the Bible, it's got many words in it that will teach you how to do unto others as you would have 'em do unto you.

EDITOR'S NOTE: This article first appeared in the July–September 1975 issue of *Goldenseal* (vol. 1, no. 2). The Lilly Brothers have built a reputation as one of the all-time great bluegrass and old-time music "brother acts." Everett Lilly still lives in Beckley and his brother Bea resides in Massachusetts. They continue to perform and make recordings, combining the old traditional ballads and folksongs with some of the best instrumentation around. Everett Lilly also appears with the band Clear Creek Crossin'.

Lynn Davis & Molly O'Day

"LIVING THE RIGHT LIFE NOW"

Abby Gail Goodnite and Ivan Tribe

EACH weekday afternoon just before one o'clock, Lynn Davis sits down in a little radio studio in his suburban Huntington home. When he presses a button, listeners on WEMM-FM radio hear the sound of a clawhammer banjo playing the familiar tune "Good Old Mountain Dew." However, as the vocal starts, a clear-voiced girl with a mountain accent begins to sing a set of sacred lyrics that are quite different from the original:

The midnight has passed, it's morning at last,
No longer in sin I bow;
My wandering is done, my life's crown is won,
I'm living the right life now.
—from "Living the Right Life Now" by William York
(used by permission of Ft. Knox Music, Inc., and Trio Music Co., Inc. All rights reserved.)

You wouldn't know from his appearance, but Lynn Davis is 83 years of age. In his many-faceted career, Lynn has been a coal miner, grocer, record retailer, restaurateur, investment counselor, and realtor in between known occupations. For over half his life, he has been a Church of God minister, but earlier he spent some 18 years in radio as a full-time announcer and entertainer. Lynn was husband and bandleader for the late Molly O'Day, whom many considered the greatest female country singer who ever lived.

Molly's recording of "Living the Right Life Now" still kicks off Lynn's daily radio program. For the last 26 years, Lynn has combined radio work and the ministry on his widely heard "Country Hymn Time" program. Among other things, he is now acclaimed as America's oldest gospel deejay.

Leonard Davis was born near Paintsville in Johnson County, Kentucky, on December 15, 1914. He grew up like

Lynn Davis at home in Huntington in 1998. Photograph by Michael Keller.

Dixie Lee Williamson and her brother Skeets, c. 1938. Photographer unknown.

many mountain youth of his era, and acquired the shortened nickname of "Lynn" along the way. His father and uncle both played old-time music and as a child Lynn learned to play the guitar and banjo. Later, his family moved to Wheelwright, Kentucky. Lynn was fortunate to grow up in an area alive with traditional music, and can recall such memorable experiences as seeing and hearing the fabled mountain fiddler, Blind Ed Haley. In his youth, Davis enjoyed tuning in to WFIW Hopkinsville, Kentucky, where he listened to programs featuring early country singers such as "Bluegrass Roy" Freeman.

In 1932, Lynn and a friend from Kentucky, Guy Ferrell, went to Huntington and got a weekly radio show on WSAZ as "Guy and Lynn, the Mountaineer Twins." Lynn played lead guitar and Guy played rhythm. Their music leaned toward the style of the Delmore Brothers featuring smooth

duet harmonies and ambitious twin guitar instrumentation. The boys enjoyed their small taste of fame on the Saturday morning show, and before long they secured another job doing a Saturday afternoon program on Charleston's WCHS. Lynn and Guy still worked as coal loaders during the week in Wheelwright, Kentucky. Once a week the Mountaineer Twins traveled to West Virginia to be on radio.

Lynn sold a couple of songs to Asher Sizemore and in 1936 he took the opportunity to become a full-time performer. After traveling around for a short while, Lynn wound up at WHIS in Bluefield, where Guy decided to quit and return home. Lynn remained in radio, traveling to Virginia and Pennsylvania for a time. By now he had become an excellent lead guitarist, and his strong voice made him a persuasive radio salesman and announcer.

Late in 1936, Gordon Jennings wrote Lynn a letter inviting him to come and play the guitar for his band at Bluefield. Although the pay would be meager, Davis decided to leave Harrisonburg, Virginia, and head back to West Virginia. Two weeks later Lynn arrived only to find that Jennings had already hired another guitarist for his band. Disheartened, he decided to go home to his mother and father in Kentucky. Lynn stopped by radio station WHIS on his way out of town. The announcer informed him that the manager of the station, Jim Shott, wanted to speak to him. Mr. Shott wanted to hire Lynn to take charge of a whole new program advertising Bi-Tone Products. He accepted the position and was responsible for hiring the talent and paying their salaries. As Lynn recalls the incident:

"Shows you how things work out, you know, when you have somebody sort of let you down. . . . I was back on the job with more money than these boys could have paid, and then I had them to hire, if I was going to hire them. . . . Of course they wondered about that after they offered me a job and then hired somebody else. I called everybody, and the next morning when they all gathered in, these boys said, 'Well, I guess we're out.' I said, 'No, I'm going to hire you and I'm going to pay you $12 more a week than you offered me!'"

Lynn organized a band called the Forty-Niners in Bluefield. The members included several musicians and a pair of yodeling cowgirls, Sue and Ann Mason. Lynn recalls that times were tough in those Depression days. In the mining camps, musicians often had to sell tickets for coal company scrip which they then discounted in converting to cash. In impoverished farm communities, folks would bring in vegetables and chickens to exchange for the price of tickets.

The early years of radio offered an unusual but exciting lifestyle for an entire generation of pioneering musicians like Lynn Davis. During the 1930s and early 1940s, radio stations played no recorded music, relying instead on the voices and talents of musicians who broadcast live from their

Lynn Davis met his match in 1940 when young Dixie Lee Williamson joined his band. They married in April 1941; she took the name "Molly O'Day" the following year. This photo was taken about 1942 in Renfro Valley, Kentucky. Photographer unknown.

Molly O'Day signs autographs in 1947, while Lynn Davis (far right) smiles at the camera. Photograph by McLemore Studio, Irvine, Kentucky.

studios. As radio stations proliferated, there grew to be an unprecedented demand for performers.

While a lucky few were paid by sponsors for their appearances, most radio entertainers used their airtime to promote local show dates or to sell song folios or other items. After several months on one station, when performers felt that the area had been "played out," they moved on. Like gypsies, they traveled from town to town or state to state, staying a few months, then moving again. According to Lynn Davis, securing a new show on a radio station at that time was relatively easy. Musicians frequently "swapped" shows, or recommended one another to sponsors or station managers. As a result, many small town musicians amassed impressive itineraries and developed a far-flung network of valuable friends and contacts.

About 1939, the Forty-Niners relocated to WPTF in Raleigh, North Carolina, and soon after moved to KVOO in Tulsa, Oklahoma. They also played in Texas where one of the yodeling cowgirls was married. They returned to Bluefield in the summer of 1940 and the other female vocalist decided to quit and return to Pennsylvania. The Lynn Davis band lacked a girl singer.

Forty-five miles of rough road to the north in Beckley, LaVerne "Dixie Lee" Williamson was the female vocalist for Johnny Bailes's group, the Happy Valley Boys. The Happy Valley Boys were in the process of disintegration, and young Dixie Lee applied for a job with Lynn Davis's band, which she had admired for quite some time. Dixie Lee, who was only 17 years old, was not allowed to leave home alone, so Lynn hired her and her brother, Skeets. Dixie Lee and Lynn fell in love and became husband and wife six months later on April 5, 1941.

Dixie Lee was born Lois LaVerne Williamson in Pike County, Kentucky, on July 9, 1923. From childhood, she and her older brother Cecil, known as "Skeets," had dreamed of careers as radio country musicians. Learning the songs she heard the female vocalists sing on WLS Chicago, the young mountain girl emulated Patsy Montana, Lulu Belle Wiseman, and Lily May Ledford, developing a powerful voice that reflected deep sincerity. Before coming to Beckley and Bluefield, she had a few months of experience at WCHS Charleston and WBTH Williamson. Skeets played the fiddle and did comedy.

Following the tradition of "radio hillbillies" at the time,

the Forty-Niners traveled from station to station and town to town. The summer after Lynn and Dixie's wedding, they returned to Beckley where they were sponsored by Dr. Pepper. That fall, they relocated to WAPI Birmingham, Alabama, to fill a spot being vacated by the Delmore Brothers. In this new locale they renamed themselves the Sunshine Hillbillies and for a time their band included the Bailes Brothers along with the late Marion Sumner on fiddle. The show went out over a regional network including stations in Nashville, Memphis, Montgomery, Mobile, Tuscaloosa, and Jackson. They stayed there for a year, and made the acquaintance of young Hank Williams, an association which eventually proved to be beneficial for both parties. Hank often sang "Tramp on the Street," a 1939 country gospel song written by Hazel and Grady Cole. Hank sang it to a different tune from the original, which greatly impressed Dixie Lee who asked him to teach her the words. She began singing it in the Williams manner, also. Soon after, it became her most popular song.

For Hank's part, the Davises were among the first artists to record his songs in the lean years before his own meteoric career took hold. According to Lynn, Hank wrote "When God Comes and Gathers His Jewels," "The Singing Waterfall," "Six More Miles," and "I Don't Care If Tomorrow Never Comes," primarily for them to record.

The Davis group left Alabama after a year and headed for Kentucky, where they got a daily show at WHAS Louisville and worked on Saturday nights at the "Renfro Valley Barn Dance." Although wartime gasoline rationing kept down the number of tourists, their radio audience grew and their live shows were crowded. They also had a large overseas audience. Even General Douglas MacArthur, in faraway Australia, frequently enjoyed their program. Clayton McMichen, an artist on WAVE, told Dixie that there was already a performer in the area known as Dixie Lee, so LaVerne Davis felt she needed a new name to avoid confusion. She chose the name "Molly O'Day."

Lynn and Molly spent most of 1944 back in West Virginia on WJLS Beckley. Working once again as the Forty-Niners, they teamed up with several important West Virginia musicians. These included talented Raleigh County musicians Bea and Everett Lilly; Hinton area Dobro player George "Speedy" Krise; and Fiddlin' Burk Barbour from Virginia.

After spending a few months in Texas at KRLD Dallas, Lynn and Molly landed at WNOX Knoxville in June 1945, appearing on the popular "Mid-Day Merry-Go-Round" show. It was here that they began performing as the Cumberland Mountain Folks and where they achieved their greatest professional success. With the war finally at an end, folks were anxious for entertainment, and the Cumberland Mountain Folks gained wide popularity.

Fred Rose, who by now was the business head of the in-

Remembering Molly O'Day

Dave Peyton

I still remember that late summer day in 1970 when I first heard that Molly O'Day was alive and well and living in Huntington.

Could it be that the woman I heard on scratchy old phonograph records in my youth was still alive? After all, I hadn't heard of her in years.

My heart skipped a beat at the possibility I might meet her. And later, my heart was thoroughly blessed by knowing her.

You see, I found Molly O'Day and it made all the difference to me.

Who knows when I first heard her mournful voice singing "Tramp On The Street"? But I remember how it felt to hear that high lonesome voice, the voice of a mountain woman—one of my people—lamenting the story of Jesus Christ's crucifixion in a song that will live forever because of her.

And she lived in Huntington! How could I not seek her out, write about her and let the world know that I had found the unforgettable Molly O'Day?

It wasn't easy locating her. She had chosen an anonymous life after she left show business in 1949 to devote herself to God and the church, along with her husband, Lynn Davis.

A 1948 publicity photo of Molly O'Day by Archie Campbell.

fluential Acuff-Rose publishing company, took a vacation in Gatlinburg and heard Molly singing "Tramp on the Street" in the summer of 1946. He soon renewed his acquaintance with Lynn, whom he had met in Oklahoma years earlier. Fred helped Molly and Lynn get a recording contract with Columbia Records. They went to Chicago on December 16, 1946, and cut their first session. Of the songs released from that first session, the most popular was "Tramp On the Street," which showcased Molly's clear, emotional vocals. It sold over a million copies. Other songs featured the highly-crafted duets of Lynn and Molly, and the musicianship of band members Speedy Krise, Mac Wiseman, and Skeets Williamson, as well as Lynn's fine guitar work.

The Cumberland Mountain Folks were at the peak of their popularity. Drawing huge paying crowds at their live appearances—often two shows a night—they also sold songbooks and photographs as quickly as the printer could turn them out. They appeared on the "Grand Ole Opry" in 1947, and turned down opportunities to join the Opry as regular performers and to make a movie with the "King of Country Music," Roy Acuff.

Despite this success, and the apparent promise of even greater stardom, Molly and Lynn had reservations about the lives they had chosen in the world of country music. Dissatisfied, Lynn and Molly left WNOX in September 1947. Lynn purchased a grocery store near Wheelwright, Ken-tucky, and the pair embarked on a considerably different way of living. Although they returned to Nashville to honor their recording commitments with Columbia in December of that year, they spent most of their time and energy close to home.

Unfortunately, they had some to learn about operating a rural grocery store. After allowing credit to striking coal miners in the area, they lost a considerable amount of money by the end of 1948. They returned to radio.

Over the next year, they worked on stations in Greens-boro, North Carolina; Knoxville, Tennessee; and Versailles, Kentucky. Molly and Lynn's frustrations with professional entertainment deepened, however, and the strain took its toll. In December 1949, Molly was hospitalized. They soon moved to Huntington and bought a restaurant. Lynn Davis and Molly O'Day left show business for good. Molly believed that her pursuit of worldly fame and fortune had violated a religious commitment she had made in youth and that her show business career must be abandoned. In February, 1950, the couple were saved in a revival meeting, and found the internal peace that had eluded them in the enter-tainment world.

After their conversion, Molly only sang in churches and Lynn entered the ministry. They did two more sessions with Columbia in 1950 and 1951 to fulfill their contract, but they recorded sacred music only. The couple spent the 1950–1951

But after convincing her and Lynn that I wouldn't and couldn't let her down by writing anything that betrayed her privacy, I drove to their house on a shady Hun-tington street one late summer evening.

It was then and there I fell in love with Molly.

She was a kind, loving person, a gentle soul, a head-on-straight woman who knew what she want-ed out of life. And it wasn't star-dom. She had been there and done that and it wasn't for her.

Her smiling eyes, gentle wit, and immense wisdom made her a true joy to be around.

I'll admit that when I first met her, I didn't understand why she didn't stay in the business and become more of a superstar than she was when she dropped out of sight in 1949.

But in time and after many vis-its, she convinced me she made the right decision. Life on the road was dangerous, debilitating, and tough on the spirit, she said. It robbed people of a real life. She wanted no part of it, even if sick-ness had not forced her out of the business.

Mostly when Molly, Lynn, and I got together, we laughed. We'd laugh so hard that tears would flow. She was particularly fond of telling stories of the foolish things that happened to her when she was playing those one-night stands throughout the South and how she genuinely loved to sing for real live people.

But she cried just as quickly when she played a song on the phonograph that reached deep in her psyche and called to mind the themes of the songs she recorded and loved.

Molly lived the life she wanted to live, something that far too few of us can say. And I'm proud to say that, when all was said and done, and when I mourned at her passing, I could see that her life made a difference, even in the vir-tual anonymity she sought.

And that made her a special lady to me and millions who still can hear her plaintive voice wail-ing the mountain blues in our memories.

EDITOR'S NOTE: This article first appeared in the spring 1998 issue of *Goldenseal* (vol. 24, no. 1).

school year in Estevan, Saskatchewan, in Canada, where Lynn studied at the International Bible College. In 1954, Lynn attended the Northwest Bible College in Minot, North Dakota, and subsequently became a licensed minister in the Church of God (Cleveland, Tennessee).

Molly assisted Lynn in his evangelistic work, sometimes with singing and testimony. Lynn pastored three churches at different times in West Huntington, Martinsburg, and in Massillon, Ohio. In the early '60s, the couple opened the Molly O'Day Music Center, a gospel record store, in Williamson.

Lynn recalls that Molly continued to enjoy singing during these years and that church congregations responded enthusiastically to her occasional performances of sacred material. Lynn and Molly's music from this time period reflects their strong religious feelings as well as their ties to traditional mountain music. Molly was always an accomplished drop-thumb banjo player, and she frequently brought the banjo into church with her. Without a larger accompanying ensemble, Lynn and Molly developed an even fuller, tighter sound as a duo. This sound was captured on two local recordings made during the 1960s which have remained in print on various labels over the years. These recordings are currently available as *The Soul of Molly O'Day, Vol. 1 and 2* on Old Homestead. They include such numbers as "Living the Right Life Now," "I'll Shout and Shine," and "Sinner Man Where You Gonna Hide"—Lynn's only recorded solo performance.

Beginning in February 1974, Lynn and Molly started a radio program on the Christian station WEMM-FM in Huntington. They did the presentation from a makeshift studio in their home. The station owner believed that folks wanted to hear contemporary Southern gospel, but Lynn argued that listeners still favored the type of hard country gospel that the couple had always preferred. "Country Hymn Time" proved the correctness of Davis's viewpoint, as it became and remains WEMM's most popular program.

In addition to playing recordings, Molly would tell an inspiring story each day as well as engage in friendly chit-chat with Lynn and their listeners. They never rehearsed for the program, and Lynn believes the informal situation helped to make them so successful. He continues a tradition Molly started by announcing the names of fellow Christian shut-ins who are sick or disabled and unable to attend regular church services. He is careful to go over the spelling of names twice, along with the addresses.

Molly O'Day is baptized in the Ohio River in 1950. Lynn Davis is on the right; the Reverend Luther Painter from the Church of God is on the left. Photographer unknown.

Each day at 1:00 P.M., Lynn Davis broadcasts "Country Hymn Time" from his home studio over WEMM-FM Huntington. Photograph by Michael Keller.

During the mid-'80s, Molly's health prevented her from appearing on the show very often. Increasingly, Lynn had to do the program alone. On December 5, 1987, Molly, hospitalized for cancer but bravely maintaining a positive attitude, "went home to be with the Lord," to quote one of her popular radio phrases.

Lynn continues to do the program every weekday at 1:00 P.M. on 107.9 WEMM-FM, keeping his late wife's spirit alive by playing one of her songs and stories on each program. Reverend Davis has developed a non-denominational approach in his ministry. He does announcements for all churches at no cost, and refuses to let the larger churches buy time on the show. Recently, Lynn has even done some guest preaching in Old Regular Baptist churches. Lynn explains why he is still active in the ministry:

"I'd actually rather be somewhere fishing. . . . At my age, of course, a lot of people do quit, but I feel it's a ministry to

a lot of people, and I'm in the ministry, so I just feel like it's something I can do to be a blessing to somebody."

In his long lifetime, Lynn Davis, along with the late Molly O'Day, has furnished both entertainment and inspiration for tens of thousands of people. Even before their own conversion, the sacred songs they rendered touched the hearts of many. Both in his ministry and through "Country Hymn Time," Lynn continues to be a source of strength to many people. What better advice can anyone provide than those words of hope that Lynn and Molly always used to close their program: "Dream of a bright tomorrow and never be less than your dreams."

EDITOR'S NOTE: This article first appeared in the spring 1998 issue of *Goldenseal* (vol. 24, no. 1). Lynn Davis remains active with his ministry and radio work, broadcasting daily from his home studio over Huntington's WEMM radio.

The Currence Brothers

"THE SPARK TO PLAY MUSIC"

Jack Waugh and Michael Kline

THE miracle of the Currence brothers and their achievements in the field of West Virginia music are important elements of a story we have been longing to present for some time. With half a dozen long-playing recordings of bluegrass and gospel music to their credit, Jimmie and Loren Currence are leaders in the country music field in this state. Yet they have never allowed success to change them or to alter their unshakable vision of the Almighty. And they are still close to their father, a number of brothers and sisters, and the humble origins of the family—a remote, beautiful section on the Randolph-Upshur county line called High Germany, about 15 miles from where the Currences now live in Cassity.

When we asked the brothers and the father to participate with us in an interview for *Goldenseal,* they encouraged us to visit the homeplace in High Germany with them. "You'll have a much better understanding of us once you see that place," Jimmie insisted. And so we motored over in a four-wheel-drive Bronco on a late December afternoon, and had the benefit of their running commentary about that country and their very difficult beginning in it. The Currence family lived in the High Germany section for five generations, but they left their farm in the mid-'60s. The following reflections are excerpts from a series of interviews, the major one of which was conducted with Jimmie and Loren at the home of Jack Waugh and his mother, Pauline Waugh, on Rich Mountain in December 29, 1979. We were recounting the drive to High Germany earlier in the day.

❧

Michael Kline: It's a shame about the old house. With no one living in a place it doesn't take it long to go down.

Loren Currence: Well, it was in nice shape when we left there. In fact, when my mother and dad left it, it was in real good shape. I don't know, must be about 14 years ago. He still had some livestock on it when they lived there by theirselves for several years, and it was in good shape then.

Jack Waugh: What impressed you the most as you were growing up? Were you happy?

LC: Yeah, Yeah. Almost everything about a farm impressed me. But I liked to venture around in the woods, the edge of the fields, when I could go, you know—when I could get about and when I was growing up. I was very interested in wildlife, birds, and things like that. One of my hobbies was a-finding bird nests. I like to do that. And after I grew up we had turkeys and I'd always want to find turkey nests.

MK: You grew up with a lot of kids around the house there, didn't you? How many brothers and sisters did you have?

LC: One died when he was two years old. And there was 11 of us grew up—I think it was about a six-room house.

MK: Did you tell me they all played music?

Jimmie Currence: Every one of us.

JW: Did you all learn to play by yourselves? Nobody ever came in to teach you to play or anything?

JC: Not a note.

JW: Who started you out on it?

JC: Well, the oldest brother started us out. He got a violin from a neighbor. About three and a half miles down the road there was a store, and a guy by the name of Emry Zickefoose played the fiddle. And he got my oldest brother to fiddle. We didn't have no bow so we just whittled him a slim stick to use for a bow. From that day on we all started playing.

LC: We sorta taught each other to play, really. We started playing, and then after a while somebody got us a guitar. And then we had a mandolin, sorta, you know, just started playing and taught one another to play.

JW: Both of your parents played guitar. Did they teach you anything?

LC: No, they never taught us a thing, 'cause they didn't play in the same key that we played in. They had the guitar tuned different from what we would. And they could play, my mother could play, a harmonica, and of course they could play the Jew's harp, but that's all the musical instruments they had, you know, at the time.

MK: Where did your mother learn her music, do you think? Can you think of the names of a couple of her favorite pieces when you were children?

LC: They sang a lot of hymns, mostly gospel songs, but they played "Marching to Georgia." I liked to hear them play that on the guitar. And "Whoa, Muley, Whoa," and pieces like that, you know.

JC: I think the favorite one was "Sitting Alone in the Moonlight."

MK: They were pretty religious, weren't they, your parents? What did they think of dancing?

Jimmie (left) and Loren Currence in 1980. Photograph by William Metzger.

LC: Well, they never did—

MK: They never rolled back the rug and danced?

LC: My dad was a good tap dancer if he wanted to be. But he never would approve of us going and play for dances.

MK: There weren't dances in the community then?

LC: No, not in the community where we grew up in. They never did have the hankering to do anything like that right around close. The closest dance ever held anywhere around here was Helvetia.

JC: The most important thing to people back then, it was their church life and their religious life, because back then people didn't have what they have today. And they totally depended on their beliefs and their religion, which was really a good thing, to my opinion.

LC: And then they depended on each other. Like in the fall of the year, in the summertime, they would help one another to do all their hay harvesting. They had log rollings, syrup boilings, and things like that. People worked together back then. They didn't depend on just one particular person, they depended on each other. That's the way it was back then.

When you didn't have any electricity or anything you depended on oil lamps for light and a potbelly Burnside stove for heat, and it wasn't like it is nowadays. Everybody's, you know, mostly for hisself anymore.

MK: Loren, one of your earliest childhood memories must have been the sound of music played around the house. Because the older kids had already got a start on it, had they, by the time you came along?

LC: Oh, yeah, right. By the time we came along they had already been playing. My brother that plays the violin now —Shorty—he played the guitar some. And Carrol played the fiddle, my oldest brother. When the younger kids was born, like Jimmie and myself and my brother, we sorta teamed up and had some trio songs a-going, you know. We would learn them off the radio from Clarksburg and Fairmont. They had some old radio programs and live entertainment, and we would learn some songs, pick them out.

MK: Who was on the radio then? Who were you listening to?

LC: Oh, the Franklin Brothers and the Delmore Brothers,

Jimmie Currence, a four-time fiddle champion at the Mountain State Forest Festival in Elkins, took up the banjo when deterioration of the elbow cramped his bowing style. Photograph by William Metzger.

and Jake Taylor and the Railsplitters and a whole mess of the older stars. Buddy Starcher, Cap, Andy and Flip—I could name a lot of them there that used to be playing and singing on the radio in the late '30s and early '40s. We listened to every program on it and picked up the songs, you know, learned them by heart. We listened to Doc Williams and the Border Riders. I expect they were in the early '40s, too.

JW: Were you playing gospel music at this time?

LC: Yeah, we played some gospel music, we sang some of the older songs out of the song books.

MK: Jimmie, you said that an older brother, Junior, that he died when he was young?

JC: He died when he was two, he fell and bumped his nose as far as I know by my dad and mother telling about it. He bled somewhere, and it kept a-going, down internally. And he took inflammation on the inside, from the blood being on the inside. He died of hemophilia.

JW: Had there ever been any cases of hemophilia in your family at all before that?

JC: Not as far back as I can remember, and not as far back as my mother could remember.

MK: How old were you when you realized that you were different from your brothers and sisters?

JC: Well, when we started going to school and playing around. We knowed right then that we was different, messing around and playing games.

MK: What would happen? Would you get bruised?

JC: We would get all hemorrhaged in the joint. We would be swollen up till we couldn't do a thing, just couldn't walk. Even take spells of bleeding internally. Internal bleeding could be either inside of you or it would be internally in a joint or under the skin—caused hemorrhaging like that. And then that way it would lay you up.

MK: How much of an injury would it take to do that? Just ordinary rough-housing on the playground?

JC: Not very much, just sometimes a little bump would cause hemorrhage for weeks at a time. Just a small bump.

JW: When did your parents realize you had it? And did they know what you had?

LC: No, no, no. They knowed that our brother had died, that he bled out. And they knew that there was something wrong. My mother knowed that we were bleeders, but she still didn't know [about] hemophilia. They ain't none of us knowed, not even the doctors knew how to stop the bleeding or anything like that.

JW: You were adults before you knew?

LC: Actually we were adults. I expect I was in my late 20s or early 30s before I knew anything about how severe it was.

JW: And the hematologists there realized what you had?

LC: Right.

∾

Guitarist and singer Loren Currence manages the Currence Brothers band. Photograph by William Metzger.

What they had was one of the oldest and most dreaded of hereditary diseases, known and feared—but little understood—even in ancient Egypt and Babylon. Queen Victoria was an unsuspected carrier, and through her offspring the royal houses of England, Spain, and Russia were later ravaged by it. It became known as the "royal disease." And Jimmie and Loren Currence in High Germany, West Virginia, unaccountably had it. There had never been a history of it anywhere in the Currence family.

The crushing truth was that the Currence brothers were victims of a grim genetic mutation. And never in their early years did they or their parents—or even the rural doctors who treated them—realize the terrible deadly danger they faced daily. Only one in four hemophiliacs in those days (they were born during the Depression) survived to age 16.

As hemophiliacs, they are probably unique in the United States in the severity of their affliction, in the odds they have had to overcome, and in the degree they have excelled in the face of it. Until they were in their late 30s the only thing that really helped Jimmie and Loren were transfusions. Loren, bleeding heavily from the kidneys one time, had 16 pints of blood poured into him in a day and a half. Not until medical science learned to produce blood concentrate of Factor VIII did Jimmie and Loren experience the kind of relief denied them for the first 30 years of their lives.

To this day the disease frustrates the medical profession.

One in every 10,000 people in the world has some form of hemophilia. Some 25,000 hemophiliacs live in the United States. Not all have the severe hemophilia—near zero clotting factor—the Currence brothers have. In two-thirds of all cases the disease is inherited. But a dispiriting one-third of the time it appears mysteriously, without warning, and without precedent, from a gene mutation. Such was the case with the Currence family.

∾

MK: It's 4.2 miles (we clocked it) into where you were raised from the hard-surfaced road. Straight down and around. You were describing as we drove in there snowdrifts that a bulldozer couldn't push without a running start downhill. That an ordinary grader couldn't push out. And you were describing your childhood as being snowed in for long periods of time before there were even bulldozers to push snow. And there you were, in a condition in which at any time you could have bled to death. Were you scared all the time?

LC: No, we never give it a thought, did we?

JC: No, we just lived with, well, with faith. We didn't think nothing about it. In other words, it's hard to explain, you just lived like a person that was just normal, hoping nothing would happen.

LC: You would lay and suffer and cry and have a lot of

pain, but after you got over it you didn't think that anything would happen.

MK: What happened in the winter time when you would take these spells? How would you get out?

LC: We didn't get out, we laid in there and suffered. We never went to a doctor much till we was in our teens. And if we got a sprain, a hemorrhaged knee or arm in the winter time, we stayed at home. And we stayed at home the biggest part of the summer time. After we had grown up there was times we had to hire someone to take us out in a car. That's scary, after you think about it, hain't it?

JC: Like when we got up in our teens. I had one bleeding spell in my stomach and I had to go to a doctor in Buckhannon. The only thing that saved me was my brother-in-law giving me a pint of blood at the time. The doctor said it was a wonder I hadn't gone into convulsions and died right then. But I was doing fine after I got the pint of blood. It was off and on you would take a spell. Many times I would have a joint problem, and after it was all over with I would keep a-going. I'd go right on; should have been a-laying still. When you was a boy and you was active as we was, you just continuously kept a-getting hurt. But as soon as you got over a spell you still wanted to go. You still had the guts to keep a-going. I did. I mean, there's something about my life and the—

LC: The will.

JC: The will power. I like that farm so well. We fooled around with everything. We made rails with our daddy. We cut wood, used axes, and everything else. But now we wouldn't dare use an axe or fool around with stuff like that.

MK: To give an example of that, you mentioned one time going berry picking way back on a ridge. Were you with your sister?

JC: I was with my oldest sister. I expect it was a good mile and a half back in there. I went a-berry picking with her and caught my toe on a snag, or something, and twisted one of my knees, and it started hemorrhaging. Still yet I didn't know what it was. But before I got out of there I was in pain. Trying to carry the blackberries. My sister would keep a-saying, "Can you make it?" I would say, "Yeah, I'll try." But before I got to the house I was with severe pain. And after I did get to the house I couldn't walk a step for days and days because my knee was a swollen clean up. Full of blood from hemorrhaging into the joint.

MK: And how old were you then?

JC: I expect I was about 13 years old.

MK: Was that when you laid in a chair?

JC: No, Michael, when I laid in the chair I was married. Right after I got married I was a-cutting wood on a block and I fell on that hip and it started hemorrhaging. It never acted right after that, but it got so I could walk pretty good. And then I went back through that country a-deer hunting

after I got to going around again, and I think that made it worse. But see, I laid across a chair for about three weeks to get rest from that hip socket. It was damaged, too, in the joint, from falling so much on the ice going to school. Well, you seen where the school house was. We walked six-tenths of a mile there from home every day. I set many a time right in the school house bleeding from the teeth—just shed a baby tooth—just set there a-spitting blood right in a can and still trying to study.

LC: I had the same trouble with my teeth. A lot of times I'd go to school, like Jimmie said, I had a lot of pride about me and I didn't want the other kids to know and I would swallow the blood. Just pour the blood. I bled with my baby teeth until I was white as a sheet. So weak I couldn't hardly go. See, that's what I said about the hemophiliac bleeder. We don't have a bit of clotting in our blood.

I went one morning to school and fell on the ice. Four o'clock that evening school let out and I had to crawl almost back. I never slept three night with that knee. It was swollen up so tight it wouldn't bend a bit. It almost set me crazy. Didn't have a thing for pain. We didn't have no ice or anything to put on it. We didn't have no refrigerator, see, at that time. The doctors said that ice packs would help it, but we didn't have none to put on. And you just suffered bloody murder. Especially when a joint was a-hemorrhaging. The only things we would use we got from Blair products. It was called high-powered liniments, and a few bathing liniments, and we would use that on our joints.

JW: What was your first contact with doctors?

LC: Our first contact with doctors was when I cut my foot on a pile of glass. And I was very small. I must not have been six or seven, if that. And they taken me to the hospital in Buckhannon. And they sewed that foot up—they put four stitches in it, never numbed it, never froze it, never put me to sleep, or anything. And I laid there and screamed like a wildcat. They couldn't hardly hold me. And they sewed my foot up. When I came back from Buckhannon it kept a-seeping and a big blue knot about the size of a silver dollar came out there about two inches long. And it just healed from the inside out, that's how long it would take it to heal. That's the only way a cut could heal—we would just keep a-bleeding till we didn't hardly have any blood in our bodies. It would eventually stop after it had a scab on it. I've bled with my nose. We've had nosebleeds just poured the blood, just keep a-bleeding and keep a-bleeding.

MK: Did you ever think you were going to die when you were a kid bleeding like that?

LC: No, I never give it no thought. Well, I didn't. I don't know about Jimmie, but I didn't have the realization that I was in that kind of shape, see? That's why it never bothered me. If I had known I would have been a nervous wreck.

JW: After you did find out, how did you feel?

The home of the Currence grandparents, built of hand-hewn logs before the turn of the century, still stands in Randolph County. The children often stopped here for beans and cornbread on their way home from the High Germany School, barely visible in the background. Photograph by William Metzger.

LC: When the doctor sent me to Morgantown with an abscessed jaw, I don't know how many doctors examined me. Of course they found out what I had. They said, "Do you know what kind of a shape you are in?" I said, "Well, I think I do, I've had it long enough." They said, "No, you don't know. You're a severe hemophiliac bleeder." They said, "You could bleed to death like that (snap of the fingers)." And of course that there let the cork off. It started me to thinking. It had an effect on me psychologically—nervousness, mental, everything.

Then I was called back by a telegram after they released me. I got a telegram in the post office saying for me to report to the hematologist at the University Hospital on a certain date. Doctor Mabel M. Stevenson. She was a hematologist. I went down there and they drawed blood out of me and asked me my life history. And I said I had a brother living and a nephew living with it. And the next time all three of us went down. That was Jimmie, Malcomb Pastine, and I.

MK: What year was that?

LC: That was in the early '60s.

JW: But there wasn't any real organized concern about you until Doctor Stevenson sent you the telegram?

LC: Not a bit in the world, that's right. There wasn't no real concern about us until I got the telegram. From that time we went regular's a month come, to give blood for the lab to work with down at the University Hospital.

JW: Had Doctor Stevenson been in the first group of doctors who saw you when you went for your abscessed tooth?

LC: No, she found out after I left. She had never seen me. We were the worst hemophiliac bleeders that's been in the University Hospital, except one down in Philippi. The Factor VIII will not take a-hold of him. He built up an antibody to it. Our blood is down to zero factor.

MK: This "zero factor" refers to the ability of your blood to clot?

LC: Right. The zero factor is severe classical hemophilia.

MK: If I were normal, what would mine be?

LC: Well, anywhere from 70 to 80, maybe 100 percent. And if a man's got 30 percent in his blood he is counted a hemophiliac bleeder, but you never notice it until major surgery. He could go through the Army. There was two of them I knew in Morgantown name McBees and they was in the Army. They was hemophiliac bleeders but they wasn't severe.

JC: I would say this for a fact. I would never—even a hemophiliac growing up today—I would encourage him not to be afraid. Not to be afraid or let something like that get him down, because if you let something get you down, after a while it will throw you clean into the dumps. I would encourage them to go right about their business like there was nothing wrong.

MK: Well, you have that job ahead of you, don't you? I mean, to encourage? You have a grandson who you'll have to encourage a lot.

JC: Yeah, that's right. I noticed a blue mark on him this evening. He's going to get them things on him before long, as soon as he starts walking. He's going to be having a hemorrhaged joint, hemorrhaging an elbow or anywhere he falls and hurts hisself, till he gets up and knows how to take care of it, and learns to cope with it. After we got up a certain age and we was hurt so much we was more protective of ourselves. We limited ourselves to what we knowed we could do, and what we couldn't do. And you would have to learn that. And that's why I would advise them not to let it worry them.

It did worry me there at one time. It had me with a nervous breakdown almost. I was afraid to go anywhere. After I found out what I had I was afraid to go anywhere, to the point where I was a nervous wreck. I even went to the doctors. I thought everything. I seen I was a-going to die. I had death on my mind, because people kept a-telling me that—people who have since passed away—told me I wouldn't live no time: "You can't live no time because you're a hemophiliac." That was people I grew up with and went to school with. I was afraid to go out, I would be setting in the house all the time. So I went to the doctor and he said, "Well, did you ever stop to think that the house could cave in on you and kill you?" He said, "You might as well enjoy yourself." Of course, he snapped me out of it and I got over it. I just felt that, heck, life's life and you'll live till you die. And I figured it was a higher power, like God, would take care of me.

Pauline Waugh: Your lack of fear was your protection.

JC: Right, that's exactly right, lack of fear.

LC: Well, another thing that protected us, too. I can't keep from believing this. We had a praying mother, and a praying father, too. They was God-fearing people. My mother was, and so my daddy is yet today.

JC: My mother, she kept alert after that one boy bled to death and she cautioned us everything that we'd do. She'd say don't do this or don't do that, try to watch and not jump like the other kids and climb trees and things like that. She cautioned us not to do that, but like boys, you know, we done that. That's why we was hurt a lot. We would go out and we were adventurous. And we would have black and blue fence marks on us all the time. But we never give it no thought of being in that shape. Still, she would caution us about our condition. And we just went right ahead and did it, tried to do, what the other boys done.

LC: I think she worried a little more than Daddy. Of course, I don't know. I think a mother has got more of a test. I know a father would worry too. I worried, you know, about my kids, but I think a mother's nature is to worry more. Mom was more to worry about it than Daddy.

JW: What was the attitude of the neighbors and the other children?

JC: Some of them was a little protective with us. You know, they would watch us. But others didn't pay no attention to us.

LC: They didn't understand it really.

JC: In fact, when I started to high school—I got my eighth-grade diploma from over there at the High Germany school while we was on the farm—and then I started to high school at Coalton. But then it got to the point where I couldn't climb up and down stairs and change rooms and classes. It would hurt me so bad, I would have to skip so much, it just got next to me and I couldn't take it. When we were younger a-growing up, we was hurt more and didn't have no medicine to take. If we had the medicine and that there Factor VIII we have today I think we could have went along to school and finished it and got more of an education, which would have been good. But we couldn't get it, just on account of having no medicine, no way of paying for that kind of expensive medicine.

MK: You had this tremendous expense buying medicine and getting doctors?

JC: It cost us a lot of trips.

LC: Well, it cost a lot of trips, but we couldn't afford to pay for the medicine. There is nobody can afford to pay for Factor VIII. The state pays for that.

JW: How much Factor VIII do you have to use?

LC: It's depending on the hemorrhage you probably have to use three units. The Factor VIII is spun out of human blood, and you mix it with sterilized water and inject it with a needle in a vein. The joint gets weak before the hemorrhage comes on. You can feel it. That's when it's hemorrhaging light. And then it starts to stiffen up. If you can catch it then, you're all right. But if you don't it will get bad. I've had my joints, my ankle joints and knee joints and elbow joints to start hemorrhaging and in a matter of an hour they would be a-hurting so bad that you couldn't stand it. If you get a fast hemorrhage, look out, you're going to have a lot of pain with it, real bad pain. And the doctor said the more it hemorrhages the worse for the joint, the more it destroys the joint, the cartilage in it. We would have been in a lot better shape if we had that Factor VIII 20 years ago.

JC: Oh, yeah, but there's nothing they can do with them joints now. Nothing. But it never did destroy my spark to play music. And it never will! I'll quit having the urge to play music when they put me away for good.

MK: Well, we'll all be playing your records when that happens, so they won't be able to keep you quiet even then. Hemophilia is a condition that comes through the genes some way and it's carried by women. Is that right?

LC: Right.

MK: Do women ever get it?

LC and JC: No.

MK: You have outlived all the predictions that your neighbors and everybody said about you years ago. You've lived normal lives, you've married, you've had kids, you are now grandfathers. And each of you had three daughters.

JC: I had one boy. He died when he was five months old.

But he wasn't no hemophiliac. He just died because he took pneumonia and was too little to survive in the cold winter over there where we lived in the farm.

MK: Are your three daughters carriers?

LC: Oh, yeah, all of them, every one of ours.

MK: If you had 100 daughters they would be carriers? All carriers?

LC: Yes indeed, every one of them carriers.

JW: But if you had sons none of them would be?

JC and LC: Right.

JC: Now, see, Malcomb, he's got hemophilia. Well, he's got a son.

LC: He's got a son, and he's normal as can be.

JC: See, my wife's no carrier of hemophilia, but my daughters carry it through my genes.

MK: But then were all of your sisters then carriers? Or some of them?

LC: All of them's carriers.

MK: But all of your brothers were not hemophiliacs?

JC: Oh, no. Me and Loren and one that died.

LC: There was seven boys and three of us were hemophiliac bleeders. And four of them was normal. So it's actually a 50-50 chance. Like 50 percent chance of rain. It might rain and it might not, so that's just the way it is when a woman is pregnant with a child—if it's a bad gene or a good gene.

MK: Has anyone ever suggested that your daughters should not have children?

LC: Yeah, doctors do.

MK: What do you think about that?

LC: I say not.

JC: I advised them, before they got married not to have children, because of what I had. I mean, you know, of what I've went through and what I have experienced in my life. Of course, they've got a better chance, like I say, with the Factor VIII than I had. But still, if you can prevent suffering humanity in the world I say not.

∽

As Loren steered his Bronco over the rutted road to High Germany, old memories were rekindled. He and Jimmie exclaimed over long-remembered landmarks—the forest alongside the road, the homeplace, the dilapidated old schoolhouse, its paint peeled and gone, old and empty and weathered.

∽

MK: What was it like, though, in the one-room school? Can you describe that a little bit? You told me as many as 45 kids were going to that school at a time.

LC: All eight grades, yeah.

JC: And we had a real good time. Then, you know, the older ones on the higher grades would help the younger ones.

LC: Yeah, they helped out.

JC: And they brought teachers in. The only way they could teach over there was to board with somebody. Most of the time they boarded with us there at our farm.

MK: Do you remember a particular teacher that was outstanding in your mind?

JC: Yeah, I remember Nellie Lambert. I remember Ava Nell Loudin, and Geneva Church. And Eleanor Fahrner taught me, when we went to school.

LC: She lives in Helvetia.

MK: Was Eleanor a pretty keen teacher?

JC: She was a fine teacher. And there was several more teachers taught school in there. The schoolhouse served as our church and school activities and everything that went on. At Christmas time they'd have a Christmas play like they do in any school. I thought it was better than most schools. Back then to me it was really something, 'cause most of the time they would work up their own plays and there was people come from miles, you know, walked to see that. Them big crowds come to them and attended them. They'd be grownups take parts in it, too, as well as the kids that went to school. And they always had a Easter play and have an Easter egg hunt for the kids. And they would have eggs all over. And I never will forget they'd take the kids out on a farm, clean back on a picnic.

LC: That was the end of the school year.

JC: The end of the school year. Take us on picnics a-way back.

LC: All the families would go together.

JC: All the families would go, and go together.

LC: They would have a tremendous meal to eat, you know, they would put it on the ground on tablecloths.

MK: What games did you play as a kid?

JC: We had a game we called "base and banner." I don't know if you ever heard of that or not. Let's see, you teamed up, as well as I can remember. There would be four, five get in a team and they'd be so far apart and they'd have bases and one of them would try maybe to go around the other one. And if the other one tagged him they got him on their side. And whoever got the most people on their side was the winners.

MK: Did you have any special beliefs as kids? Did you tell stories about haunts or spells or any of that kind of stuff? Or were there beliefs like that at all in the community? Did any of the older people believe in ghosts and signs or—

JC: Yeah, signs. They believed in signs. Well, actually some of them believed in ghosts, especially my grandmother, and I couldn't doubt her words on a few things she seen. She told us one time her grandfather was a-walking from a place. He said there was another man with him. He kept a-saying there was a dog a-following him. And he said, "No, there's no dog there." But he saw the dog and he said, "Yeah, I see the dog." And after they came to this graveyard this dog just went out and disappeared. One of my grandmother's sons, my uncle, he could almost detect somebody when they died over there. I don't know if it were ESP or what. But when they was a-going to tell him somebody died, he said, "Don't tell me, I already know that somebody died."

Of course they had a big old bell over there in the church. Every time the church bell rung you know somebody died. Unless it was Sunday morning. But if somebody died they rung that church bell so many times in that community where we lived.

That same uncle had a cat. And my grandmother told him one night, said it was time for him to put the cat out and go to bed. He said, "No, I'm going to get up early in the morning. You put the cat out and come to bed." On this particular night he stayed up a little longer with the cat and she kept a-telling him to come to bed. She finally told him for the last time. (You know they only told kids back that time one or two times and that was it.) And he knowed to come. "Well," he said, "Tom, I'll put you out, but I'll never see you no more." And he never did see the cat no more. She said he never did, and I never knowed of her a-telling lies.

MK: Did he have any other kinds of special powers? What about healing? Did he do any healing or were there healers of any kind in the community?

JC: Well, there was a woman over there—

LC: They tried, they were wanting somebody in the community to try to stop the blood when one of us was cut.

JC: They never did stop it. She claimed she could heal, and she had the power, if any little kid was sick she could heal them. But I never saw it happen myself, I never really seen it. And I never saw no ghosts as they spoke of.

LC: Only one time. I remember just as well as yesterday. We were very small. And we went outside or something. Jimmie can remember it. It was before World War II and everybody, you know, they thought it was those northern lights. You've seen the northern lights shoot up. But anyway, this one particular night, I think it was in the 1940s—early '40s—we went out and I said, "Look up at the sky, it's awful peculiar." I said, "It's very interesting." It was red, just as red as it could be, and the sky was in a quiver like this.

JC: Just looked like jelly.

LC: Nobody would believe it. The people through that country was scared to death. And it was just a-quivering like this all the time. It just looked like red Jello in it. And some of them even seen the American flag in it. The younger generation, they just don't believe that. But that was the only time it ever happened. And right after that World War II broke out. It was weird. It scared people. There was people that got out of bed and run and everything. They thought the world was a-coming to an end. But it was the sky. I mean, not in one spot; it was the whole sky. And it was no northern lights.

JC: The sky was lit up. You know how Jello looks when you got it in a pan, if you chop it up. But the heavens was just in a pure quiver. This one guy had long johns on and he run from a-top that hill, he was so frightened, he run from the top of the hill way into our home hollering and screaming. They just thought the whole heavens was on fire. I mean it was all over.

MK: Do you remember any other strange goings on?

LC: You heard some tales a-going on about music going through the skies. They heard music, people did, go over their houses. They said they heard music go over the house just in the sky.

JC: Well there was some weird things happen, I mean, back when I was in there. Things that I never saw happen today.

LC: I don't know whether there was some kind of an animal, but there was a thing that hollered back in them days, of a night. They thought maybe it might be foxes. But it would scream just like a woman. And I heard it many of times. It would make cold chills, make the hair stand on your head. One time it would scream one place and the next time it would be on the other hill. It was that quick, that's how quick it was.

MK: Well, what were some of the other tales people told?

JC: Yeah, a woman that went to a church there died from some cause and they buried the body. And my grandmother said the next day or two they had to move her or something, you know, and put her somewhere else. They didn't want her there. But they had took her up and they opened her up and she wasn't dead. And she lived 15 years after that!

JW: You fellows grew up, both of you, and became fiddle champions. Is it safe to say, Jimmie, that you're probably one of the best fiddlers in this part of the country? How in the world did you become that good? At what point did the music start to become very important to you? How did you get to the caliber that you could go and win four Forest Festival fiddle contests in a row?

JC: Well, I knew that after I had the bleeding that I was going to have some activity in life that I could pass the time away, you know, for a hobby. I had to have something to do, and I just put my head to it that I wanted to play music. I worked very hard at a violin. I practiced on that fiddle all the time, at night, in my spare time. After I won them championships I got this bleeding, see, in my arms. And then I got till I couldn't use the fiddle that good anymore. I didn't let that whip me out. I went to picking my banjo.

MK: It's as though you could see it coming or something?

JC: Right. I did. I saw it coming. It was just there, something you wanted to do and you can't let it get out of your

The Currence Brothers Band (left to right): Marvin "Shorty," Loren, Malcomb Pastine (a nephew), Buddy, and Jimmie. Photographer unknown.

system. It's just something that grows in there. Like a man that's worked in the mines all his life, he wants to be there until he retires. I like music because it brings something to me, especially if I'm singing and playing anywhere for people. I like to make people happy with music. It makes me feel good. That's why I like music and that's why I'll continue to like it as long as I'm able to pick it. There's something about music to me: when you're in the worst down-hearted, in other words, depressed, I can get my banjo and pick a good old gospel tune on that thing and it will start to spark again. It takes all that away. And that's why I like to play music.

MK: Well, did you have the same kind of experience, Loren?

LC: Yeah, same thing. I always like music, always liked to fool with it. It's just like Jimmie said, it's sort of like we have an incline to play music. It was a part of you.

JC: Of course, we can't leave our sisters out either.

LC: No, we've got brothers and sisters played.

JC: Our sisters sang with us. All of them sang, from the oldest one down.

LC: And then our mother sang with us.

JC: Mother sang with us in church. We sang with her a lot of times, lots of places and all over in churches, even from the oldest one to the youngest. And we all sang together.

LC: After they got married and moved we had to reorganize, you know. Our nephew, Malcomb Pastine, he played rock 'n' roll. We got him to play the bass for us. And then we organized our band.

JW: Malcomb is a hemophiliac too.

LC: Yeah, he's just like us.

MK: Was the Currence family thought to be very special in the music line or were there other musicians around the community that you played with at all?

JC: Well, there was a few, but not that many around where

we lived. We was sort of special to that community, because they totally inclined for us to come and sing in church from the time we started. In fact, all the Currences over there, like my uncle, see, his girls and boys sang with my oldest brother before we got big enough to sing. We was something special through that part of the country. After we got to getting older and when we was able to go, people would call on us to sing in different churches all the time. Then I met Woody Simmons when I was young enough to date girls. I got to going over to his restaurant there at the 76 station in Mill Creek. We played around with him a lot when we was kids growing up. I fiddled a lot of times for him. Like the Log Cabin Inn. Played down there with him. But of course that's been years ago.

MK: Did you used to hear Woody on the radio when you were home?

JC: Oh, yeah. We listened to him all the time. Daddy always pulled the chair up close—they were on at a certain time. I think it was in the evening, about supper time. Mom would always have supper for us. We would all gather around the old battery radio to listen to him. Then Woody got to knowing us, too, you know. He got to coming over and then after we knew each other we got to fiddling around together, too, all of us.

MK: Well, apart from the enjoyment of music, has it also been a source of income for both of you?

LC: No, if you had depended on it for a living I would have starved to death a long time ago.

MK: How in the world have you made it, financially speaking?

LC: Well, nobody would hire us. And we couldn't get a job at manual labor because we just couldn't stand it. I even tried to get school bus driving jobs. My doctor wouldn't allow it—Dr. Stevenson. But I went ahead anyway and tried to get a job driving a school bus, but they wouldn't hire me, said it was too big of a risk. And we can't get a drop of insurance or nothing. We thought we would get life insurance, but they turned us down.

JC: People's Life. It's been tough, Michael—on Supplemental Social Security. It ain't that much, but it's the only little bit of regular income we have. Maybe if somebody donates you a few dollars when you are out in church.

MK: For singing?

JC: Singing. But you don't count on that all the time, 'cause months and months go by and you don't have no place to play music.

MK: But in another way of looking at it, you've had a pretty rich life, haven't you?

JC: Yeah, I would actually say my life has been a benefit to the world. I've made a lot of people happy.

LC: Yeah.

JC: In fact, we've sang at funerals that I didn't think I

would be singing for. I thought they would be singing at mine. I always questioned my mother when she was alive. I said, why did I have to be this way and my other brothers didn't have to be? "Well," she said, "you have brought just as much joy to me as they have, or more, because you do a lot of singing in church, whereas the others don't."

JW: Were there other musicians, styles of music, that influenced or had an effect on you that changed your music in some way?

JC: Definitely, Jack. When, well, in the early '40s when I was a kid, I always listened to the "Grand Ole Opry." Every time I would hear somebody like Smiley and Reno play it always put a spark into me, where I wanted to play music. And it had an influence over me. Every time I would hear Reno, Smiley, or Bill Monroe singing, especially some of them old songs like "Danny Boy," I always had an urge to play and sing. There was a spark there.

Music to me is something that is caught, just like building a fire. It built a fire under my life to hear some singing and hear good music. It was so much joy for me to make another person enjoy it, like the older people when they get to smiling and a-tapping their feet. That means that I want to keep playing as long as I can pick music. It's a gift, a talent that was give, and I won't bury it as long as I'm able to fool with it. When I was low in the hospital at times, there was times I wanted to give up, you know, but then my wife and my kids would come, I would think of my banjo at home. And I would think of being home with them, and then I would think about getting back to where I would get that banjo. And that always brought life to me again.

When I thought of the music and the family and the kids, I think that's what kept me a-going, really. Just like I told my wife this evening. We was a-talking about 25 years together. She was reading me something from the proverbs, how a woman was a backbone of a man. "Well," I said, "you are the backbone of me, plus my music." I like my music and she has never kicked on me a-playing. You know, she has never been like some: "You ain't a-going to this place to play music," or "I don't want you a-leaving." Naturally she hated to see me be gone when I'm away at times. But still it's a duty that we have to fulfill, having a gift to playing music. Just like if this man is desperate to hear good music, I ain't a-going to turn him down, 'cause I like to play the music if it makes him happy. I do that for people on the CB radio, too. They like to hear it. And I'll play them a tune.

JW: What part does CB play in your life?

JC: Well, sir, in fact, me and Loren has made a lot of friends at that there radio. It plays a big role. I get in contact with people I like in Buckhannon that I don't get to see much. And then somebody on there will holler back and say, "Well, I would like to hear a good banjo tune!" It always lifts them up.

JW: Your handle is "Banjo Picker"?

JC: Right. The first radio I got I just thought, well, I'll pick a banjo. I hollered at Troy Simmons, been paralyzed for 30 years from his waist down, shut in. He just hollered back, "Hello, Banjo Picker!" I said, "How did you know that was my handle?" "Well," he said, "I figured that was what you would go by, Banjo Picker." And he knowed my voice, you know, and of course that's what I used as a handle on the CB ever since.

JW: Larry Groce told me one time that you played together with the first violin of the Charleston Symphony. He said that was a fairly memorable occasion. Here was the West Virginia fiddle champion playing with the first violin of the Charleston Symphony. Can you remember that and describe what it was like?

LC: Yeah, up at Elkins, remember?

JC: Yeah, that's right, I remember playing. Right, we played together with him. I played one tune was called "Bill Cheatham." He played off the notes, you know, and everything, and I played "Leave Something Special" with him and I played "Maple Sugar." He was amazed at the tunes I played on the fiddle. Of course, he was a good violinist from down at Charleston. He was a really fine fiddler.

JW: Would it be possible for you to assess your role in the music of West Virginia?

JC: Well, part of it would be knowing that I had a lot of will power and knowing the people that seen me at the point of death. And then I would come right back and go to playing the banjo again. I think it had a big influence over a lot of people, me a-getting right back a-playing the music. If that's a-telling you anything, Jack.

Just like Woody Simmons, for instance. You take him there when he had that open heart surgery they didn't think he had a prayer. But he had a strong constitution. And look at him today. He's still after the fiddle, just a-yanking on the bow. He had a strong constitution to play. And the same way with me. When I was in the Morgantown University Hospital, that's been four years in February, that's when I had that real bad bleeding spell, real bad. Now I was really depressed, you see, when I went down there, 'cause I was a-getting ready for surgery. And they didn't think they could get the bleeding stopped without surgery. And the doctor just plain out and told me, "Mr. Currence, it's a matter of life or death."

Well, they did, they got it under control, but they knowed I was pretty well depressed with it. The doc he comes up and he tells me, "No, you're not well enough to go home." "But," he said, "you can bring your banjo down in the hospital if that will help you out." I said, "How can I play with an IV in my hand?" He said, "We'll fix that right up."

So my wife brings the banjo down. I got in there set up in the bed, I got to feeling good. And I picked the banjo and before it was over with I had the whole hospital, the doctors and all, come right down to my room, and people would shut off their television to listen to me pick the banjo. Even a woman up in her years was there. They wheeled them down and they set there and they enjoyed it. And the doctor he had a guitar. The next night he brought the guitar over and he played with me, and sat on the edge of the bed and played. And they really enjoyed the banjo. They could hear it up the halls echoing. A lot of the doctor staff come right there, listened at me play. Now most hospitals wouldn't allow it, but they allowed it in there. Just put me right on top of the world. It wasn't long until I was back home playing the banjo again.

EDITOR'S NOTE: This article first appeared in the summer 1980 issue of *Goldenseal* (vol. 6, no. 2). Loren Currence died in the 1980s and his brother Jimmie died in 1992. Today, surviving brothers Marvin "Shorty" Currence (fiddle) and Clyde Currence (guitar) continue to perform and play with the Bluegrass Gospel Boys, a popular group that performs in churches and get-togethers throughout West Virginia and Ohio and makes regular appearances at the Mt. Nebo gospel sings in Nicholas County. Shorty Currence says of his brothers, "I miss them. We had our own thing," but he enjoys performing with his current group and playing music that "really touches people." The Currence brothers' father, Jacob, is 99 years old and still lives by himself, down the road from Shorty.

The Welch Brothers Band

"ALWAYS COME HOME AFTER THE DANCE"

Bill Wellington

PATTERSON Creek lies east of the Allegheny Front running from south to north, in one of the beautiful valleys that make up the Potomac Highlands of West Virginia. From its headwaters in northern Grant County to its confluence with the North Branch of the Potomac near Cumberland, Maryland, the stream flows through some of the most fertile farmland in the mountains.

At Burlington, in Mineral County, Patterson Creek intersects U.S. Route 50, the original path of the pioneers who settled the eastern part of the state in the mid- to late 18th century. About two miles northwest of Burlington is the 400-acre farm that has been home to the Welch family since the 1830s. Here live Mary Welch, age 81, her brother Israel, 71, and their cousin Margaret, 67.

According to Mary, "Old Uncle Dempsy Welch bought this place and later sold it to his nephew, James P. Welch, who was my grandfather. He was a Confederate veteran. He married Sabina Leman."

James and Sabina Welch had seven children who survived infancy. Three of their sons, Millard Dillmore, Ulysses Allen, and Judson, stayed on the farm throughout their lives. Mil-

lard married Mary Etta Placka, Allen married Bertha Maude Leatherman, and Judson married Maggie May Leatherman, Bertha's sister.

While Millard and his wife remained childless, the marriages of the two other brothers to the Leatherman sisters produced 17 children. Together with their parents and Uncle Millard and Aunt Mary Etta, these children made up a large, happy, extremely close-knit family. "Everyone was either your brother, your sister, or your double first cousin," Israel explained. "At dinner we sat down to a table with 23 people. When I was in the Army, which was the first time I left the farm, I sat down at the table with about eight other fellows and I said, "Where is everybody?"

From this large and no doubt lively group of children there emerged seven who became string musicians: John Frederick, Thomas Wesley, Oscar Ulysses, Israel Cuthbert, Bonnie Charlotte, and Elwanda from Allen's family, and Creed Thurman from Judson's family. From the 1920s to the present, various combinations of these musicians have performed as "The Welch Brothers."

Of the original seven, only Israel and his older brother

Anita Combs and Israel Welch in 1980 at Anita's house near Romney. Photograph by Michael Meador.

Brothers Ike (left) and Israel Welch, after playing a 1938 reunion.
Photographer unknown.

Tom, age 75, survive. They are remarkable musicians who
continue to play with great vigor and ability. Since meeting
Tom and Israel in 1977, I have spent many music-filled hours
in their presence. The following history is the result of many
conversations during these seven years and several recent
interviews with Mary and Margaret at the Welch homeplace.

∽

"When I was young it stirred me to hear a good hornpipe," said Tom Welch recently at his home in Petersburg,
Grant County. The fiddler who played the hornpipes that
made such an impression on young Tom was "Uncle Tom"
Thrush, a neighbor and Tom's music teacher.

"He had a big white mustache and a wonderful way about
him when he played the fiddle," Tom said. "He played reels,
hornpipes, jigs, schottisches, waltzes, and clogs. He said he
knew 2,000 fiddle tunes, and I'll say he knew a few. He also
played several classical pieces. He played very smooth, and
he wanted to hit every note right."

"Tom Thrush read and wrote music," Israel recalls. "He
traveled around from place to place with his fiddle in an old

flour sack. Sometimes when he played, his niece Sally would
accompany him on the parlor organ."

Israel and Tom Welch's mother and aunt also played the
parlor organ, having learned from their cousin Sarah Cun-
ningham of Purgitsville, Hampshire County. Their Uncle
Vernon Leatherman played the five-string banjo, and Tom
recalls him accompanying Tom Thrush. He used a two-
finger rhythmic accompaniment style. Israel recalls that
their Uncle Judson was a great whistler. The whole family
loved music.

About 1920 John, then 14, sent away to Sears and Roebuck
for a fiddle and began to learn to play. Tom, who was 11,
began to pick up John's fiddle when he could. Soon John
had to send away for another fiddle from Montgomery
Ward. Tom Thrush took a particular interest in Tom's development as a fiddler.

"Uncle Tom would listen to him play and say, 'You're a-
gettin' it, Tommy, you're a-gettin' it!'" Mary said. "When he
was on his deathbed Tommy played him a tune, and Uncle
Tom asked for the fiddle and, though he could barely move,
he showed him where he'd made a mistake in it." Uncle Tom
Thrush died in 1927.

Tom Welch remembers the same touching moment, and
even the tune. "That was the 'Price Baine Waltz.' That's what
he called it, anyway, after Price Baine, a fiddler who lived
about a mile from us down on Dry Run."

By the early 1920s brothers John and Tom were playing
their fiddles, Cousin Creed was learning the banjo, and
young Israel and Oscar (Ike) were eager to join in.

"We were always after my father for something to pick,"
Israel remembers. "I would pretend to pick a banjo as I
walked to school. I'd whistle a tune and brush against my
overalls. I wore a hole out in my overalls that my mother had
to mend several times.

"One summer my father said, 'Perhaps you'll have something to pick in the fall.' We heard that all summer long, and
in the fall he showed us what he had for us to pick—three
acres of soup beans!

"Later on, he let us cut several chestnut oaks. We peeled
the bark and sold it to the tannery in Burlington. With the
money Oscar bought a guitar, and I bought a mandolin. I
played it all the time. One day Howard Hartman saw me and
said, 'By jingo, he's got him a mandolillian!'"

By the mid-1920s, the four Welch brothers (John, Tom,
Ike, and Israel) and their cousin Creed had two fiddles, a
banjo, a mandolin, and a guitar among them. I remarked to
Mary that it must have been exciting to see the boys taking
to music. "Exciting?" she said. "I tell you, they were making
such a racket that we had them build that cabin back up on
the hill so they could play and not bother anybody."

"We cut the lumber at our sawmill that we had way down
the road and carried it up here to the orchard," Israel added.

Fiddler Tom Welch surrounded by memorabilia at his trailer in Petersburg. Photograph by Michael Meador.

Mary, Israel, and Margaret Welch relaxing at home. Photograph by Michael Meador.

"One time they had a fire up there," Mary remarked. "Uncle Millard saw it and said 'Boys, you better get up there and save your house.' So they all ran. Ike filled a five-gallon pail and ran up there, and in the smoke and excitement he threw the water on Tom!" The boys managed to save their cabin, and today Israel lives there. Every Thursday night he has friends over for music.

The year 1928 was an important one for the young Welch family band for two reasons. The first was the advent of radio. "I believe that when radio came into this country it was a much bigger novelty than television was later on," Tom said. "See, we didn't have anything like that before radio."

Radio offered a phenomenal musical resource to the brothers and particularly to Tom, who had developed the ability to learn quickly by ear. According to Israel, "Tom could hear a tune at night and pick his fiddle up the next day and play it."

Also in 1928 the boys, who were already known as the Welch Brothers, were asked to play for a regular square dance in Burlington at a place called Dantzic's Pavilion. "Nat Dantzic was a vaudeville player who had traveled all over the country," Israel said. "His brother Morris had a beach people paid to go on Patterson Creek, and the pavilion was nearby. The building was built around an old locust tree cut

off at about 18 feet. From it he hung the rafters. It had a hardwood floor and could hold a lot of people.

"We played on Friday nights. Admission was 15 cents for the ladies and 25 cents for the men. Back then, of course, a dollar looked as big as a wagon wheel.

"Tom played fiddle, Creed played the five-string banjo, Ike played guitar, and I played mandolin. Ira Mankins from Keyser and Kip Webb from down here on Patterson Creek called figures. Before we started, there wasn't any regular dance around here, and it took a while to get going, like it does for any country dance."

The dance did grow, and by the early 1930s was very successful. "We'd have 55 or 60 couples every week," Tom recalls. "It seemed like the Depression brought people together then. Of course, we knew everybody there, they were all our friends. I'll tell you, a good clean square dance is a very fine thing."

After they began playing at Dantzic's Pavilion, the Welch Brothers began to get requests to play farther from home. They needed transportation to fill those requests, so they struck a deal with their Uncle Vernon Leatherman.

"You know how Melvin Wine said he cleared two acres of brush to get a fiddle?" Israel asked. "We cleared five acres on my uncle's place over on the other side of Burlington to get a Model T Ford he had.

"It had a Ruckstell axle with these bands around it, you

Elwanda, Ike, Israel, and Tom Welch—the group that performed over WTBO in the late 1930s. Photographer unknown, 1938.

know, to drive it. We weren't making enough playing to afford a regular motor oil so we put in some 70-weight oil we had for an old Minneapolis Moline tractor. We had to push start it in the winter, and with that heavy oil in it that axle wouldn't stop. We had to run up against a tree or something to stop it."

In the 1930s the band would travel to Moorefield, Romney, Keyser, and smaller towns in their area. They provided music for picnics, fairs, reunions, ice cream socials, and dances. They worked with various callers. Israel especially remembers "Hops" Bateman from Piedmont. "He had a voice like a steamboat whistle. 'Course, we didn't have no microphones back then."

In 1936 a flood washed out Patterson Beach and Dantzic's Pavilion. The Dantzic brothers closed their enterprises and moved to Cumberland, Maryland. In the same year Creed got married and moved away from the farm. Elwanda Welch joined her brothers, playing guitar. Israel switched to banjo, and Ike took up the bass.

In addition to playing dance music, Ike, Israel, and Elwanda would sing. Israel still has much of the sheet music they used: *Mountain Melodies and Old Time Songs* by Blue-

grass Roy and the Kentucky Korn Krackers; *Mountain Melodies* by Buddy Starcher; *Sweet Sentimental Songs* by the Delmore Brothers; and other collections of songs by radio personalities from the '30s.

Around 1937 the Welch Brothers began playing regularly over radio station WTBO in Cumberland, where they stayed for several years. "We played every Saturday morning at 11:00," Tom remembers. "We'd play and my brother Oscar would sing. Elwanda also could sing. We got a lot of mail from that, people really liked to hear us. I wish you could've been around in the '30s and seen what it was like. Fiddle music was a big thing."

In 1938 the Welch Brothers were offered an opportunity to become a traveling professional band. "Dick Hartman from over on Mill Creek wanted us to have a hillbilly photograph made and then go out and play," Tom said. "He had a radio program, a good program, down in Charlotte, North Carolina. He played guitar and tenor banjo himself, and he wanted us to become professional. Our parents were against it, though. They wanted us to stay on the farm. I went along with them because I figured they knew better than what I did."

The handsome young soldier in this 1943 photograph taken in Newfoundland during World War II is Israel Welch, who was away from home for the first time. Photographer unknown.

"I'm no violinist," Tom Welch modestly says, "just kind of a common fiddle player." Photograph by Michael Meador.

This incident is characteristic of the Welch Brothers story, because their home ties have always been stronger than the lure of nightlife and fame. "My father encouraged us to play," Israel said, "but he told us to always come home after the dance and not to go anywhere but to the dance."

Until World War II began the Welch Brothers continued to play for their friends and neighbors in their community. They traveled within a 30-mile radius of Burlington. "We'd play two, sometimes three nights a week," Israel recalls. "We'd go wherever they asked us."

In 1942 the war sent Tom to Panama, Israel to Newfoundland, and Ike to Europe. The brothers who had never spent a night away from the farm now found themselves thousands of miles apart.

Israel remembers his first experience at sea. "We boarded a troop ship at Boston. Of course, they didn't tell us where we were going. We thought we were going overseas. I'd never been on a boat before, and I woke up after the first night and was sick. I ran into the ship bathroom, and every place there was to get sick already had somebody getting sick in it. It was like a bunch of bumblebees in a clover field."

Israel arrived safely at Fort McAndrew in Newfoundland, and he soon found himself doing what he'd always done. "They asked me on a form what I did for recreation," Israel said, "and I wrote I played for square dances. A Red Cross woman saw what I wrote and asked me to put together a band. I had to borrow a fiddle from a man named James D. Allison. We started playing on the base and the town people heard about us, and asked us to play for their dances, and we did."

I asked Israel what kind of dancing they did. "It seems to me," he replied, "that they came at each other in lines, like two buck sheep butting heads."

Israel thus became the fiddler for a dance band. He had played the fiddle before he came to Newfoundland, but in the Welch Brothers band he had always backed up John or Tom on guitar, banjo, or mandolin. At the same time that this opportunity arose, Israel began to listen to the local fiddle music of the Canadian Maritime Provinces.

"Don Messer and his Islanders played every week over the radio from Prince Edward Island," recalls Israel. "He was a good fiddle player. On hard stuff like 'Money Musk' he could really shake it."

Israel began to learn Maritime Canadian tunes from Don

"A Good Clean Square Dance Is a Very Fine Thing"
SATURDAY NIGHT AT NEW CREEK FIRE HALL

Bill Wellington

It's almost 9:00 by the clock in the New Creek Fire Hall. Across the smooth wooden floor on a slightly raised stage the members of the Welch Brothers are talking quietly among themselves. Israel Welch is fine-tuning his fiddle while Vance Staggs strums a chord on his guitar. Vance's wife, Virginia, plunks out several notes on her washtub bass while Dick Everett sets the volume on the amplifier attached to his combination banjo/guitar.

The hum of their conversation continues above the sound of the strings as they ask after families, discuss their schedule, and speculate on the size of tonight's crowd. People are coming in and moving to the long rows of tables and chairs on both sides of the hall. Some are carrying buckets of ice,

bags of chips, and bottles of soda pop from the kitchen to the tables. At 9:00 the lights dim and caller Harry Steele rises from a table near the band, walks over to his microphone, and nods to Israel. It's time for the dance to begin.

Israel launches into the "Kanawha March," one of Clark Kessinger's tunes. The band is thumping out the beat as the music fills the room. People are already heading toward the floor when Harry Steele calls out, "Everybody up, let's go, let's dance, make a big circle." The dancers start moving to the left, even before the circle closes. Once all the couples have joined hands, Mr. Steele calls out, "The other way back in an Indian line, ladies in the lead and gents behind."

The dancers respond, with the

gent holding his partner's hand at her shoulder. "Every other couple out" is the call, and each couple finds another so that small circles of four form all around the hall. "Birdie in the Cage" is the figure, so one lady stands in the center while the others join hands and circle left around her. "Bird hop out and the crow hop in" is the next command, and the "birdie's" partner jumps in the middle. Several "crows" around the room caw.

At the call "Swing your opposite," everybody begins a long, vigorous swing. Many are using an up-and-down motion, a trademark of the New Creek dance, which gives their swinging amazing energy. "Now swing your partner," and the couples are rejoined. After this swing they circle to the left, and

Messer and other fiddlers. His interest in Canadian dance music continued after the war, and today Israel still loves to hear Canadian fiddling. "I'd say that half of what I play is Canadian," Israel said recently.

After the war Israel would still listen to Don Messer over Canadian station CFCY every week. "We could hear his program right here on the farm up through the '50s," Israel explained. "I sent away for his records from Toomb's Music Store on Prince Edward Island." When I was in Israel's cabin recently he showed me several letters from Toomb's Music, postmarked 1955.

While Israel was far to the north during the war, Tom had gone south to Panama. He also went away without an instrument, and he also acquired a fiddle while in the service. He still has the fiddle he bought in Panama.

While there, Tom learned to play in third position on the neck from a violinist he met. Tom had already become interested in classical violin technique before the war. "In 1937," Tom recalls, "I sent away for a subscription course in violin playing from the U.S. School of Music in Chicago."

Although the war sent its principal members far away, the Welch Brothers band continued under the direction of John Welch. John had always stayed close to the band. He started working construction jobs off the farm in the '30s, so he was not always available to play with the others. He would spell Tom on the fiddle if he was there. When he wasn't playing, John danced. He must have paid close attention to the caller, for he once told Israel that Ira Mankins, the caller at Dantzic's Pavilion, knew 26 or 27 figures. Later on John got into calling, about the time that the New Creek dance started in the mid-1960s. During the war, John's widow Hazel recalls, "the band consisted of Kelton Roten from the Romney School for the Blind on the piano and Bill Wolford on guitar. John played fiddle, and I played bass."

After the war Ike got married, moved away from the farm, and began working construction jobs. Tom got a job working bridge construction on a crew that traveled all over West Virginia, Virginia, and Maryland. From 1945 on, he worked away from home. In 1953 he married Wilda Hogbin and moved to Petersburg. Tom did not play regularly with the band until after he retired from bridge construction in 1973. Elwanda had gone to West Virginia University just before the war. While in college she studied music and became an accomplished pianist, but she did not play with the band on

The New Creek Fire Hall on a Saturday night. Photograph by Michael Meador.

one couple goes on to the next while the other remains and waits for a new couple to repeat the figure with. Each dance has a different figure. These include "Right Hands Across"; "Eight Hands Up and Box the Dice"; "Take a Little Peek"; "Around That Couple and Through That Couple"; as well as others. Each dance starts and ends with a big circle.

Between every "big circle" dance there is a slow waltz which allows everyone a chance to rest and to

dance close. Couples move slowly around the floor doing a one-step to Israel's crying fiddle and the band's steady rhythm. There are people of all ages dancing, from young teens to older folks, some of whom have danced to the Welch Brothers all their lives. During the breaks, 71-year-old Israel makes his rounds about the hall greeting old friends and meeting new ones. The lights go up while firemen hold a raffle, and go back down for the dancing to begin anew.

After the second break the band plays a rock 'n' roll number, and everybody "boogies" to the beat. Later in the evening Israel plays a hot "Orange Blossom Special" for one of the last big circle dances. As couples swing at the end of the dance, Harry Steele calls, "Step right back and watch her smile, step right up and swing her a while." Several dancers display some fancy flat-footing and clogging. The last call is "Promenade right off the floor; that's all there is, there ain't no more," and the dancers return to their tables.

At midnight Mr. Steele says, "That's it, good night, see you next week." The dancers put on their coats, the band packs up, people slowly file out, and the lights go out until next week.

EDITOR'S NOTE: This article first appeared in the summer 1984 issue of *Goldenseal* (vol. 10, no. 2).

a regular basis until 1942. Israel returned to the farm after he was discharged from the army in 1945, and he joined the band John had formed.

In 1947 a young man from Keyser named Joe Blundon, who was then a sophomore at Harvard University, recorded members of the family at John's home in Burlington. "I had been to dances where the Welch Brothers played when I was growing up," Mr. Blundon explained recently. "When I was at Harvard I really got interested in traditional dancing through Ralph Page. I got a grant from the Archive of Folksong to make some recordings of West Virginia musicians for the Library of Congress. I recorded John, Israel, Elwanda, Hazel, and Ike Welch. They switched instruments around a lot, but Israel mainly played the fiddle. I recorded 25 or 30 pieces on an old disc recorder that actually cut a record."

After college and service in the Korean War, Joe Blundon returned to Keyser with his wife Gwynne. From 1954 to 1966 they ran the Allegheny Square Dance Club. Joe taught Scottish, English, European, New England, and Appalachian dances to recorded music every week. Once a month the Welch Brothers would play for the club at the Keyser Mosse Hall. Albert Schwinabart of Elk Garden and Smokey Householder from Keyser would help with the calling. Joe and Gwynne Blundon moved to Washington, D.C., in 1966, and the club went out of existence.

From 1945 until John's death in 1978, Israel and John were the core of the Welch Brothers Band. They switched off on piano and fiddle, which they both played. Hazel, John's wife, played bass for over 20 years, until the mid-1960s. The band picked up many other fine musicians as needed. As Israel said recently, "Bands down through the years kind of get split up. You have to get a new one as you go along."

Since 1945, the Welch Brothers have performed almost exclusively as a dance band. Nearly every week, and sometimes two and three times a week, there has been a Welch Brothers dance somewhere in the vicinity of Burlington. They've played at Moose clubs in Moorefield, Romney, and Keyser; VFW halls in Romney and Fort Ashby; the American Legion at Moorefield and Romney; and the Briggs Motor Company in Romney. "We've played at just about every place there is to play around here," Israel figures.

Until the mid-1960s, when John began calling, the band worked with different callers at the different dances. They played for Gladsen Allamong of Romney, Smokey Householder from Keyser, and Albert Schwinabart from Elk Garden. Rumsey Shank over in McCool, Maryland, also called dances. Strong lungs were a necessity for the caller's job, as Israel says of the Whipp brothers, Maurice and Maxwell of Burlington. "They didn't need no microphones. You could hear them from here to Mechanicsburg Gap when they hollered. They'd just make the wind shake. They's auctioneers. They had awful voices."

The dance at Mineral County's New Creek Fire Hall began in 1967 and continues today as the longest running dance in the Welch Brothers' career. In 1971 the dance stopped long enough for the fire company to add a second floor to their building, paid for in part by the success of the dance. When the dance started Israel and Creed Welch and Vance and Virginia Staggs played, and John called figures. In the 1970s the dance became something of a reunion of the original band as Tom Welch would often join them. Brother Ike had died in 1966.

Both Tom and Israel Welch are primarily dance musicians. As fiddlers, each has strong rhythm, clear phrasing, energetic drive, and buoyancy.

"I'm no violinist. I'm just kind of a common fiddle player," Tom said with characteristic modesty. In spite of what he says, Tom plays with a rich tone that is the result of his interest in classical technique. His bow motion comes from the shoulder, which gives his fiddling great strength. With his left hand he plays precise scales and doesn't slide up to notes, as Israel does. Tom generally plays in first position, although he does use third position to get a fuller sound on waltzes. He uses trills, triplets, and turns to ornament many of his tunes.

Tom's fiddling really shines on hornpipes. One of Tom's favorite tunes is the "Cincinnati Hornpipe," which he learned from his old teacher, Tom Thrush. This tune is characteristic of many hornpipes with its rapidly ascending and descending arpeggios.

On waltzes and slow tunes, Tom puts his whole body into playing the piece. He uses the full length of the bow to produce long sweet notes. He is a stately, handsome man, and when he plays a slow waltz like the "Kentucky Waltz" on stage, there are murmurs among the ladies. Tom plays songs and hymns with great fervor as well. I once heard him play a breathtaking version of "O Come All Ye Faithful" at a Christmas gathering.

Tom reads music, although he generally plays by ear. He plays in the keys of D, G, C, A, F, and B-flat. His repertoire includes reels, hornpipes, waltzes, polkas, several jigs, and at least one clog and schottische. He plays the standards—"Liberty," "Soldier's Joy," "Old Joe Clark," "Red Wing," and so forth. He also plays lesser known tunes, such as "Blue Mountain Hornpipe" and "Blackthorn Stick," which are from Maritime Canada.

Although Tom did not play with the Welch Brothers Band for many years, he never stopped fiddling. He would take his fiddle with him on the road and play with different musicians he met.

In 1962 Joe Bussard recorded Tom on fiddle with Israel on banjo. He recorded eight tunes which were made into four 78 rpm records under the Fonotone label. "The records sold well," Mr. Bussard explained. "He's a real good fiddle player, I thought."

Israel Welch approaches the Mineral County farmstead that has been home to his family for a century and a half. Photograph by Michael Meador.

Like his brother, Israel Welch also reads music. He plays in all the "fiddle keys"—D, G, A, C—plus F and B-flat, and he plays a variety of tempos. Beyond these basic similarities, the differences between the two fiddlers are profound.

"Canadian fiddlers and Texas fiddlers," Israel said last fall, "are the two types of fiddlers I like the best." This is interesting because Israel doesn't sound anything like a Canadian or a Texas fiddler. His repertoire, which is enormous, includes many Canadian and Texas tunes, but his style is his own.

I asked Virginia dance caller Jim Morrison, who is a great admirer of Israel's fiddling, to describe his style. "It's real forceful fiddling that makes great dance music," Jim said. "Like certain other West Virginia fiddlers such as Melvin Wine and Rob Propst, Israel has a distinct driving quality. His notes are highly articulated and clear. He explores the tonal possibilities on a fiddle to an astonishing degree by his heavy use of slides. It's very effective fiddling."

Israel has played mandolin, banjo, piano, and guitar with the band over the years, and he still plays guitar much of the time. He is always aware of the chord structure of a tune while he plays.

When Tom and Israel play together they trade off on the fiddle. They hardly ever play two fiddles together. The brothers both have said that two fiddlers should not play in unison but that one should "second" for the other by playing a harmony line. Tom and Israel have great respect for each other's music. They are fine gentlemen as well as wonderful musicians.

I first met the brothers at a New Creek dance in 1977. I told Baltimore musicologist Bob Dalsemer about the dance. Bob was researching West Virginia traditional dances, and was very impressed by New Creek. In his book *West Virginia Square Dances* he had this to say: "The quality of dancing at New Creek is very high. Swings are long, smooth and full of vigor. The dancers flow from one movement to the next. Their body movements are efficient and seemingly effortless, sure signs of long experience." He added, "The Welch Brothers have worked long and hard to create the good atmosphere and high level of dancing. It has been truly a labor of love."

After John Welch died in 1978, Harley Hogbin from Romney called figures for about two years until poor health made him retire. Today, Harry Steele from Mount Storm calls the figures. Lately several young musicians have become interested in the dance. Eddie and Bonnie Meyers from Burlington come and call figures. Their friend, Ernie Brummage, who is Israel's neighbor, has been learning to play the fiddle from Israel, and he has high regard for his teacher. "The best compliment someone could give me," Ernie said recently, "would be to tell me I sound like Israel."

I've come to know the Welch story in part through warm conversations at the home of Anita Combs, Israel's girl-friend. My wife, Carlotta, and I have shared many meals with Israel and Anita, and as we sit down to eat, I've noticed that Israel jokes around more than at other times. It's almost like he's back with his 22 brothers, sisters, cousins, parents, aunts, and uncles around the kitchen table at the farm. It was at Anita's that Israel told us one of the secrets of his success. "I don't know why, but a couple of people down through the years said, 'You made the best square dance fiddler I ever saw. There's nobody comes in the hall but that you didn't get around and say a few words to them.'" Israel chuckled. "So you see, if they didn't like your music then they liked your personality, and they'd come back to see you again."

It's a fine theory and it must work. For after 50 years and several thousand dances, people are still coming back for good times with the Welch Brothers.

EDITOR'S NOTE: This article first appeared in the summer 1984 issue of *Goldenseal* (vol. 10, no. 2). Tom Welch died on July 3, 1986, in Elkins, West Virginia, at the age of 63. Israel Welch continues to appear each week at the New Creek Fire Hall dance in Keyser and at folk music festivals in the eastern panhandle of West Virginia.

SUGGESTED LISTENING

The Music Never Dies (Elderberry Records ER 004), a double CD/cassette compilation from the Vandalia Gathering, 1977–87. Includes live performances by Elmer Bird, John Johnson, Sylvia O'Brien, Melvin Wine, Ernie Carpenter, Russell Fluharty, Blackie Cool, Nat Reese, Carl Rutherford, Woody Simmons, Andy Boarman, Wilson Douglas, Aunt Jennie Wilson, and Israel and Tom Welch. Highly recommended. Available from the West Virginia Division of Culture and History, 1900 Kanawha Boulevard East, Charleston, WV 25305.

ELMER BIRD
Elmer's Greatest Licks, Home Sweet Home, Bumble Bee Waltz, Turkey Creek, My Most Requested, and *George How I Miss You,* available on cassette or CD from Hurricane Music, Route 2, Box 130, Hurricane, WV 25526.

ERNIE CARPENTER
Elk River Blues (AHR 003C), available on cassette from the Augusta Heritage Center, Davis and Elkins College, Elkins, WV 26241-3996.

BLACKIE COOL
Back Memories (AHR 002C), available on cassette from the Augusta Heritage Center, Davis and Elkins College, Elkins, WV 26241-3996.

LYNN DAVIS & MOLLY O'DAY
Molly O'Day and the Cumberland Mountain Folks (Bear Family Records BCD 15565). Complete Columbia recordings reissued in a double CD package. Available from County Records, P.O. Box 191, Floyd, VA 24091.

Sacred Collection (OHCS 101), *Early Radio Favorites* (OHCS 140), and *The Heart and Soul of Molly O'Day,* volumes 1 and 2 (OHCS 312 and 313), available on cassette from Old Homestead Records, Box 100, Brighton, MI 48116.

WILSON DOUGLAS
Hot from the Kitchen, featuring Wilson Douglas and Gruder Morris, reissued from the 1973 field recordings. Available on cassette or CD from Roane Records, Route 3, Box 293, Spencer, WV 25276.

Boatin' up Sandy (AHS 1), available on cassette from the Augusta Heritage Center, Davis and Elkins College, Elkins, WV 26241-3996.

WORLEY GARDNER
Mountain Melodies, volumes 1 and 2, available on cassette from Margaret Gardner, 1332 Cain Street, Morgantown, WV 26505.

JOHN JOHNSON
Fiddlin' John (AHR 001C), available on cassette from the Augusta Heritage Center, Davis and Elkins College, Elkins, WV 26241-3996.

CLARK KESSINGER
Kessinger Brothers: Complete Recorded Works in Chronological Order, volumes 1–3 (DOCD 8010, 8011, and 8012), and *The Legend of Clark Kessinger* (County CD 2713), available through County Records, P.O. Box 191, Floyd, VA 24091.

LILLY BROTHERS
Early Recordings, Smithsonian Recordings, and *Live at Hillbilly Ranch,* with Don Stover; *Savannah's Not in Georgia* and *It Is Almost Heaven,* from Everett Lilly and Clear Creek Crossin'. Available on CD or cassette from Daniel Lilly, 3669 Clear Fork Road, Beckley, WV 25801.

PATTY LOOMAN
Nothing Fancy: Old Favorites for the Hammered Dulcimer and *Mountain Laurel Memories: The Hammered Dulcimer of Patty Looman,* available on cassette from Patty Looman, 1345 Bitonti Street, Morgantown, WV 26505.

Nat Reese

Just a Dream (AHR 005C), available on cassette from the Augusta Heritage Center, Davis and Elkins College, Elkins, WV 26241-3996.

Carl Rutherford

The Last Handloader, Home to West Virginia, Praise God, Love Can't Fly on Broken Wings, Blues and S'Mor, and *How to Play Guitar Like Carl,* available from Carl Rutherford, World Country and Gospel Productions, P.O. Box 30, Warriormine, WV 24894.

Woody Simmons

Simmons Sampler, available on cassette from Woody Simmons, Box 152, Mill Creek, WV 26280.

Sarah Singleton

Old-Time Fiddling of Braxton County, volume 1 (AHR 012). Leland Hall, Sarah Singleton, Ernie Carpenter, and Ward Jarvis play 23 tunes. Available from the Augusta Heritage Center, Davis and Elkins College, Elkins, WV 26241-3996.

Welch Brothers

Tearin' Down the Laurel (AHR 018), featuring Israel Welch. Available on cassette from the Augusta Heritage Center, Davis and Elkins College, Elkins, WV 26241-3996.

Doc Williams

Various recordings available from Doc Williams, P.O. Box 902, Wheeling, WV 26003.

Melvin Wine

Hannah at the Spring House (AHS 2) and *Vintage Wine* (AHS 6), available on cassette from the Augusta Heritage Center, Davis and Elkins College, Elkins, WV 26241-3996.

Related Recordings

Ed Haley

Forked Deer (Rounder CD 1131/1132), reissued field recordings in a double CD package. Available from Rounder Record Corp., One Camp Street, Cambridge, MA 02140.

Hammons Family

The Hammons Family: The Traditions of a West Virginia Family and Their Friends (Rounder 1504/05). Reissued double CD (first issued on LP records in 1973). Available from Rounder Record Corp., One Camp Street, Cambridge, MA 02140.

Frank Hutchison

Frank Hutchison, volume 1 (DOCD 8003). Original 78 rpm recordings remastered on CD by Document Records. Available through County Records, P.O. Box 191, Floyd, VA 24091.

CONTRIBUTORS

Mark Crabtree was born in Brooke County, West Virginia, and earned a B.S. degree in journalism from West Virginia University. Crabtree, who now lives in Morgantown, works extensively as a photographer and served as project coordinator for the West Virginia Coal Life Project photography exhibit in the 1970s.

John A. Cuthbert, curator of special collections for West Virginia University Libraries, now heads the West Virginia and Regional History Collection at WVU.

Carl Fleischhauer documented much of West Virginia's traditional life during the 1970s when he worked for West Virginia University's film unit and public television station. He and folklorist Alan Jabbour also produced a double record album, *The Hammons Family: A Study of a West Virginia Family's Traditions*, for the Library of Congress. In 1976 Fleischhauer joined the American Folklife Center at the Library of Congress, where he works today.

Jerry Galyean and his brother Brent were involved in the return of Clark Kessinger to the world of fiddling during the 1960s. In addition to arranging for numerous appearances and public events, Jerry Galyean took many photographs of Kessinger during his comeback years. Jerry Galyean lives in Knoxville, Tennessee.

Paul Gartner, a native of Ohio's Mahoning Valley, moved to West Virginia in 1977 and now lives in Lincoln County. An old-time banjo player and a regular at West Virginia festivals, he works as a freelance writer and is a copy editor and writer for *The Charleston Gazette*.

Abby Gail Goodnite is an undergraduate student at the University of Rio Grande in Ohio with "paternal roots in Mason County."

Richard Gross was a freelance photographer in Los Angeles, California, at the time the article about Sylvia O'Brien was first published.

Teresa Hamm, a native of Charlottesville, Virginia, moved to Buckhannon, West Virginia, in 1986. She studied fiddling under Sarah Singleton through the West Virginia Folk Arts Apprenticeship Program and describes herself as a singer and songwriter with a "wide interest" musically.

Pam Hutton is an old-time guitarist from Charleston, West Virginia. She is a stockbroker by day and, she reports, "a photographer in my dreams."

Peggy Jarvis taught and lived in Mercersburg, Pennsylvania, during the late 1970s. She received a B.A. degree in English from Earlham College, studied in France, and holds an M.A. degree in French.

Michael Keller is chief of photographic services for the West Virginia Division of Culture and History.

Dick Kimmel, who holds a Ph.D. degree in biology and was formally trained as a wildlife biologist, lives in Minnesota. He performs and writes original bluegrass tunes and writes articles about the history of bluegrass music. His work has been published in *Bluegrass Unlimited, Inside Bluegrass,* and many other publications.

Michael Kline, who spent childhood summers in Hampshire County, West Virginia, graduated from George Washington University in 1964 and worked in various social programs in Kentucky and West Virginia. An assistant editor for *Goldenseal* in 1978, he went on to work for the Mountain Heritage Center in North Carolina and the Pioneer Valley Folklore Society in Massachusetts. He and his wife, Carrie Nobel Kline, live in Elkins, West Virginia, and operate Talking Across Lines: Worldwide Conversations, which produces books and radio programs devoted to oral history.

Rick Lee is a commercial photographer, formerly director of photographic services for the West Virginia Department of Culture and History. He is a frequent contributor to *Goldenseal*.

Susan Leffler is the former folk arts specialist for the West Virginia Division of Culture and History. She worked as a freelance correspondent in Central America for five years and is now a special projects producer with West Virginia Public Radio, documenting the culture of various ethnic groups in the Mountain State.

John Lilly, who has a degree in arts administration from Davis and Elkins College, in Elkins, West Virginia, is the editor of *Goldenseal,* a position he has held since 1997. Formerly an associate editor of *Old-Time Herald* magazine and a tour guide at the Country Music Hall of Fame and Museum in Nashville, Tennessee, he has also served as publicist for the Augusta Heritage Center of Davis and Elkins College. A native of Illinois, he is an accomplished old-time musician, singer, and dancer.

Kip Lornell Jr. is an associate professorial lecturer in American studies and music at George Washington University and a research associate at the Smithsonian Institution, where he works on projects for Smithsonian/Folkways records. Interested in American vernacular music since the late 1960s, he is the author or coauthor of six books, including *The Life and Legend of Leadbelly* (with Charles Wolfe), which won the ASCAP–Deems Taylor Award in 1993.

Deborah Marks was a freelance photographer in Boston, Massachusetts, at the time the article about the Lilly Brothers was first published.

Nancy McClellan, who grew up on a small farm near Ashland, Kentucky, graduated from the University of Kentucky in 1954 with an A.B. degree in ancient languages. She earned master's degrees in classical language from the University of Chicago and in English from Marshall University and was a professor of English and the humanities at the University of Kentucky–Ashland Community College until her retirement in 1997. The founder of Kentucky's Mountain Heritage Folk Festival (1970–76), she is now a presenter of Appalachian lore and tales for Elderhostel programs in Kentucky and emcees Ashland's annual Ed Haley fiddle contest.

Jim McGee, a Presbyterian minister in Kanawha City, West Virginia, is completing work on a master's degree in folklore from the University of North Carolina at Chapel Hill. His story in this book was written in conjunction with his research into coal-mining songs.

Michael Meador, whose interest in photography emerged during his high school years in Oceana, West Virginia, holds a degree in photojournalism from Marshall University and an M.B.A. degree from Cornell University. His work has appeared in numerous Appalachian publications and has been exhibited in several galleries in West Virginia. Now the vice president of a telecommunications company in upstate New York, he makes time in his busy schedule to photograph his favorite subject: his family.

William Metzger is a graduate of the Ohio Institute of Photography in Dayton, Ohio. He lives in Bucyrus, Ohio, and works as a freelance photographer.

Gerald Milnes is the folk arts coordinator for the Augusta Heritage Center of Davis and Elkins College, in Elkins, West Virginia. He is a regular contributor to *Goldenseal,* a fine old-time musician, and the author of *Play of a Fiddle: Traditional Music, Dance, and Folklore in West Virginia* and the children's book *Granny Will Your Dog Bite and Other Mountain Rhymes.*

J. Roderick Moore, a native of Fincastle, Virginia, was raised in Welch, West Virginia. He is the director of the Blue Ridge Institute and Museum at Ferrum College in Virginia.

Rick Osborn was a freelance photographer in Charleston, West Virginia, at the time the article about Wilson Douglas was first published.

Blanton Owen grew up in southeast Tennessee, played old-time banjo throughout the Upland South, toured with fiddler Tommy Jarrell, and worked at folklife programs in Virginia, North Carolina, Tennessee, and Florida. In 1985 he moved to Reno, Nevada, where he inaugurated the Folk Arts Program with the Nevada Arts Council. At the time of his death in June 1998 he was a commercial pilot, a writer for the general aviation press, an archaeology technician, and a student of western vernacular architecture.

Dave Peyton, a native West Virginian, is a columnist for *The Herald Dispatch* in Huntington, where he has worked for more than 30 years.

Sam Rizzetta, born in Oak Park, Illinois, earned a B.A. degree in art and biology from Ripon College and an M.A. degree in botany from Western Michigan University. He has worked as an artist, a biologist for the Smithsonian Institution, a musician, and a designer and builder of musical instruments. In 1974 he formed the group Trapezoid, a hammered dulcimer quartet. Since 1984 he has made his home in Inwood, West Virginia, where he works as a musical instrument designer, musician, and composer.

Tom Screven, the founding editor of *Goldenseal*, edited the magazine from 1975 until 1979.

Robert Spence was born and raised in Logan, West Virginia, where his family has lived since 1790. A graduate of Marshall University with a B.A. degree in journalism, he worked for the *Logan News* for 11 years and is now a freelance writer. A descendant of Ephraim Hatfield, Spence is working with Coleman Hatfield on *The Tale of the Devil,* a definitive Hatfield family history.

Ken Sullivan, executive director of the West Virginia Humanities Council, was the editor of *Goldenseal* from 1979 until 1997. He earned a B.A. degree from the University of Virginia, an M.A. degree from the University of Rochester, and a Ph.D. degree in industrial history from the University of Pittsburgh.

Phil Swango is an old-tme musician and freelance photographer in Albuquerque, New Mexico. He is a frequent participant in the Augusta Heritage Arts Workshops in Elkins, West Virginia.

Bobby Taylor is a librarian for the Archives and History Section of the West Virginia Division of Culture and History. A fifth-generation West Virginia fiddler, he performs and teaches Clark Kessinger–style fiddling throughout the state.

Ivan Tribe attended Ohio University and earned his Ph.D. degree from the University of Toledo. He has published many articles on old-time and early country music and authored the book *Mountaineer Jamboree: Country Music in West Virginia.* He teaches at the University of Rio Grande in Ohio.

Jack Waugh spent 17 years as a staff correspondent and bureau chief for the *Christian Science Monitor,* leaving the paper in 1973 to join Vice President Nelson Rockefeller's staff

as a media specialist. From 1978 to 1983, Waugh worked as a freelance writer in West Virginia, during which time he wrote his article about the Currence Brothers for *Goldenseal.* In 1989 he began work on *The Class of 1846,* an account of the West Point class that gave the American Civil War many of its generals. Waugh moved to Texas in 1994, where he continues his work as an author. His most recent book is *Reelecting Lincoln: The Battle for the 1864 Presidency.*

Bill Wellington, a Massachusetts native, has a B.A. degree in religion from Middlebury College in Vermont. He moved to West Virginia in 1976, residing in Grant and Pendleton counties for nine years. He now lives in Staunton, Virginia, with his wife, Lynn Mackey, who is a pianist, and their daughter, Sophia. A banjoist, fiddler, and guitarist, Wellington calls, teaches, and plays for traditional dances and is a well-known children's performer.

Dave Wilbur lives in Baker, West Virginia, where he is employed by the Hardy County Board of Education as an attendance director and substitute teacher, in addition to his job as a sports reporter for *The Moorefield Examiner.* Originally from New York State, he studied philosophy at Antioch College in Ohio and in France. A self-described "bluegrass nut," he attends bluegrass festivals and concerts in West Virginia, North Carolina, and Washington, D.C., on a regular basis.

Danny Williams, a native of Wayne County, West Virginia, lives in Morgantown and publishes *High Notes,* a newsletter of West Virginia traditional music. Formerly a folk arts specialist for the West Virginia Division of Culture and History, he is an active performer and teacher of West Virginia music and a regular contributor to *Goldenseal.*

Charles Wolfe, a professor of English at Middle Tennessee State University in Murfreesboro, is one of the world's most respected and prolific writers on traditional folk and popular American music. He has authored more than a dozen books on American music and written liner notes for more than 100 record albums.

Doug Yarrow, a resident of West Virginia since 1966, now lives in Virginia Beach, Virginia. He has taught photography, video production, drama, and English. His photographs have appeared in many publications, including on the cover of *Newsweek* in 1978.

INDEX

The letter "s" following a page number indicates the material appears in a sidebar.

accordion, 12, 16, 119, 152, 173; and Afro-Americans, 82–83
Acuff, Roy, 65, 193
Adkins, Jim, 46
Afro-American music, 171–78; rural, 81–86
alcohol, 46. *See also* moonshine
Allamong, Gladsen, 216
Allegheny Square Dance Club (Keyser, W.Va.), 216
Allen family, 46
Altizer, Lee, 167
aluminum disks, 54s
"Amazing Grace," 54s, 165
American Folklife Center. *See* Library of Congress
American Indians, 67, 68, 70, 71, 88, 156
"Amos 'n' Andy" (radio show), 176
Appalachian dulcimer. *See* dulcimer, mountain
Appalachian String Band Festival (Clifftop, W.Va.), 2, 101, 170
Archive of Folk Song. *See* Library of Congress
Arizona Rangers, 161
"Arkansas Traveler," 28, 28s, 83, 99
Armstrong, Chaney, 51
Armstrong, Rob, 140
Ashland, Ky., 27, 42, 98–99
Augusta Heritage Arts Workshops and Festival (Elkins, W.Va.), 2, 11, 124, 144, 164, 170
Augusta Heritage Center (Elkins, W.Va.), 48; Spring Dulcimer Week, 48
autoharp, 110, 112, 113, 114

Bacon, Frederick J., 112
ballads, 8, 37s, 41, 42, 43, 54s, 103, 105, 107s, 165, 167
Ballard, Maggie, 135
Baltimore, Md., 92, 161
bands, family. *See* names of specific family bands
banjo: Afro-American instrument, 81–86; on CB radio, 206; in churches, 194; contests, 12, 18, 99, 101; fretless, 83, 122; groundhog hide used in making, 13, 83, 119; learning to play, 96–97, 104, 114; making, 13, 39, 83, 94, 110, 119; plectrum, 112; Wilson Douglas and, 36, 37s; Worley Gardner and, 136–37. *See also* banjo playing styles; *names of specific banjo players*

—types of: Bacon & Day, 21; Dixie Grand, 109; Gibson, 21
banjo playing styles: bluegrass, 81, 99; classical, 110, 112, 114, 162; clawhammer/frailing, 13, 81, 85, 96, 97, 99, 101, 112, 120; "double drop-thumb," 96, 101; picking techniques, 13, 84, 114, 122, 158; two-finger, 14, 97, 99, 136–37, 167. *See also* dances and dancing; square dances and square dancing; *names of specific banjo players*
"Banjo Man from Turkey Creek." *See* Bird, Elmer
"Barbara Allen," 54s, 158. *See also* "Barbry Allen"
"Barbry Allen," 37s, 107s. *See also* "Barbara Allen"
bass fiddle, 112, 215
Bateman, "Hops," 212
"Battle Hymn of the Republic, The" 182
"Beautiful, Beautiful Brown Eyes," 99
Becky's Creek, W.Va., 12, 14, 18
Bell, Bobby, 16
Bell, Charlie, 16, 159
Bell, Howard, 16
Bell, Lee, 16
Berkeley County, W.Va., 109
"Betty Baker," 78
"Beyond the Sunset," 152
Bible, 181, 184, 187
"Billy in the Low Ground," 22
Bird, Andrew Jackson, 96
Bird, Beulah, 96, 98, 102
Bird, Elmer, 3, 96–102
Bird, George, 98, 99, 101, 102
Bird, Vedious, 102
Bird Brothers, The, 99
"Birdie," 29
Birmingham Entertainers, 29. *See also* Kessinger Brothers, The
"Black-eyed Susie," 40s
blacks. *See* Afro-American music
blacksmithing, 13
"Blackthorn Stick," 216
Blake, Basil, 47, 48
Blake, John Jackson, 43, 45, 47
Blevins, Charlie, 2, 116–24
Blevins, Dana, 62
Bluegrass Gospel Boys, 207
bluegrass music, 23, 65, 72–73s, 99–100, 113, 115, 183, 186–87, 196

Bluegrass Unlimited (magazine), 109, 181
"Blue Mountain Hornpipe," 216
"Blue Ridge Drive," 169
"Blue Ridge Mountain Home," 14
blues music, 106, 108, 162, 164, 165, 175
"Blue Yodels," 2
Blundon, Joe, 216
Boarman, Ada Lee Stump, 112
Boarman, Andrew F., 3, 109–15
Boarman, Charles, 113
Boarman, Harry, 112
Boarman, James, 112
Boarman, Joseph, 112
"Boatsman," 49
"Bonaparte's Retreat," 8
bones (as musical instrument), 83, 84
Booger Hole, W.Va., 34, 37s
"Bootlegger's Blues," 86
Border Riders, 149–54, 198
Boston, Mass., 183–84, 185, 186
Bowles, Daner, 96–97
Bragg, Biddie Jane, 43
Bragg's Run, W.Va., 43
Braxton County, W.Va., 7, 10, 43, 48, 73
"Brown Skin Blues," 167
"Brownstone Girl," 29
Brunswick (record label), 25, 27–29, 31
Brunswick-Balke-Collender (record company), 27
Buckhannon, W.Va., 46, 159
"Buffalo Gals," 110
"Bull Pup," 136
Burlington, W.Va., 208
Burnsville, W.Va., 9
Bussard, Joe, 216
"Bye Bye Blues," 162
Byrd, Robert, 3, 62–65, 109
Byrne, William, 73

"Camp Chase," 55s
"Camp Run," 78
Canadian Broadcasting System, 21
Canady, William J., 114
canning, 10, 35, 36, 44, 91
Capitol Music Hall (Wheeling, W.Va.), 154, 155
carnival acts, 17, 84. *See also* circuses
Carpenter, Benjamin, 67, 68, 71
Carpenter, Carl, 77–78
Carpenter, Ernie, 3, 66–78

Carpenter, French, 32, 40s, 41s, 42, 93
Carpenter, Goldie, 77–78
Carpenter, Hemp, 17
Carpenter, Jake "Squack," 72–73
Carpenter, Jeremiah, 66, 67, 68, 70, 71
Carpenter, Mabel, 76
Carpenter, Shelt, 74, 76
Carpenter, Sol, 50, 68, 70
Carpenter, William, 73, 75, 78
Carr, Bob, 17
"Carry Me Back to Old Virginny," 84
Carson, John, 16
Carte, Joe, 49, 53
Carter Family, 16, 18, 144; guitar style of, 38s, 41
"Casey Jones," 84
Catching Up with Yesterday (documentary), 115
Centralia, W.Va., 68
Chappell, Louis Watson, 54s
Charleston, W.Va., 25, 26, 51, 57–58
Charleston (W.Va.) Symphony, 207
"Cheatham County Breakdown," 56s
"Chicken in the Barnyard," 28
"Chinky Pin," 29
Christian faith: conversion to, 10, 193; expressed through music, 181, 187, 188, 193–95; ministry of, 188, 194, 195; as social outlet, 197. See also names of specific churches
Christmas: music, 13, 14; school programs, 13, 14, 203
church. See Christian faith
Church of God (Cleveland, Tenn.), 188, 194
"Cincinnati Hornpipe," 216
"Cindy," 85
circuses, 61, 160. See also carnival acts
"Clarence C. Tross" (song), 86
clawhammer banjo. See under banjo playing styles
Clay, W.Va., 53, 57
Clay County, W.Va., 34–42, 49, 53
Clear Creek, W.Va., 181
Clear Creek Crossin' (band), 187
Cleveland, Ohio, 147
Cliffside Casino, 99
Clifftop, W.Va., 101. See also Appalachian String Band Festival
clogging, 215s. See also dances and dancing
Cline, Ezra. See Ezra Cline and the Lonesome Pine Fiddlers
coal mining: accidents, 10, 103, 107, 161, 165–66; black lung disease and, 8, 119, 175; camps, 36, 189; children in, 156; songs about, 2, 167; technique, 119, 173–74; working in, 9, 10, 18, 116, 132, 156, 165–67, 172–74, 189
"Cold Frosty Morning," 8
Columbia Records, 27, 193
"Columbus Stockade Blues," 99
Commerce Department of West Virginia, 133, 135

competitions/contests, music. See under names of specific instruments
"Coney Isle," 106–7s
Cool, Blackie, 156–64
"coon dog truth," 120
Cooper, Wilma Lee, 18, 152
Copas, Cowboy, 159
Copeland, Leonard, 167
Copen, W.Va., 7
Copen (W.Va.) United Methodist Church, 10
cornstalk fiddles, 44
Corridor G highway, 116, 124
"Corrine, Corrine," 176
Cottrell, Jenes, 32, 39, 87, 92, 93, 94
Cottrell family, 88
Country Dance and Song Society of America, 138
"Country Hymn Time" (radio show), 188, 194–95
country music, 16, 21, 26, 106, 147–55, 165, 183, 187
Country Music Ambassador. See Williams, Doc
Country Store (Wheeling, W.Va.), 154, 155
County Records, 33, 65
courting customs, 106–7
"Courtin' in the Rain," 149
craft festivals, 94
"Cripple Creek," 85. See also "Goin' Up Cripple Creek"
Crupe, Fred, 150
Crupe, Jessie. See Williams, Chickie
"Cumberland Gap," 54s, 63
Cumberland Mountain Folks (band), 192–93
Currence, Clyde, 207
Currence, Jimmie, 23–24, 196–207
Currence, Lody. See Currence, Loren
Currence, Loren, 23–24, 196–207
Currence, Marvin "Shorty," 197, 207
Currence Brothers, The, 3, 196–207
cylinder recordings, 14

Dalsemer, Robert G., 138, 217
dances and dancing, 17, 26, 44, 97–98, 162, 196–97, 214, 215s; Afro-American, 83, 84; and alcohol, 46; banjo used for, 97; contests, 17; fiddle used for, 16, 18, 26, 32, 37s, 47, 48, 73s, 77; jitterbug, 175; mandolin used for, 14; moral value of, 196–97; music for, 169, 171; as social events, 9, 14, 46, 47, 104, 175, 197, 211, 214–15s. See also square dances and square dancing
"Dancing Waves Schottische," 110
Dantzic's Pavilion (Burlington, W.Va.), 211, 212, 215
"Darktown Dandies," 110
Davidson, Ken, 32–33
Davis, Lynn, 3, 188–95
Davis and Elkins College, 116, 172
Dean, Gerry, 47

"Devil's Dream," 28
Dickens, Hazel, 165, 169
Dickerson, Gene, 99–101
"Dickson County Blues," 54s, 56s
Digman, Gander, 17. See also Digman, Gandy
Digman, Gandy, 162. See also Digman, Gander
Dillon, Tom, 73s
Dillons, George, 26
"Dill Pickle Rag," 29, 52
Distinguished West Virginian. See Williams, Doc
"Done Gone," 29
"double drop-thumb" banjo style. See under banjo playing styles
Douglas, Delma, 34, 37, 42
Douglas, Martin Stephenson Van Buren, 37s
Douglas, Wilson, 30s, 34–42
"Down Yonder," 54s
drums, 46, 84
dulcimer, hammered, 127–35, 136–40, 141–44; learning to play, 138; making, 139–40, 142–43; in Michigan, 142; technique, 138; tuning, 142. See also names of specific dulcimer players
dulcimer, mountain, 48, 103, 122–23, 134–41; making, 48. See also names of specific dulcimer players
Dundon, W.Va., 49, 53, 55
"Durang's Hornpipe," 28s
Durgon, W.Va., 81, 82

"Echoes from the Hills," 99
Eck Gibson and the Mountaineer Ramblers, 99
Edison Victrola, 14
education: higher, 142; importance of, 37, 55. See also schools
Efaw, Solomon, 128
Elkins, W.Va., 3, 18, 19
Elk River, 3, 49, 53, 66–76 passim
Elks Club (Princeton, W.Va.), 173, 177–78
Evangelical United Brethren Chapel (Fairmont, W.Va.), 129
Everett, Dick, 214
"Everybody to the Puncheon," 30
Ezra Cline and the Lonesome Pine Fiddlers, 20

Fairmont, W.Va., 9, 18–19, 159
Fairmont State College, 142
fairs and festivals, 9, 12, 25, 30, 32, 108, 113, 115, 142. See also names of specific fairs and festivals
Falling Waters, W.Va., 113
Falls Mills, W.Va., 47s
family bands. See names of specific family bands
farming, 14, 43, 51, 89–91, 98, 103–4, 129; corn, 10, 38, 43; tobacco, 89–90, 92, 96

"Fee-be-l," 12
Festival of American Folklife, 139. *See also* Smithsonian Folklife Festival
festivals. *See* fairs and festivals
fiddle: bowing, 9, 28–29s, 30, 55–65s, 216; bows, 9, 29s, 38s, 57, 196; cornstalk, 44; learning to play, 9, 15, 16, 28s, 30–31, 37–41s, 45, 48, 50, 73s, 196, 209; making, 15; noting, 30, 31, 56s, 216, 217; as political campaign tool, 3, 63–64; Texas style, 29, 30, 55s, 57, 217; tuning, 16, 22, 38s; twin, 159, 217. *See also* names of specific fiddlers
fiddle contests: banjo, 99; Clark Kessinger and, 26, 32; guitar, 158–59; Sarah Singleton and, 45; Melvin Wine and, 9, 11; Woody Simmons and, 17–18, 22, 24
fiddle tunes: Canadian Maritime, 214–15, 216, 217; East Central European, 147; origins of, 11; Scottish, 65. *See also* dances and dancing; fiddlers, female; square dances and square dancing; violin, classical; *names of specific fiddlers*
fiddlers, female, 45
"Fiddler's Hornpipe," 23
fife, 84
"Fire on the Mountain," 22
"Fisher's Hornpipe," 54s
fishing, 17, 67, 70, 72–73, 74–75
Fleischhauer, Carl, 154
Fleming, John, 123–24
Fluharty, Marjory Ice, 132
Fluharty, Russell, 127–35, 141, 142, 144
Foley, Elva, 137, 138
folk culture (in W.Va.), 1–3; as influence on cultural identity, 3; regional influences on, 2, 3
folklore, study of, 108
Folk Promotions (record label), 32. *See also* Kanawha
folk revival, 2, 25, 107–8, 183–84
Folkways Records, 33
Fonotone, 216
"Footprints in the Snow," 23
Forest Festival. *See* Mountain State Forest Festival
"Forked Deer, The," 53, 54s, 56s. *See also* "Forky Deer"
"Forky Deer," 28. *See also* "Forked Deer, The"
Forty-Niners, The (band), 189, 191, 192
Foster, George, 84
Foster, Stephen, 84
frailing. *See under* banjo playing styles
Fraley, J.P., 42
Future Farmers of America, 98

Gainer, Patrick, 108, 134
Galax, Va., 32
Galax Old-Time Fiddlers Convention, 30s, 32
Gallagher, John, 11

games: base and banner, 203; Fox and Geese, 129
Gardner, Asel, 138–39, 142–43
Gardner, Margaret (née Tennant), 137
Gardner, Worley, 136–40, 141, 142–43, 144
Garfield, James, 28
"Garfield March," 28, 29, 56s
"Garfield's Funeral March," 28
Gassaway, W.Va., 9, 47
Geer, John, 15
George, Frank, 135, 144
"George Washington March," 22
Georgia Wildcats, 164
"Georgie Buck," 85, 86
German immigrants, 83
ghost stories, 71–73, 95, 106, 203–4
Gibson, Eck. *See* Eck Gibson and the Mountaineer Ramblers
"Girl I Left Behind Me," 28
Glenn, Abe, 28
Glenville Festival. *See* West Virginia State Folk Festival
Glens, Bob, 26
Glens, Dave, 26
"Going Back to Baltimore," 85
"Going Up Brush Fork," 30
"Goin' Up Cripple Creek," 158. *See also* "Cripple Creek"
Goldenseal (magazine), 1
"Golden Slippers," 14, 78, 143
"Gold Rush," 23
"Good Old Mountain Dew," 188
gospel music, 173, 187, 194, 196, 198, 205. *See also* hymns; sacred music
gramophone. *See* records, phonograph
"Grand Ole Opry" (radio show): musical influence of, 16, 39s, 46, 98, 206; playing on, 65, 150, 193
"Granny Will Your Dog Bite," 54s
"Great Speckled Bird," 65
"Green Grow the Lilacs," 58
"Groundhog," 120
guitar: blues, 171–78; Carter Family style, 38s, 41; with fiddle, 27, 37s; learning to play, 16, 160, 173, 196; making, 14; other playing styles, 38s, 108, 158, 167; Spanish, 160; steel, 46; tuning, 156, 158, 167. *See also* square dances and square dancing; *names of specific guitarists*
Gum, Ham, 19–20
"Gunboat Going Through Georgia," 37s

Haley, Ed, 26, 39–40s, 42, 52, 189
Hammers and Strings, 144
Hammons, Burl, 22, 42, 185
Hammons, Edden, 51, 73s, 159. *See also* Hammons, Edwin
Hammons, Edwin, 18, 22. *See also* Hammons, Edden
Hammons, George, 78

Hamrick, Alex, 50, 58
Hamrick, Aretus, 158, 163
Hamrick, Dewey, 18, 22, 158, 159
handsaw (as musical instrument), 119
"Hannah at the Springhouse," 8
Hardy County (W.Va.) Heritage Weekend, 86
Harmer, Bill, 176
harmonica, 51, 106s, 196
harp. *See* string harp
Hartford, John, 97, 101
Hartman, Dick, 212
Harvey, Roy, 167
Hauser, Wayne, 30s
"Hawaiian Sunset," 162
Hayseed, Hiram, 152
"Hell Among the Yearlings," 28, 28s, 29, 30, 56s
Helvetia, W.Va., dances in, 197
hemophilia, 3, 198–203
Henlawson, W.Va., 103, 106
Henry, John, 54s
Heritage Arts Festival (Harpers Ferry, W.Va.), 114
Hicks, Lorie, 39s, 50
"High Cost of Living, The," 55
High Germany, W.Va., 196
Hilders, Jim, 24
Hill, Dorvel, 52
hillbilly music, 16, 26, 187
"Hipple Creek," 85
Hogbin, Harley, 217
"Home Place, The" (radio series), 116, 172
"Home Sweet Home," 109, 159
"Honeysuckle Rag," 54s
honky-tonk music, 165, 167–68, 184
"Hop Light Ladies," 54s
hornpipes, 47, 209, 216
Householder, Smokey, 216
Humanities Foundation of West Virginia, 116, 172
Humphreys, Mike, 30s
hunting, 14–15, 17, 67–70, 74, 91, 132
Huntington, W.Va., 188, 193
Hurt, John, 86
Huston, Richmond, 27
Hutchinson, Zillah, 18
Hutchison, Frank, 106–8s, 167
Huttonsville, W.Va., 12, 14, 17, 19
hymns, 8, 12, 18, 24, 54s, 181, 196. *See also* gospel music; sacred music

"I Don't Care If Tomorrow Never Comes," 192
"I'd Rather Be an Old-Time Christian," 2
"I'll Shout and Shine," 194
instrument making. *See under* names of specific instruments
instrument repair, 3, 41, 109, 112
"In the Pines," 167
"Irish Washer Woman," 12

Jabbour, Alan, 2, 65
Jake Taylor's Radio Ranch (Grafton, W.Va.), 152
"Jamboree U.S.A." (radio show), 2, 101, 154, 155. *See also* "Wheeling Jamboree"; "World's Original Jamboree"
Japan, 185–86
Jarvis, Reece B. "Sam," 30s
jaw harp, 43. *See also* Jew's harp
jazz music, 175
Jefferson, Thomas, as fiddler, 64
Jew's harp, 196. *See also* jaw harp
"Jimmy Johnson," 55s
Joe Phillips and the Dixie Pals, 18
"John Brown," 93
"John Hardy," 85, 120, 167
"John Henry," 167
Johnson, Charles, 51
Johnson, Cletus, 13
Johnson, George Seymour, 49
Johnson, John, 2, 30s, 49–61
Johnson, Missouri Edith Hamrick, 53–54
jug (as musical instrument), 119
"Jump Jim Crow," 11
Justice, Dick, 108

Kanawha (record company), 33. *See also* Folk Promotions
"Kanawha County Rag," 30
"Kanawha March," 28, 214s
"Katy Hill," 23. *See also* "Sally Ann Johnson"
"Kentucky Waltz," 216
Kessinger, Bob, 33
Kessinger, Clark, 3, 25–33, 52, 56s, 62, 158
Kessinger, Dan, 33
Kessinger, Luches "Luke," 26–33
Kessinger, Robin, 33
Kessinger, Rosie, 28s
Kessinger Brothers, The, 26–33
Keyser, W.Va., 216
Keystone, W.Va., 175
King, Tom, 28–29s
Knight, "Little Howard," 46
Knotts, Noble, 51
KQV (radio station), 148, 149
Kreisler, Fritz, 30–31
Krise, George "Speedy," 192
Kuhn, Bernard, 16

"Lady's Waistribbon," 8
lap bass, 177
Laurel Creek, W.Va., 66–67, 68, 70
Leary, Jake, 18
"Leather Britches," 83
Leatherman, Vernon, 209
"Leave Something Special," 207
Legg, Ernest, 28
Legg, Lee, 51
Lemley, Buckwheat, 138
Les Deux Paroissiens, 29. *See also* Kessinger Brothers, The

"Liberty," 216
Library of Congress, 65, 104, 108, 216; American Folklife Center, 65; Archive of Folk Song, 216
"Life Is Like a Mountain Railroad," 181
Lilly, Bea, 181–87
Lilly, Everett, 181–87
Lilly, Everett Alan, 185
Lilly, John, 1
Lilly Brothers, The, 2, 3, 181–87, 192
Lions Club (Elkins, W.Va.), 24
"Listen to the Mockingbird," 56s. *See also* "Mockingbird"
"Little Betty Brown," 29
"Little Birdie," 37s
"Little Blossom, The," 37s
"Little Brown Jug," 29
"Living the Right Life Now," 188, 194
Logan County, W.Va., 103, 105, 107
logging. *See* timbering
log rollings, music for, 9, 75
Longacre, Lloyd, 110
Looman, Edith, 143
Looman, Patty, 141–44
"Lost John" and his Allied Kentuckians, 64
Louvin, Charlie, 101
lumbering. *See* timbering
lunar phases: for planting, 14, 38; for preserving, 38–39; for roofing, 14, 38
Lynn Davis & Molly O'Day, 188–95
Lyons, Jim, 50

Macon, Uncle Dave, 156, 157
Mahans Run, W.Va., 127
mandolin, 9, 14, 18, 20, 24, 196
Mankins, Ira, 211, 215
Mannington, W.Va., 141, 142
Mannington District Fair, 142
Mannington Round Barn, 128
"Maple Sugar," 207
"Marching Through Georgia," 158. *See also* "Marching to Georgia"
"Marching to Georgia," 196. *See also* "Marching Through Georgia"
Marilla Recreation Center (Morgantown, W.Va.), 138
Marion County, W.Va., 127, 129
Marlinton (W.Va.) Pioneer Day, 22
Martin, Asa, 98–99
Mason, Ann, 189
Mason, Sue, 189
Mayfield, Ira, 134
Maynard, Delpha, 104
McAuliffe, Harry "Big Slim," 148, 149
McCall, Ernie, 46
McDonald, James, 183–84
McDowell County, W.Va., 165, 170
McElwain, "Uncle Jack," 73s, 78
McGee, Ballard, 15
McGee, Clint, 15
McGee, Gus, 12, 15

McGee, Wren, 15, 22
McKenzie, Karen, 154
McMichen, Clayton, 16, 25, 164, 192
Meade, Gene, 30s, 32, 33
Meade, Guthrie, 32
medicinal roots, 169; ginseng, 1, 52, 169; yellowroot, 1, 169
medicine shows, 84
Mercer County, W.Va., 171
"Merry Maiden Polka," 152
Messer, Don, 214–15
Methodist Episcopal Church (Sutton, W.Va.), 7
Meyers, Bonnie, 218
Meyers, Eddie, 218
Meyers, Simon, 136, 138
Mill Creek, W.Va., 12, 13, 14, 16, 17, 19
Milnes, Gerry, 24, 164
Mineral County, W.Va., 208, 216
Mingo County, W.Va., 116
mining. *See* coal mining
ministry. *See under* Christian faith
"Minner on the Hook," 93
minstrel shows, 84
"Mississippi Sawyer," 18, 28s, 29
Mississippi Sheiks, 86
"Miss Lucy Neal Down in the Cotton Field," 85
Mitchell, French, 26, 30s
"Mitchell Clog," 15
"Mockingbird," 31. *See also* "Listen to the Mockingbird"
Molly O'Day Music Center (Williamson, W.Va.), 194
"Momma Tried," 101
"Money Musk," 214
Monongalia County, W.Va., 136
Monroe, Bill, 20, 21, 23, 29, 62, 114
Montana, 92
Montgomery, Willard, 48
moonshine, 112, 113, 123–24, 136, 175. *See also* alcohol
Moore, Arch, 135, 155
Moore, Frankie, 19
Morgantown, W.Va., 136
"Morning Roundup, The" (radio show), 99
Morris, Dave, 101
Morris, George, 43
Morris, "Jinks," 162
Morris, John, 30s
Morris, Reece, 73s
Morrison, Jim, 217
Mountaineer Days Festival (Morgantown, W.Va.), 22
Mountaineer Dulcimer Club, 135, 143
Mountaineer Dulcimer Convention, 143
Mountaineer Ramblers, 99
Mountaineer Twins, 189
Mountain Melodies (songbook), 212
Mountain Melodies and Old Time Songs (songbook), 212

Mountain Music Association, 170
"Mountain Scene Tonight" (television show), 115
"Mountain Stage" (radio show), 2, 101
Mountain State Art and Craft Fair (Ripley, W.Va.), 108, 140
Mountain State Forest Festival (Elkins, W.Va.), 18, 159, 204
mouth organ. *See* harmonica
movies, silent: music for, 141
movie theaters, live music in, 9, 182
Muncey, Iser, 167
Muncey, Will, 167
music: as expression of local culture, 2; as political campaign tool, 3, 63–64; reading, 9, 16, 20, 93, 103, 110, 209, 216, 217
—playing for money, 7, 24, 39–40s; in bars, 58, 167, 184–85; in the coalfields, 175; for college students, 184; contracts for, 177; for dances (*see also* dances and dancing; square dances and square dancing), 16–17, 18, 21, 26, 32, 57, 112, 211–18; at movie theaters, 9, 182; for radio (*see also* radio), 20, 27, 32, 182, 212; for record companies (*see also under* recordings), 27–30, 33, 216
—teaching, 29, 72s, 114; banjo, 108; fiddle, 11, 29, 218; guitar, 151; hammered dulcimer, 143, 144. *See also* West Virginia Folk Arts Apprenticeship Program
—types of. *See* bluegrass music; blues music; country music; gospel music; hillbilly music; honky-tonk music; hymns; jazz music; ragtime music; rock 'n' roll music; sacred music; swing music
musicians: community attitudes toward, 41, 120; and work, 41
Musselman's Grove, Pa., 152

N&W Railroad, 118, 119
Nashville, Tenn., 65, 98, 153, 193
Natchee the Indian, 32, 52, 158, 159, 182
National Endowment for the Arts, 11
National Folk Festival (Covington, Ky.), 32
National Folk Festival (Washington, D.C.), 32
National Heritage Fellowship, 3, 11
Native Americans. *See* American Indians
"Nellie Gray," 48
New Creek Fire Hall (Mineral County, W.Va.), dancing at, 214–15s, 215, 216, 217, 218
Newfoundland, 21, 214–15
"Newsmark Magazine" (radio show), 140
"Ninety Days in Georgia," 15

O'Brien, Sylvia, 87–95
"O Come All Ye Faithful," 216
O'Day, Molly (LaVerne "Dixie May" Williamson), 2, 3, 188–95, 192–93s
"Oh, Susanna," 84
oil and gas industry, 129–31, 136

O'Keefe, James, 27
"Old Black Cat," 45
Old Choice Collection (songbook), 181
"Old Farm Hour" (radio show), 32, 98, 182
"Old Jake Gillie," 29
"Old Joe Clark," 62, 216
"Old Man Can I Have Your Daughter?" 85
"Old Sledge," 78
"Orange Blossom Special," 99, 101, 152, 215s
organ, 17, 112, 141, 176, 209

Painter Knob, W.Va., 34, 35
Parker, Eleanor, 20
Parker, Rex, 20
Pastine, Malcomb, 205
Patterson Beach (Burlington, W.Va.), 212
"Payday," 86
Pelferry Brothers, The, 21
"Peppermint Twist," 46–47
Phillips, Joe. *See* Joe Phillips and the Dixie Pals
phonograph. *See* records, phonograph
piano, 119, 141–42, 175, 176, 215
Pittsburgh, Pa., 148
Pocahontas County (W.Va.) Fair, 17
"Poca River Blues," 28s, 29
poetry, 53–55, 57
politics. *See under* music; *see also* rallies, political
"Polka Four," 30
polkas, 29, 47, 162, 175, 216
"Pop Goes the Weasel," 128
"Portsmouth," 29
Poss, Barry, 65
Potomac River, 109–10, 113
"Preacher and the Bear," 176
"Pretty Little Girl Get Your Foot Out of the Sand," 85
"Pretty Polly," 37s
"Prince Baine Waltz," 209
Pritchard, Wallace, 78
Propst, Rob, 217
Puckett, Riley, 159, 160
Putnam County, W.Va., 96

Radcliff, Whitey, 46
radio, 16, 39s, 98, 136, 176; announcing, 188–95; as musical resource, 2, 198, 211; transcribed programs for, 151
—live music for: Blackie Cool and, 159–60; Clark Kessinger and, 27; Doc Williams and, 149–55; Elmer Bird and, 98–99; John Johnson and, 51; Lilly Brothers and, 182; Lynn Davis & Molly O'Day and, 189–93; Nat Reese and, 176; Welch Brothers and, 212; Woody Simmons and, 18, 20
radio stations. *See* call letters of specific stations
"Rag, A," 159
"Ragtime Annie," 25, 28s, 52
ragtime music, 112, 162

railroads, 118, 119, 161, 172, 176
Raleigh County, W.Va., 62, 181
Raleigh (W.Va.) Register, 63, 64
rallies, political, 63–64
Randolph County, W.Va., 12, 13, 159, 162, 196
Reagan, Ronald, 135
recordings: for archives, 54s, 72–73s, 108, 216; for radio, 140, 151, 152
—for sale: Andrew Boarman and, 114–15; Aunt Jennie Wilson and, 108; Clark Kessinger and, 27–30, 32; Doc Williams and, 152, 153; Elmer Bird and, 101, 102; Frank Hutchison and, 108s; Lilly Brothers and, 185; Lynn Davis & Molly O'Day and, 193, 194; Patty Looman and, 144; Robert Byrd and, 65; Welch Brothers and, 216; Woody Simmons and, 21
records, phonograph, 11, 14, 16, 62, 150. *See also* recordings
"Red Bird," 28s
"Red River Valley," 138
Red Robin Inn (Borderland, W.Va.), 116, 124
"Red Wing," 99, 143, 144, 216
Reed, Blind Alfred, 163
Reese, Nat, 171–78
Reisler, Paul, 164
"Renfro Valley Barn Dance" (radio show), 192
Richmond, Va., 51
"Richmond Polka," 29
"Rickett's Hornpipe," 28s
Rockefeller, Nelson, 135
rock 'n' roll music, 20, 21, 32, 183, 205, 215s
Rodgers, Jimmie, 2, 16
rolls. *See* cylinder recordings
Rose, Fred, 192–93
Rosencrantz, Bill, 17
Rosencrantz, Ethel, 14
Ross, Brownie, 18, 158
Rounder Records, 25, 33, 85
"Roundtown Gals," 84
"Rovin' Gambler," 167
"Roxanna Waltz," 24
Rush Creek, W.Va., 34
Rutherford, Carl, 2, 165–70

sacred music, 193–95. *See also* gospel music; hymns
"Sagebrush Roundup" (radio show), 18
"Saint Louis Blues," 164
"Sally Ann," 15–16, 85
"Sally Ann Johnson," 25, 56. *See also* "Katy Hill"
"Sally Goodin," 15, 29
"Salt Creek," 29
"Salt River." *See* "Salt Creek"
Samples, Mack, 7
sawmills, 10, 14, 51, 60–61, 104, 131
schools: as community centers, 203; quitting, 91, 98, 156, 202; singing in, 182. *See also* education

schottische, 113, 216
Schwinabart, Albert, 216
Scott, Harry, 72s
Screven, Tom, 1
Sears, Roebuck and Co., 38s, 39s, 53, 122, 209
See, Clyde M., Jr., 86
See, Ralph, 16
Selman, Arnold, 19, 20, 23
Shafer, Emmett M. "Lefty," 30s
"Shame On You," 152
"Shanghai Chicken," 176
Shank, Rumsey, 216
"Shelvin' Rock," 55s, 71, 78
"Shoo Fly," 29
Shop Hollow, W.Va., 169
"Should You Go First," 152
Shreve, Smith, 15, 16
signs. *See* superstitions
"Silent Night," 13, 14
"Silver Bell," 152
Simmons, Laverne, 12, 18, 20, 24
Simmons, William, 20–21
Simmons, Woody, 12–24, 30s, 159, 162, 206, 207
Simplified By Ear System of Guitar Chords (Williams), 151
singing: ballads, 37s, 41, 43; in church, 3, 182, 194, 205–6; gospel, 41, 173, 193–94; importance of, in W.Va. folk culture, 2; for meaning, 183, 187; professionally, 184–85, 188–94, 212; in schools, 182
"Singing Waterfall, The," 192
Singleton, Etta. *See* Wine, Etta
Singleton, Jim, 45
Singleton, Sarah, 43–48
Singleton, William "Ace," 9
"Sinner Man Where You Gonna Hide," 194
"Sitting Alone in the Moonlight," 196
"Six More Miles," 192
"Skip to My Lou," 45
slavery, 82
Smik, Andrew John, Jr. *See* Williams, Doc
Smik, Milo. *See* Williams, Cy
Smith, Arthur, 16, 25, 46, 53, 55s, 62, 112, 150
Smith, Glen, 30s
Smith, Harrison B., 28–29
Smithsonian Folklife Festival, 133, 169. *See also* Festival of American Folklife
Smithsonian Institution, 7, 139
Smokey Jack and the Saddle Pals, 160, 161
Snap and Ginger, 19
Society for the Preservation of Bluegrass Music, 101
"Soldier's Joy," 11, 15, 29, 38s, 49, 83, 85, 110, 216
"Somewhere in West Virginia," 115
songbooks and folios, 181, 191, 212
songs. *See specific song titles*
songwriting, 169
"Sorry I Left My Father's Home," 85, 86
"Sourwood Mountain," 29

Southern Sounds of Grass, 115
"Spanish Cavalier, The," 182
spiders, writing, 54
spook stories. *See* ghost stories
spoons (as musical instrument), 84
Spring Dulcimer Week. *See* August Heritage Center
square dances and square dancing: banjo used for, 96, 158; on boats, 113; calling, 9, 25, 28, 45, 113, 137–38, 160, 211, 212, 214s, 215, 217, 218; contests, 99; in dance halls, 32, 137; fiddle used for, 45, 158, 159, 214; guitar used for, 137, 160; hammered dulcimer used for, 134, 140; quality of, at New Creek, 217; recorded music for, 28, 216; as social events, 105. *See also* dances and dancing
Staggs, Sloan, 140
Staggs, Vance, 214s, 216
Staggs, Virginia, 214s, 216
"Stardust," 176
"Steamboat Bill," 29
steam organ, 17, 84
Steele, Harry, 214s, 218
Stonewall Jackson Jubilee, 140, 170
Stony Creek, W.Va., 71–72
Stotesbury, W.Va., 62
Stover, Don, 185
Strawberry Festival (Buckhannon, W.Va.), 159
Street, Emery, 16
string harp, 176–77
Stump, Charles Cleveland, 112
Stump, John, 110
Stump, Harry, 110
Stutler, Bill, 73s
"Sugar in the Gourd," 16
Sullivan, Ken, 1–2, 3
Sunset Ramblers, 159
Sunshine Hillbillies, 192
superstitions, 95, 203–4; involving witches, 95
"Susie's Band," 16
Sutton, W.Va., 66
Sutton Dam, 66, 76–77
Swecker, Floyd, 13
Sweet Sentimental Songs (songbook), 212
swing music, 142, 175
Szigeti, Joseph, 30–31

"Take Me Back to Tulsa," 22
Tale of the Elk (Byrne), 73
tall tales, 106
taterbug mandolin, 14
Taylor, Bobby, 28–30s
Taylor, Lincoln, 28s
teaching music. *See under* music; *see also* West Virginia Folk Arts Apprenticeship Program
television, 153, 154
Tennant, Margaret. *See* Gardner, Margaret

Texas, 55s, 56. *See also under* fiddle
theaters. *See* movie theaters
"This World Is Not My Home," 181
Thomasson, Benny, 29s, 30s, 56s, 56–57
"Three Forks of Sandy," 29
Thrush, Tom, 209
timbering, 10, 13, 39, 75–76, 116–18, 129–30, 166. *See also* log rollings, music for; sawmills
tiple (musical instrument), 176
Toney, Brian, 182
Town and Country Pickers, 48
traditional culture. *See* folk culture
"Train That Carried My Girl From Town, The," 167
"Tramp on the Street," 192, 193
transcriptions. *See under* radio
Triplett, Lee, 50, 52
Tross, Andy, 81, 82
Tross, Clarence, 81–86
"Tugboat," 29, 30
tunes. *See* fiddle tunes; *specific tune titles*
Turkey Creek, W.Va., 96, 97, 99, 102
"Turkey in the Straw," 16, 28, 85
"Turkey Knob," 28s

"Unclouded Day, The," 50. *See also* "Uncloudy Day"
"Uncloudy Day," 2. *See also* "Unclouded Day, The"
"Under the Double Eagle," 30, 52, 56s, 99
Union Grove, N.C., music festival at, 32
United States Army Corps of Engineers, 76
United States House of Representatives, 64
University of North Carolina Folklore Archives, 85
Upshur County, W.Va., 196
Utah, 58

Vandalia Award, 11, 24, 42, 78, 87, 95, 101, 102, 108, 115, 135
Vandalia Gathering (Charleston, W.Va.), 2, 11, 108, 114, 140, 165, 169
Van Epps, Fred, 14, 112
VanPelt, Arnold, 14, 159
VanPelt, Lilburn, 14
Varner, William, 133
Victrola, 16
violin, classical, 30–31, 207, 215, 216
vocals. *See* singing

waltzes, 27, 215s, 216
Warriormine, W.Va., 165, 169
washtub bass, 214s
WBTH (radio station), 191
WBUC (radio station), 46
WCHS (radio station), 51, 98, 182, 189, 191
WCMI (radio station), 98–99
WDNE (radio station), 19, 23
"Weary Lonesome Blues," 167
Webb, Kip, 211

Webster Springs, W.Va., 162–63, 164
"Wednesday Night Waltz," 27
Welch, Bonnie Charlotte, 208
Welch, Creed, 208, 209, 211, 212, 216
Welch, Elwanda, 208, 212, 215
Welch, Hazel, 215, 216
Welch, Ike, 209, 211
Welch, Israel, 208–18
Welch, John, 208, 209, 215, 216
Welch, Margaret, 208
Welch, Mary, 208, 209, 211
Welch, Oscar, 208, 209, 212
Welch, Tom, 208, 209, 211, 215, 216, 218
Welch Brothers, The, 208–18
WEMM (radio station), 194–95
WESA (radio station), 160, 161
West Augusta Historical Society, 128
West Virginia Arts and Humanities
    Commission, 114
"West Virginia Breakdown," 165
West Virginia Commission on the Arts. See
    West Virginia Arts and Humanities
    Commission
West Virginia Department of Culture and
    History Lifetime Achievement Award, 108
West Virginia Division of Culture and
    History, 1
West Virginia Folk Arts Apprenticeship
    Program, 11, 24, 144
West Virginia House of Delegates, 63, 64
West Virginia Humanities Council. See
    Humanities Foundation of West Virginia
"West Virginia Special," 30
West Virginia Square Dances (Dalsemer),
    138, 217
West Virginia State Folk Festival (Glenville,
    W.Va.), 7, 11, 22, 94, 101, 134, 170
West Virginia University, 54s, 108, 113, 134, 137
"West Virginia Waltz," 144

Wheeler, Billy Edd, 108
Wheeling, W.Va., 101, 149–55 passim
"Wheeling Jamboree" (radio show), 135,
    147–55. See also "Jamboree U.S.A.";
    "World's Original Jamboree"
Wheeling Record Company, 152
Wheeling (W.Va.) Hall of Fame, 155
"When God Comes to Gather His Jewels,"
    192
"When I Grow Too Old to Dream," 33
Whipp, Maurice, 216
Whipp, Maxwell, 216
WHIS (radio station), 176, 189
"Whiskey Before Breakfast," 7
whistling, 209
"Whistling Rufus," 29
White, Doc, 39s
White, John, 160
"White Pilgrim, The," 54s
"Whoa, Muley, Whoa," 196
WHTN (radio station), 99
Widen, W.Va., 36, 50
"Wildcat Holler," 43
"Wild Horse and the Red Trace," 52
"Wildwood Flower," 16, 123, 160
"Will the Circle Be Unbroken," 65
Williams, Chickie, 150, 151, 152, 155
Williams, Cy, 147, 148, 152
Williams, Doc, 2, 3, 147–55, 198
Williams, Hank, 192
Williams, Helen, 20
Williams, Jack, 20
Williamson, LaVerne "Dixie Lee," 191. See
    also O'Day, Molly
Williamson, Skeets, 191
"Willow Garden," 37s
"Willy Roy," 152
Wilson, Aunt Jennie, 103–8, 135
Wilson, Jim, 106, 107

Wilson, Virginia Myrtle. See Wilson, Aunt
    Jennie
"Wilson's Hornpipe," 28s
Wine, Bob, 8
Wine, Clarence, 9
Wine, Elizabeth Sandy, 8
Wine, Etta, 7, 8, 9, 10, 11
Wine, Melvin, 2, 3, 7–11, 211, 217
Wine, Nels, 8
Wine, "Smithy," 8, 11
Winter Music Festival (Morgantown,
    W.Va.), 136, 140
Wise, Chubby, 22
Withrow, Tuck, 17
WJLS (radio station), 192
WMMN (radio station), 159
WMOD (radio station), 152–53
WOBU (radio station), 27, 32
Wolford, Bill, 215
woodslore, 37–40, 74–75
woodworking, 93–94
Workmen's Compensation, 10, 107
"World's Original Jamboree" (radio show),
    149, 150. See also "Jamboree U.S.A.";
    "Wheeling Jamboree"
World War II, 99, 137, 150, 151, 214
"Worried Blues," 167
WRVA (radio station), 51
WSAZ (radio station), 98, 189
WSM (radio station), 39s, 98, 150
WTBO (radio station), 212
WTRF (television station), 153
WWVA (radio station), 2, 3, 147, 149, 151,
    152, 154

"Yew Piney Mountain," 78
"You Are My Sunshine," 84

Zickefoose, Emry, 196

Music in American Life

Only a Miner: Studies in Recorded Coal-Mining Songs *Archie Green*
Great Day Coming: Folk Music and the American Left *R. Serge Denisoff*
John Philip Sousa: A Descriptive Catalog of His Works *Paul E. Bierley*
The Hell-Bound Train: A Cowboy Songbook *Glenn Ohrlin*
Oh, Didn't He Ramble: The Life Story of Lee Collins, as Told to Mary Collins *Edited by Frank J. Gillis and John W. Miner*
American Labor Songs of the Nineteenth Century *Philip S. Foner*
Stars of Country Music: Uncle Dave Macon to Johnny Rodriguez *Edited by Bill C. Malone and Judith McCulloh*
Git Along, Little Dogies: Songs and Songmakers of the American West *John I. White*
A Texas-Mexican *Cancionero:* Folksongs of the Lower Border *Américo Paredes*
San Antonio Rose: The Life and Music of Bob Wills *Charles R. Townsend*
Early Downhome Blues: A Musical and Cultural Analysis *Jeff Todd Titon*
An Ives Celebration: Papers and Panels of the Charles Ives Centennial Festival-Conference *Edited by H. Wiley Hitchcock and Vivian Perlis*
Sinful Tunes and Spirituals: Black Folk Music to the Civil War *Dena J. Epstein*
Joe Scott, the Woodsman-Songmaker *Edward D. Ives*
Jimmie Rodgers: The Life and Times of America's Blue Yodeler *Nolan Porterfield*
Early American Music Engraving and Printing: A History of Music Publishing in America from 1787 to 1825, with Commentary on Earlier and Later Practices *Richard J. Wolfe*
Sing a Sad Song: The Life of Hank Williams *Roger M. Williams*
Long Steel Rail: The Railroad in American Folksong *Norm Cohen*
Resources of American Music History: A Directory of Source Materials from Colonial Times to World War II *D. W. Krummel, Jean Geil, Doris J. Dyen, and Deane L. Root*
Tenement Songs: The Popular Music of the Jewish Immigrants *Mark Slobin*
Ozark Folksongs *Vance Randolph; edited and abridged by Norm Cohen*
Oscar Sonneck and American Music *Edited by William Lichtenwanger*
Bluegrass Breakdown: The Making of the Old Southern Sound *Robert Cantwell*
Bluegrass: A History *Neil V. Rosenberg*
Music at the White House: A History of the American Spirit *Elise K. Kirk*
Red River Blues: The Blues Tradition in the Southeast *Bruce Bastin*
Good Friends and Bad Enemies: Robert Winslow Gordon and the Study of American Folksong *Debora Kodish*
Fiddlin' Georgia Crazy: Fiddlin' John Carson, His Real World, and the World of His Songs *Gene Wiggins*
America's Music: From the Pilgrims to the Present (rev. 3d ed.) *Gilbert Chase*
Secular Music in Colonial Annapolis: The Tuesday Club, 1745–56 *John Barry Talley*
Bibliographical Handbook of American Music *D. W. Krummel*
Goin' to Kansas City *Nathan W. Pearson, Jr.*
"Susanna," "Jeanie," and "The Old Folks at Home": The Songs of Stephen C. Foster from His Time to Ours (2d ed.) *William W. Austin*
Songprints: The Musical Experience of Five Shoshone Women *Judith Vander*
"Happy in the Service of the Lord": Afro-American Gospel Quartets in Memphis *Kip Lornell*
Paul Hindemith in the United States *Luther Noss*
"My Song Is My Weapon": People's Songs, American Communism, and the Politics of Culture, 1930–50 *Robbie Lieberman*
Chosen Voices: The Story of the American Cantorate *Mark Slobin*
Theodore Thomas: America's Conductor and Builder of Orchestras, 1835–1905 *Ezra Schabas*
"The Whorehouse Bells Were Ringing" and Other Songs Cowboys Sing *Guy Logsdon*
Crazeology: The Autobiography of a Chicago Jazzman *Bud Freeman, as Told to Robert Wolf*
Discoursing Sweet Music: Brass Bands and Community Life in Turn-of-the-Century Pennsylvania *Kenneth Kreitner*
Mormonism and Music: A History *Michael Hicks*
Voices of the Jazz Age: Profiles of Eight Vintage Jazzmen *Chip Deffaa*
Pickin' on Peachtree: A History of Country Music in Atlanta, Georgia *Wayne W. Daniel*
Bitter Music: Collected Journals, Essays, Introductions, and Librettos *Harry Partch; edited by Thomas McGeary*

Ethnic Music on Records: A Discography of Ethnic Recordings Produced in the United States, 1893 to 1942
    Richard K. Spottswood
Downhome Blues Lyrics: An Anthology from the Post–World War II Era Jeff Todd Titon
Ellington: The Early Years Mark Tucker
Chicago Soul Robert Pruter
That Half-Barbaric Twang: The Banjo in American Popular Culture Karen Linn
Hot Man: The Life of Art Hodes Art Hodes and Chadwick Hansen
The Erotic Muse: American Bawdy Songs (2d ed.) Ed Cray
Barrio Rhythm: Mexican American Music in Los Angeles Steven Loza
The Creation of Jazz: Music, Race, and Culture in Urban America Burton W. Peretti
Charles Martin Loeffler: A Life Apart in Music Ellen Knight
Club Date Musicians: Playing the New York Party Circuit Bruce A. MacLeod
Opera on the Road: Traveling Opera Troupes in the United States, 1825–60 Katherine K. Preston
The Stonemans: An Appalachian Family and the Music That Shaped Their Lives Ivan M. Tribe
Transforming Tradition: Folk Music Revivals Examined Edited by Neil V. Rosenberg
The Crooked Stovepipe: Athapaskan Fiddle Music and Square Dancing in Northeast Alaska and Northwest Canada
    Craig Mishler
Traveling the High Way Home: Ralph Stanley and the World of Traditional Bluegrass Music John Wright
Carl Ruggles: Composer, Painter, and Storyteller Marilyn Ziffrin
Never without a Song: The Years and Songs of Jennie Devlin, 1865–1952 Katharine D. Newman
The Hank Snow Story Hank Snow, with Jack Ownbey and Bob Burris
Milton Brown and the Founding of Western Swing Cary Ginell, with special assistance from Roy Lee Brown
Santiago de Murcia's "Códice Saldívar No. 4": A Treasury of Secular Guitar Music from Baroque Mexico Craig H. Russell
The Sound of the Dove: Singing in Appalachian Primitive Baptist Churches Beverly Bush Patterson
Heartland Excursions: Ethnomusicological Reflections on Schools of Music Bruno Nettl
Doowop: The Chicago Scene Robert Pruter
Blue Rhythms: Six Lives in Rhythm and Blues Chip Deffaa
Shoshone Ghost Dance Religion: Poetry Songs and Great Basin Context Judith Vander
Go Cat Go! Rockabilly Music and Its Makers Craig Morrison
'Twas Only an Irishman's Dream: The Image of Ireland and the Irish in American Popular Song Lyrics, 1800–1920
    William H. A. Williams
Democracy at the Opera: Music, Theater, and Culture in New York City, 1815–60 Karen Ahlquist
Fred Waring and the Pennsylvanians Virginia Waring
Woody, Cisco, and Me: Seamen Three in the Merchant Marine Jim Longhi
Behind the Burnt Cork Mask: Early Blackface Minstrelsy and Antebellum American Popular Culture William J. Mahar
Going to Cincinnati: A History of the Blues in the Queen City Steven C. Tracy
Pistol Packin' Mama: Aunt Molly Jackson and the Politics of Folksong Shelly Romalis
Sixties Rock: Garage, Psychedelic, and Other Satisfactions Michael Hicks
The Late Great Johnny Ace and the Transition from R&B to Rock 'n' Roll James M. Salem
Tito Puente and the Making of Latin Music Steven Loza
Juilliard: A History Andrea Olmstead
Understanding Charles Seeger, Pioneer in American Musicology Edited by Bell Yung and Helen Rees
Mountains of Music: West Virginia Traditional Music from Goldenseal Edited by John Lilly